Studying Culture

STUDYING CULTURE

A PRACTICAL INTRODUCTION

JUDY GILES AND TIM MIDDLETON

Blackwell
Publishing

BLACKWELL PUBLISHING
350 Main Street, Malden, MA 02148-5020, USA
108 Cowley Road, Oxford OX4 1JF, UK
550 Swanston Street, Carlton, Victoria 3053, Australia

First published 1999 by Blackwell Publishing Ltd
Reprinted 2001, 2003

Library of Congress Cataloging-in-Publication Data

Giles, Judy.
   Studying culture : a practical introduction / Judy Giles and Tim Middleton.
         p.   cm.
   Includes bibliographical references (p.) and index.
   ISBN 0-631-20621-3 (hc. : alk. paper)
   ISBN 0-631-20622-1 (pbk. : alk. paper)
   1. Culture.   2. Culture—Study and teaching.   I. Middleton, Tim, 1962-   II. Title.
   HM101.G39 1999
   306—dc21   98-35452
                                                                              CIP

A catalogue record for this title is available from the British Library.

Set in 10 on 12 pt Plantin
by Ace Filmsetting Ltd, Frome, Somerset
Printed and bound in the United Kingdom
by Athenaeum Press Ltd, Gateshead, Tyne & Wear

For further information on
Blackwell Publishing, visit our website:
http://www.blackwellpublishing.com

Contents

Figures

Tables

Acknowledgements

The authors would like to thank the College of Ripon & York, St John for allowing us the sabbatical leave that enabled this book to be completed. We are also indebted to those colleagues, in particular Roger Clark, whose willingness to take on extra work made it possible for us to use this sabbatical time productively. Mary Eagleton and Dave Evans and various anonymous readers commented upon the manuscript at various stages. Their imaginative and helpful suggestions always stimulated us to further thought, even when we chose not to act on them, and for this we are grateful. Thanks are also due to the many students on whom the material in this book was piloted and who told us which aspects of studying culture they found difficult, interesting or dull. Ginny Stroud-Lewis and John Taylor were helpful, efficient and good humoured in helping us to prepare the manuscript for publication, and Andrew McNeillie's advice and commitment in the later stages were essential. We owe a final debt of gratitude to Mary Eagleton, who actively initiated the project and who has, over many years, supported and encouraged both of us in different ways.

The authors and publishers gratefully acknowledge the following for permission to reproduce copyright material:

Figure 1.1, by A. F. Kersting, copyright © Pitkin Unichrome. Figure 2.1, by Corinne Dufka, copyright © Popperfoto/Reuters. Figure 3.1 courtesy of Midland Bank plc. Figure 3.2 courtesy of Posy Simmonds. Figure 3.3 courtesy of the Jo Spence Memorial Archive. Figure 4.1, copyright © *The Independent*/Andre Buurman. Figure 4.2, © Crown Copyright, courtesy of Her Majesty's Stationery Office. Figures 5.1 and 5.2, reproduced from Ordnance Survey Motoring Atlas of Great Britain 1995, with the permission of the Controller of Her Majesty's Stationery Office, © Crown Copyright MC 88448M0001. Figure 5.3, reproduced from Ordnance Survey Outdoor Leisure Map 27, with the permission of the Controller of Her Majesty's Stationery Office, © Crown Copyright MC 88448M0001. Figure 6.1, copyright © The Hulton Getty Picture Collection. Figures 6.3 and 6.4, reproduced with the permission of the Controller of Her Majesty's Stationery Office, © Crown Copyright MC 88448M0001. Figure 6.5 reproduced by courtesy of the London Transport Museum. Table 6.1, from P. Oliver et al. (eds), *The Dunroamin House* (London: Barrie and Jenkins, 1981), courtesy of Random House. Figure 6.6, copyright © National Trust Photographic Library/Geoffrey Frosh.

Figure 8.1, courtesy Carol Day, IHBC, BABTAC. Figure 9.2, text by Kathy Marks, *The Independent*, 21 October 1997; photograph courtesy of North News and Pictures, Newcastle-upon-Tyne. Figure 9.3 reproduced by courtesy of Tilda Foods. Figure 10.2 courtesy of Orange. Figure 10.3 reproduced by courtesy of Blackwell's Online Bookshop.

Reading 3.1, from Catherine Belsey, *Critical Practice* (London: Methuen and Co., 1980), courtesy of the publisher. Reading 3.2, from Stuart Hall (ed.), *Representation: Cultural Representations and Signifying Practices* (Milton Keynes: Open University, 1997), courtesy of the publisher. Reading 3.8, from Richard Dyer, *The Matter of Images: Essays on Representation* (London: Routledge, 1993), courtesy of the publisher. Readings 4.7 and 4.8, from Raphael Samuel, *Theatres of Memory* (London: Verso, 1994), courtesy of the publisher. Reading 6.3, from John Burnett, *A Social History of Housing 1815–1985* (London: Methuen, 1986), courtesy of the publisher. Reading 7.6, from *English in the National Curriculum: Draft Proposals 1994*, © Crown Copyright, is reproduced with the permission of the Controller of Her Majesty's Stationery Office. Reading 8.2, 'Recognition' by Carol Ann Duffy, with permission of Anvil Press. Reading 8.4, from Rosalind Minsky, 'Lacan', in Helen Crowley and Susan Himmelweit (eds), *Knowing Women: Feminism and Knowledge* (Milton Keynes: Open University, 1992), courtesy of the publisher. Reading 8.7, from Emily Martin, 'Body narratives, body boundaries', in Lawrence Grossberg, Cary Nelson and Paula Triechler (eds), *Cultural Studies* (London: Routledge, 1992), courtesy of the publisher. Reading 8.8, from Susan Bordo, 'Reading the slender body', in M. Jacobus, E. Fox Keller and S. Shuttleworth (eds), *Body/Politics: Women and the Discourse of Science* (London: Routledge, 1990), courtesy of the publisher. Reading 10.4, from M. Gillespie, 'Technology and tradition – audio-visual culture among South Asian families in West London', *Cultural Studies*, volume 3, number 2, courtesy of the publisher, Routledge. Reading 10.5, from Douglas Rushkoff, *Children of Chaos* (London: HarperCollins, 1997), courtesy of the publisher. Readings 10.6, from Shannon McRae, 'Coming apart at the seams', and 10.8, from Stephanie Brail, 'The price of admission', both copyright 1996 Cherny and Weise, reprinted from *Wired Women: Gender and New Realities in Cyberspace*, edited by Lynn Cherny and Elizabeth Reba Weise and published by Seal Press (Seattle).

The publishers apologize for any errors or omissions in the above list and would be grateful to be notified of any corrections that should be incorporated in the next edition or reprint of this book.

Introduction

This book is intended as a starting point for those who are newcomers to the study of culture, whether it be in the area of sociology, literature, history, geography, communication, media or cultural studies. Our aims are threefold. First, to offer an accessible and 'beginner's' route through the sometimes bewildering mass of material, theories and information that currently constitutes the study and analysis of culture. Second, to provide you with an introductory taste of some key areas that you may encounter in your studies. Third, as you will soon discover, this is not a book to be read passively: its format is interactive, engaging you, the reader, in activities at various points. Culture is something that all of us are engaged with in our everyday lives, and is the process by which we make sense of the world we inhabit. Everyone is knowledgeable in different ways about the cultures that surround us, and you should not be deterred, because you are now 'studying' culture in an academic environment, from using your own experience as a valuable resource. We want you to bring your own ideas and thoughts to the readings and discussions we offer. In return, it is our intention to offer you a vocabulary in which to express the complex ideas towards which you may be grasping.

One of the problems as well as one of the pleasures of studying culture is that almost everything seems to be cultural and therefore available for study. Cultural studies as an area of knowledge has grown rapidly in recent years, often in tandem with other subjects such as communication, media and film studies, and there is an enormous diversity of topics that lend themselves to cultural studies approaches. However, while cultural studies may seem, at first sight, to be everywhere and nowhere, it does have a distinctive history which has emphasized its interdisciplinary nature and its commitment to appropriating from other disciplinary areas whatever theories or methods are most appropriate to its purposes. Cultural studies, in Britain, began as a wide-ranging critique of dominant views of culture and of the modes of study and academic canons that maintained this hegemony. This original challenge to cultural elitism in Britain has widened since the 1960s and 1970s to encompass political interventions in a variety of international contexts. Cultural studies now thrives, for example, in South East Asia, France, the United States and Australia. Its particularly British focus on class has extended to analyses of gender, 'race', ethnicity, nationality and the power relations that shape and are shaped by cultural practices wherever they are found. In this book we have tried to offer a range of dimensions that can be brought to the study of culture –

for example, issues of time and space that have their roots in the disciplines of history and geography. As well, we focus on so-called 'high' cultural forms, such as the literary, which are often, although by no means always, excluded from a cultural studies approach and which can, therefore, tend to remain the discrete subject matter of literary critics, art historians and music scholars, for example.

We believe this book will be useful to newcomers to the area by offering an entry point to the field of cultural studies. At the same time, it needs to be acknowledged that our particular version of this field is one that has been shaped by our teaching and thinking about cultural studies and the requirements of students over a number of years. For example, the scope of this book thus conceived has not allowed us to focus in as much detail as some might wish on the import of the ethnographic work that has been produced as part of the process of cultural studies. However, this does not mean that we would wish to favour the textual and the abstract over the lived. Implicit in the interactive format of the book is our belief that the knowledge and experiences of 'ordinary' people are an important starting point for any consideration of culture

The impetus for writing this book came directly from our teaching of first- and second-year undergraduate students. We found that, while there are a number of excellent readers available, much of the material in these requires familiarity with a vocabulary that most newcomers do not possess. Our experience has shown that students, new to the area, have difficulty assimilating and applying many of the ideas and concepts without guidance. This book is an attempt to offer the kind of help which most readers are unable to provide. We would stress, however, that the activities and readings with which we invite you to engage should not be taken as a substitute for reading and thinking about the articles to be found in many of these collections. Rather, we suggest you use this book as a complement to your wider reading, and to this end we have provided lists of further reading for each chapter.

One of the problems in writing a book of this nature is what to include and what to leave out. We have not included comprehensive accounts of particular areas of knowledge – for example, psychoanalytic theory, media theory and film theory – not because we believe these areas are of lesser import to the study of culture, but because there are excellent, detailed introductions to these topics already available. We have chosen to concentrate on areas that are less accessibly covered elsewhere, and to offer a taste of the variety and diversity of approaches that constitute contemporary cultural studies. We hope that you will find much to interest you, but we also hope that the book's format will encourage you to question and take further areas that you find particularly stimulating.

The origins of this book are to be found in the core modules we teach on the cultural and critical studies programme. Identity and difference, representation, cultural history, heritage and geography are our starting points, and have proved a firm basis for more complex work at higher levels. More recently, we have begun to introduce students to theories and ideas of material and consumer cultures and to ways of thinking about new electronic information technologies. The activities we suggest have grown out of seminar-based discussions and exercises, but can be done individually and will help you to clarify points of debate as well as your own thoughts.

Throughout the book we have addressed 'you', the reader. We can, of course, have very little idea of who 'you' might be. We have, necessarily, assumed that there is a 'typical' student whom we are addressing. However, we remain aware that all of you who read this book will bring to it your individual histories, backgrounds, your preferences and interests, and your own needs. We cannot control how you will read this book or what use you will make of it, but we have tried to allow space for as wide a range of views and preoccupations as we can, at the same time as offering what we believe to be helpful suggestions. This would also be the point at which to say something about 'we': 'we' are lecturers in higher education, one female, one male, both British and both white. Most of the time we speak collectively but occasionally, when using an example specific to one of us, we use 'I'. When we do so we have indicated which of us is speaking at that particular point. Most of our examples are taken from British culture because this is what is most accessible to us and what we know best. However, there is no intention to insist that our particular (white European/British) knowledge of the world is all there is to know, and we would urge you, as readers, to seek out and think about cultures other than the one you know best. Our aim is to suggest possible approaches to studying and analysing culture and it should prove possible to apply the ideas developed in each chapter to a range of different cultures and artefacts.

Occasionally in the readings you will come across the male pronouns, 'he', 'his', 'him', or the noun 'man', used generically to denote 'human beings'. We do not subscribe to this sexist usage of language. Rather than interrupting the flow of the text by marking each occasion, we have chosen to draw attention to this here in the introduction. Wherever such usage occurs you should get into the habit of mentally inserting, 'she', 'her', 'hers' alongside the male pronoun. You might also consider what difference this insertion makes to the meaning of any particular sentence.

How to use this book

We have divided the book into two parts. Part I deals with what we would suggest are some key areas for the study of culture. If you work through these chapters and complement this with wider reading around each area you will be well on the way to acquiring a firm foundation for further study. At the end of part I we have written a case study in which we draw on the key areas already introduced. Bringing them together in this way illustrates, we hope, how it is possible to apply abstract concepts to empirical material but, equally, demonstrates the value of working across a range of disciplines to produce an interdisciplinary piece of cultural analysis.

Part II introduces ideas, debates, theories and information that, we think, are more readily understood once the key areas of part I have been introduced. In this sense, part II builds on the foundation established in part I but, at the same time, continues the objective of introducing you to key areas in the study of culture, in this case extending the debate about culture and introducing theories about the subject and consumption. Part II ends with a short case study. This one is contemporary rather than historical, thus offering you opportunities to see how concepts can be used with both contemporary and historical material.

We recognize that undergraduate courses, while concentrating on many of the topics we have identified, are unlikely to structure the material in the same way as we have done here. We suggest that you dip into sections as and when these are relevant to your current study. There is no necessity to work through the book as we have organized it – it should be possible to move around the sections and topics as your needs and interests dictate. On occasion we link activities across the chapters or we draw your attention to connections that can be made between topics, but we also hope that you will find your own links and connections as you move around the book.

Throughout the book we offer you short readings and invite you to engage in activities that will clarify the readings or our discussions.

Readings are signalled by the symbol

and activities by

You will find it productive if you do make serious attempts at the suggested activities, even if you do not always write down your thoughts. Don't worry if you find the questions difficult to answer; the purpose is to get you thinking even if you don't come up with a final answer. Some of the activities are best carried out with another person, and we hope this will encourage you to engage in discussion with your peers outside as well as inside the seminar room. Try to get into the habit of problematizing the terms and ideas you encounter by asking questions such as 'what', 'why', 'how', 'when' and 'where'. Neither should you feel you have to agree either with us or with the authors of the various readings. If you disagree, try to work out with what in particular you disagree and why. The aim is to engage in a dialogue or conversation through which you will find it becomes possible to clarify your own thoughts and to develop an individual response to the material.

In each chapter we can offer only a taste of the various debates and you would be advised, as we have already suggested, to follow these up with wider reading. At the end of the book we have provided lists of references from each chapter and suggested further reading, as well as a list of introductory texts and readers. These make good starting points as they offer a range of material and most of them can be found in any academic library. You will always find it helpful to read, in full, the article or chapter from which the extracted readings have been taken. At the same time you might also wish to read something that offers a different perspective. If you find the material you are reading difficult, try to see it as a challenge rather than rejecting it out of hand. Take from it what you do understand or the bits that interest you, and return to it at a later date. Often you will be surprised to find that what seemed impenetrable before has started to become clearer as you have developed and extended your capacity for study. We suggest too that you acquire the habit of using reference books to fill in factual gaps in your knowledge: these can be a valuable source of information of all kinds and we have tried to suggest some titles you may find useful along with the further reading.

One final point: some words have been printed in **bold type**. The intention is to draw your attention to these concepts, as you will find they crop up regularly in your study. We would suggest you compile your own glossary of these terms, and any others that seem to you important. Attempting to produce your own glossary and your own definitions is another way of assimilating and clarifying complex concepts. You could get into the habit of adding to such a glossary and revising your initial definitions as you read more widely.

Above all, we hope this book will prove the starting point for a continuing commitment to and enjoyment of the study of culture in all its diversity and variety. Now read on . . .

PART 1

CHAPTER 1

What Is Culture?

Introduction

When you start to study any topic or subject it is always useful to think about how that topic or subject has been defined by others and what questions are raised about the subject in the process of attempting to define it. **Culture** is no exception: Raymond Williams famously asserted that 'culture is one of the two or three most complicated words in the English language' (Williams, 1976, p. 87). It is undoubtedly one of the central concepts in our understanding of how modern societies work, and for this reason it is worth spending some time considering the different ways in which the term 'culture' has been and is used. In this chapter we want to introduce you to the variety of ways in which the term can be understood and to suggest how the tensions between different meanings have informed current debates about the place of culture in the social sciences and the humanities. We also want to introduce you to a way of understanding culture that is widely accepted and used among contemporary cultural theorists and students of culture. This is not to suggest that the 'true' meaning of culture has finally been defined: because culture is one of the key concepts in our knowledge of societies both past and present, definitions are constantly being developed and refined. We can only make a start in this chapter. You, too, may want to revisit, rethink and develop your understanding of the term as you engage with the material in this book.

It would be useful to begin by noting in a sentence or two what you understand by the term culture. When you have completed this chapter you could look again at your definition and think about whether and how you would change or refine it. It would be useful to continue this exercise at various points in your studies.

1.1

You can continue to explore what is meant by the concept 'culture' by examining a number of statements using the term 'culture'. Look at the following statements and note what you think is meant by 'culture' in each. You could try to suggest an example of culture that would be appropriate in each case:

ACTIVITIES

- There are enormous cultural differences between Europe and Asia.
- She is such a cultured person.
- Pop music is often used by sub-cultures to assert their identity.
- There is a danger that mass culture may destroy the values of our society.
- This course will examine Victorian society and culture.
- Culture is the network of shared meanings in any society.
- McDonalds fosters a distinctive culture based on certain values.

As Raymond Williams points out in *Keywords* (1976), the word culture originally meant the tending or cultivation of something, in particular animals or crops – hence the noun 'agriculture'. From the eighteenth century onwards, this sense of culture as cultivation was particularly associated with the spiritual and moral progress of humanity. Involved in this meaning of culture was the idea of a process, unlike some meanings of the term, which suggest an end product. For example, the term culture is often used to mean actual products, such as opera, concerts, literature, drama and paintings; mass culture is often applied to television, Hollywood, magazines, 'pulp' fiction and newspapers; and the term 'Victorian culture' implies a body of material already available for study. However, as Williams reminds us, from the nineteenth century onwards, with the growth of nation states and the Romantic interest in 'folk art', it became necessary 'to speak of cultures in the plural' in order to distinguish between the particular cultures of different nations, but also 'the specific and variable cultures of social and economic groups within a nation' (Williams, 1976, p. 89). Moreover, anthropology, as an academic discipline, became established in the early years of the twentieth century, with its sub-branch of cultural anthropology generally understood to be 'the comparative study of preliterate people', in which culture is defined as the whole way of life of a particular society (Kuper and Kuper, 1985, p. 27). As a result, by the twentieth century, there were three broad categories of definition in general usage. Williams identifies these as follows:

- a general process of intellectual, spiritual and aesthetic development;
- a particular way of life, whether of a people, a period, a group or humanity in general;
- the works and practices of intellectual and especially artistic activity (Williams, 1976, p. 90).

What is important for our purposes is not to select one of these definitions as the 'true' meaning of the concept culture, but to begin to think about (a) the ways in which these varied definitions overlap and (b) the points of emphasis that are of interest to contemporary social and cultural theorists. In the following sections we look more closely at the ways in which these different definitions have been expressed and how these have contributed to what is often referred to as 'the contemporary turn to culture' not only in academia, but also in the worlds of business, economics and politics (du Gay et al., 1997, p. 2).

The 'culture and civilization' debate

You should now read the following extract from *Culture and Anarchy* (1869) by Matthew Arnold. Arnold (1822–88) was an inspector of schools from 1851 to 1887. He was elected Professor of Poetry at the University of Oxford in 1857 and is probably best known today as a poet. Among his most anthologized poems are 'The Scholar-Gipsy' (1853) and 'Dover Beach' (1867). As you read, try to answer the following questions:

- What do you think Arnold means when he claims that culture is 'a study of perfection'?
- Why does Arnold believe culture is so important in 'our modern world'?
- What kinds of things do you think would constitute for Arnold 'the best that has been thought and known in the world'?

1.1

I am a Liberal, yet I am a Liberal tempered by experience, reflexion, and renouncement, and I am above all, a believer in culture. Therefore I propose now to try and enquire, in the simple unsystematic way which best suits both my taste and my powers, what culture really is, what good it can do, what is our own special need of it; and I shall seek to find some plain grounds on which a faith in culture – both my own faith in it and the faith of others, – may rest securely . . .

There is a view in which all the love of our neighbour, the impulses towards action, help and beneficence, the desire for removing human error, clearing human confusion, and diminishing human misery, the noble aspiration to leave the world better and happier than we found it, – motives eminently such as are called social – come in as part of the grounds of culture, and the main and pre-eminent part. Culture is then properly described not as having its origin in curiosity, but as having its origin in the love of perfection: it is a *study of perfection*. It moves by the force, not merely or primarily of the scientific passion for pure knowledge, but also of the moral and social passion for doing good . . .

If culture, then, is a study of perfection, and of harmonious perfection, general perfection, and perfection which consists in becoming something rather than in having something, in an inward condition of the mind and spirit, not in an outward set of circumstances, – it is clear that culture . . . has a very important function to fulfil for mankind. And this function is particularly important in our modern world, of which the whole civilisation is . . . mechanical and external, and tends constantly to become more so . . .

The pursuit of perfection, then, is the pursuit of sweetness and light. He who works for sweetness and light works to make reason and the will of God prevail. He who works for machinery, he who works for hatred, works only for confusion. Culture looks beyond machinery, culture hates hatred; culture has one great passion, the passion for sweetness and light . . . It is not satisfied till we *all* come to a perfect man, it knows that the sweetness and light of the few must be imperfect until the raw and unkindled masses of humanity are touched with sweetness and light . . . Again and again I have insisted how those are the happy moments of humanity, how those are the marking epochs of people's life, how those are the flowering times for literature and art and all the creative power of genius, when there is a *national* glow of life and thought, when the whole of society is in the fullest measure permeated by thought, sensible to beauty, intelligent and alive. Only it must be *real* thought and *real* beauty; *real* sweetness and *real* light. Plenty of people will try to give the masses, as they call them, an intellectual food prepared and adapted in the way they think proper for the actual condition of the masses. The ordinary popular literature is an example of this way of working on the masses. Plenty of people will try to indoctrinate the masses with the set of ideas and judgements constituting the creed of their own profession or party. Our religious and political organisations give an example of this way of working on the masses. I condemn neither way; but culture works differently. It does not try to teach down to the level of inferior classes; it does not try to win them for this or that sect of its own, with ready-made judgements and watchwords. It seeks to do away with classes; to make the best that has been thought and known in the world current everywhere; to make all men live in an atmosphere of sweetness and light, where they may use ideas, as it uses them itself, freely, – nourished, and not bound by them. (Arnold, 1869, Introduction and chapter 1)

'The pursuit of perfection', for Arnold, is a moral, intellectual and spiritual journey 'to make reason and the will of God prevail'. Opportunities to achieve 'perfection' in this sense cannot be restricted to a privileged minority, but must be available to 'the raw and unkindled masses of humanity'. Culture, in the sense of the 'best that has been thought and known', is the conduit through which 'real thought and real beauty' will be given to 'the masses'. In modern industrial society, Arnold believes, it is the duty of those already possessing 'culture' to ensure its transmission to 'the masses' who are in danger of being offered inferior 'intellectual food': for example, 'ordinary popular literature'.

Arnold's view of culture has to be understood in the context of his time. Arnold, like other nineteenth-century commentators – for example, Thomas Carlyle, John Ruskin and William Morris – believed that mechanization, urbanization and *laissez-faire* economics would inevitably lead to a morally bankrupt society that would eventually collapse into anarchy. The 1867 Reform Act, which extended the franchise to urban working-class males, was further cause for anxiety: granting political power to an uneducated, undeferential mass of urban dwellers could, it was believed, hasten the anarchy that commentators, such as Arnold, feared. Culture offered through education – remember Arnold was a schools inspector as well as professor of poetry – is the solution because, for Arnold, it generates both a moral and spiritual aspiration to know 'the best that has been known and thought in the world'. For Arnold, to be 'cultured' means having a familiarity with that body of knowledge – philosophy, literature, painting, music – which, for him, constitutes the 'best'. In *Culture and Anarchy* culture understood as a process of humanization becomes conflated with the products through which humanization will be achieved.

1.2

- Can you suggest any ways in which Arnold's view of culture was a progressive view?
- Use a general history of Victorianism to find out more about the ideas of Arnold, Carlyle, Ruskin and Morris. For example, *The Cambridge Cultural History of Britain: Victorian Britain, Volume 9*, edited by Boris Ford, would be a useful source. For a more detailed account try the relevant chapters in Walter Houghton, *The Victorian Frame of Mind*.
- Arnold sees 'culture' and 'anarchy' as two opposing concepts. The question, as he sets it, is *either* culture *or* anarchy. How do you respond to this? What might be the political effects of this way of thinking? You could return to this when you read the extract from Said later in the chapter.

The idea that 'the best that has been known and thought' should be available to all and not simply to an educated elite is potentially democratic in that it implies a widening of access to certain forms of culture. Art galleries, theatre, opera, museums and 'great' literature should be available and accessible to all, and not the preserve of the rich or powerful. In this sense a 'cultured' person is educated and knowledgeable about history, literature, art and philosophy, with the corollary that such knowledge is both civilizing and humanizing. However, you might want to question the claim that culture, in this sense, teaches humane values: some Nazi leaders, as we know, enjoyed and understood art, literature and music. Equally, it is worth noting that the Arnoldian perspective on culture is a restrictive one. It limits the meaning of culture to scholarship and the arts: 'high' culture as opposed to 'popular' or 'mass' culture; Shakespeare but not *EastEnders*. Nevertheless, Arnold's belief in the beneficial aspects of certain forms of culture was highly influential in determining policies towards education and the arts until the 1950s, and traces still persist today in discussions about what forms of culture society should value and support. For example, the debate about a national curriculum in British schools has, from time to time, invoked an Arnoldian view of the humanizing effects of teaching 'high' culture (see chapter 7).

1.3

In order to explore further the consequences of defining 'culture' along the lines taken by Arnold, try the following activities.

1   Make a list of those products or activities which would and would not count as 'culture' according to Arnold. We have started you off.

Would count	Would not count
• Production of *Hamlet*	TV soap opera
• Sculpture	Knitting
• Paintings	Wallpaper designs

2   Can you identify any common elements amongst the items on each list? If there are commonalities do these suggest why some things might count as culture and others not?

3   Look out for articles in newspapers or magazines which seem to you to offer an Arnoldian perspective, particularly with regard to the arts or education.

4   Try to construct a set of criteria for deciding what is 'the best that has been thought and known'. Note down any problems you have in arriving at a set of criteria.

Now read the following account written by an adult education student in the 1930s.

1.2

I am a worker – a trade unionist, and for years a W.E.A. student with an ardent desire to learn. Three years ago I felt the need for advancing my education, and being interested in Literature, I attended my first W.E.A class, the subject of which was 'The Modern Novel'. As I had read all the books of Edgar Wallace, Ethel M. Dell and Rafael Sabatini.[1] I felt a very superior person, a person who could hold his own in a discussion. After two hours of hearing a lecturer, who took for granted that each member of the class was well-versed in Virginia Woolf, Aldous Huxley and D. H. Lawrence, I left the room dazed. Vague references to Freud and Behaviourism ran riot in my brain in bewildering confusion. The revelation of my colossal ignorance so stunned me that I did not even know how or where to begin. Moreover, the discussion afterwards gave me such a feeling of humiliation that I daren't even ask the lecturer for advice. My first impulse was to stop going to the classes, but curiosity conquered me; so for the first year I became an interested but dumb student. By making mistakes in written work, I began to learn and I continued to learn in the same way. But, you may ask, 'Why don't you help swell the ranks of the class by introducing new members?' This is my answer. 'Because I do not want them to experience what I experienced. I do not want to choke them by bringing them into an environment of middle class. (Cited in Jordan and Weedon, 1995, p. 41)

1.4

What are the writer's feelings about encountering 'culture'? Why does he or she feel this way? Do you recognize any aspects of this account in your own experience? Does this writer's experience suggest difficulties with Arnold's project 'to make the best that has been thought and known in the world current everywhere'?

[1]   Three popular writers of the period: for example, Wallace wrote detective fiction and Dell wrote romantic fiction.

The 'mass culture' debate

An extension of Arnold's thesis on culture was the debate about 'mass culture' that gathered momentum in the 1920s and 1930s and continued throughout the 1940s and 1950s. Developing technologies in the early twentieth century made possible a wider range of media through which communication was possible – cinema, radio, television, equipment for listening to music, newspapers, magazines and commercially produced fiction – with, as a result of compulsory universal education, an increasingly literate audience or readership. The growth of a mass media producing cultural products for a growing market of consumers created concern among those who believed in the civilizing effects of 'high' art. Arnold's fear that 'people will try to indoctrinate the masses' was one response to the spread of a so-called 'mass culture', particularly in the context of the growth of totalitarian states in, for example, Germany and Russia. Others, like F. R. and Q. D. Leavis, both academics in the English Literature Department at the University of Cambridge in the 1930s and 1940s, condemned the preference of the majority of the population for the products of the mass media. In *Fiction and the Reading Public*, published in 1932, Q. D. Leavis referred to the reading of popular fiction as 'a drug addiction' which could lead to 'a habit of fantasying [which] will lead to maladjustment in actual life' (pp. 152, 54). F. R. Leavis, in his book *Mass Civilization and Minority Culture*, attacked cinemas for offering films that 'involve surrender, under conditions of hypnotic receptivity, to the cheapest emotional appeals' (Leavis, 1930, p. 10). For cultural critics like the Leavises the concept of culture implied a distinction between culture and mass culture, an opposition in which the term 'mass culture' signified an inferior and debased form of culture (often associated with the USA and American influence).

In the years following the Second World War, as Cold War ideologies established themselves, intellectuals in the USA continued this debate in relation to concerns about 'the enemies within' American society. Mass culture, it was feared, produced fertile ground for the growth of 'unamerican' ideologies (in particular, communism) and threatened the liberalism and pluralism on which it was believed an enduring political and cultural consensus had been built. This apparent consensus was to collapse with the rise of the black civil rights movement and the countercultures of the late 1960s and 1970s (Storey, 1993, pp. 33–4). Now read the following extract from an influential essay by the American critic, Dwight Macdonald written in the 1950s. This essay is part of an anthology published in 1957, *Mass Culture: the Popular Arts in America*, edited by Bernard Rosenberg and David Manning White, which attacked what they saw as the dehumanizing effects of mass culture. As you read bear in mind the following questions and at the end note down your responses:

- What does Macdonald see as the differences between 'folk art' and 'mass culture'?
- What does Macdonald see as the dangers of 'mass culture'?
- What does Macdonald see as the characteristics of 'the mass man'?

1.3

Folk art grew from below. It was a spontaneous, autochthonous expression of the people, shaped by themselves, pretty much without the benefit of High Culture, to suit their own needs. Mass Culture is imposed from above. It is fabricated by technicians hired by businessmen; its audience are passive consumers, their participation limited to the choice between buying and not buying. The Lords of *kitsch*, in short, exploit the cultural needs of the masses in order to make a profit and/or to maintain their class rule – in Communist countries, only the second purpose obtains . . . Folk art was the people's own institution, their private little garden walled off from the great formal part of their masters; High Culture. But Mass Culture breaks down the wall, integrating the masses into a debased form of High Culture and thus becoming an instrument of political domination . . .

For the masses in historical time are what a crowd is in space: a large quantity of people unable to express themselves as human beings because they are related to one another neither as individuals nor as members of communities – indeed, they are not related to each other at all, but only to something distant, abstract, nonhuman: a football game or bargain sale in the case of a crowd, a system of industrial production, a party or a State in the case of the masses. The mass man is a solitary atom, uniform with and undifferentiated from thousands and millions of other atoms who go to make up 'the lonely crowd' as David Reisman well calls American society. A folk or a people, however, is a community, i.e., a group of individuals linked to each other by common interests, work, traditions, values, and sentiments. (Macdonald, 1957, p. 60)

For those, like Macdonald, who bemoaned the stultifying and manipulative effects of a commercially produced culture, individuals in modern industrial society were perceived as fragmented, atomized and alienated from a sense of community which had once bestowed identity and belonging. In the same year that Macdonald's essay was published (1957), Richard Hoggart, a Senior Staff Tutor in Literature in the Department of Adult Education at Hull University, published *The Uses of Literacy*, in which he argued that the urban working-class cultures of his youth were being destroyed by an Americanized mass-produced culture. Hoggart was born in Leeds in 1918 and spent his childhood in the working-class areas of that city. He gained scholarships to secondary school and later to the University of Leeds, where he gained a first class honours degree in English literature. In the 1960s, Hoggart established the Centre for Contemporary Cultural Studies at the University of Birmingham and was its first director.

1.4

I suggested earlier that it would be a mistake to regard the cultural struggle now going on as a straight fight between, say, what *The Times* and the picture-dailies respectively represent. To wish that a majority of the population will ever read *The Times* is to wish that human beings were constitutionally different, and is to fall into an intellectual snobbery. The ability to read the decent weeklies is not a *sine qua non* of the good life. It seems unlikely at any time, and is certainly not likely in any period which those of us now alive are likely to know that a majority in any class will have strongly intellectual pursuits. There are other ways of being in the truth. The strongest objection to the more trivial popular entertainments is not that they prevent their readers from becoming highbrow, but that they make it harder for people without an intellectual bent to become wise in their own way . . .

Most mass-entertainments are in the end what D. H. Lawrence described as 'anti-life'. They are full of a corrupt brightness, of improper appeals and moral evasions . . . they tend towards a view of the world in which progress is conceived as a seeking of material possessions, equality as a moral levelling, and freedom as the ground for endless irresponsible pleasure. These productions belong to a vicarious spectators' world; they offer nothing which can really grip the brain or heart. They assist a gradual drying-up of the more positive, the fuller, the more co-operative kinds of enjoyment, in which one gains much by giving much. They have intolerable pretensions; and pander to the wish to have things both ways, to do as we want and accept no consequences. A handful of such productions reaches daily the great majority of the population: their effect is both widespread and uniform. (Hoggart, 1957, pp. 281–3)

1.5

- What is your response to Macdonald's belief that people are 'passive consumers' of the products offered by a mass media? Think about how you and others known to you respond to TV programmes, what you read in the newspapers, what you see at the cinema. What about readers of the tabloid newspapers? What about those who appear on television game shows? Are they 'passive consumers'?
- Does Hoggart see the people he is discussing as 'passive consumers'? If so, are there any differences between his view and Macdonald's? If not, how would you describe his attitude to 'the great majority of the population'?

You may have thought that Hoggart is more optimistic than Macdonald. Hoggart appears to allow that, despite the fragmentation of modern urban life, 'people without an intellectual bent' can 'become wise in their own way' if they can remain untainted by the blandishments of 'mass culture', whereas for Macdonald the 'large quantity of people unable to express themselves as human beings' appear already doomed to 'a narcotized acceptance of Mass Culture' (Macdonald, 1957, p. 73). The idea that the mass of population in modern society consumes passively, accepting without question the diet of ideas, images, stereotypes offered by the mass media, needs to be questioned, and we shall return to this in more detail in later chapters (see chapters 7 and 9). For now it is worth noting that, while Hoggart is concerned about the possibly enervating effects of a mass culture on the British working class, he does allow them wisdom and intelligence. Macdonald, on the other hand, appears to have little faith that people have any resources to resist their positioning as the 'passive dupes' of an all encompassing mass media. In order to appreciate more fully the similarities and differences between the two arguments you should consider these extracts in context by reading more widely in the books from which they are taken.

Although Hoggart follows Arnold in a concern for cultural decline and a belief in education as the means of stemming this, he uses a wider concept of culture than cultural critics like the Leavises or Macdonald. For Hoggart, culture is not simply 'the best that has been thought and known' but *all* those activities, practices, artistic and intellectual processes and products that go to make up the culture of a specific group at a particular time. Hoggart argues that the British urban working class developed certain cultural forms through which it could express itself at a particular historical moment (the 1930s), and that these forms were now (in the 1950s) in danger of disappearing. Hoggart's work is justly important because it paved the way for later cultural theorists to study a broader version of culture, which included mass as well as 'high' culture.

Although you are unlikely to encounter ideas about culture in the precise form expressed by Arnold, Macdonald or Hoggart in the work of contemporary cultural theorists, traces of these definitions may persist in general works, in newspaper articles and in general usage. We have introduced you to these ideas because you will find it useful to be able to distinguish these traces from the theories of culture currently employed in the academic study of culture. In the next section we shall begin to consider how theories of culture have developed in recent years. Before you move on you could try the following activities.

ACTIVITIES

1.6

- Use the list of suggested reading for this chapter to find out more about the debates over culture in the early part of the twentieth century. John Storey's *An Introductory Guide to Cultural Theory and Popular Culture* would be a useful starting point. We have focused on British and American responses but the debate was carried on with different emphases in other European countries. In chapter 9 we look at the contribution of the Frankfurt School, represented here by the German exiles Theodor Adorno and Max Horkheimer.

- We have, in passing, mentioned the working classes. Are there other groups in society who might have a stake in a particular culture? Do they appear in any of the analyses above?

- Does the term 'mass' adequately describe the population of a society? Make a list of the senses in which the term is used and compare the differences. Whenever you come across the word 'mass' or 'masses' in your reading check it against your list of meanings and think about how it is being used.

Social definitions of culture

Of the three definitions of culture that we quoted in the introduction to this chapter, we have so far been concerned with two:

- a general process of intellectual, spiritual and aesthetic development;
- the works and practices of intellectual and especially artistic activity (Williams, 1976, p. 90).

In *The Long Revolution* (1961), Raymond Williams outlines a theory of culture that attempts to link these two definitions with the third: that is, 'a particular way of life, whether of a people, a period, a group, or humanity in general' (Williams, 1976, p. 90). Williams called this:

> a 'social' definition of culture, in which culture is a description of a particular way of life, which expresses certain meanings and values not only in art and learning but also in institutions and ordinary behaviour. The analysis of culture, from such a definition, is the clarification of the meanings and values implicit and explicit in a particular way of life, a particular culture. Such analysis will include . . . historical criticism . . . in which intellectual and imaginative works are analysed in relation to particular traditions and societies, but will also include analysis of elements in the way of life that to followers of the other definitions are not 'culture' at all: the organization of production, the structure of the family, the structure of institutions which express or govern social relationships, the characteristic forms through which members of the society communicate. (Williams, 1961, p. 57)

Like Richard Hoggart's, Raymond Williams's origins were working class. Williams was born in the Welsh border village of Pandy and his father was a railway signalman. Like Hoggart, Williams gained scholarships, enabling him to continue his education at Abergavenny Grammar School and later at Trinity College, Cambridge. He became Professor of Drama at Cambridge University and is a central figure in the development of ideas about the relationship between culture and society.

Williams's definition above proposes that culture is a system by which meanings and ideas are expressed, not only in 'art and learning', but also in 'ordinary behaviour'. This breaks with Arnold's version of culture as 'the best that has been thought and known', and posits culture as a more inclusive and wider ranging phenomenon. The purpose of cultural analysis, according to Williams, is to clarify and identify the meanings that are expressed in not only 'art and learning', but also 'ordinary behaviour', 'the structure of the family' and the institutions of a society. Now read the following extract from an earlier essay by Williams, first published in 1958.

1.5

The bus stop was outside the cathedral. I had been looking at the Mappa Mundi, with its rivers out of Paradise, and at the chained library, where a party of clergymen had got in easily, but where I had waited an hour and cajoled a verger before I even saw the chains. Now, across the street, a cinema advertised the *Six-Five Special*[2] and a cartoon version of *Gulliver's Travels*. The bus arrived, with a driver and a conductress deeply absorbed in each other. We went out of the city, over the old bridge, and on through the orchards and the green meadows and

---

² A pop music TV programme popular in the late 1950s and early 1960s.

the fields red under the plough. Ahead were the Black Mountains, and we climbed among them, watching the steep fields end at the grey wall, beyond which the bracken and heather and whin had not yet been driven back. To the east, along the ridge, stood the line of grey Norman castles; to the west, the fortress wall of the mountains. Then, as we still climbed, the rock changed under us. Here, now, was limestone, and the line of the early iron workings along the scarp. The farming valleys, with their scattered white houses, fell away behind. Ahead of us were the narrower valleys: the steel-rolling mill, the gasworks, the grey terraces, the pitheads. The bus stopped, and the driver and conductress got out, still absorbed. They had done this journey so often, and seen all its stages. It is a journey, in fact, that in one form or another we have all made.

I was born and grew up halfway along that bus journey. Where I lived is still a farming valley, though the road through it is being widened and straightened, to carry the heavy lorries to the north. Not far away, my grandfather, and so back through the generations, worked as a farm labourer until he was turned out of his cottage and, in his fifties, became a road man. His sons went at thirteen or fourteen on to the farms, his daughters into service. My father, his third son, left the farm at fifteen to be a boy porter on the railway, and later became a signalman, working in a box in this valley until he died. I went up the road to the village school, where a curtain divided the two classes – Second to eight or nine, First to fourteen. At eleven I went to the local grammar school, and later to Cambridge.

Culture is ordinary: that is where we must start. To grow up in that country was to see the shape of a culture, and its modes of change . . .

Culture is ordinary: that is the first fact. Every human society has its own shape, its own purposes, its own meanings. Every human society expresses these, in institutions, and in arts and learning. The making of a society is the finding of common meanings and directions, and its growth is an active debate and amendment under the pressures of experience, contact and discovery, writing themselves into the land . . . We use the word culture in . . . two senses: to mean a whole way of life – the common meanings; to mean the arts and learning – the special processes of discovery and creative effort. Some writers reserve the word for one or other of these senses; I insist on both, and on the significance of their conjunction. The questions I ask about our culture are questions about our general and common purposes, yet also questions about deep personal meanings. Culture is ordinary, in every society and in every mind. (Williams, 1958a, pp. 5–6)

1.7

1 Why do you think Williams stresses and repeats the phrase 'culture is ordinary'? Can you think of examples from your own knowledge of culture as the ordinary?

2 Make a list of the things Williams identifies as culture. Can you suggest some of the meanings that might be expressed by the cultures he identifies? We have started this off for you, you carry on.

● The cathedral[3] expresses ideas about religion and worship, Christianity, the importance of religion and worship in the past.

³ The cathedral referred to in Williams's article is Hereford Cathedral.

Figure 1.1 Hereford Cathedral

- The steel rolling mill expresses the significance of heavy industry to Britain's economic prosperity now and in the past.
- The Norman castles express . . .
- The life stories . . .
-
-

If we take one example from the list above we can explore further what Williams has in mind when he talks about 'meanings and values'. A cathedral is a large building in which people congregate for an act of worship. If we belong to a

European or Western society, we will probably recognize a cathedral as a specifically Christian house of worship. If we come from a society that has very different kinds of religious buildings we know what it stands for by relating it to similar buildings in our own cultures – temple, mosque etc. We may also understand a cathedral as a place of historic interest: it tells us about the importance of Christianity in society in the past and the ways in which it was practised. Equally, a cathedral can be understood as a work of art. Visitors come from all over the world to study its architecture, to look at its fine art, to appreciate the beauty and craftsmanship of its stained glass windows. A cathedral can also mean a tourist attraction, spawning tea rooms, gift shops, guided tours – a piece of European heritage that can be marketed at home and abroad. Moreover, specific cathedrals may have another layer of local and particular meanings. Think, for example, of Canterbury Cathedral or Sacré Coeur in Paris. You may well be able to think of other meanings that attach themselves to the idea of a cathedral.

The diverse meanings that come to mind when we think or read about cathedrals do not present themselves as intrinsic to the physical presence of the building. We can think about cathedrals, as you are probably doing now, without actually looking at or being present in one. The meanings that attach themselves to physical objects as well as abstract concepts grow out of the ways in which objects or concepts are used by a particular group or society. There was no pre-existent idea of cathedral that preceded the actual design and building of one, although there were strong religious feelings and creative impulses which found their expression in the physical construction of a cathedral. Equally, the ways in which an object or concept may be used can be shaped by the meanings that have grown up around that object or concept. If we take cathedrals as an example, the growth of cathedrals as tourist attractions has come about in part because they have been and are perceived as places of great beauty. An understanding of cathedrals as works of art has led to the practice of making them accessible as places to visit as well as places to worship. You may also have noted that different meanings conflict with and contradict each other. For example, there is surely a tension between understanding a cathedral as a sacred place of worship for the believers of a particular religion and understanding it as a place of beauty that should be accessible to all, or as a marketable tourist attraction. Thinking about this tension and analysing how the tension manifests or resolves itself in actual behaviour and practice can help us to understand the complex relations between religion, the arts, economics and consumerism in secular, contemporary society. The processes by which meanings evolve and interact with behaviour and practice is one that we shall return to throughout this book.

ACTIVITIES

1.8

Try thinking about some of the other forms of culture mentioned by Williams in the way we have discussed cathedrals. Consider the meanings that attach to these. Good examples would be: the cinema, the cluster of industrial images (steel rolling mill, gasworks, terraces, pitheads), the village school, Cambridge University.

In *The Long Revolution*, Williams expands and develops his assertion that 'culture is ordinary'. At the same time, he spells out very clearly the task of cultural analysis. Now read the following extract from chapter 2 of *The Long Revolution*.

1.6

Again, such analysis ranges from an 'ideal' emphasis, the discovery of certain absolute or universal, or at least higher and lower, meanings and values, through the 'documentary' emphasis, in which clarification of a particular way of life is the main end in view, to an emphasis which, from studying particular meanings and values, seeks not so much to compare these, as a way of establishing a scale, but by studying their modes of change to discover certain general 'laws' or 'trends', by which social and cultural development as a whole can be better understood . . .

I think we can best understand this if we think of any similar analysis of a way of life that we ourselves share. For we find here a particular sense of life, a particular community of experience hardly needing expression, through which the characteristics of our way of life that an external analyst could describe are in some way passed, giving them a particular and characteristic colour. We are usually most aware of this when we notice the contrasts between generations, who never talk quite 'the same language', or when we read an account of our lives by someone from outside the community, or watch the small differences in style, of speech or behaviour, in someone who has learned our ways yet was not bred in them . . .

The term I would suggest to describe it is *structure of feeling*: it is as firm and definite as 'structure' suggests, yet it operates in the most delicate and least tangible parts of our activity. In one sense, this structure of feeling is the culture of a period: it is the particular living result of all the elements in the general organization . . . I do not mean that the structure of feeling, any more than the social character, is possessed in the same way by the many individuals in the community. But I think it is a very deep and very wide possession, in all actual communities, precisely because it is on it that communication depends. (Williams, 1961, pp. 42, 48)

Here, Williams is concerned to offer a form of cultural analysis that does not have evaluation or comparison as its function but seeks to 'discover certain general "laws" '. Later in the chapter from which this extract is taken, Williams uses Sophocles' *Antigone* to illustrate his point. Let's take two contemporary examples: an RSC production of Shakespeare's *Hamlet* and a pop concert. The aim of the analysis, according to Williams, would not be to produce a comparison of the two events in which one or other is discovered to be superior. Instead, the task would be to seek out similarities as well as differences in content, form and production, and to relate these to the wider structures of the society or community which produced these performances. In so doing, the analysis might reveal the shared attitudes and values of a particular society, community or group. For example, the cultural analyst might be interested in the links between Hamlet, as cynical outsider and/or tormented rebel, and the similar identities often attributed to pop stars, and might then go on to suggest how these identities function in modern societies. However, in order for these identities to be recognized, it is necessary for a group or society to share certain, often tacitly understood, values and attitudes – in this case the various connotations of the rebel/loner/misfit figure – what Williams refers to as 'structure of feeling'.

1.9

- Can you think of any values, attitudes in your family, or community, or social group, that could illustrate Williams's 'structure of feeling'?
- Can you widen this to identify examples of structures of feeling in British society, or other societies more generally?

Williams stresses that it is structures of feeling that enable communication. If we did not share certain common understandings of the world, we would find it extremely difficult to communicate. We used the example of the cathedral, in our discussion above, because we were able to assume that most readers would share with us certain ideas about what a cathedral stands for.

Language, of course, is central to any theory of communication: language is the medium through which shared meanings or structures of feeling are communicated. Verbal language is not the only medium of communication; we also use visual, musical and body languages, often in conjunction with words. Recent developments in sociology and cultural studies have developed Williams's emphasis on the links between culture, language and meaning. However, rather than seeing culture (meanings, beliefs, language) as a reflection of economic and social conditions, which Williams tends to do, these have stressed the ways in which culture itself creates, constructs and constitutes social relations (such as those between men and women, children and parents) and economic relations (for example, those between business and the arts or between industry and environmentalism). Moreover, subsequent developments in the disciplinary areas most concerned with the analysis of culture (social sciences, cultural studies, literary studies, history) have begun to ask questions about how meanings are produced, how they are communicated, which meanings are shared and by which groups, what happens when meanings are contested by different groups. One contemporary definition is that culture is 'the production and circulation of meaning' – the processes by which culture is produced and the forms it takes, rather than simply the 'structure of feeling' or 'way of life' it reveals.

Recent theorists in social theory and cultural studies have put much greater stress on the centrality and the relative autonomy of culture. We cannot just 'read off' culture from society. We need to analyse the role of 'the symbolic' sphere in social life in its own terms ... This critique gives the production of meaning through language – what is sometimes called *signification* – a privileged place in the analysis of culture. All social practices, recent critics would argue, are organized through meanings – they are *signifying practices* and must therefore be studied by giving greater weight to their cultural dimension. (du Gay et al., 1997, p. 13)

Culture and power

Whether we choose to see culture as 'the production and circulation of meaning' or as 'a particular way of life', we need to consider carefully its place in constructing, sustaining and reproducing structures and relations of power. A 'structure of feeling' – a particular way of seeing the world – has political implications. The ways in which societies or groups see the world have direct results for how members of a particular society or group treat non-members and are themselves treated. For example, a 'structure of feeling' based on certain ideas about the nature and roles of women and men or on concepts of 'racial' difference can produce practices and behaviours which lead to oppression and discrimination. **Discourses** of gender or race – the ways in which sexual and 'racial' differences are defined, talked about, represented visually – create the conditions in which men and women experience their lives. If we see culture as 'the production and circulation of meaning' then culture is a significant site for the formation of discourses by which one social group or community (a sex, 'race', nation or society) legitimates its power over another group or community.

Equally, culture becomes an important place where power, and the meanings that uphold power, can be resisted. We shall explore the concept of discourse further in chapter 3. Now read the following extract from Edward Said's *Culture and Imperialism*. It may help you to know that 'the administrative massacre' Said refers to occurred in 1865, when the British Governor of Jamaica, F. J. Eyre, ordered the killing of many black people in Jamaica as a means of 'controlling' social unrest and rioting among Jamaican Blacks. Said's use of the term 'narrative' is close in meaning to the term 'discourse' used above, and very broadly speaking can be taken to mean the stories we tell, the stories we are told, the stories that circulate in a particular culture through literature, art, music. He is, it should also be noted, mainly concerned with those elements of culture that Arnold would have categorized as 'the best that has been thought and known', and has less to say about the narratives or discourses constructed in other forms of culture.

1.7

Introduction

. . . The main battle in imperialism is over land, of course; but when it came to who owned the land, who had the right to settle and work on it, who kept it going, who won it back, and who now plans its future – these issues were reflected, contested, and even for a time decided in narrative. As one critic has suggested, nations themselves *are* narrations. The power to narrate, or to block other narratives from forming and emerging, is very important to culture and imperialism, and constitutes one of the main connections between them. Most important, the grand narratives of emancipation and enlightenment mobilized people in the colonial world to rise up and throw off imperial subjection; in the process, many Europeans and

Americans were also stirred by these stories and their protagonists, and they too fought for new narratives of equality and human community . . .

Arnold believed that culture palliates, if it does not altogether neutralize, the ravages of a modern, aggressive, mercantile, and brutalizing urban existence. You read Dante or Shakespeare in order to keep up with the best that was thought and known, and also to see yourself, your people, society, and tradition in their best lights. In time, culture comes to be associated, often aggressively, with the nation or state; this differentiates 'us' from 'them', almost always with some degree of xenophobia. Culture in this sense is a source of identity . . .

Chapter 2

. . . Most modern readers of Matthew Arnold's anguished poetry, or of his celebrated theory in praise of culture, do not also know that Arnold connected the 'administrative massacre' ordered by Eyre [the British Governor of Jamaica in 1865] with tough British policies towards colonial Eire [Ireland] and strongly approved both; *Culture and Anarchy* is set plumb in the middle of the Hyde Park Riots of 1867, and what Arnold had to say about culture was specifically believed to be a deterrent to rampant disorder – colonial, Irish, domestic, Jamaican, Irishmen and women, and some historians bring up these massacres at 'inappropriate' moments, but most Anglo-American readers of Arnold remain oblivious, see them – if they look at them at all – as irrelevant to the more important cultural theory that Arnold appears to be promoting for all the ages (Said, 1993, pp. xiii, 157–8)

1.10

- Try to express in your own words why Said is critical of Arnold's theory of culture.
- How would you respond to the statement 'culture is civilizing' in the light of Said's argument?
- Can you find or think of any stories or cultural forms which appear to uphold British imperialism? The nineteenth-century novel, old films, travel writing, poetry or news reports could prove illuminating.
- Said states that culture is 'a source of identity': what do you understand him to mean by this?

In chapter 2 we shall explore the relationship between culture and identity further. For now, it is enough that you begin to be aware of how culture ('the production and circulation of meanings') can play a part in constructing a sense of who 'we' are in relation to 'them' – in European imperialism this is the colonial encounter between European and non-European. And the act of writing, as we have done, 'European' and 'non-European' is itself complicit in the production and circulation of certain meanings which legitimate the idea of the European as superior. To identify someone as 'non-European' is to define her or him against the implicit normality of 'European' and to consolidate that 'structure of feeling' in which Europe is represented as the centre of the world, around which other countries and identities place themselves.

You may also have noted that even those who theorize about culture and the purpose of its study are involved in the legitimation of certain ways of understanding and knowing the world. Said argues that Arnold's defence of culture had a political aim that was specific to the historical moment that produced *Culture and Anarchy*. He suggests that sections of Victorian Britain believed that the civilizing effects of 'the best that has been thought and known' would act as a deterrent to the growing unrest among diverse groups, both at home and abroad. This unrest took the form of demands for political and civil rights and/or independent status from Britain: Arnold, Said suggests, was concerned that these democratic demands would threaten social stability and therefore required suppression by political as well as cultural means. Said, himself of Palestinian origin, is committed to rendering visible the repressive and oppressive nature of imperialism, and the ways in which cultural products, particularly the novel, sustain this. Williams, whose ideas we looked at in the previous section, writes from a socialist and Marxist position, in which he seeks to redress the inequalities and injuries of the British class system. Feminist cultural theorists have in mind the particular subordination of women. There is nothing inherently sinister in developing theories from within, or to serve a particular political purpose. Indeed, it could be argued that all academic theories are grounded in struggles over power. Knowledge, Pierre Bourdieu has argued, is part of that 'cultural capital' which, along with financial resources, enables certain groups in society to exert and maintain a privileged position (Bourdieu, 1984; see chapters 7 and 9). In order to challenge dominance and privilege it is necessary to produce 'new' knowledge, as both Said and Williams have done. If you read further in the writings of Williams or Said you will find that both of them make their own political position clear and explicit – the same cannot be said of all theorists. Cultural theories, like all cultural forms, are always related, albeit in complex ways, to the particular historical moment when they are produced and the political climates in which they circulate. As a student of culture you will learn to contextualize the material you encounter, both historically and politically.

The final extract in this chapter is from an essay by the feminist anthropologist Sherry Ortner, published in 1974: 'Is female to male as nature is to culture?' Use the following questions as a guide to your reading:

- What is the problem that Ortner identifies as in need of explanation?
- In what senses is the concept of culture used in this extract?

1.8

The secondary status of woman in society is one of the true universals, a pancultural fact. Yet within that universal fact, the specific cultural conceptions and symbolizations of woman are extraordinarily diverse and even mutually contradictory. Further, the actual treatment of women and their relative power and contribution vary enormously from culture to culture, and over different periods in the history of particular cultural traditions. Both these points – the universal fact and the cultural variation – constitute problems to be explained . . .

It is important to sort out the levels of the problem. The confusion can be staggering. For example, depending on which aspect of Chinese culture we look at, we might extrapolate any of several entirely different guesses concerning the status of women in China. In the ideology of Taoism, *yin*, the female principle, and *yang*, the male principle, are given equal weight . . . Hence we might guess that maleness and femaleness are equally valued in the general ideology of Chinese culture. Looking at the social structure, however, we see the strongly emphasized patrilineal descent principle, the importance of sons, and the absolute authority of the father in the family. Thus we might conclude that China is the archetypal patriarchal society. Next, looking at the actual roles played, power and influence wielded, and material contributions made by women in Chinese society – all of which are, upon observation, quite substantial – we would have to say that women are allotted a great deal of (unspoken) status in the system. Or again, we might focus on the fact that a goddess, Kuan Yin, is the central (most worshipped, most depicted) deity in Chinese Buddhism, and we might be tempted to say, as many have tried to say about goddess-worshipping cultures in prehistoric and early historical societies, that China is actually a sort of matriarchy. In short, we must be absolutely clear about *what* we are trying to explain before explaining it (Ortner, 1974, pp. 86–7)

1.11

- Can you list the different aspects of Chinese society and culture that Ortner draws on to make her point?
- Use a similar list to attempt the same exercise with regard to your own society. Do you find a similar range of diverse and contradictory meanings about 'woman in society'?

Ortner, rightly, draws attention to the often contradictory ways in which woman is represented in Chinese culture. At this stage in her analysis she doesn't attempt to connect the 'actual roles' played by women in China to the 'symbolization' of woman in culture, but she does stress the importance of being clear about precisely what is being explained. As students of culture you too should aspire to this kind of clarity. Make sure when you read, write or speak about women, or indeed any other social group, that you are clearly distinguishing between **symbolizations** and lived experience. Beware of assuming that films, TV, novels, paintings, advertisements and newspaper reports offer a direct reflection of the actual roles played and experience lived. In chapter 3 we shall take up further the points just made, by exploring what we mean by representation and how it works to produce meaning.

Conclusions

For now, we hope that this chapter has enabled you to begin thinking about how the concept of culture is defined. The process of definition that you have engaged in here should continue as you read and study. You will, we hope, want to revisit and refine your understanding of the term culture as an on-going process. You could begin this now by returning to the sentences about culture that you wrote at the very beginning of this chapter. Have your ideas altered? Would you add to or qualify your original statement?

CHAPTER 2

Identity and Difference

Introduction

In chapter 1 we examined a range of meanings for the term 'culture'. Culture, as we saw, is inextricably linked with the social groupings and social institutions which constitute society at any given time and in any specific place. Hence culture requires and implies interactions between people, between groups of people and between institutions. All of this might seem to suggest that individuals, you and I as unique, autonomous human subjects, have very little to do with the workings of culture. None the less, although the cultural forms and practices produced in any society are shaped by the structures of that society, they are also shaped by the **subjectivities** of individual women and men in our roles as social actors. For example, in chapter 1 we suggested that Matthew Arnold was part of the social grouping (the gender and class positions he occupied at a specific historical moment) whose interests his version of culture expressed. Yet he was also an individual who experienced himself in daily life as a unique human being with the ability to act autonomously, despite the social structures within which he was necessarily located. This ability to act independently is often referred to as **agency**. Equally, the **identities** that individuals adopt in order to define themselves are produced, at least in part, from the cultural and social contexts in which we find ourselves and from which we draw certain assumptions about 'human nature', 'individuality' and 'the self'.

By the end of this chapter we shall have explored more precisely what is meant by the concepts of identity and difference and why they are significant for the study of culture. (Although we have mentioned subjectivity here we shall deal with this more fully in chapter 8.) You will also have a brief opportunity to consider how these differing ideas about individual identify are represented in a specific representational form: the personal life narrative or autobiography. This will lead into the next chapter, which takes up and develops further the idea of representation and its relation to reality.

Who am I?

2.1

Write a short paragraph – no more than two or three lines – describing your-self. Alternatively, make a list of things which comprise the way you see yourself.

It would be impossible to cover all the possibilities you may have included but the following are probably some of the things you mentioned. You may well have mentioned things not listed here. If so, try to identify which aspects of identity they are concerned with. Here is our list:

- sex, age, occupation, ethnicity, sexual orientation (social);
- hair colour, skin colour, eye colour, bodyshape, physical disabilities, height, kind of clothes worn (physical appearance);
- lively, quiet, shy, concerned for others, morose, a loner, gregarious (personality);
- Irish, Chinese, American, Nigerian (nationality);
- Catholic, Jewish, Muslim (religion);
- mother, father, daughter, son, niece, grandfather (family relationships);
- barman, waitress, postman, student, teacher, architect (occupation);
- interested in music, a film goer, football-mad, politically committed (cultural).

These categories, as you have probably realised by now, are not watertight. Skin colour can also be a mark of social identity; physical disability may not simply be about appearance, but may have ramifications for all other aspects of identity; sex may have some bearing on how far appearance is important to identity (women are more likely to experience their identity as linked to how they look); political commitment may derive from being born into a certain class or nationality. Some of you may have defined yourselves according to a specific religious faith, and this could be linked to nationality, to ethnicity, to personality and to cultural markers. Or you may have felt that your occupational identity (for example, 'student') is currently the most significant marker of who you are. On the other hand, you may feel that none of these categories captures the 'real you'. You might see yourself as a self detached from society, nation, faith – an individual defined less by the categories above than by an inner sense of a unique self that is the 'true' you and that cannot be fitted easily into these external categories. We shall return to the ways in which identities are marked, but for now we want to explore further the idea that at the heart of each individual there is a 'real' self in which resides some essence of authentic personhood.

However we describe ourselves and however many categories we draw upon (social, personal, biological, cultural etc.), we tend and want to believe that there is a 'real me' in which resides the essence or core of our nature. We want to believe that this 'real' self pre-exists or is independent of the categories mentioned above. We sometimes believe that this 'real me' is hidden or suppressed by the demands of social roles or cultural conventions that require a public facade. A persistent narrative found in novels, films and TV plays is the man or woman whose story traces a quest for this kind of private, inner identity. How often have you heard people say, and you may well have said it yourself, 'I need time to find myself? This belief that a unique 'true' selfhood lies within the psyche of each individual and that each individual has the right to express and protect that uniqueness has provided the basis of **humanism**, the predominant philosophy of the individual over the past two centuries in the Western world.

Matthew Arnold appealed to humanist beliefs when he argued that culture could offer every human being the means to a fully realized moral life. Arnold assumed that human beings, more or less evolved, are the same everywhere and in all times, and that culture, as defined by him, would speak to some essential human nature that transcends social, historical and biological differences. Arnold also espoused **liberalism**, in that he believed that education and 'Culture' were the keys which would unlock individual potential and that such opportunities should be open to all, regardless of social distinctions.

ACTIVITIES ✓

2.2

How far do you think this is true, i.e. that access to culture (as defined by Arnold) will provide opportunities for self-fulfilment? Can you see any problems with this argument? Can you think of any examples where culture, in Arnold's sense, might have different meanings for different groups? Look at reading 1.2 and reading 3.3. How are the experiences narrated here linked to a sense of identity?

It does seem that a belief in a fundamental, ahistorical human nature is problematic. Historical moment, nationality, ethnicity, sex and social circumstances do make a difference, and therefore do determine the way we see ourselves and the way we think and act. Yet we continue to experience ourselves as individuals with the feelings, beliefs and attitudes that make us autonomous, unique beings, and prefer to believe that we are not simply the products of external forces such as social structures or historical circumstances. Perhaps it is more accurate to understand identity as the interface between a private sense of self that includes conscious and unconscious feelings, rational and irrational motivations, personal beliefs and values, and those factors that constitute the social context in which we experience those feelings and motivations (for example, age, ethnicity, sex). If our deepest desires and our most personal experiences constitute an individual consciousness, then identity is the way we may choose to represent ourselves and act out our thoughts, beliefs and emotions in the social world.

One of the differences between individual consciousness and identity is that individual consciousness, despite its acquisition in a social context, is an internalized combination of ideas and feelings, while identity may be bestowed by others as well as chosen by ourselves. For example, a woman experiencing her first child-birth may find herself identified by medical experts, midwives and health visitors as a mother, long before she herself has consciously adopted this identity. Another example is the identity of patient which is conferred upon those in hospital; an identity which requires and expects certain behaviours which may be at odds with other aspects of the individual. Throughout our lives we are offered a variety of possible social identities as part of our experience of work, family, sexuality, culture and leisure. Sometimes different identities are contradictory and seemingly impossible to reconcile; nearly always identity positions are located in relations of power, in the binary opposition 'us/them'. Now read the following extract by the artist Rasheed Araeen. Araeen is the founding editor of a quarterly journal, *Third Text*, published in Britain since 1987. *Third Text* provides a space in which 'Third World perspectives on contemporary art and culture' can be expressed, debated and heard (Jordan and Weedon, 1995, pp. 316, 435–42).

2.1

I was born in India, when India was under the British Raj. As a teenager I grew up, spent my early youth and was educated in Pakistan. At the age of 29, inspired by the West's achievement in art in the 20th century, and to fulfil my own aspirations to be a modern artist, I left my country to live in Europe. I have now lived and worked in London for 27 years. I often travel to Pakistan to see my mother, brothers and sisters, and also some friends. I can say I'm Asian, Indian, Pakistani, British, European, Muslim, Oriental, secular, modernist, postmodernist, and so on . . . But what do these things mean? Do they define my identity? Can I accept all of them as part of my life, or must I choose one thing or another according to someone else's notion about my identity? I have no problem in saying that I'm all of these things, and perhaps none of these things at the same time . . .

In the summer of 1970 we had a grand party, to which hundreds of people from the art world were invited . . . As I was having drinks and chatting with my friends in my studio, an elderly well-dressed gentleman moved towards us . . . 'I like your work very much' he said as we began to talk. I thanked him and we moved around together in the studio. As we were looking at various works something suddenly occurred to me, and I asked him. 'How did you know that this was my work?' 'Aren't you an Arab?' he replied looking at my face. 'No, I'm from Pakistan,' I said, becoming rather puzzled by all this: 'Oh, it's all the same. You are Muslim.' 'Yes,' I said reluctantly. 'You see, this kind of work could have been conceived only by a Muslim. I cannot imagine a European doing this work,' he began to explain politely.

Next day somebody told me that the person I had met was the Professor of Fine Art at the Slade School of Art, and that he was an important member of the art establishment . . . It was the first time that I became aware that my work had something to do with Islamic tradition. It was a disturbing discovery, because I have never made any connection between my work and my being a Muslim. They were two different things. Moreover I was never interested in Islamic art, or concerned with the expression of my cultural identity. My interest was in modernism. (Rasheed Araeen, 'How I discovered my Oriental soul in the wilderness of the West', cited in Jordan and Weedon, 1995, pp. 439–40)

As Jordan and Weedon suggest, in this extract Rasheed Araeen is forced to confront the way in which his work and, by extension, his identity is defined by others. He aspires to be 'a modern artist' working in the European tradition of modernism. However, the professor of fine art sees him as 'Arab', producing Islamic art, and insists that his work cannot be seen as 'European'. The professor's comments, despite his praise and kindness, fix Araeen in a particular identity that by definition excludes him from other possible identities. Because he is perceived as 'Muslim' he cannot, at the same time, be 'European'. To be identified as 'Muslim' is to be identified as 'not-European', 'not-Christian'. Identity definitions function to classify and categorize: the identity 'Muslim' is a marker of **difference** from those who are categorized as 'European' or 'Christian'. That Araeen sees himself as both non-religious and Muslim, as Pakistani, Indian and British, and his work as modernist, doesn't matter. Because the professor represents the British art establishment he has the power to define what is and what is not art, how it should be valued and how Araeen and his art fit into this. The binary logic of Western thought insists that it is impossible to be simultaneously 'Oriental' and 'Western' – each identity depends upon the other for its meaning. Identity and difference are about inclusion and exclusion. If you are British you cannot also be Japanese, if you are male you cannot also be female, if you are young you cannot also be old. Or can you?

2.3

Can you think of any occasions when you have been given an identity that did not fit? Have the identity labels you use changed over your lifetime?

The point to grasp is that identities are relational and contingent rather than permanently fixed. They depend upon what they are defined against, and this may change over time or be understood differently in different places. In Britain in the 1960s, Araeen is defined by the professor as 'Arab', a generic identity that signifies his difference from Europeans. In other circumstances, possibly when he visits his family in Pakistan, he might find himself defined as Pakistani in order to mark his difference from Indians. The other point to note is that the identity positions within which we locate ourselves or are located by others are neither neutral nor equal. The act of naming, as we saw with the professor of fine art, is, however liberal and kindly meant, an act of power. It is he who defines and places Araeen from his position as a representative of Western Eurocentric knowledge, and it is Western logic and knowledge that have defined the ways in which it is possible for us to think about who we are. For example, have you ever heard Europeans described as non-Asians, have you ever heard white people described as non-blacks? Yet the terms 'non-European' and 'non-white' are frequently used to define those from Asia or Africa.

Going back to the account by Araeen, did you notice how the professor of fine art was able to define Araeen by reference to his appearance ('"Aren't you an

Arab?" he replied looking at my face')? Differences are marked symbolically as well as experienced socially. In the case of Araeen, the symbolic marker of difference is his physical appearance and skin colour. Henry Louis Gates Jr, a professor of African-American studies in the United States, argues, in the extract that follows, that 'race' is not a biological given but a linguistic construct that functions to mark symbolically difference and 'otherness'. Race, Gates insists, is not an objective term of categorization but 'a dangerous trope'. As he comments, later in the article from which this extract is taken, 'who has seen a black or red person, a white, yellow, or brown? These terms are arbitrary constructs, not reports of reality' (Gates, 1986, p. 5).

2.2

Race, as a meaningful criterion within the biological sciences, has long been recognized to be a fiction. When we speak of 'the white race' or 'the black race,' 'the Jewish race' or 'the Aryan race,' we speak in biological misnomers and, more generally, in metaphors . . .

The sense of difference defined in popular usages of the term 'race' has both described and *inscribed* differences of language, belief system, artistic tradition, and gene pool as well as all sorts of supposedly natural attributes such as rhythm, athletic ability, cerebration, usury, fidelity, and so forth. The relation between 'racial character' and these sorts of characteristics has been inscribed through tropes of race, lending the sanction of God, biology, or the natural order to even presumably unbiased descriptions of cultural tendencies and differences . . . In 1973 I was amazed to hear a member of the House of Lords describe the differences between Irish Protestants and Catholics in terms of their 'distinct and clearly definable differences of race.' 'You mean to say that you can tell them apart?' I asked incredulously. 'Of course,' responded the Lord. 'Any Englishman can.' (Gates, 1986, p. 4)

Identity also operates through social and material conditions. The symbolic markers of difference will have real effects on the lived experience of people's social relations. So, for example, in eighteenth- and nineteenth-century Europe and America black Africans were symbolically and socially marked by their colour as 'inferior' to white people. As a result, they were treated as less than human, sold into slavery and transported from their homelands, prevented from learning to read and write, physically abused and materially and socially disadvantaged long after the specific practices of slavery were abolished. The ways in which groups are symbolically marked (represented) will shape the social relations and practices that constitute lived experience. Equally, social practices of inclusion and exclusion are based on classification systems (e.g. man/woman, black/white, European/American/Eastern, First World/Third World, lesbian/homosexual/heterosexual) that rely on symbolic representation for their maintenance. For example, the assertion of national identities is frequently represented symbolically by national flags or songs. In Britain the monarchy has stood as a symbolic marker of national identity for over 300 years. In some countries the carrying of a small handbag by a man would be seen as a symbol or marker of his 'effeminacy': 'real' men don't carry handbags. Femininity has been symbolically marked in a variety of ways at different times and in different places. In nineteenth-century Europe a tiny waist was a mark of femininity. In the 1950s blonde hair and an hourglass figure were the symbols of femininity, with Marilyn Monroe as its cinematic epitome. The things people use, the rituals they follow, the way they dress and appear function to define who they are and, importantly, who they are not. Symbolic markers are vital to the construction and maintenance of identities and differences and are inextricably intertwined and interdependent with social processes and practices. Thus, the man carrying a handbag can be seen to be 'effeminate' and can therefore be treated in certain ways; Araeen can be seen to be 'Oriental' and this, in the eyes of the art establishment, legitimates the exclusion of his work from the modernist tradition of European art and his exclusion from the category 'European modern artist'.

This discussion of identity would not be complete without considering the tension between **essentialist** and **non-essentialist** perspectives on identity. By essentialist we mean the idea that identity is fixed in an originating moment, that there is a 'true', authentic, unchanging set of characteristics that belong to, say, Asians, and an equally authentic, fixed set of characteristics that can be attributed to Europeans. An essentialist perspective would maintain that these characteristics do not change across time and are shared by all Asians and all Europeans. An essentialist perspective would maintain that there is something intrinsically 'Asian' or 'British' or 'Japanese' that transcends history or is inherent in the person. The English lord cited by Gates had adopted an essentialist position with regard to Irish Protestants and Catholics. A non-essentialist perspective questions whether it is possible to speak of a 'true' identity that is fixed for all time and in all places. For example, in what sense is it possible to define a third-generation Japanese woman, living in America, who is unable to speak Japanese, as 'Japanese'. What is it that determines her identity as Japanese or not-Japanese? Is it biological genes, citizenship in the sense, for example, of holding an American or Japanese passport as a naturalized citizen, language, place of birth, place of current residence or a personal and subjective sense of herself as 'Japanese' or 'American'?

To complete your work on this section you should now read the following extract from Trinh T. Minh-ha's *Woman, Native, Other: Writing, Postcoloniality, and Feminism*. Trinh T. Minh-ha is a filmmaker and composer, as well as a writer and teacher, living in the USA.

2.3

A critical difference from myself means that I am not i, am within and without i. I/i can be I or i, you and me both involved. We (with capital W) sometimes include(s), other times exclude(s) me. You and I are close, we intertwine, you may stand on the other side of the hill once in a while, but you may also be me, while remaining what you are and what i am not. The differences made *between* entities comprehended as absolute presences – hence the notions of *pure origin* and *true self* – are an outgrowth of a dualistic system of thought peculiar to the Occident (the 'ontotheology' which characterizes Western metaphysics). They should be distinguished from the differences grasped *both between* and *within* entities, each of these being understood as multiple presence. Not One, not two either. 'I' is, therefore, not a unified subject, a fixed identity, or that solid mass covered with layers of superficialities one has gradually to peel off before one can see its true face. 'I' is, itself, *infinite layers*. Its complexity can hardly be conveyed through such typographic conventions as I, i, or I/i. Thus, I/i am compelled by the will to say/unsay, to resort to the entire gamut of personal pronouns to stay near this fleeing *and* static essence of Not-I. Whether I accept it or not, the natures of *I*, *i*, *you*, *s/he*, *We*, *we*, *they*, and *wo/man* constantly overlap. They all display a necessary ambivalence, for the line dividing I and *Not-I*, *us* and *them*, or *him* and *her* is not (cannot) always (be) as clear as we would like it to be. Despite our desperate, eternal attempt to separate, contain, and mend, categories always leak. Of all the layers that form the open (never finite) totality of 'I', which is to be filtered out as superfluous, fake, corrupt, and which is to be called pure, true, real, genuine, original, authentic? Which, indeed, since all interchange, revolving in an endless process? . . . *Authenticity* as a need to rely on an 'undisputed origin,' is prey to an obsessive fear: that of *losing a connection*. Everything must hold together (Minh-ha, 1989, p. 90)

2.4

- What do you think Minh-ha means when she says that the 'line dividing *I* and *Not-I*, *us* and *them*, or *him* and *her* is not (cannot) always (be) as clear as we would like it to be'?
- Think about the pronouns Minh-ha refers to: what meanings are associated with these? Can you think of circumstances in which the use of these pronouns and their meanings might shape how a person is treated or treats others? Try to find specific examples from your own experience.
- Why do you think Minh-ha distinguishes between 'I' and 'i'?
- Do you think Minh-ha is right when she says we make a 'desperate, eternal attempt to separate, contain, and mend'? If you agree with her, why do you think this is? Who is the 'our' she refers to here?

ACTIVITIES

Social constructivist approaches to identity

Individuals experience their lives within a particular society at a particular time. The ways in which we act and experience ourselves are shaped by the social environment within which we exist and our relations with others. We are defined and define ourselves in terms of how others see us, how we see others, how we act with other people and how other people respond to us, not only on an individual basis but also within social institutions such as the family, the workplace, the school. Equally, the ways in which we are able to act, respond and see ourselves may be shaped by the material and economic circumstances of our environment. Karl

Marx famously asserted that 'It is not the consciousness of men that determines their being, but, on the contrary, their social being that determines their consciousness' (Marx, 1859). Marx was particularly concerned with the relationship people had to modes of economic production and exchange, but in order to argue this he first had to show that human consciousness did not pre-exist the actual circumstances and experiences of people's lives, but was produced by those circumstances and experiences, what is sometimes called a **materialist** view of society. In order to clarify for yourself what this means you should attempt the exercise below.

ACTIVITIES

2.5

Imagine you are a woman with no educational qualifications, a low-paid job and a family to care for, living in a rural village, many miles from the nearest town, and you want to become a writer. In what ways might these circumstances influence your realization of this ambition? Be as specific as possible in detailing the ways in which you might be constrained or aided in your aspirations.

You may have noted any of the following:

- Lack of money might make it impossible to purchase the equipment you would need, e.g. word processor, typewriter, books, paper.
- The necessity of earning an income, however small, might make it impossible to find the time to write.
- The lack of formal education might mean limited access to other books from which to discover the tricks of the trade. It might also mean difficulties with reading and writing generally.
- The lack of formal education might have developed a sense that 'people like me don't become writers' and a consequent lack of confidence.
- A sense of guilt that the time being used to write rightfully belonged to the family; the belief that it is a mother's role to give time and care to her family and that spending time in activities outside this role is 'selfish'.
- The physical isolation and distance from the centres of publishing would be an obstacle to getting anything into print.

It does seem, doesn't it, as if material circumstances would determine the way in which this woman viewed herself and would mitigate against her becoming a writer. It does seem as if 'her social being' would foster a consciousness of her own limitations and 'the place' she should occupy in society. Yet . . .

Women with similar circumstances to those detailed above have written and published books. For example, Evelyn Haythorne, who grew up in a Yorkshire mining village during the Second World War, wrote and published an autobiographical account of her childhood (Haythorne, 1990). She kept diaries, despite her mother's discouragement, wrote in secret and only showed the book to her husband when it was ready to be published. While Evelyn Haythorne may have been an exceptional woman, her story does suggest that while consciousness is, in part, formed from material circumstances, this does not preclude individuals from acting against the grain of the structures which shape and determine consciousness. Social forces might predispose individuals like our fictional woman or Evelyn Haythorne not to realize their ambitions, but that does not mean no one in such circumstances will ever become a writer. The possibility of some human agency, choice and self-determination remains, however constrained by social structures.

The point we are making is that social factors have an impact on our sense of identity in a variety of complex ways. Little girls, it is claimed, learn what it means to be a women as a result of their experience in the family, at school and later in the workplace, as well as from books, magazines, newspapers, TV, films and other media. Feminist approaches to gender have argued that girls align themselves with femininity and men with masculinity as a result of the social relations experienced in childhood and adolescence. Girls are not 'naturally' feminine, nor boys 'naturally' masculine. These are learned identities. **Social constructivist** approaches to gender have been justifiably influential in breaking the link between sex and biological destiny – all women are not inherently 'maternal', for example. However, more recently writers have questionned the idea that masculinity and femininity are polarized constructs into which individuals are neatly slotted as a result of the lessons learned at school and home. Rather than there being a single form of femininity or masculinity, it has been suggested that we should think in terms of a range of femininities or masculinities that may be taken up by individuals. Moreover, rather than being socialized into one specific gender identity that remains fixed and unchanging, it is possible for individuals to change their sense of identity over time (Crowley and Himmelweit, 1992). Again, the idea that we achieve a stable gender identity at maturity is at odds with many people's experience: both women and men resist some elements of gender identity, while accepting others. Many women gain satisfaction and enjoyment from their maternal and caring roles, but react strongly against the idea that this should be their primary role, while at the same time feeling guilty if they are not 'perfect' mothers. Many men reject the idea that to be masculine they need to be dominant and aggressive, yet complain of feeling 'threatened' by assertive women. Material and social factors can explain the construction of particular identities at specific historical moments, but they do not explain why individuals invest in identity positions that are not always in their best interests, or the depth of attachment to a particular identity, to the extent that an individual is willing to die or kill to maintain that identity.

Louis Althusser developed Marx's work on ideologies in order to try to explain why particular positions are taken up by individuals. In his essay 'Ideology and ideological state apparatuses', Althusser revises Marx's model in which the base – the economic mode of production of a society – is seen as determining the superstructure – social relations, ideologies, political and social institutions (Althusser, 1971). In place of the Marxist model, Althusser emphasizes the ways in which individuals are **interpellated** into subject positions by a process of identification. For example, the new mother sees herself in a variety of representations of motherhood within her society, and is 'recruited' to the subject position 'mother' by an act of recognition: 'yes, that's me, yes, that's how it is'. For Althusser, ideology exists in everyday commonplaces, in what we call 'common sense', as well as in religious, political and philosophical systems of thought. Ideology is apparent in all that strikes us as self-evident and 'obvious', in what Althusser calls 'obviousnesses which we cannot fail to recognize and before which we have the inevitable and natural reaction of crying out (aloud or in the "still, small voice of conscience"): "That's obvious! That's right! That's true!"' (Althusser, 1971, p. 161). This process of interpellation takes place at the level of the unconscious as well as consciously, and is the means by which subjects are constructed. For Althusser, the subject is not the same as the individual. Subjectivity is a constructed category produced by ideology, 'the category of the subject is constitutive of all ideology, but at the same time and immediately I add that the category of the subject is only constitutive of all ideology in so far as all ideology has the function (which defines it) of "constituting" concrete individuals as subjects' (Althusser, 1971, p. 160).

Althusser's essay emphasizes the role of symbolic systems in the production of identities. In particular, he drew on the work of Jacques Lacan (see chapter 8) in order to link the psychoanalytic and material dimensions in explanations of why individuals take up, attach themselves to and invest in particular identity positions. In chapter 8 you will have the opportunity to explore further the ideas of Lacan and the concept of subjectivity. Now read the following account by Alison Fell, a feminist novelist and poet. This is taken from a collection of autobiographical essays by women who grew up in the 1950s.

2.4

In spite of my staunch teenage vows against marriage, during the five years at Edinburgh [Art College] I was married, divorced, and finally pregnant, so that in 1967 I found myself in Leeds as a faculty wife, mother and depressive. In 1968 I got involved in the beginnings of the Welfare State theatre group, and then, in 1969, with one of the first Women's Liberation groups, which was a revelation, and saved me from a weight of guilt about how badly I fitted into my womanly role. It also provided outlets for daring. To speak at a male-dominated meeting or occupy a pub in those scornful days required a certain reckless edge. (Still does.) In 1970 I left the Welfare State and moved to London in search of all-woman theatre. The Women's Street Theatre group did its first performance on the 1971 Women's Day march, and members of the group later went on to found Monstrous Regiment, the Women's Theatre Group, etc. Then a report I'd done on our arrest at the right-wing 'Festival of Light' led to a job on *Ink*, one of the more radical papers of the underground press. So, by accident (or was it?), I was a journalist, just as my father had wanted. For me the next few years were one long fever of feminist and libertarian politics, campaigning, militating, organising women's centres, working on *Red Rag*, the marxist feminist journal, and on the *Islington Gutter Press*. In 1974 a breakdown forced me to withdraw from activity for a year, but perhaps also gave me the inner permission I needed to write poetry again. In fact, that year marks the start of a serious commitment to writing.

Since then I've worked for four years on *Spare Rib*, and as a Writer-in-Residence in two London boroughs. In 1981 Collins published my children's novel *The Grey Dancer*, and in 1984 Virago brought out my adult novel *Every Move You Make* and my first individual poetry collection, *Kisses for Mayakovsky*. Currently I'm writing, teaching and trying to believe I'm forty. (Heron, 1985, pp. 24–5)

2.6

- Can you trace the ways in which the writer's identity has changed over time?
- What material factors appear to have been significant in forming her identity over time?
- Does Alison Fell's account of herself confirm or otherwise the idea that gender identity, in her case femininity, is learned once and for all in childhood and adolescence?
- Can you suggest any points in her life story that could be explained by Althusser's theory of interpellation?

2.7

Taking the question 'What is a woman?' or 'What is a man?', brainstorm as many possible answers as you can. We have started you off.

What is a woman?	*What is a man?*
- Someone with long hair	Physically strong
- Career girl	New man
- Lesbian	Lover of football
-	
-	
-	
-	
-	
-	
-	

Simone de Beauvoir famously asserted that 'one is not born but rather becomes a woman' but, if you have completed this activity, it may have surprised you to see how many different, and sometimes contradictory, versions of 'becoming a woman' are possible. Do you think this is equally true of 'becoming a man'?

Social constructivism is the term used to describe approaches that reject essentialist explanations of identity. A social constructivist perspective claims that gender identity is formed through interaction with social factors, and is not simply the result of biological differences. Such an approach does not deny biological differences, but attempts to understand and explain them in terms of social context, rather than seeing individuals as limited and bounded by their biology. In order to complete your work on this section, we want to introduce you briefly to some ideas from sociobiology. Read the following short extract from an article by Richard Stevens. According to Stevens, what do sociobiologists identify as the origin of human behaviour and what function does this serve?

2.5

A useful principle is that, if you want to understand something, it is worth looking at its origins, its history. One approach to understanding human behaviour is to look at it as a species pattern. Can we gain any insights into identity by considering how human behaviour might have evolved?

The theory which argues that we can is called sociobiology. This is an approach concerned with understanding the social behaviour of animals. Humans are regarded as another animal species and as being, like them, the product of evolutionary development. Sociobiologists are interested in understanding why social behaviours evolved in the way that they did – what functions did they serve in ensuring the survival of the species and passing on genes to future generations? . . .

Their [sociobiologists'] position is that psychological and behavioural characteristics have been shaped by the process of evolution. Those behaviours which in the past have facilitated survival and reproduction are those which have been selected for. (Stevens, 1994, pp. 158, 166)

Sociobiological explanations of behaviour take as their starting point the idea that humans are a highly complex and evolved species of animal life. 'Even if we allow for major differences between ourselves and other species, given the continuity of evolution, is it not arrogant, the sociobiologist might argue, to presume that we should be *totally* exempt' (Stevens, 1994, p. 168). If, as research has shown, genes and genetic development determine, at least in part, the behaviour and responses of animals, might they not also determine human behaviour? The sociobiological approach argues that biological imperatives, and in particular the impulse to ensure survival of the species, ensured that those behaviours which facilitated survival and reproduction of the species were the behaviours most likely to be adopted and most likely to evolve into highly complex patterns of response.

Explanations of human actions which are rooted in biology will have particular relevance for theories of gender identity because of the significance such theories place on sexual reproduction. Thus, it may be argued, as women are limited in the number of children they can bear, the characteristics and behaviours of our female ancestors might have been those most likely to ensure the survival of their (relatively few) offspring, whereas men, who are able to father as many offspring as they can find partners, might have developed those responses most likely to produce an optimal number of descendants. You may well want to reject such arguments on the grounds that they appear to justify inequalities between the sexes, and biology has often been used as an explanation for the different behaviours of men and women. For example, in the nineteenth century it was argued that women's reproductive capacity rendered them physiologically unfit for the kind of intellectual study required in higher education except at enormous cost to their potential motherhood. Sociobiology is contentious because it does suggest that human responses are more determined than most of us like to imagine. It seems to claim that our actions are the result of deep-seated and innate natural factors over which we may have little control. However, sociobiologists do acknowledge the limitations of their claims. As Stevens goes on to say, a 'more intermediate position sees human social life as a complex interplay between social process and biological predispositions, each affecting the other in complex interaction' (Stevens, 1994, p. 168). He gives the example of crying: weeping is a spontaneous act for children, it is not something they are required to learn; what they do learn is when and where it is inappropriate to cry. 'The meanings attributed to weeping are shaped by social practice and convention rather than by biology' (ibid.). In the same way, we might want to say that the meanings attributed to masculine and feminine behaviours are shaped by social practice and cultural expectations and that these are linked in certain ways to the biological functions of the sexes, male and female.

Biological differences between people have often been used as the basis for social divisions and the injustices which can stem from these. For example, genetic arguments were used until recently to explain alleged differences between the intelligence of white and black people and, as we saw above, arguments from biology were used to hinder women's access to higher education in nineteenth-century Britain and America. Yet we cannot deny our biological selves – our bodies and their workings do shape how we feel about ourselves, what we are able to do and how we are seen by others. We may want to argue that social and cultural environment plays a greater part in how we develop as human beings (the nature/nurture debate as it is often called), but we cannot forget that we do have biologically programmed bodies, that we are not simply the sum of our thoughts and emotions. For example, the inevitability of ageing and the prospect of our own mortality may shape our consciousness and our sense of personal identity in profound ways, and many people explain their desire to have children as a way of leaving some trace of their existence for future generations. Such responses to mortality do not stem simply from either biological imperatives or cultural conventions, but include elements of both. Lynda Birke has argued that we need to think outside the conventionally accepted polarizations biology/culture, body/mind, animal/human. We end this section by asking you to read the following extract and to consider carefully your response.

2.6

[One] problem with denying our biological selves has to do with the relationship between humans and animals. We know, of course, that we have some things in common with other animals: all female mammals, including women, produce milk with which to feed their young. But we usually draw the line when it comes to behaviour; human behaviour, it is generally assumed, is not really the concern of biology. Indeed, this is why biological determinism is a problem for feminism – we do assume that human (and specifically women's) behaviour is shaped by culture.

The behaviour of animals, by contrast, is included squarely within the domain of 'biology'. Everything about animals, that is, constitutes *their* biology, while only some things in feminist accounts (our anatomy or physiology) constitute ours. As far as behaviour is concerned, we thereby imply that we are not like other animals.

This distinction is not very satisfactory. Are we to assume that evolution has shaped our bodies, but not our minds, while shaping both bodies *and* minds for other species? This is simply another way of recasting the distinction (so prevalent in Western culture) between body and mind. Animals are basically bodies with little in the way of mind; we are minds busily denying that we have bodies.

Yet we cannot simultaneously hold two contrasting positions. If animals' behaviour *is* their biology, then we have to assume that the behaviour is caused directly by something inside the animal. If this was said about women, we would immediately cry foul and accuse someone of biological determinism. But if it is only animals, it is all right. Isn't it?

My short answer is no – I do not think that other mammals (at least) are mere puppets of their genes, any more than I think people are. But biologically determinist arguments always rely on drawing parallels between human and animal societies . . . So, as long as animals are wholly seen as 'biological', then the parallel will lead inevitably to seeing humans in the same way. An alternative way of drawing parallels would be to point to the extent to which individuals learn to be social – in both humans and other animals. This possibility is rarely considered, so we are left with either (a) accepting parallels based on biological determinism, or (b) denying any parallels or similarity at all. (Birke, 1992, pp. 72–3)

Recent work in sociology and cultural studies has begun to suggest alternative ways in which we can understand the relationship between the physical bodies people inhabit and the formation of identities. These perspectives reject the idea of the body as simply a biological organism, and stress instead that people's experience of their physical bodies is shaped by social structures and expectations, as well as 'natural' functions. For example, we consume food in order to survive, but what we eat, when and how, as well as how far we can choose (or not) to shape our body through eating, is a result of a range of social variables. These might include which part of the globe we inhabit (the industrialized or developing world), whether we are male or female and historically specific 'ideal' body shapes. The current vogue for body-building is another example of the links between cultural practice and physical bodies. Our bodies, recent writers have argued, are an integral part of our identities, shaping and shaped by the meanings ascribed to them. They are more than a physical shell within which is contained the non-physical 'real' self, as anyone who has suffered anorexia or experienced obesity can testify (Bordo, 1993; Featherstone et al., 1991; Shilling, 1993; and chapter 8 in this book).

Hence the classifying categories that are used to distinguish between people – for example, 'race' and gender – are not immutable aspects of the natural world but social constructs. Racial difference, as the reading from Gates (above) argued, is not a biological phenomenon but a means of categorizing people that uses certain bodily characteristics as markers of 'race'. The persecution and mass slaughter of Jews in Nazi extermination camps during the Second World War is an extreme example of the barbarous practices that can be legitimated by reference to socially constructed 'racial' differences. Differences based on social constructs, such as 'race', gender, sexual orientation, age or disability, can be construed so as to exclude, marginalize or, in extreme forms, slaughter those perceived as 'different' or 'other'. As we write, the Indian government is planning to offer financial incentives to families who produce daughters in order to halt the widespread practice of aborting female foetuses. The recognition that 'race', gender, sexual orientation and disability are socially constructed has enabled new social movements, such as black civil rights, the women's liberation movement, gay and lesbian rights and disability rights, to challenge the negative stereotyping that reinforces 'otherness' and difference. Instead, differences have been celebrated as enriching sources of energy and diversity, as in slogans such as 'Glad to be gay' and 'Black is beautiful'.

2.8

You could keep a file of images, articles, TV programmes etc. in which stereotyping is used to reinforce a particular social category, e.g. Asian, French, English, Irish, single parent, homosexual, lesbian, AIDS sufferer, feminist, secretary, drug addict. There is more on stereotyping in chapters 3 and 9. Try to identify the precise elements that create recognizable stereotypes of your chosen category.

'Identity crisis' and the modern world

Identity, however, is not only experienced at the level of the individual. Collective, ethnic and national identities are important ways in which people negotiate a sense of belonging and, often allied to this, political solidarity. Asserting national, religious or ethnic identities can lead to political conflict, as in the case of Northern Ireland, where identities based on religion have divided the province. In the former Yugoslavia, established identities fragmented under the pressures of economic and political conflict, and the re-emergence of national identities around older forms of ethnicity – Serb and Croat – has led to devastating upheaval and war. In Britain, right-wing politicians have been concerned to reaffirm a sense of national identity in the face of what they perceive as threats from European unity. In England, as in many parts of the industrialized world, international migration and a loss of certainty about what constitutes 'Englishness' has brought with it the possibility of new identities that are less firmly aligned to the older boundaries of nation-states. Since the 1950s immigration has produced Asian communities in many parts of Britain that were previously the province of white working-class groups, notably in Bradford and parts of London. Many young people whose parents or grandparents came to Britain in the 1950s or the 1970s from the Caribbean or Asia do not see themselves as either wholly British or wholly Indian or

West Indian. In his novel *The Buddha of Suburbia*, Hanif Kureishi has his narrator begin with a discussion of his identity:

> My name is Karim Amir, and I am an Englishman born and bred, almost. I am often considered to be a funny kind of Englishman, a new breed as it were, having emerged from two old histories. But I don't care – Englishman I am (though not proud of it), from the South London suburbs and going somewhere. Perhaps it is the odd mixture of continents and blood, of here and there, of belonging and not, that makes me restless and easily bored. (Kureishi, 1990, p. 3)

Karim sees himself as English but not in the way 'English' has been defined in the past. He sees himself as a 'new breed' – a hybrid produced by his Indian background and his English upbringing (his father is a first-generation Indian in Britain and his mother is white, British, working class). He reflects on the effects of this both in terms of biology (blood) and in terms of the groups he can and cannot belong to. He wonders if the consequences of this 'mixing' have produced the sense of restlessness and boredom he feels. The following reading is from a series of articles in *the Independent* between 17 and 22 November 1997, in which the findings of a large-scale survey of young people, aged 17–24, were discussed and analysed.

2.7

The extent of isolation felt by this generation is astonishing in a country that until recently called itself Christian and prided itself on local loyalties. Just one in five feels part of a community, while only one in ten identifies with a religion or race. Two per cent see themselves as belonging to a political party, while 13 per cent feel part of a social class.

'I'm very much a creature of the planet,' says Mr Reza, born in Glasgow of Mauritian parents. 'I don't belong to any particular land mass. My skin is brown but I don't feel Mauritian. I feel more British when I go abroad. I don't belong to any religion. I'm open to the existence of anything but I don't believe in God. Some of the Buddhist philosophies I find quite palatable. I don't want to be a member of a class. I'm a person. I've never followed one political party. I'm not a believer in one though if you had to label me I would probably fall somewhere between Labour and the Liberal Democrats'. (*Independent*, 22 November 1997)

2.9

- What do you see as the advantages and disadvantages of belonging to an identifiable grouping such as gender, ethnic group, class, political allegiance, religion, nationality?
- The *Independent* report suggests that the loss of clear-cut cultural identities is a cause for concern. How do you respond to this?

The idea that contemporary societies are characterized by crises of identity, such as those exemplified in the former Yugoslavia or, in a different form, by Kureishi's narrator and Mr Reza, is one that has been argued by a number of social and cultural theorists in recent years. In a collection of essays on this topic, published in 1990, Kobena Mercer comments,

> Just now everybody wants to talk about 'identity'. As a keyword in contemporary politics it has taken on so many different connotations that sometimes it is obvious that people are not even talking about the same thing. One thing at least is clear – identity only becomes an issue when it is in crisis, when something assumed to be fixed, coherent and stable is displaced by the experience of doubt and uncertainty. (Mercer, 1990, p. 43)

Let us consider some of the features of contemporary life that have been suggested as reasons for a 'crisis of identity'. Some recent writers have argued that the search for collective and individual identities has become more intense in the face of increasing **globalization** (Giddens, 1990; Robins, 1997). The modes of economic production and consumption that have placed McDonalds, the burger chain, in almost every city in the world, made it possible to buy a can of Coca-Cola in the remotest corner of the globe and allow us to cross continents in hours rather than weeks have led, it is argued, to a fragmentation of the characteristics that once distinguished specific identities and nationalities. According to some writers, instead of identities based on groupings of community or nation, we all now share a common identity as global consumers, as a consequence of what Kevin Robins calls the 'transnationalization of economic and cultural life' (Robins, 1997, p. 12). For example, the management consultant, Kenichi Ohmae believes that national boundaries and the identities aligned to these are no longer significant in a world dominated by global corporations and organized around a global economy: 'The nation state has become an unnatural, even dysfunctional, unit for organizing human activity and managing economic endeavour in a borderless world. It represents no genuine, shared community of economic interests; it defines no meaningful flows of economic activity' (Ohmae, cited in Robins, 1997, p. 26).

In the face of these global movements people may feel detached from the older identities that defined previous generations and may, like Mr Reza, see themselves as 'creatures of the planet'. This may express a sense of alienation and detachment or it may involve resistance to the socio-cultural effects of global capitalism through the assertion of a new ethics based on a sense of global citizenship and responsibility. An example of such citizenship would be allegiance to environmental and ecological movements concerned with the future of the planet. There is further consideration of this in chapter 9, but for now the point to grasp is that increasing global trends in terms of the goods that are produced and consumed, the speed and accessibility (for some) of world travel, the development of electronic technologies that allow us to communicate immediately with Tokyo or New York and the movement of people, as a result of occupation, poverty or war, will have far-reaching consequences for the ways in which we define ourselves and are defined by others. Before going any further, you could attempt the following activity in order to extend your understanding of what is being argued in debates about globalization.

2.10

- Use a dictionary or reference book to find out what is meant by the term 'nation-state'.
- Can you think of any examples of how the 'transnationalization of economic and cultural life' has shaped the area you live in? Who lives in your neighbourhood? Do you have a sense of belonging to a particular community that bestows identity in your neighbourhood, in the workplace or elsewhere?
- Has globalization had any impact on your work, your family, your neighbourhood?

The trend towards a global economy has led to changes in the migration of labour. Often forced by poverty, and sometimes by war as well, people have moved across the globe. Of course, migration has always occurred, but the late twentieth century has seen an acceleration of this phenomenon. Most large cities in the industrialized world have an ethnically diverse population. For example, as mentioned above, London and Bradford in Britain have large, well established Asian communities that have brought to Britain their own cultures and religious faiths. This dispersal of people across the globe produces new forms of identity, as well as tensions as a result of cross-cultural differences. For example, in the extract above from *The Buddha of Suburbia*, the narrator, Karim, describes himself as 'a funny kind of Englishman, a new breed as it were'. For many centuries Jewish people have been dispersed across the globe. Since the Second World War Jews have struggled to create 'a home' in the Middle East. One of the consequences of this has been to displace Palestinians from what they perceived as their home. Yet for many Jewish people 'home' is the USA or France or wherever they were born and have lived for most of their lives. Thus, for some, Jewish identity is closely aligned to a specific place, a particular geographic area, a bounded land mass; for others, their sense of identity may be created from their upbringing as American (or British or Polish) as well as their Jewish culture and religion. And all Jewish people in the late twentieth century live in the shadow of the Holocaust, whether they see their roots in Israel, Europe or America.

The term **diaspora** is used to conceptualize the forced dispersal of people across the globe. Literally the term means: *dia*, through, apart, across; *spora*, from the Greek 'to scatter'; therefore to scatter apart, across, through. The Africans who were brought to the Caribbean or to North American to be sold as slaves from the late sixteenth to the early nineteenth centuries were displaced and dispersed in multiple ways, and the experience of transportation, colonization and slavery caused a profound discontinuity in terms of cultural identity. Taken from different villages, different parts of Africa, different tribes, speaking different tongues, worshipping different gods, the African people of the Caribbean and

North America nevertheless shared the experience of exile and slavery. The cultures and identities developed by black Africans in the Caribbean and North America may draw on their African 'roots', but they also draw on a shared history of slavery *and* the experience of living in the industrialized North or under European colonization. Edouard Glissant has commented on this as follows:

> There is a difference between the transplanting (by exile or dispersion) of a people who continue to survive elsewhere and the transfer (by the slave trade) of a population to another place where they change into something different, into a new set of possibilities . . . I feel that what makes this difference between a people that survives elsewhere, *that maintains its original nature*, and a population that is transformed elsewhere *into another people* . . . is that the latter has not brought with it, not collectively continued, the methods of existence and survival, both material and spiritual, which it practiced before being uprooted. These methods leave only dim traces or survive in the form of spontaneous impulses. This is what distinguishes, besides the persecution of one and the enslavement of the other, the Jewish Diaspora from the African slave trade. (Glissant, 1992, p. 14)

In more recent times, the wars in Vietnam or in the former Yugoslavia, in the Middle East, South America or Africa have resulted in myriad displacements. In the contemporary world this process of dispersal and displacement has accelerated, and produces cultural identities that are shaped by different places and located in diverse parts of the world. Identities produced in these circumstances cannot be traced back to a single origin or homeland (Africa or Indochina), but are produced from a range of cultures, locations and experiences.

2.11

Think about the ways in which the following might *share* a sense of cultural identity and the ways in which their different experiences might have produced *variations* of identity:

- South African blacks in the 1990s.
- Jamaicans living in Jamaica.
- Third-generation black British whose grandparents emigrated from Jamaica in the 1950s.
- Black Americans living in the southern states of the USA.
- Black Americans living in New York.
- Tutsi refugees from Rwanda now living in Zaire (1994 conflict).

You may need to find out more about these groups from newspaper reports, reference books or the following texts (full details are in the further reading): Fanon (1986), Gilroy (1987), Rutherford (1990), African Rights (1994).

The third feature that can be linked to the idea of 'identity crisis' is the political disruption in Eastern Europe and the former USSR. The break-up of the USSR and the collapse of communism in 1989 left a political void that was quickly filled by the re-emergence of earlier forms of national identity, ethnicity and religion. Without communism as a central reference point, people in the USSR and Eastern Europe found themselves fragmented and uncertain or in a position to claim identities that had been lost or suppressed under communism. The collapse of communism also had consequences for the ways in which writers and academics saw the future. The spread of capitalism across the globe and the end of the Cold War made it difficult to think and talk in terms of two structuring and opposing centres: capitalism and communism. In the 1960s and 1970s, conflict was frequently discussed and analysed in terms of a small number of 'master' ideologies, such as communism and capitalism. In the 1990s, with the collapse of communism, this is no longer tenable and there is a growing tendency to seek explanations for conflict in terms of competing identities, whether between large social groupings or at the level of the individual.

In recent years there has been a growth in social movements based on **identity politics**: feminism, the black civil rights movement, gay and lesbian movements have used a sense of collective identity as women, black people, homosexuals and lesbians to challenge subordination and oppression. Some strands of these movements base their politics and strategies on the uniqueness of a particular identity. For example, some members of the Greenham Common Peace Camp movement that actively protested against nuclear warfare and American missile bases in Britain during the 1980s based their politics on a radical feminism that held that women as women have a greater investment in peace as a consequence of, among other things, their social and biological role as mothers. Attempts on the part of white, Western feminists to advocate a universal female identity have been criticized by black feminists for failing to recognize the differences between women of different cultures, classes and ethnicities. Black feminist critiques have shown how the class and ethnic identities of some white, middle-class feminists are frequently at odds with the desire of such feminists to speak to and for a universal female identity,

> Many black women had been alienated by the non-recognition of their lives, experiences and herstories in the WLM [women's liberation movement]. Black feminists have been, and are still, demanding that the existence of racism must be acknowledged as a structuring feature of our relationships with white women. Both white feminist theory and practice have to recognize that white women stand in a power relation as oppressors of black women. (Carby, 1982, p. 215)

Now read the following extract, by Jeffrey Weeks.

2.8

READING

Identity is about belonging, about what you have in common with some people and what differentiates you from others. At its most basic it gives you a sense of personal location, the stable core to your individuality. But it is also about your social relationships, your complex involvement with others, and in the modern world these have become ever more complex and confusing. Each of us live with a variety of potentially contradictory identities, which battle within us for allegiance; as men or women, black or white, straight or gay, able-bodied or disabled, 'British' or 'European' . . . The list is potentially infinite, and so therefore are our possible belongings. Which of them we focus on, bring to the fore, 'identify' with, depends on a host of factors. At the centre, however, are the values we share or wish to share with others . . . Identities are not neutral. Behind the quest for identity are different and often conflicting values. By saying who we are, we are also striving to express what we are, what we believe and what we desire. The problem is that these beliefs, needs and desires are often patently in conflict, not only between different communities but within individuals themselves.

All this makes debates over values particularly fraught and delicate: they are not simply speculations about the world and our place in it; they touch on fundamental, and deeply felt, issues about who we are and what we want to be and become. They also pose major political questions: how to achieve a reconciliation between our collective needs as human beings and our specific needs as individuals and members of diverse communities, how to balance the universal and the particular. (Weeks, 1990, pp. 88–9)

2.12

- Look back at the description you wrote of yourself at the start of this chapter. Try to identify which aspects of your description are about collective identity in the sense discussed by Weeks above. Consider how significant these are for your sense of yourself, which ones 'you bring to the fore'.
- Look out for newspaper reports or news items on TV that refer to collective identities. You could collect a portfolio of such material. Figure 2.1 suggests a transnational identity around the issue of AIDS that is based on a political cause rather than global consumerism.

Representing and narrating identity

The extract from Alison Fell in reading 2.4 was from a piece of **autobiographical** writing. The word 'autobiography' is made up of three distinct parts, each with its own meaning: auto meaning 'I', bio meaning 'life' and 'graphy' meaning writing. Autobiography is therefore generally understood as the written account of an individual's life. As such, it offers a self-representation: a representation of a particular identity created by the self who is thus represented. The writer looks back (usually) on the past and narrates that past from the standpoint of the present. Of course, not all self-representations are literary or even written. People tell stories about their lives in many ways: in conversation, in oral accounts, in therapeutic case histories, in visual images, even in a CV for a job application. Personal narratives, whether produced as written autobiographies or in other forms, are an attempt to impose meaning and coherence on the often random and chaotic

Figure 2.1   World AIDS Day

experiences which constitute lives as they are lived, to order experiences by placing them within a narrative frame. Telling or writing a life story involves interpretation. The act of selecting, from the mass of lived experience, which events and people to include and emphasize is itself an act of interpretation. Alison Fell, you will recall, highlights her work with feminist organizations in the theatre and journalism. In doing so she constructs a specific identity for herself and a particular set of meanings to which her life testifies. The personal narratives we tell are never simply mirror reflections of a lived reality, but are mediated by the need to represent the self as possessing a sense of identity and control. Think about the result if you tried to tell a friend about every event, emotion or person you could recall encountering. Apart from the fact that your friend would undoubtedly quickly tire of listening, wouldn't you feel the account was incoherent, contradictory and meaningless? Autobiographical representation is one of the ways in which we shape our experiences into some form of meaning and construct particular identities for ourselves. Now read the extract below, in which Margaret Woollard, a London teenager, gives her reasons for writing autobiography.

2.9

I chose to write an autobiography basically because I just love writing about myself. I have kept a detailed diary now for four years because I want my children and my children's children to look back on it and find out what I was like as a teenager and what life was like in the 1980s. I also keep it for my own personal records as to how I have changed. But not only that; even if I never looked back on it again I shall never forget the satisfaction it gave me to put down my deepest thoughts on paper.

It took me a while to work out what to include in my autobiography: how personal I should make it, and what aspects of my personality I should portray. My life has been fairly uneventful compared to some; apart from moving to London and my parents' separation. There are few single events that I can pinpoint as landmarks in it, so I decided to write about the periods I went through and my attitudes and opinions, rather than tell a straight narrative from the day I was born up until the present day.

I have been very frank in my autobiography. I may come across as 'weird': I don't think my life is in fact very different to the average London teenager and I have maybe exaggerated the differences to make a more interesting story. I am not afraid to portray myself as an individual and express what I really feel. I would like other young readers to enjoy reading about my life: to laugh at the funny incidents and be moved by the sad ones, and to try to accept and understand me and see me as a young person similar to themselves. (Simons and Bleiman, 1987, p. 81)

Activity 2.13

- Why does Margaret want to write about herself?
- What decisions does she make about the story she will tell?
- What 'message' or meanings is she trying to convey about herself?

As we have suggested, there may be a gap between identity as it is represented and identity as it is lived, but this does not mean that representation and reality are two mutually exclusive categories. Personal life narratives may be informed by the ways in which we think 'tales of lives should be told'; that is, they require moments of drama, interesting characters and a coherent meaning in order to communicate with a reader/listener (Stanley, 1992, p. 12). At the same time, a personal life narrative, whatever form it takes, does involve a real rather than a fictional life, it is about people who actually existed rather than imaginary characters and it does refer to events which did occur, however mediated these are by the narrator's shaping influence.

> And more complex still, 'lives as they are lived' exist symbiotically with the written representation of lives: we expect our and other people's lives to have troughs and peaks, to have 'meaning', to have major and minor characters, heroes and villains, to be experienced as linear and progressive, and for chronology to provide the most important means of understanding them, all of which are characteristics of fiction. (Stanley, 1992, p. 14)

Many of the issues introduced in this section will be taken up in chapters 3 and 8. There are connections too with the discussion about history in chapter 4.

Conclusions

This chapter has introduced you to the concepts of identity and difference. You will have the opportunity to consider further some of the ideas raised here in later chapters. For now we offer you a summary of the main ideas introduced here.

- Social as well individual factors create people's sense of themselves, the ways in which they can be seen by others and the lives they may expect to live. Although social factors provide the parameters within which lives are lived and identities experienced, these may not be inevitably determining; there remains scope for individual action and agency. We are able to construct identities from a diverse and sometimes conflicting range of possibilities. However, identities are bestowed as well as chosen, and this may give rise to conflicting identities.
- At the same time, however, material factors alone cannot explain the investment that individuals have in specific identities. Althusser's theory of the subject attempts to incorporate psychoanalytic explanations into a materialist perspective.
- The formation of identities can involve essentialist claims about biology (e.g. the statement 'I have British blood'). Non-essentialist perspectives argue that identity is relational and contingent, and depends upon the symbolic marking of one group as different from another (e.g. man/woman or Asian/European).
- Identities are formed through classification systems that define social groups in terms of similarities and differences. To be Asian is to be not-European. 'Race', gender, age, sexual orientation are socially constructed categories that are **relational** rather than biologically inherited. Such categories may, however, use biological features as symbolic markers by which to classify individuals.
- Identities and differences can shift over time, circumstances and place. For example, the assertion of national identity during wartime may attempt to transcend those gender, age, class, religious and ethnic differences that in peacetime may have engendered conflict. Thus identities are **contingent** upon time, circumstance and place.
- Social and material effects follow from the symbolic marking of one group as different from another.
- Identities may be formed collectively as well as individually, and can be used for political purposes: for example, the women's liberation movement, 'Glad to be gay', Black Power.
- Accelerated globalization, increased migration and the collapse of an alternative ideology to capitalism have led to what some writers see as 'a crisis of identity' at the end of the twentieth century.
- The perspectives we explored also raised the question of a conceptual split between body/mind, animal/human, nature/culture. Lynda Birke suggests that this conceptual polarization constrains the ways in which we are able to understand the relationship between biological imperatives and cultural identity.

- Cultural representations, in this context autobiography and personal life narratives, are one of the ways in which we can construct self-definitions and identities out of the 'raw material' at our disposal. Cultural representations offer forms within which we can choose to narrate ourselves and our lives in order to produce a sense of identity and meaning.

Later chapters take up many of the issues raised here in further detail and in relation to specific topics. For example, the next chapter has a section on gay and lesbian representations, chapter 8 extends the discussion by focusing on the concept of subjectivity and chapter 9 thinks about our identities as consumers. Indeed, issues of identity are central to the study of culture: how we define ourselves and how we are defined by others is inextricably related to the 'production and circulation of meaning' in a particular society at a particular time.

CHAPTER 3

Representation

Introduction

Stuart Hall, one of the founders of cultural studies in Britain and a leading contributor to many of the debates in cultural studies since the 1970s, argues that culture

> is not so much a set of *things* – novels and paintings or TV programmes and comics – as a process, a set of *practices*. Primarily, culture is concerned with the production and the exchange of meanings – 'the giving and taking of meaning' – between the members of a society or group. (Hall, 1997, p. 2)

Representation is one of the key practices by which meanings are produced. By the end of this chapter we hope you will have begun to understand what we mean by 'representation' and something of how it functions. Working through the readings and activities that follow this introduction will enable you to recognize the often complex ways in which meanings are produced through systems of representation – primarily, in this chapter, written language, visual images and objects. We begin by considering what is meant by the term 'representation', and then move on to consider how the links between meanings, representation and culture might be explained.

ACTIVITIES

3.1

Spend a few minutes thinking about what is meant by the word 'represent'. You might find it helpful to use a dictionary.

There are three possible senses to the word 'represent'.

- To 'represent' meaning to stand in for, as in the case of a country's flag, which when flown at a sporting event, for example, signals that country's presence at the event. The flag stands for or symbolizes a nation, distinguishing France from China or Ireland from the USA. In Britain, the Royal Standard represents/symbolizes the royal family and the institution of monarchy.

- To 'represent' meaning to speak or act on behalf of, as in the sentence 'A spokesperson on behalf of lesbian mothers voiced the concerns of the group on television.' Members of Parliament represent the concerns of their constituents. A person who represents a group in this sense may also serve a symbolic function. An example might be the Pope, who speaks and acts on behalf of the Roman Catholic community but might also stand as a symbol of Roman Catholicism.
- To 'represent' meaning to re-present. In this sense, a biography or historical writing re-presents the events of the past. Equally, a photograph re-presents a moment or event which has already occurred – it presents the occasion again. A photograph or painting can also, of course, represent someone or something in the sense of standing in for. Posters of rock stars, religious paintings and public statues all fulfil this function. Images that function in this way are said to be **iconic**.

In practice the three meanings we have identified frequently overlap and merge. None the less, it is worth spending a few moments thinking about further examples of each meaning from your own experience. In which sense is a photograph of a child's birthday party working? What about road signs? What about the red 'M' sign used by the hamburger chain McDonalds? In what sense is a written autobiography a representation? Is a novel or a TV soap opera a representation and, if so, of what?

Language and representation

Language is an arbitrary system of **signs** in which we tacitly agree to accept, for example, that the letters/sounds d.o.g. will represent (stand in for) those animals we wish to classify as different from, say, elephants or mice. It is only at the moment when we agree that the **signifier** d.o.g. equals a mental concept of a certain animal (the **signified**) that an animal known to us as 'dog' and therefore not 'elephant' or 'mouse' exists. Signifier plus signified produce the sign, dog. Furthermore, we understand d.o.g. as dog because it is not the letters or sounds c.a.t. nor l.o.g. rather than because there are physical differences between cats and dogs that fall into naturally pre-existent categories of what constitutes a dog or a cat. Language works through a system of differentiation 'readily experienced as natural, given, but in reality constructed by the language itself' (Belsey, 1980, pp. 39–40). Prior to its constitution in language (the sounds/letters d.o.g.) we do not possess a *shared* conception of dog that can be socially communicated. This does not mean that we are unable to see or think about certain animals with certain characteristics, but that such animals are not known specifically as dogs or cats or elephants or mice that can be talked, thought and spoken about as different, until language constitutes them as such. Now read this extract from Catherine Belsey's *Critical Practice*, which expands the ideas that we have just glossed.

3.1

We use signifiers to mark off areas of a continuum. The [colour] spectrum again illustrates this point. It is not that I cannot distinguish between shades of blue but that the language insists on a difference, which readily comes to seem fundamental, *natural*, between blue and green. The world, which without signification would be experienced as a continuum, is divided up by language into entities which then readily come to be experienced as essentially distinct. The way in which we use signifiers to create differences appears in the labelling of otherwise identical toothmugs, 'his' and 'hers' . . .

Only a social group can generate signs. Noises which have no meaning may be purely individual, but meaning intelligibility, cannot by definition be produced in isolation. The sign is in an important sense arbitrary – the sound *dog* has not more necessary or natural connection with the concept *dog* than has *chien* or *Hund*. Even onomatopeic words, which seem to imitate the sounds they signify, are by no means international: French dogs say *ouaoua*; *to splash* in French is *éclabousser*. And it is the arbitrariness of the sign which points to the fact that language is a matter of convention. The linguistic community 'agrees' to attach a specific signified to a specific signifier, though in reality, of course, its agreement is not explicitly sought but merely manifested in the fact that certain linguistic units are used and understood. 'The arbitrary nature of the sign explains in turn why the social fact alone can create a linguistic system. The community is necessary if values that owe their existence solely to usage and general acceptance are to be set up' (Saussure, 1974, p. 113). And conversely, of course, a community needs a signifying system: social organization and social exchange, the ordering of the processes of producing the means of subsistence, is impossible without the existence of a signifying system. Language therefore comes into being at the same time as society . . .

Language is not, of course, the only signifying system. Images, gestures, social behaviour, clothes are all socially invested with meaning, are all elements of the symbolic order: language is simply the most flexible and perhaps the most complex of the signifying systems. Thought, if not exclusively dependent on language, is inconceivable without the symbolic order in general. 'Thought is nothing other than the power to construct representations of things and to operate on these representations. It is in essence symbolic' [Benveniste, 1971, p. 25]. (Belsey, 1980, pp. 39–45)

Activity 3.2

- Look up the word 'nice' in the *Oxford English Dictionary*. Look in particular at its etymology – the way its meaning has changed over time. (This information is given in square brackets at the end of the entry).
- Can you think of examples of language marking differences that have social meaning? For example, the forms of address, Miss, Ms, Mr, Dr, Reverend.
- Think about the concept of 'race'. Is this an instance where 'the language insists on a difference, which readily comes to seem fundamental, *natural*'? Is 'race' a form of linguistic differentiation and classification rather than a natural phenomenon?

Communicating meaning

You should now read the following passage by Stuart Hall.

3.2

Members of the same culture must share sets of concepts, images and ideas which enable them to think and feel about the world, and thus to interpret the world, in roughly similar ways. They must share, broadly speaking, the same 'cultural codes'. In this sense, thinking and feeling are themselves 'systems of representation', in which our concepts, images and emotions 'stand for' or represent, in our mental life, things which are or may be 'out there' in the world. Similarly, in order to *communicate* these meanings to other people, the participants to any meaningful exchange must also be able to use the same linguistic codes – they must, in a very broad sense, 'speak the same language' . . . They must also be able to read visual images in roughly similar ways. They must be familiar with broadly the same ways of producing sounds to make what they would both recognize as 'music'. They must all interpret body language and facial expressions in broadly similar ways. And they must know how to translate their feelings and ideas into these various languages. Meaning is a dialogue – always only partially understood, always an unequal exchange.

Why do we refer to all these different ways of producing and communicating meaning as 'languages' or as 'working like languages'? How do languages work? The simple answer is that languages work *through representation*. They are 'systems of representations'. Essentially, we can say that all these practices 'work like languages', *not* because they are all written or spoken (they are not), but because they all use some element to stand for or represent what we want to say, to express or communicate a thought, concept, idea or feeling. Spoken language uses sounds, written language uses words, musical language uses notes on a scale, the 'language of the body' uses physical gesture, the fashion industry uses items of clothing, the language of facial expression uses ways of arranging one's features, television uses digitally or electronically produced dots on a screen, traffic lights use red, green and amber to 'say something' These elements – sounds, words, notes, gestures, expressions, clothes – are part of our natural and material world, but their importance for language is not what they *are* but what they *do*, their function. They construct meaning and transmit it. They signify. They don't have any clear meaning *in themselves*. Rather, they are the vehicles or media which *carry meaning* because they operate as *symbols*, which stand for or represent (i.e. symbolize) the meanings we wish to communicate. To use another metaphor, they function as *signs*. Signs stand for or *represent* our concepts, ideas and feelings in such a way as to enable others to 'read', decode or interpret their meaning in roughly the same way that we do. (Hall, 1997, pp. 4–5)

In order to explore what Hall is saying more fully, let us take a simple example. The word 'star' can mean, among other things, an extra-terrestial form in the galaxy, a celebrity, an award for good work or behaviour, an architectual formation. It all depends on the meaning attributed to the sign 'star' in a particular context. The letters s.t.a.r. have no intrinsic meaning in themselves – as Hall says, words are important not for what 'they *are* but what they *do*, their function'. They are a symbol or sign to which we tacitly agree to attach certain meanings. Taking the first meaning, until a group or society 'agrees' to use the letters s.t.a.r. to signify the shiny dots that can be seen in the sky at night, the word star has no meaning. The letters s.t.a.r. represent (stand in for) the physical objects we can see in the night sky, and allow us to communicate this meaning to others who use the same language. To use the word 'star' to represent (symbolize) a particular kind of celebrity is to understand 'star' as a metaphor – it suggests a connection or likeness between a star in the firmament and certain 'brilliant' people. Stars are also physical shapes used for buildings, decorations, swimming or dancing formations. Here, they are being used as a visual sign, rather than a verbal one, but one which works through shared ways of seeing: we recognize a particular shape as 'star' because we share the same codes of communication. A star used as a reward can function as both a visual and a verbal symbol – a symbol of, or a way of representing, special achievement. The point to grasp is that the concept 'star' has no fixed or single meaning for all time. What it means will depend upon the context in which it is used, how it is represented and the codes which govern that representation. For example, schoolchildren do not believe that the award of a gold star will mean being presented with a star from the galaxy; they understand the meaning of star within the context of its use and the codes of representation in the British education system, which designate stars as symbols of excellence. Again, if asked to form a star in a dance class they would not confuse this with the award for achievement. In summary, meaning is produced via **signifying practices**, in which signs are assembled according to sets of codes in order to represent, in material form (speech, the written word, visual images, music, body language, clothing, the environments we live and work in), the mental conceptualizations shared by a particular grouping of people.

ACTIVITIES

3.3

- List as many meanings for the sign 'star' as you can think of.
- Collect some visual images of stars (in any of the senses used). Do they connect with the words and stories used about stars?
- Can you think of physical gestures that function as signs in the particular body language you recognize? For example, in Britain a nod of the head signifies assent, but it might signify differently in another culture.

In order to interpret the world we inhabit, we need a framework of meanings that will enable us to place people, objects and events in ways that make sense for us. Think back to chapter 1, where we made the point that it was possible to know what a cathedral was without actually being in or looking at one. We have a mental concept of 'cathedral' that we can access even when we are nowhere near an actual, bricks and mortar cathedral. The same is true of objects like tables, chairs or computers. It is also true of less tangible things, like love, loyalty, justice or cruelty, and even of things that we have never experienced or seen, such as dragons, fairies or prehistoric cavemen. This ability to conceptualize mentally even abstract things allows us to represent the world to ourselves in ways which are meaningful, and to communicate those meanings to others who share broadly similar systems of representation. Try explaining Father Christmas to someone from a culture in which this figure does not exist. In order to understand Father Christmas we need a shared concept and a way of communicating this or, if we belong to a culture which does not have Father Christmas, we will try to relate the concept of Father Christmas to something similar in our own culture in order to classify it as 'similar to'/'different from'. The concepts we use to make sense of the world are arrived at by a process of **categorization** and **classification**. Signs only operate to produce meaning within a system of other signs that signify along chains of similarity and difference. For example, night means not-day, a dark room means not-night because it is created by artificial means – no electric light, drawn curtains – whereas night signifies a natural state, but a dark room is like night in that both a dark room and night are unlike a lighted room or daytime. In this way we are able to form complex meanings that can be communicated to others through systems of representation that are constituted in:

- the signs we use, such as s.t.a.r., a nod of the head;
- the categorization and classification of signs according to similarity or differ-ence, e.g. the sign w.o.m.a.n. signifies in relation to other signs, such as m.a.n. or a.n.i.m.a.l. or h.u.m.a.n.;
- the codes that govern how we assemble the signs to produce meaning, e.g. the context in which 'star' means a heavenly body or a symbol of achievement;
- the signifying practices through which meanings are communicated, e.g. sounds, writing, visual images, musical notation, physical gestures, clothing.

So far this may seem somewhat abstract. Let us demonstrate what we have been saying with a practical example. Look carefully at figure 3.1 and try to follow the discussion that follows. For your information, the background is a deep red, blurring into a yellowy orange, with the doormat a lighter shade of yellowy or-ange, blurring into yellowy gold along its fold. The writing is black on the door-mat and white elsewhere, with the yellowy orange colour used for the bullet points.

3.4

ACTIVITIES

Figure 3.1 is a picture of the cover of one of the booklets produced by the Midland Bank (now renamed the HSBC) to provide information for custom-ers. What is this cover 'saying'? Don't simply offer an overall impression. Try to analyse precisely how the various signs are assembled in order to signify a particular meaning. What does the sign 'doormat' signify here? What about the use of colour? What does the word 'home' signify?

The cover is promoting Midland's range of mortgages, loans and insurance. It suggests that Midland ('the listening bank') welcomes the opportunity to help

Figure 3.1   The cover of a booklet produced by Midland Bank plc

and advise potential home owners to find the right financial services. The door-mat, which occupies the centre of the cover and draws our eyes, is intended to signify as an invitation: 'come on in', in the sense of both reading the booklet and entering a home. The word 'welcome' confirms the intended meaning of the door-mat: in another context a doormat can signify someone who is willing to be walked all over. Using words or a caption to ensure the meaning of a visual image is referred to as **anchoring** the meaning. On this cover the words 'welcome' and 'home' ensure that a certain meaning is secured. It is worth noting that the caption says 'Buying a home' rather than 'Buying a house'. Home has certain **connotations** that are not present in concepts of 'house': safety, family, place of origin, comfort, haven, not-work etc. The use of the colours red and gold confirms these meanings: red and gold in this context suggest warmth, even firelight, and this links directly to the idea of home that the cover is promoting. Midland, 'the listening bank', becomes associated with the values of security, warmth and welcome that are represented by the particular assemblage of signs used here.

This booklet is one of a series providing information on the services offered by Midland. Each booklet cover represents a different set of services and the values or meanings attached to these. Yet the series has a whole is held together by a certain housestyle – the graphics use the same font and are placed in the same position on each cover. Different colours are used for each booklet in order to signify certain ideas, but also to distinguish each booklet. Taken together, the series of booklets represents in visual and written form the range of services offered by Midland. The signs used here are **encoded** so as to suggest particular meanings. By encoding we mean using them in certain ways and in particular relations to other signs so as to convey a specific meaning or 'message'. A doormat could be encoded in ways that signify 'to be walked over' or 'to wipe your feet on'. The colours red and gold can signify pomp and majesty in other contexts. Red, in the sequence of traffic lights, represents stop. Used with other signs and encoded differently, red can suggest passion.

Activity 3.5

- Search through magazines, brochures and advertisements to try to find examples of representations that encode red and/or gold in different ways from the Midland booklet cover.
- What signs might you use in conjunction with a doormat to suggest meanings other than 'welcome home'? Think about objects, colours, words, context etc.

By now you may be thinking that it is all very well to encode a meaning by placing signs in particular relation to each other, but how can we know that this encoded meaning will be received (decoded) in precisely the form intended, given the range of possible meanings of even an apparently straightforward sign such as 'star'. In his essay 'Encoding/decoding in television discourse', Hall argues that 'decodings do not follow inevitably from encodings', that there is no natural symmetry between encoders and decoders (Hall, 1990, p. 100). TV news producers, for example, may encode events in ways that point to an intended or preferred meaning, but these encodings may be decoded or 'read' differently. The Midland Bank cover, for example, encodes a 'preferred' meaning but the producers of the cover can only attempt to persuade us into reading the meaning they intend. As 'readers' we bring our own histories, understandings, place in the world to our reading of the cover, and therefore possibly produce meanings from it which were not intended by the cover designers. Hall uses the word **articulation** to suggest the point at which encoding and decoding meet. This is a useful word to convey the process he is attempting to describe. To articulate means two things: to express something and to link two things in a way which retains the independence of each. Think of an articulated lorry in which the cab and container are interdependent but not permanently joined; each can be articulated to another vehicle if needed. Now read the extract from Jacqueline Bobo's study of black women's readings of the Steven Spielberg film of Alice Walker's book *The Color Purple*.

From political sociology, the encoding/decoding model was drawn from the work of Frank Parkin, who developed a theory of meaning systems [Morley, 1989, p. 4]. This theory delineates three potential responses to a media message: dominant, negotiated or oppositional. A dominant (or preferred) reading of a text accepts the content of the cultural product without question. A negotiated reading questions parts of the content of the text but does not question the dominant ideology which underlies the production of the text. An oppositional response to a cultural product is one in which the recipient of the text understands that the system that produced the text is one with which she/he is fundamentally at odds [Grossberg, 1984, p. 403].

A viewer of a film (reader of a text) comes to the moment of engagement with the work with a knowledge of the world and a knowledge of other texts or media products. What this means is that when a person comes to view a film, she/he does not leave her/his histories, whether social, cultural, economic, racial, or sexual at the door. An audience member from a marginalized group (people of colour, women, the poor, and so on) has an oppositional stance as they participate in mainstream media. The motivation for this counter-reception is that we understand that mainstream media has never rendered our segment of the population faithfully. We have as evidence our years of watching films and television programmes and reading plays and books. Out of habit, as readers of mainstream texts, we have learned to ferret out the beneficial and put up blinders against the rest.

From this wary viewing standpoint, a subversive reading of a text can occur. This alternative reading comes from something in the work that strikes the viewer as amiss, that appears 'strange'. Behind the idea of subversion lies a reader-oriented notion of 'making strange' [Gledhill, 1984]. When things appear strange to the viewer, she/he may then bring other viewpoints to bear on the watching of the film and may see things other than what the film-makers intended. The viewer, that is, will read 'against the grain' of the film. (Bobo, 1988, p. 55).

Bobo's interviews with black women who saw *The Color Purple* demonstrate the ways in which these women read the film 'against the grain' of dominant critical readings that condemned the film for its negative representation of black people. She suggests that, rather than finding the portrayal of the black community stereotypical and negative, as argued by numerous critics, these women 'discovered something progressive and useful in the film' (Bobo, 1988, p. 54).

A further example: advertising that uses images of white, young, slim, attractive and healthy females to sell a product is encoding a particular version of femininity. In these adverts femininity equals whiteness, youth, beauty, slenderness and health. A reader who straightforwardly accepts that whiteness, youth, beauty and a slender, healthy body connote femininity can be said to be reading from within the dominant code in which this image is encoded. An unquestioning acceptance of these **dominant** codes of femininity may lead to a continuing quest for youth, beauty and slenderness and, if one is non-white, possible attempts to 'pass as white'. A **negotiated** decoding may accept the encoded definition of femininity at the level of the advertisement, possibly as an unattainable ideal or fantasy, but this meaning of femininity may have minimum impact on or bear little relation to everyday experience. A woman who decodes from a negotiated position may enjoy looking at the femininity offered in advertisements and magazines but may, quite happily, spend very little time or money in her daily life attempting to emulate these. Neither, however, is she likely to question the underlying structures that posit femininity in these terms – as Bobo writes, she 'does not question the dominant ideology which underlies the production of the text'. Someone who decodes the images of femininity from an **oppositional** position would read such images as harmful to women, in that they render women of colour, older women, large women, poor women and women with disabilities invisible and promote a dominant ideology of heterosexuality. They might actively seek to change the ways in which advertisements represent women through the politics of feminism and black rights movements (see chapter 2; Betterton, 1987; Bonner *et al.*, 1992; McCracken, 1993; Dines and Humez, 1995).

3.6

- Collect a variety of brochures, booklets, pamphlets etc. from a range of sources (banks, travel agents, museums, publishers etc.). Have a go at analysing these as we did the Midland booklet cover above.
- Select an advertisement or series of advertisements. Try to work out how the advert might be read from: (a) a dominant decoding position; (b) a negotiated decoding position; and (c) an oppositional position.
- Watch a film with friends, family or fellow students. Try to identify the preferred meanings that are being conveyed. Discuss the film with the other viewers. Does the discussion demonstrate examples of dominant, negotiated or oppositional positionings? Dominant and oppositional will probably be the easiest to identify, but have a go at identifying negotiated decoding positions both in the discussion and in your everyday life.

ACTIVITIES

Representation and discourse

You may have begun to wonder how and why dominant meanings are sustained, often consistently over a long period, when it is possible for people to produce alternative and oppositional meanings that may be subversive. In order to think about this we need to turn our attention to how meanings 'circulate', and the way we have chosen to explore this is through the concept of discourse developed by Michel Foucault. Discourse moves the focus from an examination of the relation of signs within a signifying system to asking questions about how certain ways of thinking about an area of knowledge acquire authority, how certain meanings attach themselves to certain signs in specific historical periods and how meaning and knowledge produce and sustain power relations. Discourse is a social act, in that it links systems of representation with the real world in which people experience social relations. Foucault argues that how human beings understand themselves in relation to the social world is not fixed or universal, but that this knowledge is produced differently at different historical moments. Such knowledge, he claims, is produced through discourse, and is inextricably linked with the ways in which power operates,

> power produces knowledge (and not simply by encouraging it because it serves power or by applying it because it is useful); that power and knowledge directly imply one another; that there is no power relation without the correlative constitution of a field of knowledge, nor any knowledge that does not presuppose and constitute at the same time power relations. (Foucault, 1975, 27)

Before we go on to think about discourse, let us consider what is meant by 'there is no power relation without the correlative constitution of a field of knowledge'.

ACTIVITIES

3.7

Look back to the extract from Said in chapter 1, in which he writes of imperialism's need to differentiate 'us' from 'them' (reading 1.7). What particular knowledges or way of seeing the world are connected with the power relations of imperialism?

In order for one area of the globe to colonize and rule another it is necessary for the colonizers and colonized to know and represent the world in certain ways. For example, in the nineteenth century, British imperialists understood Africa as 'the dark continent', a primitive and unknowable place, to be 'civilized' by Christianity, science and the 'forces of reason'. Such knowledge constructed oppositions in which Europe represented enlightenment, reason and civilization, while Africa was the scene of ignorance, irrationality and savagery. This 'knowledge' legitimated the practice of slavery in the southern states of North America, the slave trade that operated in a triangle comprising Africa, North America and Britain, and the European colonization of Africa. In the eighteenth and nineteenth centuries power relations between black and white people, in which black signified subordination and servitude, while white signified superiority and ownership, were represented as the 'natural' order of things, thus closing off any discussion of these relations. Blacks were 'by nature' lazy, 'primitive' and childish, and this legitimated the subjection of their bodies, as well as their work, homes, leisure and environment, to white authority. This 'knowledge', often validated by scientific findings about the 'true nature' of Black Africans, was crucial to the white imperialist project. Once black inferiority was accepted as 'true', certain practices – economic and social – could be carried out in the name of that 'truth' (Mackenzie, 1986; Gates, 1988; hooks, 1992; McClintock, 1995; Hall, 1997). And we might also ask how the colonized saw *themselves* in the education system. The next extract is taken from a collection of life stories by Jamaican girls published in 1986, and describes the feelings of a creole woman when she read *Jane Eyre* as a schoolgirl receiving a British education in Kingston, Jamaica.

3.4

In third form, they gave us *Jane Eyre* to read. It was the only piece of literature in which there was any mention of the Caribbean. It was also the only book by a woman which they had given us to read. We liked the bits about school and then we came upon the mad heiress from Spanish Town locked up in the attic. At first we giggled, knowing that it was Jane we were supposed to identify with and her quest for independence and dignity. Then we got to the part where this masterpiece of English Literature describes Bertha Mason as 'inferior, blue skinned . . . etc.' Someone was reading it out loud in the class as was the custom. Gradually the mumbling and whispering in the class room crescendoed into an open revolt with loud choruses of 'It's not fair, Miss!' Miss admitted it seemed unfair but she went on to do nothing with that insight . . . I couldn't put it down . . . anxiously looking for a chapter, a paragraph or a sentence that might redeem the insane animal inferiority of the Caribbean. It was a women's novel and I had liked so much of the earlier part, but I couldn't stomach the way I had been relegated to the attic. I felt betrayed. (Cited in Duncker, 1992, p. 26)

Novels, like *Jane Eyre*, are one of the ways in which 'truth' and knowledge are circulated. So 'naturalized' are these 'truths' that we often fail to see the power relations they uphold until someone, like this Jamaican schoolgirl, reading from a different position makes these visible. White European students reading *Jane Eyre* are often shocked and sometimes resistant when they first encounter the passage above.

3.8

- Whether or not you have read *Jane Eyre*, what was your reaction to the idea expressed above that this 'masterpiece of English Literature' represented the Caribbean, through the figure of Bertha Mason, as 'insane', 'animal' and inferior. If you were shocked, try to work out why. If you were resistant to the idea that a writer like Charlotte Brontë could express racist sentiments, ask yourself why you find it hard to believe.
- Can you think of other cultural forms (novels, paintings, films, TV programmes etc.) in which the non-European is represented as different, 'abnormal' or 'deviant'? These could be contemporary or from another historical period.

Constructing, sustaining and reproducing 'truths' is essential to the maintenance of power. Until recently, women's 'natural destiny' was seen as motherhood: this was a 'truth' that required no comment (although, of course, in any age, such ideas have been challenged, as the schoolgirl above challenges the norm that allows the Caribbean to be represented as 'other' and inferior). The 'truth', that a woman's 'destiny' was motherhood, validated the exclusion of women from many spheres of public activity, at the same time making it difficult for those excluded to question publicly the knowledge on which their exclusion was based.

Thus certain knowledges about women could be maintained and reproduced by those whose interest was best served by such 'truths'.

According to Foucault, knowledge and 'truth' are produced through discourses. There are no pre-existent 'truths' that representations simply reflect. The numerous representations of mother and child in Western art, in advertising, in newspapers, are not a mirror reflection of an already existing 'fact' – that is, that women's highest destiny is motherhood – but are one element of the system of representation that constructs women as primarily mothers. Discourse is the term used to describe the network of statements, images, stories and practices by which certain beliefs or a set of ideas about a particular topic are circulated and sustained in order to **naturalize** these as self-evident or common sense. Thus, we could speak of a patriarchal discourse of gender in which it is perceived as 'natural' that women should exhibit a predisposition to mothering as a result of their biology (see also, in this connection, our references in chapter 2 to essentialism). We could equally refer to a feminist discourse of gender that has contested what were perceived as common-sense beliefs about the 'nature' of women. Now read the extract by John Fiske.

READING

3.5

Discourse is a language or system of representation that has developed socially in order to make and circulate a coherent set of meanings about an important topic area. These meanings serve the interests of that section of society within which the discourse originates and which works ideologically to naturalize those meanings into common sense. 'Discourses are power relations' (O'Sullivan et al. 1983: 74). Discourse is thus a social act which may promote or oppose the dominant ideology, and is thus often refered to as a 'discursive practice'. Any account of a discourse or a discursive practice must include its topic area, its social origin, and its ideological work: we should not, therefore, think about a discourse of economics, or of gender, but of a capitalist (or socialist) discourse of economics, or the patriarchal (or feminist) discourse of gender. Such discourses frequently become institutionalized, particularly by the media industries in so far as they are structured by a socially produced set of conventions that are tacitly accepted by both industry and consumers.

Discourses function not only in the production and reading of texts, but also in making sense of social experience. A particular discourse of gender, for example, works not only to make sense of a television program . . . but also to make a particular pattern of sense of gender in the family, in the workplace, in school, in social clubs – in fact, in our general social relations. (Fiske, 1987, pp. 14–15)

ACTIVITIES

3.9

Try to think of some specific examples of how and where discourses of gender, either feminist or patriarchal, are produced. We have started you off; you carry on and add to our examples.

How	Where
● By making statements	In parliament, in the newspapers, in studies of gender
● Through representations	In novels, advertisements
● By teaching	In schools and in the family
● By social practices	Marriage, parenting, jobs
●	
●	
●	

Looking at your list, select those examples which, you think, would be most likely to authorize the patriarchal discourse of gender. Why? Are there any examples that might offer a space in which the patriarchal discourse could be challenged?

A discourse operates across a range of diverse practices, texts and the institutions in which these are located. Discourse, as a way of understanding representation, extends the **semiotic** concern with signs and symbols beyond systems of language by linking representation to the ways in which power operates in specific social situations and historical periods. Although Foucault recognizes that language is the medium through which discourses produce knowledge, he is also concerned to stress that since 'all social practices entail meaning, and meanings shape and influence what we do – our conduct – all practices have a discursive aspect' (Hall, 1992, p. 291). Hence, it is not language alone that produces discourse, but also behaviours and practices. For example, the star-shaped piece of gold paper kept in the teacher's desk or stationery cupboard becomes 'a gold star for achievement' not only when it is named as such but also when it is awarded to a pupil. The meaning of 'gold stars' is produced through specific social acts, as well as linguistic naming and visual objects. Gold stars take on a particular meaning within a child-centred discourse of education, which includes, *inter alia*: statements about the value of schooling and the importance of achievement; authorization of the practice of rewards and encouragements by psychologists and other 'experts'; and rules that prescribe when and how such awards will be made.

Let us look at another example. The sixteenth and seventeenth centuries witnessed widespread persecution and punishment of those people, mostly women, 'known' to be witches. If you have seen Arthur Miller's play *The Crucible*, watched the film adaptation or studied American history, you will know that in the seventeenth century, Salem, Massachusetts, experienced a ferocious witch-hunt. In order for this to occur, certain elements had to come together to produce a context in which witchcraft had particular meanings that legitimated the identification and punishment of some people as witches. For example:

1 Statements about the practices and customs of witches, providing the community with certain kinds of knowledge about what constituted witchcraft.
2 Rules which made it possible to say some things but not others about witchcraft. For example, it was not possible in the seventeenth century to understand or talk about so-called witches as wise, rational or moral beings.

3 Actual people – 'subjects' – who, because their behaviour, attributes or habits fitted the period's knowledge of witches, constructed in 1 and 2 above, could be identified as 'witch'.

4 Institutional frameworks which allowed the knowledges produced by 1, 2 and 3 to acquire authority and thus come to constitute the 'truth' at a specific historical moment: for example religious communities, the legal system, schooling and education.

Now read the following extract from Elaine Showalter's *Hystories: Hysterical Epidemics and Modern Culture.*

3.6

Preconditions of a witch-hunt were consistent, whether the events took place in Scotland or Salem. The community had to know something about the practices of witches and to be convinced of their habits. Lawyers and judges also had to believe in witchcraft, since they controlled the judicial process and could halt the hunts. For successful prosecutions, specific antiwitchcraft legislation and the establishment of jurisdiction were necessary. Witch-hunts were smaller where inquisitional procedures and torture were prohibited, as in seventeenth-century England.

In addition, witch-hunts required an emotional atmosphere stirred up by sermons, discussions and rumors. They often began with individual denunciations stemming from personal grudges. Sometimes malice played a role. Sometimes disturbed individuals confessed. In England, witch-hunts were usually limited to those originally accused. In Switzerland, Germany and Scotland, medium-sized witch-hunts . . . prevailed: the accused were tortured and implicated a group of accomplices. These panics burned themselves out when the local group of suspicious persons had been exhausted.

Large witch-hunts, 'characterized by a high degree of panic or hysteria' [Levack, 1995, p. 174] took place in France, Sweden, and of course in Salem. These were driven by both the clinical conversion hysteria of the demoniacs and the collective hysteria of the community. (Showalter, 1997, p. 25)

This passage not only suggests how witch-hunts gathered momentum in the past but also makes statements about how they can be understood in the present. Witchcraft in the seventeenth century was understood within the discourses of religion and the law, so that we can speak of the religious discourse of witchcraft or the legal discourse of witchcraft. In the late twentieth century, the same events and facts are given meaning by Showalter within the discourses of psychology, sociology and medicine – witch-hunts are now to be understood as 'collective hysteria'. It is also possible to construct a feminist discourse of witchcraft in opposition to the patriarchal discourse in which 'a witch' is a specifically gendered identity.

Let us try another example. Figure 3.2 makes a neat point about the ways in which meanings about children and childhood change over time. Take each of the elements listed above (1 to 4) and apply them to the ways your culture defines children and childhood. Our examples are taken from British culture because that is what we know best, but you should use the culture with which you are most familiar.

3.10

Where might you expect to find 'official' statements about children and child-hood? 'Official' here means those statements that are generally available, carry authority and/or are ratified by 'expert' knowledge. We have started you off; you carry on.

- Dictionary definitions.
- Legal definitions of childhood, as, for example, in the age of consent for sexual activity.
- Medical textbooks.
- Books about the psychological development of children.
-
-
-
-

Where might you find 'unofficial' statements?

- Conversations between mothers.
-
-
-
-

Where might you find visual and/or imaginative representations of children and childhood?

- TV programmes for children.
-
-
-
-

Do these visual/imaginative representations carry the same meanings as official state-ments, or do they offer different meanings of children and childhood? Or both? For example, do TV programmes about children adhere to the legal statements about the age of consent for sexual activity?

Are there things it would be unacceptable or 'unthinkable' to say about children and childhood? For example, to suggest that children might work in factories or sweep chimneys would be unthinkable nowadays in British culture, although these were common practices in the nineteenth century, and in some less industrialized coun-tries today children work alongside their parents in the fields. (For example, see the extracts from nineteenth-century reports below.) What is it about our understanding

Figure 3.2 Old rose-tinted spectacles/New dark shades, by Posy Simmonds

of childhood that makes such an idea unacceptable? In this context you might also think about childhood and sexuality.

Who are 'children'? How do we recognize and define certain people as 'children'? Think about physical attributes. What other attributes define someone as a child? (For example, see the extract from Susan Isaacs below.) What do we mean when we say of a grown man, 'He's still such a child'?

Can you identify social practices or institutions in which the statements, visual images and stories that represent children and childhood are acted out? For example, the education system authorizes an ending to childhood, as do social practices such as eighteenth birthday parties. In relation to this question, think about the part played by the family in constructing the meaning of children and childhood.

If you already have, or think one day you might have, children, where have your ideas come from about how you will bring them up?

As result of working through the above, can you identify some of the meanings that are represented by the words 'children' and 'childhood' in the late twentieth century? As you worked through the questions did your answers reveal any contradictory or conflicting meanings?

If you wanted to challenge the generally accepted meaning of children and childhood in your culture, would any of the elements above offer a potential space for doing so? Where would you begin? Try to plan a strategy that would enable new meanings to emerge.

We hope this exercise has demonstrated how the production of meaning is dispersed across a range of sites where representation occurs (statements, visual images, what can and cannot be said, the physical bodies of human beings, institutions and practices). Each element both takes from and contributes to the accepted meanings of children and childhood in a particular historical period. Taken together, the elements constitute a discourse, and each element is meaningful only within the discourse of which it is a part. The readings that follow may suggest to you how the meaning of childhood has changed over time. They offer examples of historically specific discourses of childhood.

3.7

READING

From a report by a Factory Inspector to the Home Secretary in 1852

In my last report I gave an account of the vast increase of factories during the two preceding years, and there is no cessation, for new mills are going up everywhere. It is not to be wondered at, therefore, that I should hear of a great scarcity of hands, of much machinery standing idle from the want of people to work it, and of a rise of wages. This scarcity of hands has led to a considerable increase in the number of children employed in my district which indeed has been going on, happily, for a long time; I say 'happily' without hesitation, for now that children are restricted to half a day's work and are required to attend school, I know no description of work so advantageous for them as that in a factory . . . (Golby, 1986, p. 9).

From the Second Report (1864) of the Children's Employment Commission

The introduction of the machine has necessitated the employment, on the whole, of older children and girls, the usual age for commencing being about 14, one consequence of which is that in these factories the great majority of the employed being above 13 are either adults or 'young persons' as defined by the Factory Act, and therefore entitled to work full time, thus facilitating the introduction of legislative measures. (Golby, 1986, p. 15).

From a paper given to the British Psychological Society: The Mental Hygiene of the Pre-School Child' by Susan Isaacs (1928)

[M]any of the ways of behaviour in a very young child which would at once suggest the possibility or even the certainty of neurosis to the more experienced observer are actually welcomed by the parent and educator as signs of moral development, or chuckled over as evidences of childish quaintness and precocity. A pleasing docility, the absence of open defiance and hostility, particular tidiness, a precise care in folding and arranging the clothes at bed-time, careful effort not to spill water when drinking or washing, anxious dislike of soiled hands or mouth or meticulous kindness and sensitive dislike of cruelty to other children or pet animals, ritual attention to the saying of prayers, frequent endearments and shows of affection, waiting always until one is spoken to before speaking, the offering of gifts to older and stronger children, an ardent desire to be good or clever, an intense ambition not to have to be helped, docility to punishment, drawing-room politeness, the quiet voice and controlled movements – most of these things either please or amuse the parent. Yet any one of them, and particularly several of them found together, may be and often are effects of a deep neurotic guilt and anxiety (Isaacs, 1948, pp. 3–4)

In summary, meanings are encoded in representations by the assembly of a particular set of signs in a particular context which may be decoded from a number of positions. However, there is no guarantee that the meanings encoded will be directly and unambiguously decoded. In order to communicate there must be some shared meanings that are tacitly accepted by encoder and decoder, but this process is always mediated by the possibility that the decoder will bring alternative or oppositional understandings to the exchange. Furthermore, representations only become meaningful within discourse. Discourse is all those statements, images, practices and institutions which represent a particular body of knowledge. One of the tasks of the cultural analyst is to explore how discourses are formed, how they function to constitute and sustain power relations and how and where dominant discourses have been, and are, challenged.

3.11

- We have briefly examined the concept of discourse in relation to witchhunts and to childhood. In order to extend your understanding of discourse you could explore either of these two examples further or you could look at other discursive formations. Foucault was particularly interested in 'madness', 'punishment' and 'sexuality'. You could usefully read more widely from the suggested list for this chapter.
- You might select a topic and trace how it is constructed within discourse, drawing on a range of texts, practices and institutions. Examples might be 'home', 'royalty', 'homeopathy', 'motherhood', 'Third World', 'education', 'woman' – but there are many more you could choose.

Representation, discourse and resistance

In the previous section we saw how a Jamaican schoolgirl resisted the representation of the Caribbean as 'animal' and 'insane'. Charlotte Brontë's representation of the Caribbean, for this reader, was a misrepresentation not only of her country but also of personal identity. Discourse and representation are profoundly implicated in the construction of personal identities as well as group identities, as you will recall from chapter 2, where we discussed autobiography and personal life narratives. In the previous section we discussed how producing and sustaining 'truths' was crucial to the maintenance and reproduction of power relations. Once something becomes established as 'truth' or 'common sense' it becomes naturalized and difficult to challenge. As the Jamaican black woman said, 'Miss admitted it seemed unfair, but she went on to do nothing with that insight.' Our focus in this section is on the ways in which groups who believe themselves to be consistently misrepresented have resisted or challenged the 'truths' embedded in certain discourses. Now read this extract from an article by Richard Dyer, entitled 'Seen to be believed: some problems in the representation of gay people as typical'.

3.8

'Homosexual' and 'lesbian' have been negative sexual categories, at best to be viewed pathologically, at worst as moral degeneracy, and in either case calling forth images in which such features as skin pallor, hooded eyes, and genital deformity have been used as visual correlatives of sickness and sin. Such views of lesbianism and (male) homosexuality have been challenged above all by those people who found themselves designated by the categories. There have been two predominant forms of challenge.

One has attempted to alter the object of the categories, to change the terms of what they refer to by shifting from persons to acts. The most familiar form that this argument takes is that people who perform homosexual acts are in every other respect just like everyone else: their sexuality does not imply anything else about their personality. This has been a major plank in the arguments of homosexual civil rights and law reform movements, and it is in the logic of this position that all typification is anathema. The problem was and is that the arguments about homosexuality are very hard to make on the terrain of existing definitions, which do inexorably imply categories and types. Thus a statement like 'homosexuals are just like anyone else' already reproduces the notion that there are persons designated homosexuals. Moreover, the development of gay sub-cultures meant that many homosexual people did participate in a lifestyle, a set of tastes, a language and so on that meant that their lives were, in more respects than the sexual, different from that of most heterosexual people.

The sub-cultural activity was itself a form of resistance to the negative implications of the lesbian/homosexual categories, in that it took the categories as a basis for a way of life rather than as something to be overcome or cured. From this sub-culture emerged the politics of the late 1960s gay movement, with its stress on accepting oneself as lesbian/homosexual, identifying oneself with other homosexual people under the term 'gay' and coming out, openly declaring and showing oneself as gay to society as a whole. These strategies of identifying and coming out immediately raise the problem of visibility, of being seen to be gay. Wearing badges, kissing in the streets were means of being visible, but so equally were behaving and dressing in recognizably gay ways – they brought you together in an act of sharing and they made you obvious on the streets. Typification (visually recognizable images and self-presentations) is not just something wished on gay people but produced by them, both in the pre-political gay sub-cultures and in the radical gay movement since 1968. (Dyer, 1993, pp. 20–1)

Dyer is concerned to demonstrate the difficulties involved in attempts by gay people to change the ways in which they represent themselves. Since the 1960s the gay movement has openly resisted and challenged the dominant representations of homosexuality that were produced through the discourses of medicine and religion. Homosexuality, according to these discourses, is either pathological (caused by physical or mental sickness) or a symptom of moral depravity. Both views imply that a solution to the state of homosexuality is necessary. Depending on which view is taken, this will be either cure or punishment. In the article from which the extract is taken, Dyer's focus is on the representation of homosexuality in film, and he is very much concerned with visual typification. However, he argues that, in the case of homosexuality, visual representation is all-important.

A major fact about being gay is that it doesn't show. There is nothing about gay people's physiognomy that declares them gay, no equivalents to the biological markers of sex and race. There are signs of gayness, a repertoire of gestures, expressions, stances, clothing, and even environments that bespeak gayness, but these are cultural forms designed to show what the person's person alone does not show: that he or she is gay. (Dyer, 1993, p. 19)

Within a discourse in which homosexuality is 'sickness or sin', those who are charged with cure or punishment need to be able to recognize homosexuality in order to be able to 'solve' it. Recall from the previous section that one of the elements of a discourse is that there should be people (subjects) who can be recognized as personifying the attributes assigned to them by the particular 'truth' constructed in discourse. The physical bodies of women, black people, those with disabilities and the old declare their categorization. As Dyer points out, this is not the case for gay people. As a result, a repertoire of images emerged (men dressed and acting in a feminine way, women wearing men's suits, women who make no concessions to femininity, among others) that signalled homosexuality in the way skin colour or anatomy signalled 'race' or sex. Dyer argues that there have been two strategies which the gay movement has adopted in order to challenge these visual typifications.

3.12

- Can you identify the two strategies to which Dyer is referring?
- What is problematic about each strategy?
- What do you think?

Whatever your own views, the point to note is that the gay movement has not simply rejected conventional representations of homosexuality as mis-representations. Instead, it has attempted to rework the coding of those visual typifications that produced negative meanings so as to signify dignity, pride in one's gayness and solidarity with other gay people. In this way gay people have challenged how they are represented, not by producing new representations, but by insisting on the revaluation of previously negative images. Through self-representation they are re-presenting homosexuality as a positive category. In doing so they have attempted to take control of the meanings produced, rather than allowing themselves to remain invisible and/or represented by others. Black people have used the same strategy – the word 'negro' has been appropriated as a positive term by some black people (see reading 8.6, for example).

3.13

How far do you think these strategies can counter the negative discourses of homosexuality and the discriminatory treatment of gay people in society?

We end this chapter with an extract from the work of Jo Spence. Jo Spence (1934–92) was a photographer and educator who used her photography to challenge radically, among other things, conventional representations of class, illness and women's bodies. Photography, along with TV and film, is the source of much of the visual imagery we consume now. As a consequence it has enormous power to construct 'truthful' and 'normative' ways of seeing ourselves and the world we inhabit. Photographic journalism, documentary photography, advertising and fashion photography 'make sense' of the world by representing it to us visually. As students of culture you need to remain aware of the ways in which such representations are encoded, the discourses within which they acquire meaning and the possibilities for resistance and challenge.

3.9

[C]ommercial photography . . . is still dominated by incredibly narrow definitions of photography which are straddled by news and advertising and a multitude of state uses of photography many of which employ the window-on the-world documentary mode of representation. Often these are a thinly disguised form of surveillance, a way of offering phoney evidence of surface phenomena, or of defining individual or group cultural identities which appear to be grounded in the 'real world' but are in fact total fictions offered up for consumption. We must never forget that all this is the background to any kind of radical professionalism in which we are engaged. Such images as we produce which we feel challenge the dominant ideology, even if they initially attempt to show something which has never been seen before, will soon be sucked up by the industrial machine of the mass media. We must expect this and have strategies for dealing with ways in which work is appropriated.

Equally fictitious are the fantasies (apparently more pleasurable, often engaging with our unconscious desires and traumas) offered to us by advertising. Some of us are also offered images of the fragmented female body, which are often called pornography. These images appear to present men with a kind of pseudo control over women in which they can day-dream of being dominant whilst in fact they continue to occupy a kind of childlike notion of omnipotence. This is often in contradiction to the economic and political impotence of many men. These interconnected spheres of image-making create regimes of desire in which we are always flattered into assuming positions which are difficult to escape in imagination – even if our daily lives totally differ. (Spence, 1995, p. 103)

Spence goes on to suggest that it is 'only by having a theory of what it is possible to speak about or to represent visually that we can begin to understand what is absent from all these agendas' (Spence, 1995, p. 104). This connects to our previous discussion about discourse: that which is absent, that which cannot be said, remains outside discourse. Representations have no meaning until they are made sense of through a particular discourse – even where these representations are resisting or challenging dominant knowledge. For example, Spence's photograph of an adult man sucking at a woman's breast (figure 3.3) can only be understood as challenging normative assumptions about breastfeeding, mothering and adult sexuality once we know what those normative assumptions are. And it is within discourse that these assumptions are constructed as 'the norm'.

ACTIVITIES

3.14

Try to work out precisely what assumptions about breasts, sexuality and motherhood figure 3.3 is challenging. Where do these assumptions come from? Try to identify the discourses which produce these assumptions. For example:

- Breasts are erotic playthings for men: patriarchal discourse of gender.
-
-

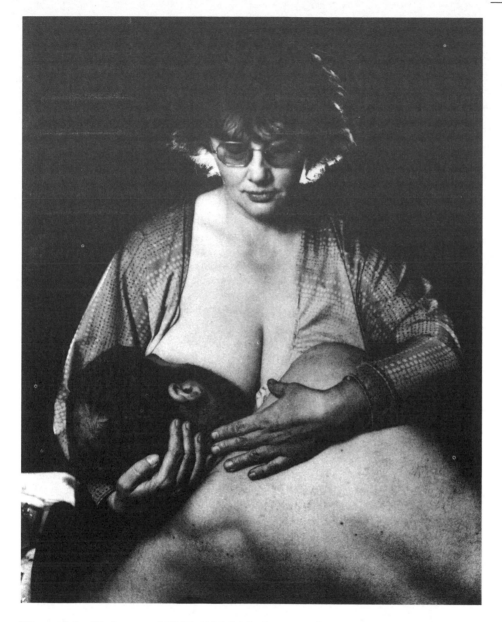

Figure 3.3 *Madonna and Child*, 1982, by Jo Spence and Terry Dennett (from the series The History Lesson)

Conclusions

In order to summarize the material covered in this chapter we have chosen to quote from Richard Dyer's introduction to *The Matter of Images: Essays on*

Representation, in which he argues that the cultural representation of social groups raises political questions about oppression and dominance. Who represents whom, where and how determines the representations available for us to look at and read, but people do not necessarily make sense of these representations in terms of the preferred or intended meaning. We bring to our viewing and reading a range of codes and conventions in order to make sense of the material offered: the codes used will depend upon the position we occupy in the social world and the ways in which we understand that world. However, despite the impossibility of single, predetermined meanings, we are limited as to the range of meanings we can bring to any text – representations do refer to realities at the same time as they affect reality. To understand a picture of a horse as representing a motor car is an error of seeing which could result in being seen as insane or visually impaired. Furthermore, as Dyer points out,

> The prestige of high culture, the centralization of mass cultural production, the literal poverty of marginal cultural production: these are aspects of the power relations of representation that put the weight of control over representation on the side of the rich, the white, the male, the heterosexual. Acknowledging the complexity of viewing/reading practices in relation to representation does not entail the claim that there is equality and freedom in the regime of representation. (Dyer, 1993, p. 2)

The relation of representation to the lives and experiences of people in the real social world is complicated, but representations do 'have real consequences for real people'. As Dyer insists,

> how social groups are treated in cultural representation is part and parcel of how they are treated in life, that poverty, harassment, self-hate and discrimination (in housing, jobs, educational opportunity and so on) are shored up and instituted by representation. The resonances of the term 'representation' suggest as much. How a group is represented, presented over again in cultural forms, how an image of a member of a group is taken as representative of that group, how that group is represented in the sense of spoken for and on behalf of (whether they represent, speak for themselves or not), these all have to do with how members of groups see themselves and others like themselves, how they see their place in society, their right to the rights a society claims to ensure its citizens. Equally re-presentation, representativeness, representing have to do also with how others see members of a group and their place and rights, others who have the power to affect that place and those rights. How we are seen determines in part how we are treated; how we treat others is based on how we see them; such seeing comes from representation. (Dyer, 1993, p. 1)

You could usefully link your work on representation with that on identity and difference by re-reading Rashid Araeen's account of his meeting with the professor of fine art (reading 2.1) in the light of Dyer's comments about the politics of representation.

CHAPTER 4

History

Introduction

Although we have referred to history and used material from the past in the previous chapters, we have not, so far, considered what we mean by 'history' and how we might approach the past as students of culture. In chapter 1 we wrote about the 'contemporary turn to culture', and in recent decades the study of history has been influenced, along with literature and sociology, by this 'cultural turn'. It is not necessary to have studied history in order to engage with the material in this chapter. If, up to now, you have not enjoyed historical study you may find that approaching the past through culture offers perspectives that stimulate a new interest. If you have enjoyed history we hope you will find material and ideas in this chapter that provoke fresh insights.

The *Oxford English Dictionary* defines 'history' as 'a continuous, usually chronological, record of important or public events'. However, we tend to use the word 'history' far more broadly than this. We say of a person, 'she has a history', meaning she has an exciting or chequered past; or we say 'anyway, it's all history now', by which we mean that certain events are over and done with – relegated to the past. History as studied in universities or at school tends to follow the dictionary definition: students study 'important or public events'. Professional historians construct the chronological record of important events, and what constitutes an important event is the subject matter of historical debate and research. The point is that history is a human construction, or perhaps more accurately a reconstruction. The past does not present itself 'as it really was': writing history involves the interpretation and selection of elements in the past to produce an account that 'makes sense' to those who read or study it in the present. Think back to chapter 3, where we introduced you to the concept of 'representation'. History is one of the ways in which we re-present the past in the present, and like all representations it requires a set of shared understandings or a discourse within which it becomes meaningful. For example, from the eighteenth century onwards there was a widespread belief in progress and evolution. Many nineteenth-century historians stressed the ways in which the past had been improved upon or could be learned from. History demonstrated the onward march of civilization and the lessons to be learned from its failures. Yet the writing of history from within a discourse of progress was itself one of the elements of nineteenth-century culture that *produced* a discourse of progress. In the twentieth century, two world wars, the threat of nuclear war and the continuing existence of poverty, starvation and barbarism have exposed the myth of progress. Contemporary accounts of the past are less likely to emphasize history as a continuing triumph of 'civilization' over 'the primitive'. Raymond Williams (1976, p. 147) comments, 'history as a tale of accidents, unforeseen events, frustration of conscious purposes . . . is probably a specific 20th century form of history as general process, though now used, in contrast with the sense of achievement or promise of the earlier and still active versions, to indicate a general pattern of frustration and defeat' (Williams, 1976, p. 147).

Nevertheless, the belief that history is a story of gradual and sustained progress is one that is often implicit in discussions about the past. We all want to believe that the world can become a more humane place. The past could be represented by a catalogue of random, arbitrary events, unconnected with each other or with the present, but this is rarely the case. History is a way of creating order out of the mass of material that is the past's legacy to the present. In chapter 2, when we looked at autobiography, we suggested that life stories were a way in which individuals shaped the random experience of their lives into something with meaning. To represent the past by selecting certain versions of events or certain personages as significant is to create an order that bestows meaning on the events, people and objects of past times. Choosing, as historians do, to represent the past in terms of cause and effect or as less evolved than the present are two of the ways in which specific meanings of the past are produced and circulated. If you recall, in chapter 1 we introduced you to the definition of culture as 'the production and circulation of meanings'. History, in all its forms, and it has many, as we shall see, is therefore a key practice in the processes of culture. In this chapter we shall be exploring history as one aspect of culture and identity. Social groups, nations and communities all have their histories. History is one of the ways in which human beings acquire identities and make sense of the world and their experience of it. Thinking about how the past is represented, and ideas about it are communicated, in the present can offer insights into the process by which meaning is produced and circulated. So we begin this chapter by posing the question 'what is history?'; we then discuss some recent challenges to orthodox **paradigms** of history, and finally, we want you to think about history as a cultural product, a commodity that is consumed and produced in the present. In order to do this, you will be invited to engage in a discussion about what is often called 'the heritage' industry.

The past 'as it really was'?

In his book *The Nature of History*, the historian Arthur Marwick identifies three senses in which the term 'history' is used. As you read this extract note down the three different meanings Marwick identifies.

4.1

'History' as commonly used has three levels of meaning. First it can connote the entire human past as it actually happened. Life, doubtless, would be simpler if this usage could be abandoned in favour of the unambiguous locution 'the past'. Language however is a common property, ill-defined, often badly cultivated, but not subject to enclosure by precious academics. Even those scholars who have publicly renounced this usage of the word will be found at some stage to betray themselves, for it is very hard to avoid such plump pronouncements as 'History is not the handwork of hero-figures', or 'Now is the time to take stock of human history'. History, secondly and more usefully, connotes man's [sic] attempt to describe and interpret that past: it is, in the words of Professor Barraclough, 'the attempt to discover on the basis of fragmentary evidence the significant things about the past'. This is the history with which we are concerned when we talk of history as a social necessity, of history being an 'industry'; which comes nearest to the original Greek meaning, 'Inquiry'. Some ventures in discovery or inquiry are clearly more successful than others: some ages have regarded as 'significant' matters which we would now relegate to the realms of superstition, myth or polemic. We can enjoy and profit from historical works spread across the entire timespan of human literary activity, such as those of Thucydides, Ssu-ma Chi'en, Bede or Machiavelli: but we must note that the systematic study of history, history as a *discipline* (the third meaning), is a very recent phenomenon, becoming established in West European and North American universities only in the nineteenth century, far in arrears of philosophy, classical languages, mathematics and natural sciences. In this book we shall be specially concerned with the development of modern historical studies; but an important theme will be the difficult, but highly exciting tensions generated between history as an academic and sometimes pedantic discipline, and history as an essential facet of human experience. (Marwick, 1970, p. 15).

The term 'history' is often used as synonymous with 'the past'. However, in its earliest use history meant a narrative of events which had passed. In this sense its meaning was very close to that of story; either history or story might be used to connote imaginative accounts of events or accounts of events which were assumed to have happened. History, meaning an account of past events, also included the idea of inquiry: why did this happen; what caused it to happen? In a third sense history connotes the academic discipline of history, in which scholarly, systematic methods are applied to the source material from which interpretations of past events are constructed and disseminated.

4.1

Read the following statements and note against each one which of the three senses of 'history' is being used.

1 I really enjoyed reading the novel, *The History of Mr Polly*.
2 It's all history now!
3 Visiting museums can teach us a lot about history.

4 That film was an excellent piece of history.
5 I hope to go on to study history at university.
6 Many of Shakespeare's plays offer a version of history.
7 Shakespeare used drama to present history.
8 The history of football in this country has yet to be written.
9 The history we were taught at school was not very interesting.

Don't worry if you found it difficult to distinguish between history as an academic discipline and history as a less scholarly account of the past, but do ensure you understand the distinction between history as the past and history as the reconstruction, narrating and interpretation of the past (whether academic or not). Points 2, 3 and 6 are using history to mean the past, 5 and 9 are using history to mean the scholarly, academic discipline, 1, 4, 7 and 8 are using history in a more generalized sense, to suggest a narrative account of the past. In the rest of this chapter it is the second and third meanings of the term 'history' with which we are concerned.

Marwick makes a distinction between the disciplined, systematic study of the past undertaken by academic historians and 'history as an essential facet of human experience'. By the latter he has in mind the ways in which the past is made sense of in a variety of ways other than the scholarly work of professional historians. While he concedes that 'superstition, myth and polemic' have been important as ways of passing on knowledge of the past, his implication is that it is only through the academic discipline of history that we can gain a 'true' understanding of past events. The nineteenth-century historian Leopold von Ranke, who pioneered the modern discipline of history, was concerned that history should be seen as a science, providing facts and objective deductions. For Ranke, history should aim to present the past as 'it actually was'. Marwick, while acknowledging that Ranke may have been somewhat optimistic in believing that history can inevitably yield an 'exact, objective, scientific account of "what actually happened" ', writes within the paradigm of history established by Ranke (Marwick, 1986, p. 16). The aim of scholarly history should be to represent as closely as possible the events of the past as 'they really happened'. In order to achieve this, the historian's task is to produce an interpretation of past events from a range of primary sources, the most important of which are written documents produced in the period being studied (manuscript materials). Autobiographies, oral accounts, folk-lore, novels and ballads, although essential in order 'to understand an age from, as it were, the inside', may not give the historian 'one single piece of concrete information' (Marwick, 1970, p. 139). In order to reconstruct and interpret the past, professional historians require a lengthy training in the analysis of primary source material and the use of footnotes and bibliographies, as well as access to archive materials. They are the 'experts' in interpreting the past: those who write autobiographies or trace their family's genealogy or collect nursery rhymes are 'amateur' historians. The history produced by 'experts' tends to be assigned a privileged place in hierarchies of knowledge, and for this reason, it can be argued, historians play a significant role in the 'production and circulation of meanings'.

You will recall that in chapter 3 we discussed the concept of discourse as a process by which certain forms of knowledge are produced. Marwick offers what was, until the 1960s, an orthodox view of historical **epistemology**; a view which concurs with a specific understanding or discourse of what constitutes valid knowledge more generally. Orthodox historical research is concerned with the systematic production of 'objective' knowledge. It is 'scientific', seeking out facts and proven hypotheses. In pursuit of 'objectivity', myth, anecdote, personal and fictional accounts are relegated to a secondary place, in which the meanings or knowledges offered through subjectivity, polemic and imagination can be categorized as less 'true'.

Now read the following extract from *The Pursuit of History*, by John Tosh.

4.2

Whereas the individual's sense of his or her past arises spontaneously, historical knowledge has to be produced. Society has a past which extends back far beyond the lives of the individuals who happen to comprise it at any one time, the raw materials out of which a historical consciousness can be fashioned are accordingly almost unlimited. Those elements which find a place in it represent a selection of truths which are deemed worthy of note. Who produces historical knowledge, and who validates it for general consumption, are therefore important questions. How well the job is done has a bearing on the cohesion of society and its capacity for renewal and adaptation in the future. That is why what historians do should matter to everyone else. Their work can be manipulated to promote desired forms of social consciousness; it can remain confined to academic circles, powerless to influence society for good or ill; or it can become the basis for informed and critical discussion of current issues. (Tosh, 1984, p. 2)

Tosh raises some important questions about the social and cultural significance of historical knowledge. Let us explore these further.

4.2

- Think back to the history you learned at school. What topics can you recall covering? Which nations' histories did you learn about? Which social groups did you learn about? Following Tosh, can you identify 'those elements' which have found a place in your 'historical consciousness'? Can you think of any period, group, place and/or ideas of which you have little historical knowledge?
- Can you think of examples of history being used as a starting point for 'informed and critical discussion of current issues'?

The point Tosh is making is that the production of historical knowledge is political, by which we mean that researching, writing and disseminating history is one of the means by which power relations can be sustained. For example, in George Orwell's novel *Nineteen Eighty-Four*, the state rewrites the history books in order to construct a version of the past in which the current totalitarian regime is presented as the best and, indeed, the only way of ordering society. Equally, writing and researching history can contest existing power relations. Tosh cites a resolution carried by the International Congress of African Historians in 1965, which stated 'that an African philosophy of history which would serve as a liberation from the colonial experience must be a vital concern of all historians studying in Africa' (Tosh, 1991, p. 5). Making visible those whom the history books have ignored can challenge the apparent 'naturalness' of a historically specific social order. Serious discussions of the position of women in society by feminists gained momentum in the late 1960s and early 1970s. Some, like Sheila Rowbotham's *Hidden from History*, took the invisibility of women in the historical record as a starting point for the recovery of a history of women (Rowbotham, 1973).

In 1963, the Marxist historian, E. P. Thompson published *The Making of the English Working Class*, in which he argued that the working class did not 'rise like the sun at an appointed time' but 'was present at its own making' (Thompson, 1963, p. 8). By this he means that working-class people in the early nineteenth century were actively involved in the process by which they acquired a consciousness of themselves as working class. They were not simply born into a pre-given 'class' but, by their own agency, created a set of relations with others whose interests were different from theirs. In terms of our understanding of culture, they were actively engaged in the process of producing certain meanings which contributed to the social phenomenon we understand as 'class'. Now read the following extract from Thompson's preface to *The Making of the English Working Class*.

4.3

This is a group of studies, on related themes, rather than a consecutive narrative. In selecting these themes I have been conscious, at times, of writing against the weight of prevailing orthodoxies. There is the Fabian orthodoxy, in which the great majority of working people are seen as passive victims of *laisser faire*, with the exception of a handful of far-sighted organizers (notably, Francis Place). There is the orthodoxy of the empirical economic historians, in which working people are seen as a labour force, as migrants, or as the data for statistical series. There is the 'Pilgrim's Progress' orthodoxy, in which the period is ransacked for forerunners – pioneers of the Welfare State, progenitors of a Socialist Commonwealth, or (more recently) early exemplars of rational industrial relations. Each of these orthodoxies has a certain validity. All have added to our knowledge. My quarrel with the first and second is that they tend to obscure the agency of working people, the degree to which they contributed by conscious efforts, to the making of history. My quarrel with the third is that it reads history in the light of subsequent preoccupations, and not as in fact it occurred. Only the successful (in the sense of those whose aspirations anticipated subsequent evolution) are remembered. The blind alleys, the lost causes, and the losers themselves are forgotten.

I am seeking to rescue the poor stockinger, the Luddite cropper, the 'obsolete' hand-loom weaver, the 'utopian' artisan, and even the deluded follower of Joanna Southcott, from the enormous condescension of posterity. Their crafts and traditions may have been dying. Their hostility to the new industrialism may have been backward-looking. Their communitarian ideals may have been fantasies. Their insurrectionary conspiracies may have been foolhardy. But they lived through these times of acute social disturbance, and we did not. Their aspirations were valid in terms of their own experience; and if they were casualties of history, they remain, condemned in their own lives, as casualties. (Thompson, 1968, pp. 11–12)

Don't worry if you don't understand many of the historical references. However, if you are interested, do follow these up in Thompson's book. For now the point to try to grasp is the significance of Thompson's challenge to 'prevailing orthodoxies'.

4.3

- Do you think history ('posterity') has represented working people in ways that are condescending? Can you think of any examples from history books, TV programmes, films?
- Why do you think it matters whether working people are represented, for example, as victims of an economic system? Are there consequences for the way in which they are treated? You could remind yourself of the conclusion of chapter 3 if you feel you need help with this question.

Thompson's history has justifiably been highly influential. As an account of the experiences, values and beliefs of 'ordinary' people at a moment of dramatic social change, *The Making of the English Working Class* contested the idea that history was inevitably about the great and good (or bad). Moreover, it demonstrated that 'ordinary' people could act as agents of social change and were not simply at the mercy of historical and economic forces beyond their control. Such a belief is important, as it can enable 'ordinary' people to believe that social change might be possible. This was important in the 1960s, as movements 'from below' challenged the dominance of the most powerful groups in society. In the 1960s, student demonstrations, the Civil Rights movement, the women's liberation movement and youth sub-cultures, more generally, questioned the right of a small, powerful elite to control access to knowledge and wealth. Writing in the 1960s, Thompson's concern for the 'poor stockinger', like Rowbotham's for the invisibility of women, is, at least in part, intimately connected to the preoccupations of their present. In the present our dialogue with Thompson as well as our dialogue with 'the poor stockinger' are equally related to our contemporary concerns. It could be argued that in the present we construct the past we would like: historians, like Marwick, Tosh, Thompson and Rowbotham, remain critically alert to the dynamics of this tension, but in less scrupulous hands history can become a powerful weapon in political struggle. None the less, an awareness of a shared history is one of the most powerful ways in which group identities, be they family, national, ethnic or social, are formed and strengthened.

4.4

- Think about your own sense of identity. Are you conscious of sharing a history with others? How would it feel if you had no knowledge of the history of the people with whom you share a sense of belonging? Look back to the discussion on identities in chapter 2 to help with this.
- Look out for examples of history being used to create bonds between people. The newspapers and TV would be useful sources for this exercise.

When you write, rewrite or read history you should aim for a critical awareness of the relation between past and present and of the part history can play in the shaping of identities. This takes us back to Tosh's point about the ways in which history can become 'the basis for informed and critical discussion of current issues'.

Challenges to objectivity: post-structuralist theories of history

In recent years the Rankean paradigm of history, within which the historians discussed above work, has been radically challenged. Indeed, the work of Rowbotham and Thompson questions the supposed 'objectivity' of history, revealing the gaps and omissions in the historical record that functioned to hide certain groups from historical scrutiny, and the significance of historical interpretation that, consciously or not, reconstructs in line with present preoccupations. However, recent post-structuralist theories have gone further, questioning the very nature of that reality the historian aims to reconstruct. The German critic, Walter Benjamin, wrote, 'The true picture of the past flits by. The past can be seized only as an image which flashes up at the instant when it can be recognized and is never seen again . . . For every image of the past that is not recognized by the present as one of its own concerns threatens to disappear irretrievably' (Benjamin, 1973, p. 257). So far we have assumed that the past is a reality that can be accessed and thus faithfully reproduced by the historian in the present. Benjamin problematizes this belief, suggesting instead that the past can never be recognized 'as it really was', but only in the ephemeral and transient form of flashing images which if not immediately grasped by the present are forever lost.

4.5

- Think of a historical period that you have some knowledge of, however limited. Could your knowledge of this period be characterized as 'flashing images'? What is missing in your mental picture of the period?
- Think back to your own childhood. How do you know what happened when you were very small?
- If the past can only be known as 'flashing images', what becomes of the historian's authority to represent the past 'as it really was'?

We want now to introduce you to another way in which orthodox **histori-ography** has been challenged in recent years. Historiography means the process by which history is written. Read the following extract by Hayden White, an American historiographer, from his book *Metahistory: the Historical Imagination in Nineteenth Century Europe*. White begins by making a distinction between histories and chronicles, where a chronicle is understood to be simply a list of events in chronological order of their occurrence.

4.4

Historical *stories* trace the sequences of events that lead from inaugurations to (provisional) terminations of social and cultural processes in a way that *chronicles* are not required to do. Chronicles are, strictly speaking, open-ended. In principle they have no inaugurations; they simply 'begin' when the chronicler starts recording events. And they have no culminations or resolutions; they can go on indefinitely. Stories, however, have a discernible form (even when that form is an image of a state of chaos) which marks off the events contained in them from the other events that might appear in a comprehensive chronicle of the years covered in their unfoldings.

It is sometimes said that the aim of the historian is to explain the past by 'finding', 'identifying', or 'uncovering' the 'stories' that lie buried in chronicles; and that the difference between 'history' and 'fiction' resides in the fact that the historian 'finds' his stories, whereas the fiction writer 'invents' his. This conception of the historian's task, however, obscures the extent to which 'invention' also plays a part in the historian's operations. The same event can serve as a different kind of element of many different historical stories, depending on the role it is assigned in a specific motific characterization of the set to which it belongs. The death of the king may be a beginning, an ending, or simply a transitional event in three different stories. In the chronicle, this event is simply 'there' as an element of a series; it does not 'function' as a story element. The historian arranges the events in the chronicle into a hierarchy of significance by assigning events different functions as story elements in such a way as to disclose the formal coherence of a whole set of events considered as a comprehensible process with a discernible beginning, middle and end.

The arrangement of selected events of the chronicle into a story raises the kinds of questions the historian must anticipate and answer in the course of constructing his narrative. These questions are of the sort: 'What happened next' 'How did that happen?' 'Why did things happen this way rather than that?' 'How did it all come out in the end?' These questions determine the narrative tactics the historian must use in the construction of his story. But such questions about the connections between events which make of them elements in a *followable* story should be distinguished from questions of another sort: 'What does it all add up to?' 'What is the point of it all?' These questions have to do with the structure of the entire set of events considered as a complete story and call for a synoptic judgment of the relationship between a given story and other stories that might be 'found', 'identified', or 'uncovered' in the chronicle. (White, 1973, pp. 7–8)

White's point is that history may be no more objective than any other form of narration: for example, fiction. Because historical narratives are communicated through the medium of language, they cannot escape those features of language that are common to all spoken or written texts. Such features include the structuring of material into a narrative with a beginning, middle and end: that is, making a story out of a series of events. And what is important for White's argument is that historians do not 'discover' or 'find' a pre-existing story; they construct a story as part of the process of communicating through language. In doing so, historians, according to White, produce completed stories by arranging and selecting events in specific ways. As a consequence there are always other ways in which the events might be organized: these remain unspoken and unwritten in the form of gaps, silences and traces. And in structuring their material in certain ways, historians produce a meaning from it: 'what it all adds up to'. Thus, the significance of historical events is produced by the historian; it does not pre-exist her or his reconstruction of the past into a series of meaningful events. For White, historiography is closely linked to the writing of fiction, using similar fictive devices, such as plot and character. White's insistence on blurring the distinction between history and fiction has raised a number of important issues and problems, but it can also prove a fruitful way of approaching both historical and literary texts.

ACTIVITIES

4.6

- If we accept White's argument that history is akin to fiction, are there any political consequences? Look back to what Tosh said about the role of historians.
- Does White's proposition have implications for Thompson's wish to rescue working people from the 'condescension of posterity'?
- Does it matter if history is seen as a fiction?

Finally, read the following extract from a paper by the historian Carolyn Steedman, on history and autobiography. Steedman is remembering herself attempting to write history as an eight-year-old. What is your response?

READING

4.5

It is at this point that I remember most clearly an eight-year-old in a crowded post-War South London classroom, writing a life of Queen Victoria in three volumes (three LCC exercise books): the holly pinned to the little princess's collar to make her sit up straight at meal times, the moment of destiny on the stairs when the men in frock coats fell at her feet. This story I write (dip pen, a good round hand: it's 1955) is me, but also, exactly at the same time, not-me. It will go on operating like that, the historical past will, as acceptance and denial.

I know that there is no 'really how it was' at all. But knowing about all the pretensions of the historical enterprise that seeks to conjure the past before our eyes, as it really was, does not stop me from wanting what all of history's readers want: the thing we cannot have, which is past time; the past 'as it really was'. The child in the 1950s South London classroom knew (she might be able to articulate this, if you asked her the right question) that the point isn't what happened, nor how the young Victoria sat at the table, nor the hurried drive through the dark to announce ascension to the throne; the point is what the child does with that history. (Steedman, 1992, pp. 46–7)

We have suggested above that we require a shared history in order to know ourselves as belonging to certain groups. Steedman seems to be suggesting that there is a deeper individual need for history, an unconscious or subconscious yearning for past time; a past that is always already lost to us and that we can never recapture. Steedman's 'historical enterprise that seeks to conjure the past before our eyes as it really was' is a long way from Ranke's systematic sifting of the evidence. For Steedman, the whole enterprise of history is located in fantasy and desire, memory and loss: our relationship with history and with the past constitutes psychological selfhood, both individually and collectively. In seeking to identify with the past we recognize both our belonging in it and our distance from it: 'acceptance and denial'. We will leave you to think about your own response to this.

The past and popular memory

In this section we want to take up the point made by Steedman about what we do with history. If, as White suggests, history is simply another fiction, another text, then the authenticity of the historian to make sense of the past is limited. If he or she cannot represent the past to us 'as it really was', what is the role of the historian? How, in Tosh's words, can 'what historians do . . . matter to everyone else'? The following extract comes from the introduction to a book entitled *Narrating the Thirties: a Decade in the Making*.

4.6

READING

The eminent Tudor historian, Geoffrey Elton, a staunch defender of methodological orthodoxy, described historical method as 'a recognised and tested way of extracting from what the past has left the true facts and events of that past, and so far as possible their true meaning and interrelation'. Even over looking the obvious questions, 'recognised and tested by whom?' and *which* facts and events?', and accepting for the sake of argument that historians can tell us fairly unproblematically 'what happened', there are still insurmountable problems with the claim that they can tell us with authority what those events *mean*. And this is a serious matter, because it is meanings, rather than factual accuracy, that the present looks for when it contemplates the past. Events may be part of a fixed past, but their meanings are part of the changing present, and cannot therefore be settled for good by the authority of professional experts. Walter Benjamin reminds us that the meaning of a historical event can be determined, 'posthumously, as it were, through events that can be separated from it by thousands of years. A historian who takes this as his point of departure stops telling the sequence of events like the beads of a rosary. Instead, he grasps the constellation which his own era has formed with a definite earlier one' [Benjamin, 1973, p. 265]. (Baxendale and Pawling, 1996, p. 8)

In the extract above, we have a suggestion that what is important about history is its meanings: history is one aspect of culture, understood as 'the production and circulation of meanings'. You will recall the discussion in chapter 3 of how meanings are produced through representation, and the processes of encoding and decoding involved in this. In their book, Baxendale and Pawling go on to analyse the ways in which a particular decade of British history, the 1930s, has been given certain meaning and significance:

> in particular, how narratives about or including the Thirties have not only been shaped by subsequent history, but also have been used to shape it, to influence subsequent events and give them particular meanings. These meanings, like the meaning of episodes in a novel, arise less from the intrinsic nature of historical events than from their position in the story – in Elton's phrase, 'their interrelations' with other events . . . disagreements about the history of the Thirties have rarely been about factual matters, but more often about the way the elements of the story have been emplotted, and thereby given meaning. (Baxendale and Pawling, 1996, p.9).

4.7

- What meanings do you associate with the period referred to as 'the sixties'? Compile a list of words, images, events, books, films and people that seem to you to connote 'the sixties'. If you can, compare your list with someone else's. Are there common elements?
- What or who were your sources?

This activity can reveal the enormous range of practices and materials from which we construct a sense of the past. You may have listed any of the following: history books, TV documentaries and drama, autobiography and biography, individual memory or the memories of older relatives, photographs, popular music, exhibitions in museums, films of the period, family saga fictions, magazines and comics of the period, local history groups, school or university study, topic work undertaken at school (the latter are less likely for the sixties, as school and university history tends to end round about 1945). This suggests, as Raphael Samuel (1994, p. 8) points out, that 'history is not the prerogative of the historian, nor even, as postmodernism [see extract above by Hayden White] contends, a historian's 'invention'. It is, rather, a social form of knowledge; the work, in any given instance, of a thousand different hands'. History, according to Samuel, is not the work of individuals, but 'the ensemble of activities and practices in which ideas of history are embedded or a dialectic of past–present relations is rehearsed' (Samuel, 1994, p. 8). Our sense of the past is not simply revealed to us by professional historians but produced from a storehouse of popular memory, which may include the works of individual historians, from which we draw the impressions and ideas that together constitute a collective consciousness of a particular historical event or period.

Let us begin to examine what is meant by the term 'popular memory' by thinking about the different ways in which history is encountered in everyday life. For example, as this is being written, the day's viewing on television offers two historical documentaries about events in the 1940s and 1950s, another programme entitled *The Complete Guide to the 20th Century*, three films made in the 1940s, a programme about a couple seeking to replace the eighteenth-century Martello tower they are currently living in with another historical building and a situation comedy based on the main character's ability to 'time travel' between the present and the 1940s. The newspaper carries three obituaries, one of which is accompanied by a photograph of the pop group Abba winning the 1974 Eurovision Song Contest, and a film about Queen Victoria, *Mrs Brown*, has been released this week. Some articles on the Irish peace process refer to events in Ireland's history. The building we work in was founded as a teaching training college for 'Christian gentlemen' in the mid-nineteenth century and overlooks York Minster, erected in the eleventh century. A local café has tables made from the bases of old treadle sewing machines, a cast iron cooking range and sepia photographs of Victorian and Edwardian street scenes. The estate agents across the road are advertising houses with 'period' features, and a trip to the outskirts of the city passes through a council estate built in the 1920s. There are shops offering replica art deco ceramics, Celtic jewellery, William Morris wallpapers, Victorian recipe books and medieval stained glass, as well as greetings cards featuring eighteenth- and nineteenth-century reproductions. Within the region it is possible to visit, for example, Eden camp, a theme museum based on the Second World War, and the Brontë Parsonage, with its museum housing a collection of Brontë memorabilia. In the town is the Jorvik Centre, which offers opportunities to 'experience' life in Viking York. The local paper advertises evening classes in local history and tracing your family tree. We are surrounded in our daily lives not only by historical buildings, landscapes and artefacts but by contemporary representations of the past in TV programmes, films, novels, advertisements, shops, furniture and wallpaper. Moreover, we are also invited to use our leisure time to engage in or 'experience' history by joining classes or local groups, and by visiting museums and theme parks.

4.8

ACTIVITIES

- Choose a week (or a day if you prefer) and keep a diary of all the different ways in which you encounter history during that time. Note, as we have tried to do, everything you come across that has anything to do with history.
- Divide your list into those things that are: (a) legacies or traces left from the past; (b) contemporary representations of the past; (c) practices which involve engagement with the past.
- Are there any periods or themes in history that feature time and again in your list? If so, do they seem to have particular meanings? Do they seem to stand for any particular values? Or do they appear to be offering lessons to be learned? Do certain personages recur again and again?
- Can you discern any patterns of meaning from your analysis so far? Have you noticed any contradictory 'messages' among the apparent jumble of popular memory? For example, the reminders of the grinding poverty in which many people existed, alongside the frequent insistence by those who experienced this that these were 'the good old days'.

Now read this extract from *Theatres of Memory*, by Raphael Samuel. Samuel argues that British culture in the 1990s is steeped in history, much of it visual.

READING

4.7

The last thirty years have witnessed an extraordinary and, it seems, ever grow-ing enthusiasm for the recovery of the national past – both the real past of recorded history, and the timeless one of tradition. The preservation mania, which first appeared in reference to the railways in the early 1950s, has now penetrated every department of national life. In music it extends from Baroque instruments – a discovery of the early 1960s, when concerts of early music began to be performed for the *cognoscenti* – to pop memorabilia, which bring in six-figure bids when they are auctioned at Christie's or Sotheby's. In numismatics[1] it has given trade tokens the status of Roman coinage. Industrial archaeology, a term coined in 1955, has won the protective mantle of 'historic' for abandoned or salvaged plant. The number of designated ancient monuments (268 in 1882, 12,900 today) also increases by leaps and bounds: among them is that brand-new eighteenth-century industrial village – product of inspired scavengings as well as of Telford New Town's search for a historical identity – Ironbridge. Country houses, on their last legs in the 1940s, and a Gothic horror in British films of the period, attract hundreds of thousands of summer visitors and have helped to make the National Trust (no more than a pressure group for the first seventy years of its existence) into the largest mass-membership organization in Britain. New museums open, it is said, at a rate of one a fortnight and miraculously contrive to flourish in face of repeated cuts in government funding: there are now some seventy-eight of them devoted to railways alone.

One feature of the historicist turn in national life – as of the collecting mania – has been the progressive updating of the notion of period, and a reconstruction of history's grand narrative by reference to the recent rather than the ancient past. Thus in TV docu-mentary, the British Empire is liable to be seen through the lens of 'The Last Days of the Raj', as it is in Paul Scott's trilogy [*The Jewel in the Crown*], or the films of Merchant-Ivory. The year 1940 – replacing 1688, 1649 or 1066 as the central drama in the national past – becomes, according to taste, 'Britain's finest hour' or a privileged vantage point for studying the national decadence. Twentieth anniversaries, these days, seem to excite as much ceremony and rejoicing as for centenaries or diamond jubilees. Very pertinent here is what Fredric Jameson calls 'nostalgia for the present' – the desperate desire to hold on to disappearing worlds. Hence it may be the growth of rock pilgrimages and the creation of pop shrines. Hence too, it may be – memorials to the fragility of the present rather than the past – the multiplication of commemorative occasions, such as 40th and 50th birthdays, and the explosive growth in the production of commemorative wares. The past under threat in many retrieval projects, as in the mass of 'do-it-yourself' museums, and self-made or family shrines, is often the recent past – the day before yesterday rather than as say, in nineteenth century revivalism, that of the Elizabethan sea-dogs, medieval chivalry or Gothic architecture. (Samuel, 1994, pp. 139–40)

Can you see the point that Samuel is making? A profound concern with the past is something that all societies, both now and in the past, share. A sometimes obsessive

---

[1] The study of coins and medals

need to engage with the past has proved common to all cultures; even non-literate cultures have orally transmitted stories, legends and myths handed down from generation to generation. You might want to think about this need in the light of the suggestions made by Steedman in the extract with which we ended the previous section. The point Samuel is making is that in our own time this concern with the past has taken a particular form – an emphasis on the recent past – that is different from, for example, the form taken by nineteenth-century historicism. In the nineteenth century, painting, poetry, architecture and design looked back to the medieval and Tudor periods of British history for inspiration and values. For example, the Pre-Raphaelite Brotherhood, a group of young artists in the mid-century, aspired to a standard of art which they believed existed prior to the emergence of the style of art associated with the painter Raphael, and which had subsequently been lost. In their art they aimed to recapture what they saw as the purity of medieval art. In the 1990s, Samuel claims, our concern is not with the distant past but with what he calls 'the day before yesterday'. He goes on to argue that what societies do with the past, which aspects of it are emphasized in popular memory and what forms these take are all themselves historically specific. Society in eighteenth-century England used different aspects of history in different ways from nineteenth- or twentieth-century society. The eighteenth century, for example, used the civilizations of ancient Greece and Roman as models for architecture, literature and intellectual thought. The same civilizations are studied today by schoolchildren, constructing a model of, say, a Roman villa, in terms of how ordinary people lived in the past. Even in the same period there may be competing versions: in the 1990s the National Trust promotes a version of English history which has the country house as a key feature, while museums like the ones at York Castle or Wigan Pier, or the Black Country Museum, offer a version of the past rooted in the urban experience of 'ordinary' people. Samuel's wider point is that a study of the popular forms in which history is presented can tell us much about the values, aspirations, beliefs and tensions of the present and the relationship of these to the values, aspirations, beliefs and tensions of the past.

4.9

Did the exercise you carried out for activity 4.8 confirm or not Samuel's claim that in the 1990s much of our concern with the past is focused on 'the day before yesterday'? Can you identify any specific period(s) as offering particular values for the present?

Now read the following letter to *the Daily Telegraph*.

4.8

Sir – I have recently visited HMS Victory in Portsmouth Dockyard, and was both perplexed and disappointed by the commentary given by the guide.

As a child I remember being fascinated by the description given by the sailor who was then our guide, not only of the function of the ship's equipment and weapons and the duties of all who sailed in her, but of the battle of Trafalgar and its place in our history.

But now Victory is presented simply as an ancient artefact. The guide dwells mainly on the dreadful conditions suffered by the men below deck and the punishments meted out to them by the officers, who enjoyed great comfort on the deck above.

No mention is made of the fact that all these officers, including Nelson, would have gone to sea as midshipmen, aged as young as 10, they would have lived and worked on the same decks as the men, going aloft with them to handle the sails. There was no purchase of commissions in the Royal Navy, so they would have risen to become officers only if they had mastered the skills of seamanship required to sail and fight.

Nelson's death is now presented as little more than an incident at the battle of Trafalgar. Anyone without historical knowledge might think he died just because he was standing carelessly on deck at the time. There is no explanation of why Nelson and his flagship have been held in such esteem by the nation. No reference is made to his genius, the signalling innovations he used, or his new tactics which enabled him to win his great battle.

This is deplorable today, when so little history is taught in many schools. We need our national heroes as never before. (Jean Gordon, Petersfield, Hants, 'Letters to the Editor', *Daily Telegraph*, 14 March 1994; cited in Samuel, 1994, p. 164)

4.10

1. To what does Jean Gordon object in the commentary accompanying her visit to HMS Victory?
2. Why is she concerned about the treatment of Nelson as a historical figure?
3. What is your response to her claim that national heroes are needed as 'never before'?
4. Can you think of other heroes or heroines of popular memory? What are they remembered for? We have started you off, you carry on.

Hero/heroine	Remembered because
● Martin Luther King	Fought for civil rights for black Americans
● Emily Davison	Died for the cause of women's right to the vote
● Joan of Arc	
● Robin Hood	
●	
●	
●	

Those historical figures who become established in popular memory as heroes or heroines often acquire mythical status. Stories circulate which affirm their lives and actions as especially virtuous, courageous or inspiring and, often despite detailed and painstaking research by historians to reveal them as complex three-dimensional human beings, they remain symbolic figures in the collective consciousness of the group for whom their significance is particularly relevant. For example, while closely argued historical scholarship has attempted to represent a

balanced account of the strengths and limitations, as well as the long and chequered career, of Winston Churchill, many people who lived through the Second
World War prefer to remember him as the man who, according to the myth,
almost single-handedly saved Britain from Nazi invasion. This is not to suggest
that the myths which surround a figure such as Churchill offer a completely false
representation. Many people who experienced the Second World War accepted
that Churchill was one, albeit very important, factor in Britain's victory but were,
nevertheless, reassured and inspired by the representations and practices that produced his mythical status. He came to represent a belief in the power of the individual against the forces of evil, a belief that, however embattled, 'good' will triumph
and that the essence of this 'goodness' was a particular Englishness.

The Churchillian myth offers a particular way of interpreting and narrating
history, in which individual figures are seen as responsible for the destinies of
whole nations, and conflicts between nations are struggles between the forces
of good and evil. **Myths** are another of the signifying practices we introduced you
to in chapter 3: their function is to produce meaning by assembling a set of signs
that can be read symbolically. In the case of popular memory, certain figures
acquire the status of hero or villain or certain events are invested with particular
significance, thereby representing or standing in for a whole nexus of determining
factors, motivations and interests. The media, in particular, rely on myth as a way
of representing past events. Think, for example, of photo-journalism, which often
uses a single image to represent a whole cluster of ideas and meanings.

4.11

Look carefully at Figure 4.1. This photograph of Buckingham Palace was taken
in the week following the death of Diana, Princess of Wales, in August 1997.
Can you suggest some of the encoded meanings here?

Roland Barthes, in his highly influential book *Mythologies*, first published in
France in 1957, argued that myth is one of the most significant ways in which
human beings deal with the complexities of experience.

4.9

[M]yth is constituted by the loss of the historical quality of things: in it, things
lose the memory that they once were made. The world enters language as a
dialectical relation between activities, between human actions; it comes out of
myth as a harmonious display of essences. A conjuring trick has taken place; it
has turned reality inside out, it has emptied it of history and has filled it with
nature, it has removed from things their human meaning so as to make them signify a
human insignificance. The function of the myth is to empty reality: it is, literally, a ceaseless
flowing, a haemorrhage, or perhaps an evaporation, in short a perceptible absence . . .

Figure 4.1 Buckingham Palace

> Myth does not deny things, on the contrary, its function is to talk about them; simply, it purifies them, it makes them innocent, it gives them a natural and eternal justification, it gives them a clarity which is not that of an explanation but that of a statement of fact. If I state the fact of French imperiality without explaining it, I am very near to finding that it is natural and goes without saying: I am reassured. In passing from history to nature, myth acts economically: it abolishes the complexity of human acts, it gives them the simplicity of essences, it does away with all dialectics, with any going back beyond what is immediately visible, it organizes a world which is without contradictions because it is without depth, a world wide open and wallowing in the evident, it establishes a blissful clarity: things appear to mean something by themselves. (Barthes, 1973, pp. 142–3)

The function of myth, according to Barthes, is not so much to falsify events or deeds but to reduce them to essences in order to render them comprehensible and significant. As Barthes says, myth 'abolishes the complexity of human acts, it gives them the simplicity of essences . . . it organizes . . . a world wide open'. This is particularly relevant for our consideration of popular memory, since our collective sense of the past is frequently organized around myth. For example, the story that, on hearing that the Spanish Armada had set sail for England, Sir Francis Drake insisted on finishing his game of bowls has outlasted the historical accuracy of scholars who have demonstrated that, while it is likely that a game of bowls was being played, it is most unlikely that an astute 'sea dog' such as Drake would waste time finishing the game at such a critical moment. The myth that has Drake saying 'Time to finish the game' captures some perceived essence of 'Englishness' which can 'explain' more 'naturally' than detailed historical evidence why the

Armada was defeated by the English. The victory over Spain becomes the victory of good over evil, rather than the outcome of a nexus of historical, political and economic factors – complex, fallible, human actions are represented as natural forces or, in Barthes's words, myth 'has turned reality inside out, it has emptied it of history and has filled it with nature'. As Barthes says, myth 'does not deny things': the main elements of the story are true, there was a game of bowls, the Armada was sailing for England, Drake was at Plymouth. What myth does is 'to talk about them . . . it gives them a natural and eternal justification, it gives them a clarity which is not that of an explanation but that of a statement of fact' – and it does so by arranging the elements of the story in certain ways, by creating heroic characters and by reducing the complex interplay of myriad determinations to a statement of fact (in this case victory over Spain). And this statement of fact requires no explanation: it goes without saying, for example, that it was a victory and that it was self-evidently the triumph of good over evil.

4.12

Consider figure 4.2, which reproduces the cover picture of a 1942 leaflet designed to stir up hatred for the 'enemy' against whom Britain was waging war. How does this representation contribute to myths of the Second World War?

To cultural historians the ways in which myths become established at any particular moment are worthy of study: exploring how and why a myth developed can yield insight into the meanings ascribed by popular memory to historical events. Furthermore, as Angus Calder, the historian, comments, 'Myth may distort what has happened. But it affects what happens' (Calder, 1992, p. 14). In the Second World War, the people of Britain were encouraged to believe that they were making history, that this was Britain's 'finest hour', the moment for which all the years of 'our island's history', a historical mythology that included heroes like Drake and Nelson, had prepared them. Because it is important and inevitable that in wartime people make sense of what is chaotic and frightening by reference to heroic mythologies, many people tried to conduct themselves in accordance with these myths, and in doing so helped to sustain and legitimate the story of Britain's heroic stand against the forces of barbarism. As Calder (1992, p. 14) neatly puts it, 'Heroic mythology fused with everyday life to produce heroism.' We cannot simply dismiss myth as falsehood, lies, fiction. Instead, we need to engage with the discourses (see chapter 3) in which specific myths can be understood and the ways in which myth interacts with everyday life to produce certain behaviours and understandings of the world at a specific moment.

History as 'heritage'

Finally, we want to introduce you to the contemporary debate around the idea of heritage in England. We have focused upon England here because there is a

The great majority of men and women are peaceable and law-abiding; only a few are criminals. And that is fortunate for civilisation, because if the bad out-numbered the good, the police would be faced with an impossible task, and neither life nor property would ever be safe. In the same way, most of the nations in the world are peaceable and orderly, desiring only to live as " good neighbours " with one another. The three " Axis Powers " are like three gangsters trying to hold up and rob all the rest of us. For years they have prepared their weapons and plotted together, so that they could strike without warning and gain the advantage of surprise. This was a very real and important advantage, and it gave them great successes at first—so great, indeed, that Hitler, after knocking out France in June, 1940, prophesied that he would be in London by the following August. However, the Battle of Britain put an end to that dream, and Hitler was forced, in his search for quick victories, to invade Russia instead—only to find that Moscow was equally difficult to reach. The civilised world is proving stronger than the gangsters after all.

Figure 4.2 'The Battle for Civilisation'

very specific relationship between Englishness and a sense of the past. Unlike the Scots or Irish, for many of whom there is an intimate and personal connection with the past, the English are both strangely reluctant to celebrate the nation's actual history and very keen to commemorate an imagined past, shorn of most of its historical reality (Paxman, 1998, pp. 234, 264–5; Giles and Middleton, 1995, pp. 3–9).

Although the term 'heritage' means in its broadest terms that which is inherited, it has increasingly come to mean those material artefacts, places and buildings left by the past which are worthy of preservation. English Heritage and the National Trust, the two major organizations committed to the conservation and preservation of the past's legacy, have large memberships, many of whom are willing to work voluntarily on conservation or restoration projects, as well as contributing to fund raising along with the general public. Furthermore, such organizations command royal patronage and substantial financial subsidies. On the one hand, 'heritage' has been attacked for shoring up a decaying and beleaguered aristocracy by subsidizing the upkeep of their country homes and a certain level of luxurious living (Hewison, 1987). On the other hand, 'heritage' has been criticized for opening historic monuments and sites to the dangers of mass tourism, as more and more historical sites, bygones and memorabilia are preserved and crowds of people spend their leisure time and holidays visiting country houses, theme parks, living history museums and working farms. Equally attacked is the proliferation of historical replicas for purchase, from Victorian christmas cards to 'art deco' ceramics, from reproduction fireplaces to replica storage jars. Those who oppose what they see as the commodification of the past for the purposes of a profit-making tourist and leisure industry point to the ways in which the country is being turned into a giant Disneyland-type museum, catering to a 'vulgar English nationalism'.

> Where there were mines and mills, now there is Wigan Pier Heritage Centre, where you can pay to crawl through a model coal mine, watch dummies making nails, and be invited 'in' by actors and actresses dressed as 1900 proletarians. Britain, where these days a new museum opens every fortnight is becoming a museum itself . . . The Total Museum, though it can entertain, is a lie. Pretending to open a window into the past is a technique which weakens imagination much in the way that colour television weakens the intuition, whereas radio – by its incompleteness – so strongly stimulates it. (Ascherson, 1987, cited in Samuel 1994, p. 262)

The arguments put forward in condemnation of 'heritage' resemble in some ways the debates over mass culture that we encountered in chapter 1. Richard Hoggart railed against 'the candy floss world' of milk bars and juke boxes for its tendency, as he perceived it, to entertain rather than educate. A similar charge is brought against 'heritage'. Visits to living history museums or working farms are a social practice engaged in as a leisure pursuit: as such, it is argued, they encourage the passive consumption of images and impressions rather than the active engagement of reading or study. Equally, to purchase replica 'period' crockery or furniture is to engage in a celebration of the past rather than critical inquiry. The consumption of history in the form of 'heritage', so it is argued, is a popular activity of 'the masses' and, therefore, by its very nature is degraded and degrading. Historians, as well as arbiters of aesthetic taste, have attacked the 'heritage' industry for offering sanitized and sentimentalized versions of the past which avoid confronting the complexities of human motivation and the fragmentary, often contradictory, nature of the historical record. In his book, published in 1985, *On Living in an Old Country*, the cultural critic Patrick Wright argued that the contemporary British obsession with 'heritage' was symptomatic of a wider malaise, in that it represented a pervasive nostalgia for the 'good old days' of British ascendancy. Such nostalgia, he argued, supported a collective mentality that was backward looking rather than fostering a more dynamic and radical engagement with the present (Wright, 1985). Wright's argument, which is a complex one and has to be placed in the context of mid-1980s Thatcherite Britain, has been critiqued by the historian Raphael Samuel, most memorably in *Theatres of Memory*, in which he mounts a provocative defence of 'heritage' and calls for a reassessment of 'the sources of its energies and strengths' (Samuel, 1994, p. 274). Now read the following extract from *Theatres of Memory*.

4.10

The hostility of historians to heritage is possibly exacerbated by the fact that they are in some sort competing for the same terrain. Each, after its own fashion, claims to be representing the past 'as it was' ... Interpretation, the privilege of the archive-based historian, and 're-creation', the ambition of heritage, also share a common conceit; the belief that scrupulous attention to detail will bring the dead to life ...

Whatever the reasons, history and heritage are typically placed in opposite camps. The first is assigned to the realm of critical inquiry, the second to a merely antiquarian preoccupation, the classification and hoarding of things. The first, so the argument runs, is dynamic and concerned with development and change, the second is static. The first is concerned with explanation, bringing a sceptical intelligence to bear on the complexities and contradictoriness of the record; the second sentimentalizes, and is content merely to celebrate ...

The perceived opposition between 'education' and 'entertainment' and the unspoken and unargued-for assumption that pleasure is almost by definition mindless, ought not to go unchallenged. There is no reason to think that people are more passive when looking at old photographs or film footage, handling a museum exhibit, following a local history trail, or even buying a historical souvenir, than when reading a book. People do not simply 'consume' images in the way in which, say, they buy a bar of chocolate. As in any reading, they assimilate them as best they can to pre-existing images and narratives. The pleasures of the gaze ... are different in kind from those of the written word but not necessarily less taxing on historical reflection and thought. (Samuel, 1994, pp. 270–1)

4.13

- Think about the various arguments put forward here about 'heritage': (a) the 'heritage' industry supports the aristocracy in a certain lifestyle which is not appropriate in a democratic society; (b) Britain is becoming one huge museum in which crowds of visitors and tourists spend their leisure time passively and uncritically viewing historic spectacles or buying replicated historical products and gifts; (c) 'heritage' does not simply offer passive spectacle but can provide valuable opportunities for discovering history. Can you put forward evidence and argument for each position?
- What is your own experience of 'heritage'? How do you respond to the different standpoints on it? What do you think?
- Think about the use of 'living history' and themed museums in schools. Do you think these offer a valuable experience of history or not? Give reasons for your answer.

ACTIVITIES

Conclusions

This discussion of 'heritage' has brought us back to Tosh's point that history 'can become the basis for informed and critical discussion of current issues'. Wright and Samuel are both concerned with the relationship between the current political climate and the ways in which the past is represented and used in the present. In relation to this you might think about recent calls to teach a particular kind of history in English schools – put crudely, kings, queens, heroic figures and English successes, rather than the histories of other cultures or the histories of so-called ordinary people – and consider whether, how and why this connects to wider political issues both nationally and globally.

Many of the ideas raised in this chapter will be taken up again in different ways later, notably in the case study which completes part I, where you will find discussion of a particular example of 'heritage'. As students of culture you will frequently find yourselves having to engage with the historical past, whether it be in the form of popular memory and myth, archival research, fiction, politics and identities or 'heritage'. Remind yourself when you encounter any form of history to ask questions about the paradigms of knowledge within which it is located and the purposes it serves in the present.

CHAPTER 5

Spaces and Places

Introduction: exploring the connotations of place

Early on in James Joyce's novel *A Portrait of the Artist as a Young Man*, we find the central character, Stephen Dedalus, day-dreaming during a geography lesson:

> He turned to the flyleaf of the geography and read what he had written there: himself, his name and where he was.
>
> Stephen Dedalus
> Class of Elements
> Clongowes Wood College
> Sallins
> County Kildare
> Ireland
> Europe
> The World
> The Universe
> (Joyce, 1916, pp. 212–13)

Stephen's sense of identity ('himself') is closely linked to his name ('Stephen Dedalus') and, importantly for our purposes, a listing of ever larger geographical spaces. Just as they affirm his own identity, the places in which he locates himself also shape our response to him, because we take into account the connotations of the places he mentions. How would your view of him alter if the address was Tokyo, Japan, or Cape Town, South Africa or, even, Eton, Berkshire, England? As we saw in chapter 2, a sense of identity is derived from a number of sources, one of which will be the connotations that given locale or region has for an individual. What cultural geography does is to focus on the context from which such connotations arise. It is concerned with teasing out the ways in which places and spaces are shaped by and can themselves come to shape the beliefs and values of those who inhabit them. As Peter Jackson (1989, p. 23) argues, 'cultural geography . . . focuses on the way cultures are produced and reproduced through actual social practices that take place in historically contingent and geographically specific contexts.'

In this chapter we will be discussing some of the ways in which an awareness of the role and meanings of place in shaping individual and group identities can help you to study both represented and actual environments.

5.1

Work with someone else if you can – preferably someone from a different part of the world or country to you. Jot down a list of places or locations which have particular meaning for you (and your community), and then get your partner to write down his or her views of the same places. We have started you off with an example.

Place/locale	Your view	Partner's view
• Majorca	Holiday place	Place of employment
•		
•		
•		
•		

Take an example on which you had particularly divergent opinions and discuss what differences emerged? What caused these?

What we imagine this exercise points up is that you have different views about a particular place. For a Christian, the local church might be a location with associations of communal support, a place of particular significance as a space in which one's beliefs and values can be nourished. For an atheist, the church might be an architecturally interesting old building, but is unlikely to be seen to have any bearing upon her or his behaviour in and around it. Another perspective on this emerges if you talk to people from different generations: your grandmother, for example, may well have very different ideas about the meaning and purpose of a pub from your own.

Places are filled with meanings, and cultural geography is concerned to ensure that the relationship between places and the meanings that adhere to them are not lost sight of. It has also been interested in exploring the ways in which places take on and are shaped by ideas and beliefs which may run counter to those of the people inhabiting a given locale. We can examine this further by thinking about the relationship between maps and the places they represent.

Maps and mapping

Representations of spaces, whether in our minds or in the material form of map or plan, are abstractions (on this distinction see Lefebvre, 1991, pp. 33–46) that emerge from a particular cultural context. For example, what we may have imagined the location 'university' to be like will depend upon our experience of 'universities' and the experiences (and beliefs and values) of our immediate networks of family, friends and social contacts. Real or imagined, places are products of specific cultural conditions and as such not simply arenas for action but actually always a part of the action and its meanings. Over time a place becomes part of what Raymond Williams calls the documentary record of a society. At this point, you might look again at Williams's description of his bus journey in reading 1.5. In conducting a cultural geography one is often re-reading other people's representations – in the form of maps, reflections, paintings, photographs etc. – in the hope of producing a fuller sense of the complex processes by which a given culture can be characterized; in effect, the cultural geographer makes a map of the cultural phenomenon being investigated.

Such maps do not, it must be stressed, claim to be complete or direct reflections of 'reality'. As Smith and Katz (1993, p. 70) explain,

> Although geographers and cartographers habitually give lip service to the selectiveness involved in mapping and to the realisation that maps are strategic social constructions, they more often proceed in practice from traditionally realist assumptions. Only recently have a few geographers and cartographers begun a . . . critique of cartographic conventions of positioning, framing, scale, absence and presence on the map, and, a critique of the absent if omniscient cartographer.

ACTIVITIES

5.2

Can you suggest what is meant by the 'absent if omniscient cartographer'?

Now read the following extract from an influential book on spatial politics by the French social theorist Henri Lefebvre.

READING

5.1

To compare different maps of a region or country . . . is to be struck by the remarkable diversity among them. Some, such as maps that show 'beauty spots' and historical sites and monuments to the accompaniment of an appropriate rhetoric, aim to mystify in fairly obvious ways. This kind of map designates places where a ravenous consumption picks over the last remains of nature and of the past in search of whatever nourishment may be obtained from the *signs* of anything historical or original. If the maps and guides are to be believed, a veritable feast of authenticity awaits the tourist. The conventional signs used in these documents constitute a code even more deceptive than the things themselves, for they are at one more remove from reality. Next, consider an ordinary map of roads and other communications . . . What such a map reveals, its meaning – not, perhaps, to the most ingenious inspection, but certainly to an intelligent perusal with even minimal preparation – is at once clear and hard to decipher . . .

These spaces are *produced*. The 'raw material' from which they are produced is nature. They are products of an activity which involves the economic and technical realms but which extends well beyond them, for these are also political products, and strategic spaces. (Lefebvre, 1991, p. 84)

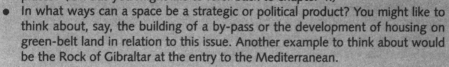

5.3

- What would you say was the main point of Lefebvre's argument?
- Lefebvre was writing in France in the 1970s: to what extent can his remarks about the relation to the past here be applied to contemporary Britain's attitudes towards its national monuments and other 'historic' places? (On this you might like to refer back to chapter 4.)
- In what ways can a space be a strategic or political product? You might like to think about, say, the building of a by-pass or the development of housing on green-belt land in relation to this issue. Another example to think about would be the Rock of Gibraltar at the entry to the Mediterranean.

The extract from Lefebvre suggested that the meanings of spaces/places on a given map are produced in complex ways. You can test his claim, and the argument he puts forward in the extract as a whole, by examining a sequence of maps.

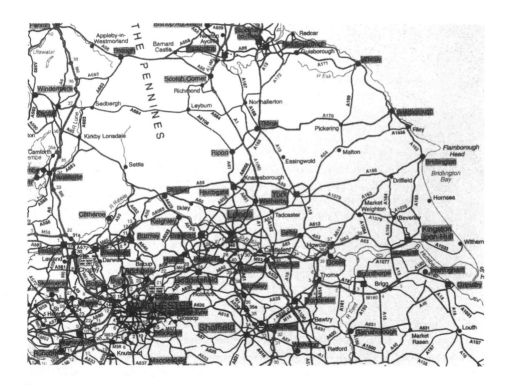

Figure 5.1   Ordnance Survey map of North East England

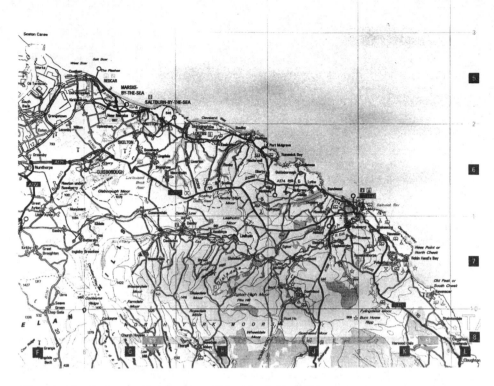

Figure 5.2 Ordnance Survey map of the North York Moors

5.4

- Look at the map in figure 5.1. What features strike you? What does it tell you about the area?
- Now look at the larger scale map of the North York Moors (figure 5.2): what information do we get here that was absent from the previous map; in addition to the detailing of towns, villages, roads and landscape features, note and comment upon the proliferation of symbols.
- Finally, look at the very large scale map of the Moors showing Goathland and the surrounding area (figure 5.3) and compare this with the previous two maps.

It is perhaps worth noting that the area marked 'MOD Property' at the bottom right of figure 5.3 is, in fact, Fylingdales Listening Station, and that from the road you would see a huge white pyramid and a collection of buildings, rather than the featureless moorland the map suggests is there. You may also want to reflect upon the fact that the village of Goathland has an alternative existence as the village in Yorkshire TV's *Heartbeat*: thus adding another layer to the meanings of the place.

Lefebvre's approach to maps seeks to unpack the ways in which what may

Figure 5.3 Ordnance Survey map of Goathland and Grosmont, North York Moors

appear to be a fixed, stable locale is in fact overlain and shaped by ideology. As Peter Vujakovic notes, 'All maps can be regarded as "propagandist" in the widest sense of the world . . . [and] national atlases can be seen as important ideological devices, telling the story of a nation and locating the national identity in both time and space' (Vujakovic, 1995, pp. 129–30); this is as true of the *Ordnance Survey Motoring Atlas of Britain* as it is of the *Concise Atlas of the Republic of Croatia*, which Vujakovic analyses. The Route Planning Map (figure 5.1) suggests that neither Pickering nor Malton is a Primary Route destination, yet if you are interested in steam trains you might be making a trip to the North Yorkshire Moors Railway in Pickering, so your use of the map and relationship with the place would be different from that which we might want to attribute to the map maker. The route planning map prioritizes getting from A to B, usually by car, and, as such, omits much detail. By contrast, the next map (figure 5.2) is packed with information: it designates not only towns, roads, and villages but also viewpoints, tourist features, caravan and camp sites, youth hostels, railway stations and picnic sites. This map constructs a landscape whose primary function might seem to be leisure – looking at the view, camping, eating sandwiches etc. The highly detailed map (figure 5.3) reveals something of this location's economic life beyond tourism and leisure – we see various farms, sheep pens, disused quarries and grouse butts, as well as schools, hotels and the like – but once again it is a representation that foregrounds certain uses of the landscape (it is taken from a map 'specially designed' (cover blurb) by the Ordnance Survey to promote the recreational use of the area). This map tells us much about contemporary British culture's perception of the countryside as a site of leisure, but tells us very little about the experiences of the people who live and work in the landscape. Thus a concern with the representation of culture through maps depends to a large extent on an assessment of whom the map was made for and the purposes of the map-maker.

Real spaces are no less constructed or shaped by powerful ideologies than maps. In the next section we examine the phenomenon of supermarket shopping from a cultural geography point of view.

Going shopping

The great expansion of retail parks and out-of-town shopping centres may, in the late 1990s, have slowed, but many people still spend a great deal of time shopping and increasingly many people shop at these centres. Out-of-town shopping centres offer a constructed locale and a site of consumption (see chapter 9) which can tell us much about contemporary culture – not least because they are sites that are so often utilized in ways which subvert the intentions of their planners and owners. Much recent work on shopping centres has focused upon them as a specific phenomenon of contemporary culture in industrialized societies (Kowinski, 1985; Morris, 1988). In particular, shopping centres have been studied as spaces in which individuals interact with powerful, often global, commercial forces at a local level. As John Fiske comments in an essay on the culture of everyday life,

'The supermarket is an arena full of the goods and information produced by the political economy of capitalism, but within it, shoppers construct for the period and purposes of shopping their own settings' (Fiske, 1992, p. 160). Fiske examines the ways in which individuals redefine the space of a supermarket in their own terms and distinguishes between setting and arena – settings are defined as 'repeatedly experienced, personally ordered and edited versions of the arena' (Lave, 1988, p. 151, cited in Fiske, 1992, p. 160) – linking these ideas to the distinction between place and space found in the work of Michael de Certeau (1984). Fiske's summary can help us think through the ways in which individuals can use space in a subversive or, at least, unintended way.

5.2

For . . . [de Certeau] place is an ordered structure provided by the dominant order through which its power to organise and control is exerted. It is often physical. So cities are places built to organise and control the lives and movements of the 'city subjects' in the interests of the dominant. So, too, supermarkets, apartment blocks, and universities are places. But within and against them, the various formations of the people construct their spaces by the practices of living. So renters make the apartment, the place of the landlord, into their space by the practices of living; the textures of objects, relationships, and behaviors with which they occupy and possess it for the period of the renting. Space is practiced place, and space is produced by the creativity of the people using the resources of the other. De Certeau stresses the political conflict involved, the confrontation of opposing social interests that is central to the construction of space out of place. Lave focuses more on the functional creativity of the activities involved in constructing a setting out of an arena. But her argument shows that a setting is a material and cognitive space where the inhabitant or shopper is in control, is able to cope successfully. (Fiske, 1992, p. 160)

5.5

- Can you think of any ways in which Fiske's claims about the freedom of the shopper might be challenged?
- Fiske suggests that renters can make a place their own space: can you think of some constraints on their ability to do this?
- Think about a place which you habitually utilize: are there ways in which you use it that suggest that you are creating your own space? Are there any constraints on your ability to do this?
- As Meaghan Morris notes, individual stores often work to create settings in the wider arena of a shopping centre (Morris, 1988, p. 316). Can you think of some examples from your own experience of shopping, and perhaps suggest some reasons for why they might do this?

Let us debate further Fiske's arguments about the creation of personal space via some more detailed work on supermarket shopping.

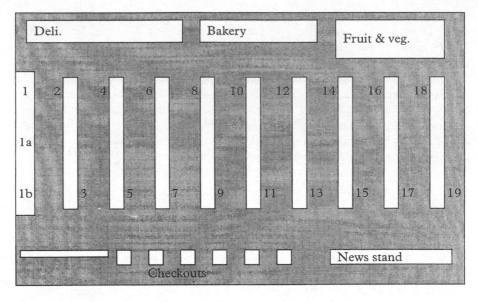

Key: shelf number and stock

1 Beers and ciders.
1a Wines.
1b Spirits.
2 Soft drinks, crisps and snacks.
3 Dairy, fruit juices, milk yoghurt.
4 Chilled meals, including pizza, curries etc.
5 Frozen veg./frozen foods
6 Fresh poultry and speciality meats (game and exotic, e.g. ostrich).
7 Beef, lamb, pork.
8 Dried herbs, spices, cooking sauces etc.
9 Cooking oils, vinegars.
10 Tinned vegetables and cooking sauces, dried pasta and rice.
11 Tinned meat and fish, dried vegetables, pulses.
12 Tea, coffee and other beverages; flour and home baking.

13 Biscuits, chocolate and cakes.
14 Washing liquid, powder etc.; cleaning products.
15 Soap, shampoo, sanitary towels, deodorant, toothpaste, non-prescription medicine and health care (including condoms and femidoms).
16 Household: bin liners, cloths, food wrap, foil, toilet paper, kitchen paper. Eggs.
17 Jam, honey, spreads.
18 Organic produce: dried and tinned; organic beer and wine.
19 Organic fruit and vegetables; organic chilled products, butter, milk meat.

The fruit and vegetables unit stocks basic varieties and bunched flowers.
The bakery stocks fresh and pre-wrapped bread, cakes etc.
The deli stocks cold meat, cheese, bacon, sausages etc.
The news stand stocks local and national papers and magazines.

Figure 5.4 A small supermarket

5.6

Copy the diagram in figure 5.4 and then track the likely routes of the shoppers listed below when they complete a shopping trip; using different coloured pens will help you to keep each shopper's journey distinct (you could work on an acetate). Shoppers:

- A family (Mum, Dad, two small children) doing a weekly shop
- A single person doing a weekly shop
- A vegetarian doing a weekly shop
- A well off couple preparing for a dinner party
- A student buying lunch
- An office worker buying lunch

Having tracked each shopper's journey read the following quote and then consider the questions below:

> We all make meanings with the commodities we use and bestow. But the meaning possibilities are already inscribed in the history of commodity production and exchange. The school of popular culture criticism that promotes meaning-making as the redemptive aspect of our relationship to a commodified culture sometimes goes so far as to imply that we can make wholly new meanings. (Willis, 1991, p. 136)

- How far does the supermarket as a space ultimately differ for each shopper? How far does an individual's use of the place actually represent the creation of the kind of personal space that Fiske discussed?
- What factors operate when you do your own shopping (ethical, financial, moral, religious, racial, gendered etc.). How far is your 'journey' around the supermarket determined by these factors; how is it determined by the supermarket itself; how much free choice do you have about how you use the supermarket?

We need to strike a judicious balance between seemingly optimistic claims that we are free agents who can boldly remake in our own image the places we inhabit and move through, and apparently pessimistic claims that we are all the pawns of a capitalist system (for further discussion of these issues see chapters 8 and 9).

In the act of going shopping in the kind of setting we have been discussing individuals are fundamentally implicated in the processes of late twentieth-century Western consumer culture. Not only does what we buy have meanings through which we signal identity and are identified by others, in going shopping we are actors in a corporate space which stages encounters. The various people who work in a supermarket are carefully constructed by their employers through particular uniforms or specific activities. Susan Willis writes about this in an American context.

5.3

The current practice in many supermarkets is to put a theatrical form of production on display, while the real work that goes in to maintaining the store and serving the customers is either hidden from view or made to appear trivial because of deskilling. The work of pricing the merchandise, stocking the shelves, cleaning the store, and preparing the meat and produce for sale is accomplished by a largely invisible workforce, whose members labor behind the scene in a backroom warehouse, or at night after the store is closed. The work of managing, which includes decisions over purchases and personnel, is conducted by a number of upper-level employees whose photos sometimes decorate the store's service counter, but who are seldom seen by shoppers. The work of checking, which in a bygone era would have anchored the customer's apprehension of work in the supermarket, has today been greatly undermined by the installation of computerized scanners that weigh and price the commodities and often speak to the customer. The supermarket checker has been deskilled to the point of becoming a human robotoid extension of the checkout system.

As if to compensate for the marginalization and in some cases the erasure, of productive labor, the supermarket offers an array of theatrical labors, whose importance has more to do with the spectacle they create than the actual services they render. Most supermarkets today offer in-store bakeries, deli-counters, florist shops, and gourmet food sections. These are staffed by a corps of store-personnel whose uniforms are more theatrical than practical. Often, the employees' pert hats and aprons mimic the colours and patterns of the store's interior decor, making the supermarket something of a stage for sales and the costumed employees the actors enacting service. If we take the supermarket as the place where we most commonly come into contact with the festishized commodities of daily life, then all the strategies developed by a supermarket to render service personal, to make it visible, rebound in a theatricality whose effect is to create the appearance of use value in the commodities we buy. (Willis, 1991, p. 17)

5.7

- Think about the organization of supermarkets you have visited. Can you identify any of the features Willis discusses?
- Do you agree that the labour on show is purely theatrical? How does buying bread from a section of a store labelled Bakery or meat from a section labelled Butchers give a different set of meanings to the transaction and product from what would adhere if we simply picked the items out of a chill cabinet or off a shelf? Note down some of the meanings that are 'added' by the kind of theatrical organization Willis describes.

Willis offers a Marxist reading of capitalism (for more on this see chapter 9) which seems to suggest that everyone is positioned and defined by the vast impersonal forces of economics. Meghan Morris has argued: 'Shopping centres illustrate very well, I think, the argument that you can't treat a public at a cultural event as directly expressive of social groups and classes, or their supposed sensibility. Publics aren't stable, homogenous entities' (Morris, 1988, p. 304). This is because when we shop we do so in our own terms, and central to our experience of shopping centres is the construction of our own mental map of the place determined by our habitual needs (Fiske, 1992, p. 160). That this map is never simply of our own making underlines the ways in which our experience of culture is very much built upon processes and interactions.

Place and identity

By focusing upon the competing and changing meanings of places for different individuals, cultural geography focuses upon the contingent nature of identity. The problem of identity as either complicit with or subversive of the ideologies which shape a given locale is, at root, based on the logic of **binary opposition**. What might be needed, then, is a way of thinking which doesn't stop at 'either/ or' but allows many more shades of opinion: for example, hot *and* cold, rather than hot *or* cold. It is exactly this kind of non-binary based logic that can be identified in the postmodern Marxism of Laclau: 'Identity depends on conditions of existence which are contingent, its relationship with them is absolutely necessary' (Laclau, 1990, p. 21, cited in Keith and Pile, 1993, pp. 27–9).

As we move into different arenas of activity, the shifting meanings attached to these locations inform the ways in which we operate and, as such, help to shape our experience of a given place. For Laclau, the ethical dilemma we may experience over whether or not to buy imported fresh vegetables produced as a cash crop in a country whose need for foreign currency outweighs the needs of its people for food staples is an important factor of our identity. That we can both buy the mange tout and be opposed to the extension of airport runways is part of the way in which we can operate across different settings and actually present different identities (for more on this see chapter 8). As Keith and Pile (1993, p. 30) argue, by accepting the multiplicity of identities an individual can inhabit we must not lose sight of the ways in which location informs a subject's identity.

The act of leaving your home to go shopping does not seem a very huge shift in location, and so may appear unlikely to occasion any great change in identity. In fact, as Michael de Certeau has argued (cited in During, 1993, pp. 157–8), to trace an individual's actions – glancing in store windows, stopping to look at an item, reading an advertising hoarding, asking a sales assistant for information, interacting with other shoppers – and their impact upon identity is almost impossible. If, as we suggested in chapter 3, everything signifies, then all the action and interactions of an individual shopper become part of the shifting arena in which his or her identity ought to be read. At a simplified level, you can trace the larger shifts by thinking through the ways in which who you are subtly changes as you move through a set of locations.

ACTIVITIES

5.8

Think about the different ways in which you see yourself and are seen by others in the following settings. Try to identify as many factors as possible informing the way in which a given setting informs your identity.

1   At the bus queue
2   Queuing in the university library to return textbooks
3   Queuing in the student union shop
4   Discussing a film in a seminar group
5   Discussing the same film with friends in a pub
6   Visiting a foreign country for a holiday
7   Working or studying in a foreign country

The differences you are able to identify may be slight, but we should not neglect these micro details of daily life as part of the 'structure of feeling' of our culture. Sometimes historical distance or a shift in context may allow the ways in which place impacts upon identity to become much more visible for analysis. In this area we would direct you to the extensive work that has been done on colonialism and on travel and exploration as occasions when we are often actively mapping (literally and metaphorically) a new terrain, but often at a loss to make sense of our experiences because the relationship which exists between context and identity has become so removed that we struggle to bring the two together. (For an introduction see Boehmer, 1995. For more detailed work see, among others, Bhabha, 1994, Ryan, 1994.) Even in our daily lives we can experience something of this dislocation: when we first start school, university or a job there is a short period when the strangeness of our environment has an impact on how we feel and interact with others. This dislocation can lead to an intensification of the rituals and practices which shaped an individual's identity in another context; to bafflement or, even, madness. All three responses can be found in Joseph Conrad's novella *Heart of Darkness*, which examines the impact of colonial practices in Africa on various white men and the native peoples they encounter and exploit.

Heart of Darkness was first published in Britain in a conservative literary magazine called *Blackwood's* in 1899. The narrative centres on Charlie Marlow, an English sea captain, who is telling the story of his adventures in Africa to a group of friends on board a sailing ship which is moored on the Thames. Marlow travels from Europe to Africa and then journeys up-river in search of the enigmatic Mr Kurtz. For Marlow, the journey to the river's 'farthest point of navigation' (Conrad, 1902, p. 141) marks 'the culminating point in my experience'. Marlow's initial interest in Africa is the result of his encounter with a map:

> Now when I was a little chap I had a passion for maps. I would look for hours at South America, or Africa or Australia, and lose myself in all the glories of exploration. At that time there were many blank spaces on the earth, and when I saw one

that looked particularly inviting on a map (but they all look that) I would put my finger on it and say, 'When I grow up I will go there.' . . . there was one . . . the biggest, the most blank, so to speak – that I had a hankering after.

True, by this time it was not a blank space any more. It had got filled since my boyhood with rivers and lakes and names. It had ceased to be a blank space of delightful mystery – a white patch for a boy to dream gloriously over. It had become a place of darkness. (Conrad, 1902, p. 142)

Marlow already has ideas about the nature of the place he is to travel to, and some of these appear as the oppositions which are a feature of this extract (and of the book as a whole): between emptiness and fullness, between whiteness and darkness. Marlow, the white Englishman, already has a very clear set of expectations about what the reality of Africa will be and, initially, it would seem that these are borne out in his experiences there. In this second extract, Marlow has just arrived at the company's base in Africa:

I met a white man, in such an unexpected elegance of get-up that in the first moment I took him for a sort of vision. I saw a high starched collar, white cuffs, a light alpaca jacket, snowy trousers, a clear necktie, and varnished boots. No hat. Hair parted, brushed, oiled, under a green lined parasol held in a big white hand. He was amazing, and had a penholder behind his ear.

I shook hands with this miracle, and I learned he was the Company's chief accountant, and that all the book-keeping was done at this station. He had come out for a moment, he said, 'to get a breath of fresh air.' The expression sounded wonderfully odd, with its suggestion of sedentary desk-life . . . I respected the fellow. Yes; I respected his collars, his vast cuffs, his brushed hair. His appearance was certainly that of a hairdresser's dummy; but in the great demoralisation of the land he kept up his appearance. That's backbone. (Conrad, 1902, pp. 157–8).

In this next extract Marlow describes the African who works as the fireman on the ship he takes up-river:

He was an improved specimen; he could fire up a vertical boiler. He was there below me, and, upon my word, to look at him was as edifying as seeing a dog in a parody of breeches and a feather hat, walking on its hind legs. A few months of training had done for that really fine chap. He squinted at the steam-gauge and at the water-gauge with an evident effort of intrepidity – and he had filed teeth, too, the poor devil, and the wool of his pate shaved into queer patterns, and three ornamental scars on each cheek. He ought to have been clapping his hands and stamping his feet on the bank, instead of which he was hard at work, a thrall to strange witchcraft, full of improving knowledge. He was useful because he had been instructed; and what he knew was this – that should the water in that transparent thing disappear, the evil spirit inside the boiler would get angry through the greatness of his thirst, and take a terrible vengeance. So he sweated and fired up and watched the glass fearfully (with an impromptu charm, made of rags, tied to his arm, and a piece of polished bone, as big as a watch, stuck flat-ways through his lower lip). (Conrad, 1902, pp. 187–8)

117

5.9

In his important essay on the novella, Chinua Achebe remarks that much of the story uses the idea of Africa as a 'place of negation' (Achebe 1977, p. 250), in which European values are shown to be superior. Compare the descriptions of the two men and comment on the ways in which Marlow's perception of them is grounded in his English origins.

To get to grips with the ways in which perceptions of place are shaped by an individual's tendency to 'map' new terrain in terms of that which is already familiar to him or her, you might like to read the whole novella or Conrad's short story 'An outpost of progress', and then to consider to what extent the representation of places is dependent upon specifically English or European values. In his highly influential book, *Orientalism*, Edward Said, speaking not of Africa but of the Far and Middle East, observes that

> the Orient was almost a European invention, and had been since antiquity a place of romance, exotic beings, haunting memories and landscapes, remarkable experiences . . . The Orient is not only adjacent to Europe; it is also the place of Europe's greatest and richest and oldest colonies, the source of its civilizations and languages, its cultural contestant, and one of its deepest and most recurring images of the Other. In addition, the Orient has helped to define Europe (or the West) as its contrasting image, idea, personality, experience. (Said, 1978, p. 1)

Africa, 'the Orient' and Europe are geographically contingent land masses, but they are also places that 'form a reservoir of meanings which people can draw upon to tell stories about and thereby define themselves' (Thrift, 1997, p. 160). You could usefully spend some time thinking about the meanings that have been and are circulated about Africa, Europe, America, China, Japan or the Middle East, and from whose point of view these 'stories' are told.

Now read the extract from an article by the cultural geographer Doreen Massey.

5.4

This is an era – it is often said – when things are speeding up, and spreading out. Capital is going through a new phase of internationalization, especially in its financial parts. More people travel more frequently and for longer distances. Your clothes have probably been made in a range of countries from Latin America to South East Asia. Dinner consists of food shipped in from all over the world. And if you have a screen in your office, instead of opening a letter which – care of Her Majesty's Post Office – has taken some days to wend its way across the country, you now get interrupted by e-mail . . .

It is a phenomenon which has been called 'time-space-compression'. And the general acceptance that something of the sort is going on is marked by the almost obligatory use in the literature of terms and phrases such as speed-up, global village, overcoming spatial barriers, the disruption of horizons, and so forth . . .

To begin with, there are some questions to be asked about time-space-compression itself. Who is it that experiences it, and how? Do we all benefit and suffer from it in the same way.

... We also need to ask about its causes: what is it that determines our degrees of mobility, that influences the sense we have of space and place? Time-space-compression refers to movement and communication across space, to the geographical stretching-out of social relations, and to our experience of all this. The usual interpretation is that it results overwhelmingly from the actions of capital, and from its currently increasing internationalization. On this interpretation, then, it is time space and money which make the world go round, and us go round (or not) the world. It is capitalism and its developments which are argued to determine our understanding and our experience of space.

But surely this is insufficient. Among the many other things which clearly influence that experience, there are for instance, race and gender. The degree to which we can move between countries, or walk about the streets at night, or venture out of hotels in foreign cities, is not just influenced by 'capital'. Survey after survey has shown how women's mobility, for instance, is restricted – in a thousand different ways, from physical violence to being ogled at or made to feel quite simply 'out of place' – not by 'capital' but by men. (Massey, 1991, pp. 232–3)

5.10

- Can you suggest which social groups from which parts of the world are more likely to be mobile in the sense described in the first paragraph of the reading?
- Can you think of groups who move around the world but are less in charge of their mobility? Who or what does control the mobility of such groups?
- Massey mentions race and gender as things that influence our experience of time-space-compression. Can you think of an example of how race might determine this? Can you think of other social factors that might influence the experience of time-space-compression?

Your answers to these questions are likely to have suggested that the ways in which people experience time-space-compression are varied and complex. It is not enough to say that it is caused solely by the effects of global capitalism: for example, global corporations such as Mars, Coca-Cola or McDonalds or global networks of communication like the Internet, MTV and Hollywood. Those who control, organize and distribute international currency, international markets or international media are often those who have access to electronic technology, long-haul flights and worldwide contacts through fax, e-mail and conference calling. These groups are the ones who see the benefits of time-space-compression and whose power and influence is increased by the growth of global economies and global media. However, there are other groups, such as refugees from the recent war in Rwanda, whose mobility is enforced not by the movements of international 'capital', but by tribal war and fears of genocide. Moreover, even where the movement of a group from one place to another is the result of economic forces, as in the case of migrant workers from Mexico who attempt to enter the USA in search of work, the people 'on the move' may not be in control of this mobility or its outcomes. Their movements are as likely to be controlled by immigration laws and racial prejudices as by capitalism. Massey also notes another group: those on the receiving end of time-space-compression. She cites as an example the pensioner trapped in an inner-city bedsit by fear of what lurks outside, who eats British fish and chips from a Chinese take-away and watches an American film on a television made in Japan. The cosmopolitanization of culture has done little to improve the lives of people like this.

We touched on the issues around globalization in chapter 2 and will return to these in chapter 9 in the context of consumerism and chapter 10 in relation to electronic technology. For now, you could think about the ways in which the world appears to be becoming a 'smaller' space or, as some commentators call it, 'a global village'. Do you think this is true for you or the people you know? Do you see it as a positive or negative thing? Can you see any evidence that people are trying, in the face of this, to retain or imagine a sense of **local**, individual place in which they can counter the supposedly homogenizing effects of global cultures? For example, might the popularity of soap operas like EastEnders and Coronation Street be to do with the fictional 'communities' they create? How important is place to these 'communities' and do they represent homogeniety or diversity or what? What about the place you live – where are the meeting places, what connections do you make with this place and the rest of the world by phone, by letter, through your memories and in your imagination?

Space and place in Hardy's *Jude the Obscure*

We want to end this chapter with an analysis of Thomas Hardy's *Jude the Obscure*: to suggest how some of the ideas of cultural geography may be used to illuminate a literary text; to offer you a fictional representation of place at a moment when new ideas about space and time were emerging (as they are also at the end of the twentieth century – see the discussion in the previous section about globalization); and to suggest the ways in which writers of fiction can act as cartographers of the imagination. Hardy's Wessex is as much a part of contemporary culture as of the late nineteenth century, though differently understood, as anyone who has visited Dorset recently could testify. You might pause here and think about the ways in which areas of Britain have been identified with writers, famous people or fiction: Warwickshire is 'Shakespeare's county'; the area around Tyneside and Newcastle is called 'Catherine Cookson country'; Nottinghamshire is linked with Robin Hood; and Swaledale in the north Pennines is 'James Herriot country'.

Hardy's late fiction was written and produced at the end of the nineteenth century, a time in which a 'distinctively different culture and consciousness of space, time and modernity emerged' (Soja, 1989, p. 31), and *Jude the Obscure* can be seen to offer an account of subjectivity in the context of a changing social order. It tracks Jude's movement through the fictional Wessex from the village of Marygreen to the city of Christminster, and on to the towns of Melchester, Shaston and Aldbrickham. In each case Hardy's narrator is at pains to set out the social structures of these locales and their associated ideologies, not as the backdrop to Jude's situation but as fundamental factors which shape and structure his experiences. As Hardy noted,

> the book is all contrasts – or was meant to be in its originally conception. Alas, what a miserable accomplishment it is, when I compare it with what I meant to make it – e.g. Sue and her heathen gods set against Jude's reading the Greek testament. Christminster academical, Christminster in the slums; Jude the saint, Jude the sinner, Sue the pagan, Sue the saint, marriage, no marriage, etc. etc. (Cited in Hardy, 1928, pp. 272–3)

The novel obsessively stages the encounter of self and society via a registration of the tensions which are generated between an individual and the space that he or she inhabits. Below is reprinted the opening chapter of *Jude the Obscure*: as you read through think carefully about the ways in which various places are given particular meanings or associations.

5.5

The schoolmaster was leaving the village, and everybody seemed sorry. The miller at Cresscombe lent him the small white tilted cart and horse to carry his goods to the city of his destination, about twenty miles off, such a vehicle proving of quite sufficient size for the departing teacher's effects. For the school house had been partly furnished by the managers, and the only cumbersome article possessed by the master, in addition to the packing case of books, was a cottage piano that he had bought at an auction during the year in which he thought of learning instrumental music. But the enthusiasm having waned he had never acquired any skill in playing, and the purchase article had been a perpetual trouble to him ever since in moving house.

The rector had gone away for the day, being a man who disliked the sight of changes. He did not mean to return till the evening, when the new school-teacher would have arrived and settled in, and everything would be smooth again.

The blacksmith, the farm bailiff, and the schoolmaster himself were standing in perplexed attitudes in the parlour before the instrument. The master had remarked that even if he got it into the cart he should not know what to do with it on his arrival at Christminster, the city he was bound for, since he was only going into temporary lodgings just at first.

A little boy of eleven, who had been thoughtfully assisting in the packing, joined the group of men, and as they rubbed their chins he spoke up, blushing at the sound of his own voice:

'Aunt have got a great fuel-house, and it could be put there, perhaps, till you've found a place to settle in, sir.'

'A proper good notion', said the blacksmith.

It was decided that a deputation should wait on the boy's aunt – an old maiden resident – and ask her if she would house the piano till Mr Phillotson should send for it. The smith and the bailiff started to see the practicability of the suggested shelter, and the boy and the schoolmaster were left standing alone.

'Sorry I am going, Jude?' asked the latter kindly.

Tears rose into the boy's eyes, for he was not among the regular day scholars, who came unromantically close to the schoolmaster's life, but one who had attended the night school only during the present teacher's term of office. The regular scholars, if the truth must be told, stood at the present moment afar off, like certain historic disciples, indisposed to any enthusiastic volunteering of aid.

The boy awkwardly opened the book he held in his hand, which Mr Phillotson had bestowed on him as a parting gift, and admitted that he was sorry.

'So am I', said Mr Phillotson.

'Why do you go, sir?' asked the boy.

'Ah – that would be a long story. You wouldn't understand my reasons, Jude. You will, perhaps, when you are older.'

'I think I should now, sir.'

'Well – don't speak of this everywhere. You know what a university is, and a university degree? It is the necessary hall-mark of a man who wants to do anything in teaching. My scheme, or dream, is to be a university graduate, and then to be ordained. By going to live at Christminster, or near it, I shall be at headquarters, so to speak, and if my scheme is practicable at all, I consider that being on the spot will afford me a better chance of carrying it out than I should have elsewhere.'

The smith and his companion returned. Old Miss Fawley's fuel-house was dry, and eminently practicable; and she seemed willing to give the instrument standing room there. It was accordingly left in the school till the evening, when more hands would be available for removing it; and the schoolmaster gave a final glance round.

The boy Jude assisted in loading some small articles, and at nine o'clock Mr Phillotson mounted beside his box of books and other *impedimenta*, and bade his friends good-bye.

'I shan't forget you, Jude,' he said, smiling, as the cart moved off. 'Be a good boy, remember; and be kind to animals and birds, and read all you can. And if you ever come to Christminster remember you hunt me out for old acquaintance sake.'

The cart creaked across the green, and disappeared round the corner by the rectory-house. The boy returned to the draw-well at the edge of the greensward, where he had left his buckets when he went to help his patron and teacher in the loading. There was a quiver in his lip now, and after opening the well-cover to begin lowering the bucket he paused and leant with his forehead and arms against the frame-work, his face wearing the fixity of a thoughtful child's who has felt the pricks of life somewhat before his time. The well into which he was looking was as ancient as the village itself, and from his present position appeared as a long circular perspective ending in a shining disk of quivering water at a distance of a hundred feet down. There was a lining of green moss near the top, and nearer still the hart's-tongue fern.

He said to himself, in the melodramatic tones of a whimsical boy, that the schoolmaster had drawn at that well scores of times on a morning like this, and would never draw there any more. 'I've seen him look down into it, when he was tired, just as I do now, and when he rested a bit before carrying the buckets home. But he was too clever to bide here any longer – a small sleepy place like this!

A tear rolled from his eye into the depths of the well. The morning was a little foggy, and the boy's breathing unfurled itself as a thicker fog upon the still and heavy air. His thoughts were interrupted by a sudden outcry.

'Bring on that water, will ye, you idle young harlican!'

It came from an old woman who had emerged from her door towards the garden gate of a green-thatched cottage not far off. The boy quickly waved a signal of assent, drew the water with what was a great effort for one of his stature, landed and emptied the big bucket into his own pair of smaller ones, and pausing a moment for breath, started with them across the patch of clammy greensward whereon the well stood – nearly in the centre of the little village, or rather hamlet of Marygreen.

It was as old-fashioned as it was small, and rested in the lap of an undulating upland adjoining the North Wessex downs. Old as it was, however, the well-shaft was probably the only relic of the local history that remained absolutely unchanged. Many of the thatched and dormered dwelling houses had been pulled down of late years, and many trees felled on the green. Above all, the original church, hump-backed, wood-turreted, and quaintly hipped, had been taken down, and either cracked up into heaps of road-metal in the lane, or utilized as pig-sty walls, garden seats, guard-stones to fences, and rockeries in the flower-beds of the neighbourhood. In place of it a tall new building of modern gothic design, unfamiliar to English eyes, had been erected on a new piece of ground by a certain obliterator of historic records who had run down from London and back in a day. The site whereon so long had stood the ancient temple to the Christian divinities was not even recorded on the green and level grass plot that had immemorially been the church-yard, the obliterated graves being commemorated by eighteenpenny cast-iron crosses warranted to last five years. (Hardy, 1896, chapter I-i)

5.11

In the opening chapter, Hardy not only sets up the story, he also establishes the vital role of place in the novel. Having read the chapter, jot down the ideas and perspectives associated with:

- Marygreen
- Christminster
- London
- England

The novel begins by setting in motion a number of ideas which are going to be developed throughout the text. The community is losing its schoolmaster 'and everybody seemed sorry': the community is represented here by the blacksmith, a farm bailiff, the absent rector and a small boy. In itself this is a minor point but it does construct a place in which hierarchies exist (a farm bailiff collects rents and manages the land for a landowner) and in which the Church or, at least, its local representative is opposed to change. The community's sorrow is perhaps only superficial (the rector doesn't like change, so might be more angry than sad), but is genuinely felt by Jude, one of the teacher's night-school pupils who seems to be a favoured individual in as much as he has been given a present by the departing Mr Phillotson.

Phillotson is leaving because his ambition to achieve impels him to move closer to Christminster, where he may eventually become an undergraduate. This is regarded as a rather grand undertaking, and Phillotson asks Jude not to speak of his ambition publicly: thus intellectual advancement is set up as a subject for secrecy and embarrassment. The schoolmaster leaves having pledged to remember Jude and offered him the parting advice: 'be kind to animals and birds and read all you can'. These opening pages serve to establish some important facets of Jude's individuality: already we might identify a tacit opposition between Jude and the community he inhabits; for Jude, intellectual ability is now firmly in opposition to the culture of Marygreen; as he puts it, Phillotson 'was too clever to bide here any longer – a small sleepy place like this'.

As several commentators have pointed out, Jude is no simple peasant, and nor is Marygreen a crudely drawn cliché of rural England (Eagleton, 1974, p. 10). It is only its well that links the village to its history, for: 'Many of the thatched and dormered dwelling houses had been pulled down of late years and many trees felled on the green. Above all . . . the original church had been taken down, and either cracked up into road metal in the lane or utilised as pig sty walls, garden seats, guard stones to fences and rockeries.' This 'obliteration' of the historic centre of the village has occurred despite the rector disliking change and has, we note, been caused by a London architect. The chapter ends, then, by rewriting (albeit subtly) the placing of the church within this community: it now stands revealed as powerless; as no longer central. The last paragraph of the chapter changes the version of Marygreen we may have constructed at the start, and portrays a community in flux. Ironically, then, the act of moving away (of breaking up the village's social order) is not the oddity it might have at first seemed, as Marygreen stands revealed not as a seamless coherent 'community' but as a place that is in a state of near permanent flux.

5.12

You could continue your investigation of places and spaces in Hardy's novel by thinking about some of the following locations.

1   Christminster: part I, chapter 3; compare part II, chapter 6 (the Crossway), part III, chapter 8
2   Christminster: part II, chapter 1; compare part II, chapter 2
3   Melchester (esp. the Training School): part III, chapters 1, 3
4   Shaston: part IV, chapter 1; compare part IV, chapter 6 (as a space in which to read Sue and Phillotson?)

In your work on these locales you might like to concentrate upon the following issues:

● How a place shapes an individual's opinions
● How a place is used to help us understand how an individual feels
● Note the ways in which we are given access to the dominant meanings of a place
● Comment on the extent to which an individual is in conflict with the dominant ideologies of the place – does anyone ever get to represent the multiple voices

and identities that constitute particular places, or is the dominant view of a locale too powerful?

- Do the central characters suffer because they have a utopian view of the places they inhabit, which fails to take into account the competing versions through which it takes on meaning?
- You could also consider the ideologies associated with places outside of Wessex (for example, Australia or London) or examine the ways in which even seemingly minor places are woven into the thematic concerns of the novel – think about places like Aldbrickham or Stoke Barehills, and how they provide more than mere backdrops to the action.

Conclusions

Throughout this chapter we have focused upon the relationship between place and identity, and have drawn upon the work of social theorists and cultural geographers to help us to tease out the often complex ways in which human subjects interact with their physical environment. We have concentrated upon contemporary and historical examples mainly based in British culture, but many of the sources cited in the recommended further reading will help you to work on the intersection of place and identity in other cultures.

Our survey has not made much use of approaches to the geography of culture in terms of landscape studies. We have, however, tried to strike a balance between an engagement with the materiality of cultural experience and more abstract approaches to the processes at work in shaping individual identities. In this chapter we tackle one of the central problems for cultural studies: how to describe and analyse what is often fleeting, ephemeral and prosaic but none the less fundamental to the ways in which human subjects make sense of themselves and the world they inhabit. The importance of cultural geography to cultural studies is that it forcibly reminds us that a culture cannot be reduced to a set of discourses, but has to take account of the physical places in which those discourses operate. In order to explore some of these ideas further, you could do worse than reflect upon your own experience and understanding of a range of places and spaces – those you have lived in, those you have visited, those you have worked in, those you have imagined, those you have seen represented in pictures, films or TV, those you have read about, those you would like to visit, those you wouldn't, those that produce goods and services for you to purchase, those that are in the news. Think about the ways in which these places and spaces are linked in your consciousness – is it through memory or imagination, or through relatives, or by international media, or through what you buy? Think about the social relations that certain spaces produce (classrooms, for example) but also think about the ways in which a particular place or space could be produced as a result of a set of social relations (two friends sharing a house might produce a different 'place' to a married couple sharing a house). Some of the ideas in this chapter feed into discussions in chapters 6, 8 and 9, and there are suggestions for further reading if you are interested in this topic.

CHAPTER 6

Case Study 1. The Suburban Semi-detached in Interwar Britain

Introduction

This chapter comprises a case study in which you can begin to apply the concepts introduced in the previous five chapters: culture, identity, representation, history and cultural geography. We have chosen to focus on the suburban semi-detached houses built in Britain during the interwar period. The interwar 'semi' has been chosen for a number of reasons: it allows us to explore both history and geography, as well as identity and representation; a large number of these semi-detached houses can still be seen on the outskirts of most large towns and cities in Britain; and it has accrued, in its more than sixty-year history, a cluster of meanings that go beyond its practical function as medium to lower income housing. Before we try to make sense of all this, let us begin by thinking about how we 'read' or make sense of the interwar semi.

ACTIVITIES

6.1

Look at figure 6.1, which shows a typical street of semi-detached houses built in the 1930s.

What words, ideas or meanings come to mind when you look at this picture? Who lives in these houses? What do they do – for jobs, for leisure? Do they have children? Have you lived in a house like this? Would you like to? If you would, why? If not, why not? Have you come across any novels, films, TV dramas or sitcoms in which houses like these are featured? Make up a story about this street and the people who live there. Can you describe the interiors?

If you are not familiar with British culture you may have had difficulty with this activity. The reason for this may be that while the interwar semi-detached house is a feature of many British towns, the meanings that have adhered to this type of housing are closely associated with the dominance of 'Englishness' within the British cultural milieu of that epoch and later. It is not a well known object of global culture in the way that temples, Coca-Cola, McDonalds, Levi's or, even, English country houses are. Tourists do not generally flock to visit examples of

Figure 6.1   Elmer Gardens, Isleworth

this particular architecture, although, as we shall see later, this may change in the future. However, if you are familiar with British culture, you were probably able to make sense of the street, albeit in a number of different ways. This is because this particular house is an aspect of social knowledge that, for the most part, we take for granted. We are able to make sense of the picture because we share certain understandings about what it means. Few of you, we imagine, linked these houses with either wealth or abject poverty. Many of you will have peopled them with families and we wouldn't be surprised if a considerable number of you could draw a plan of the inside. Some of you may have ascribed a certain set of values to the people who live in this street. You may have found it a strange exercise and/or felt that it was all rather obvious. This is because making sense of these houses is something we are not often called upon to do. We don't need to explain or analyse them because 'everyone knows what they mean': their meanings are part of our generally unexamined 'common-sense' knowledge, part of our everyday understandings of the world we inhabit. Think back to chapter 1 and our discussion of 'what is culture?' The shared understandings, the 'everybody knows, it's obvious' feeling that *can* enable those of us familiar with British culture to 'interpret' the semi-detached house, even if we resist doing so, are culture in the sense of Williams's 'structure of feeling' and in du Gay's sense of meanings that are produced and circulated within society. The semi-detached house has no inherent meaning that is present in it simply as a physical object. Instead, the ways in which it can be understood are structured and framed within a network of meaning (when the houses were built and why, who lives in them, where they are, what they stand for) that is cultural. This network of meaning is produced from a range of discourses that enable us to understand and communicate ideas about, among other things, home, family, work and leisure, specific social identities and the nation.

For those who are less familiar with British culture, it is still possible to 'make sense' of the streets of semi-detached houses as a particularly English form of suburbia. Suburbs are to be found throughout the industrialized world. Los Angeles has five thousand square miles of suburbs, Brisbane's suburbs continue to expand across its large hinterland, the suburbs of Paris or Oslo are unlike those of England or Scotland, yet all are recognizably identifiable as suburbs (Thorns, 1972). Now read the short extract below and list the features which the author uses to define suburbia.

6.1

The plot sizes tend to be fairly uniform: often six or up to a dozen to the acre among those owned by the average wage-earner; the houses perhaps standing alone in a half, or even an acre of ground in the suburbs of the more affluent. Industries are seldom seen among them; golf courses are often closer at hand than are factories. But there are corner shops serving the neighbourhood and big stores can be reached by private or public transport in the downtown areas.

Progressively, the opening of malls and precincts and large, drive in shopping centres to serve the weekly needs of the suburbs are to be found throughout the United States and Canada, often in Australia, and with increasing frequency in Europe, including England. (Oliver et al., 1981, p. 11)

We shall explore the meanings signified by the particular form of suburbia found in England later in this chapter. For now the point to grasp is that 'suburbia' is not a specifically English concept but one common to industrialized countries, especially those in the West. The word 'suburb' originally comes from the Latin term, *sub urbe*, which means 'under city control'. Suburbs grew wherever and whenever there was a shift from a predominantly agricultural economy to a largely industrialized economy. As cities became centres of industry, finance and administration, housing for those who worked in the cities was built on the outskirts with transport links to the centre accompanying this building. In an agricultural economy people tended to live and work in the same place – home and work were not separated as they have become with industrialisation. In the industrialized world this separation has taken the form of out of town (suburban) housing from which people travel daily to their workplaces. In the more recently developed cities of Asia and Latin America, different patterns of suburban development have occurred. Read the description below of Mexico City and note the differences.

6.2

The major Latin American cities are similarly surrounded by large-scale shanty neighbourhoods, whose occupants include both recent migrants and families displaced from other sections by urban renewal and highway construction. In Mexico City, over a third of the population live in dwellings or neighbourhoods without running water, and nearly a quarter of these buildings lack sewerage. The city contains an old centre, business and entertainment districts, and affluent housing areas (which are all most tourists see). Almost all the outer perimeter, however, is occupied by shanty or slum dwellings. There is a large amount of state-subsidized housing, but this demands a level of income that no more than 40 per cent of the city's population can afford. Only about 10 per cent of the inhabitants are able to buy or rent on the private housing market. The majority of the city's population, therefore are excluded from access to available housing . . . Most housing is provided by the occupants themselves, who have cleared the land and built their own homes. The majority of these housing settlements are in fact illegal, but tolerated by the city authorities. (Giddens, 1989, p. 571)

Can you see the point we are making? Suburbanization has occurred in many industrialized areas of the world, notably the United States, Australia, Britain and Western Europe. However, despite similar patterns of development, the forms and, most importantly for our analysis, the meanings that have attached themselves to these forms are diverse. Nor should we forget that suburbanization may be, for a number of reasons, a geographically and historically specific pattern. The description of the way in which Mexico City has developed bears little resemblance to the common features identified in the (earlier) growth of suburbia in Western Europe or the United States. When you come to consider the English 'semi' in its suburban setting it is important to locate it globally. It is one form of suburbia among many in the world, producing specific meanings and identities for those who live there, as well as for those who represent its meanings in language and discourse. The English suburban semi of the interwar period was a local response to a transnational phenomenon.

Because, as we argued above, the semi-detached house is a cultural product – that is, it becomes meaningful within a network of interpretation – we can analyse and explore how it has become **inscribed** in popular or collective knowledge and what this process can tell us about the production of social knowledge. The rest of this chapter is devoted to exploring questions about the ways in which these houses have been represented in language and discourse; questions about how the geographical location of these houses contributes to their meanings and to the organization of housing space generally; and questions about how certain social groupings and lifestyles have become associated with these particular houses. In attempting to answer these questions we shall necessarily engage with a historical perspective and questions about how we can 'know' what these homes meant in the past. Moreover, we can extend the discussion of heritage from chapter 4, as a late nineteenth-century example of a suburban semi-detached was recently left to the National Trust. We begin our analysis by briefly sketching out the historical circumstances in which these homes were designed and built.

The story of the semi

6.3

Between the two world wars new shapes on the ground began to appear all over England on the edges of towns and cities, in the suburbs, along the arterial roads, in the coastal resorts and even in the remote villages, which by their number and external similarity might seem to suggest to an outside observer that some new race or class had suddenly appeared, clamorous for accommodation. In the development of English housing types, middle-class housing of the inter-war period, most typically represented by the semi-detached villa situated in a newly developed suburban area, seems to mark a disjunction with the past, and an entry into a new era of mass housing still today the most characteristic expression of English domestic architecture. It has been estimated that about half the population of Britain now lives in suburbs, and that of these the largest proportion lives in houses which are semi-detached, three-bedroomed dwellings.

Such housing was, in fact, the response of the building industry to the needs of a middle class which had greatly swollen in size but was poorer than its Edwardian predecessor . . .

Between the wars private building made a remarkable effort to meet the housing demands of this group, extending the possibility of home-ownership well down into the lower middle classes and even into the upper levels of the working classes. By the 1930s, a regular salary or wage of £200 a year was widely regarded as adequate security for a mortgage which might involve repayments of as little as 9s [45p] a week, well within the reach of engineers, fitters, printers, engine-drivers and other skilled workers. New houses have probably never been so cheap or so widely available as in the mid-thirties, when, it has been calculated, the length of time that a man earning the average industrial wage would have to work in order to buy one was 2.5 years. In total between 1919 and 1939, 3,998,000 new houses were built, 2,886,000 by private builders and 1,112,000 by local authorities. Starting practically from standstill in 1919 after five years' dislocation by war, the building industry delivered no fewer than 1,617,000 houses in the boom period 1935–9, with private-enterprise housing reaching particular peaks of 287,500 houses in 1935 and 275,000 in 1937. Thus some 72 per cent of all houses built between the wars were built by private enterprise, and of these the vast majority were built for sale rather than rent. The consequence was an important shift in the tenure of property towards house-ownership. (Burnett, 1986, pp. 250–2)

6.2

- What are the main reasons John Burnett gives for the emergence of the 'semi-detached villa' as a new form of domestic architecture?
- What does he see as the historical significance of this phenomenon?

Burnett claims that the efforts of private builders to provide semi-detached houses in suburban areas was a response to the needs of a particular social group: the middle class. In the 1930s mortgages were cheap and, for those in work, particularly in the South East of England and the Midlands, salaries and wages were gradually increasing. The effect of this building boom, according to Burnett, was twofold: a shift from a housing market that dealt predominantly in rented housing or accommodation to one based on home ownership and 'entry into a new era of mass housing' that was to change the landscape of British cities, towns, seaside resorts and even villages. For Burnett, the advent of the semi-detached house heralded major social and topographical change. As students of culture we will want to ask if and how these changes were interrelated, what meanings were thus produced (for example, about home ownership, domesticity, social status) and how these were represented in the discourses of the period. We might also think it is worth asking questions about the role of culture in shaping the circumstances in which about half the population of England came to live in the suburbs (Oliver et al, 1982, p. 9). The development of suburban estates did not simply produce new meanings about home ownership and domesticity; these estates came into being, in part, because of new meanings in the period about home and family, about social responsibility and about citizenship. The interaction between culture (meanings), social practices (home ownership and identity formation) and physical environment (houses, landscape) is best represented as a circle rather than a straight line of cause and effect. At whatever point you start on the circle you are connected to all the other points: there is no one starting point, nor is there an end point. One thing does not precede another but interacts to create a circular or web effect (see figure 6.2).

We shall need to examine the geography of suburbia and the social practices not only of home ownership, but also of suburban living, but before we do so let us explore what the houses were like, why they were designed in the way they were and who built them. In other words we are going to look at how they were

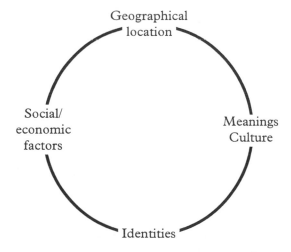

Figure 6.2   A circle of interaction

produced before we consider how they were **consumed** (lived in, understood) and represented.

Burnett's account suggests that builders responded to a perceived need for a certain kind of housing by a particular social group. This was undoubtedly the case: there was a housing shortage after the First World War and increased wages for some made home ownership a very real possibility. However, it also needs to be remembered that builders needed to make a profit and that private investors with funds in house-building enterprises demanded a return on their investment. Before the First World War, investment in housing consisted in the main of buying properties for rent. Soaring building costs, high interest rates and restrictions on the rents that could be charged rendered investment in properties for rent financially unattractive. As a result, private investment went into building societies, and builders found the market for their properties diminishing. In the immediate post-war period government subsidies were made available to builders to encourage private enterprise house building in order to meet the housing shortage. In economic terms, the increased building society funds available for mortgages and government aid with building costs combined to produce a buoyant market for house builders and favourable conditions for would-be purchasers (Rowntree, 1941, pp. 223–4; Bentley, 1981a, pp. 70–1).

The three bedroomed semi-detached was the most common type of house built between the wars by private builders. It consisted of a hall with doors off to a separate parlour, dining-room and small kitchen, three bedrooms, one often only big enough to hold a baby's cot, a bathroom and toilet, and gardens back and front. Many had space to erect a garage and a driveway for a car. The most common design, which can be seen on the arterial roads of any largish town, had bay windows at the front and a canopied front door. These houses differed from what had gone before in having lighter, sunnier rooms, amenties such as hot water and electricity and larger gardens. The Victorian terraced house had more space, to accommodate larger families and domestic servants, but was frequently dark, difficult to keep clean and lacking in 'modern' amenities such as a streamlined kitchen or electric light and heating.

The semi-detached was designed to house a smaller family with no or fewer servants. From the late nineteenth century onwards, family size in Britain had been falling. A middle-class family in 1930 were likely to have no more than two children, as opposed to the five or more common sixty years earlier. The large Victorian households with a full staff of servants were disappearing as young women found alternative employment and as middle-class incomes made it difficult to sustain such households. The semi was designed in contrast to the older terraced villa of the Victorian suburbs – it was well ventilated and lit and designed to be run without the help of servants. Equally importantly, semi-detached housing was located on the outskirts of city and town centres, providing a semi-rural environment in which people could escape the hazards and pressures of urban life. Semi-detached houses proved extremely popular and by the mid-thirties it seemed likely that market saturation was within reach – all those who could afford and wanted such a property had bought one (Oliver *et al.*, 1981, p. 74).

6.3

In order to consolidate your reading, list the social and economic factors that were influential in the construction of the semi. To help you we have provided headings under which you could group different factors.

- Economic/financial
- Demographic, i.e. changes in population and household size
- Housing design
- Other

The geography of English suburbia

6.4

Look carefully at the two maps reproduced in figures 6.3 and 6.4. These are of the village of Northfield in 1917 and 1936. Northfield is approximately five miles from Birmingham city centre. List the differences between the two. What do these maps tell us about Northfield in 1917 and 1936?

The most obvious difference is the proliferation of new housing, particularly along the main road (Bristol Road South). Pigeon House has disappeared, The Grange has become a hotel, Cock Lane has been renamed Frankley Beeches Road and new roads have been built to serve residential housing: Sylvan Avenue, Hill Top Road, Park View Road. A pub, the Black Horse, has appeared, as well as the swimming baths opposite, and a tram line has been installed along the length of Bristol Road. The 1917 map represents a predominantly rural area dominated by large houses (The Grange, Beechcroft, Quarry House) and farms: the 1936 map represents an environment functioning as a mainly residential area with associated transport networks and leisure facilities. Maps, as we discussed in chapter 5, do not simply describe and record certain features of geography, they represent the ways in which geographical locations are also social places. As Nigel Thrift points out, 'we do not live our lives in a space which is made up of locations which are simply neutral coordinates. We live in *places*. The difference between location and place is that places have meanings for us which cannot be reduced to their location' (Thrift, 1997, p. 160).

Northfield is not simply a geographical space: it is a place which has meant different things to different people at different times. At one time it was understood by those who lived there as the north field; later, as church and houses were established, it was known as the village of Northfield; from the 1900s onwards it became the suburb of Northfield and part of the City of Birmingham as the city boundaries were extended to encompass it. Yet the older meanings remain as traces both on the landscape and in the perceptions of those who live in Northfield. For example, the church still exists as a reminder that once it was the centre of the

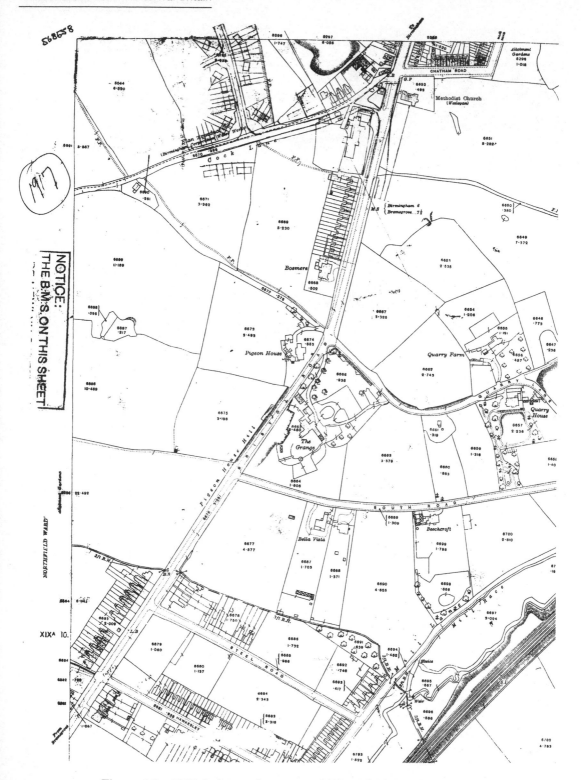

Figure 6.3   1917 Ordnance Survey map of Northfield, Birmingham

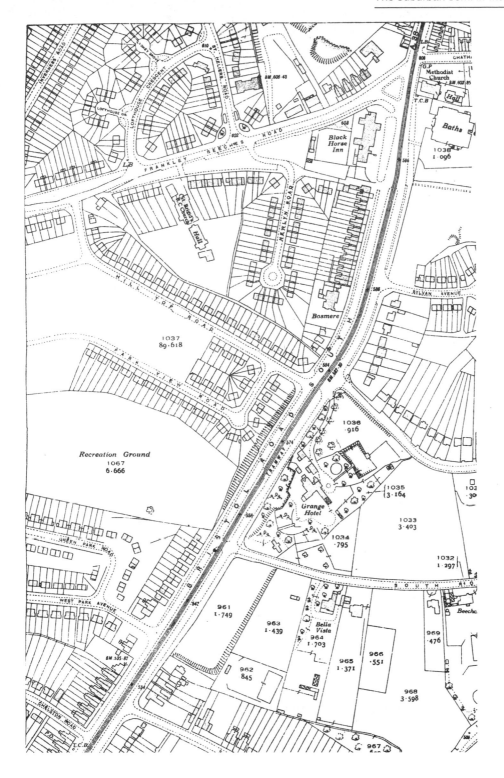

Figure 6.4 1936 Ordnance Survey map of Northfield, Birmingham

village; road names suggest previous uses of the land (Mill Lane, for example); local historians have produced pamphlets and books on the history of Northfield; and, as recently as ten years ago, older people living in the area would talk of 'going to the village' when they went to the shopping parade on the main road. The ways in which the environment, Northfield, changed between 1917 and 1936 were experienced socially and culturally as well as physically, by those who witnessed and were involved in the changes.

6.5

Can you speculate as to how different groups might have understood the changes? What arguments for or against the changes might they have put forward?

- The various economic interests: private builders, local authorities that began to provide council housing in Northfield, the brewery that built the Black Horse, the farmers and landowners who had land to sell.
- The city planners and officials who were involved in policy decisions about the regulation and provision of services to the area: for example, water, electricity, transport, swimming baths.
- The people who moved out from the city centre to live in the new housing.
- Those people who had lived in the area before its development as a residential area and continued to live there.
- Those who were able to find work on the buses and trams which ran along Bristol Road.
- The clergy involved in the churches in the area.
-
-
-

All of these groups will have understood the suburbanization of Northfield from different perspectives, but they will also have drawn on shared meanings about suburbanization to rationalize decisions made and to make sense of their experience. This nexus of shared meanings, individual experience, economic interest, policy decisions and geographical location produces the **created environment** known as the suburb of Northfield. You will recall that in chapter 3 we argued that representation is one of the ways in which meanings are produced and that meanings are circulated and shared in discourse. In the next section we can begin to explore the role of representation and discourse in producing and circulating certain meanings about suburbia. Before you start on this section it might be useful to remind yourself of the discussion in chapter 3.

Representing suburbia

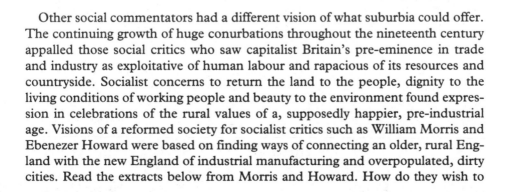

6.4

In 1909, C. F. G. Masterman, author, journalist and Liberal politician, wrote of those he called 'the Suburbans'.

They form a homogenous civilization – detached, self-centred, unostentatious – covering the hills along the northern and southern boundaries of the city [London], and spreading their conquests over the quiet fields beyond. They are the peculiar product of England and America: of the nations which have pre-eminently added commerce, business and finance to the work of manufacture and agriculture. It is a life of Security: a life of Sedentary occupation; a life of Respectability; and these three qualities give the key to its special characteristics. Its male population is engaged in all its working hours in small, crowded offices, under artificial light, doing immense sums, adding up other men's accounts, writing other men's letters. It is sucked into the City at daybreak and scattered again as darkness falls. It finds itself towards evening in its own territory in the miles and miles of little red houses in little, silent streets, in number defying imagination. Each boasts its pleasant drawing-room, its bow-window, its little front garden, its high-sounding title – 'Acacia Villa' or 'Camperdown Lodge' – attesting unconquered human aspiration. The women, with their single domestic servants, now so difficult to get, and so exacting when found, find time hangs rather heavy on their hands. But there are excursions to shopping centres in the West End, and pious sociabilities, and occasional theatre visits, and the interests of home. The children are jolly, well-fed, intelligent English boys and girls, full of curiosity, at least in earlier years. (Masterman, 1909, pp. 57–8)

6.6

- What are the main characteristics of 'the Suburbans' as identified by Masterman?
- What do you think is Masterman's attitude to this group? For example, does he approve of them? Pay careful attention to the tone of voice he adopts in this extract.

Other social commentators had a different vision of what suburbia could offer. The continuing growth of huge conurbations throughout the nineteenth century appalled those social critics who saw capitalist Britain's pre-eminence in trade and industry as exploitative of human labour and rapacious of its resources and countryside. Socialist concerns to return the land to the people, dignity to the living conditions of working people and beauty to the environment found expression in celebrations of the rural values of a, supposedly happier, pre-industrial age. Visions of a reformed society for socialist critics such as William Morris and Ebenezer Howard were based on finding ways of connecting an older, rural England with the new England of industrial manufacturing and overpopulated, dirty cities. Read the extracts below from Morris and Howard. How do they wish to solve the problems of large cities? The first reading is taken from William Morris's *News from Nowhere* (1890), in which he presents his utopian vision of a reformed England. In this passage the narrator is being told about the ways in which the utopian society of Nowhere has combined the best of town and country and solved the problem of urban sprawl. The second extract is by Ebenezer Howard, whose *Garden Cities of Tomorrow*, published in 1902, set out his vision of a 'social city' based on the principles of cooperative ownership.

6.5

As to the big murky places which were once, as we know, the centres of manufacture, they have, like the brick and mortar desert of London, disappeared . . . People flocked into the country villages, and, so to say, flung themselves upon the freed land like a wild beast upon his prey; and in a very little time the villages of England were more populous than they had been since the fourteenth century, and were still growing fast. Of course, this invasion of the country was awkward to deal with, and would have created much misery, if the folk had still been under the bondage of class monopoly. But as it was, things soon righted themselves. People found out what they were fit for, and gave up attempting to push themselves into occupations in which they must needs fail. The town invaded the country; but the invaders, like the warlike invaders of early days, yielded to the influence of their surroundings, and became country people; and in their turn, as they became more numerous than the townsmen, influenced them also; so that the difference between town and country grew less and less; and it was indeed this world of the country vivified by the thought and briskness of town-bred folk which has produced that happy and leisurely but eager life of which you have had a first taste . . .

England was once a country of clearings amongst the woods and wastes, with a few towns interspersed, which were fortresses for the feudal army, markets for the folk, gathering places for the craftsmen. It then became [in the nineteenth century] a country of huge and foul workshops and fouler gambling-dens, surrounded by an ill-kept, poverty-stricken farm, pillaged by the masters of the workshops. It is now a garden, where nothing is wasted and nothing is spoilt, with the necessary dwellings, sheds, and workshops scattered up and down the country, all trim and neat and pretty. (Morris, 1890, pp. 58–61)

And this principle of growth – this principle of always preserving a belt of country round our cities would be ever kept in mind till, in course of time, we should have a cluster of cities . . . grouped around a Central City that each inhabitant of the whole group, though in one sense living in a town of small size, would be in reality living in, and would enjoy all the advantages of, a great and most beautiful city; and yet all the fresh delights of the country – field, hedgerow, and woodland – not prim parks and gardens merely – would be within a very few minutes walk or ride. And *because the people in their collective capacity own the land* on which this beautiful group of cities is built, the public buildings, the churches, the schools and universities, the libraries, picture galleries, theatres, would be on a scale of magnificence which no city in the world whose land is in pawn to private individuals can afford. (Howard, 1902, p. 142, original emphasis; extracted in Giles and Middleton, 1995, p. 199)

You will have noticed that both writers emphasize the importance of combining the best of rural and urban life to provide an environment that can justly be called 'garden' Morris calls his reformed England 'a garden' and Howard uses the term as the title for his book. The Garden City Movement, pioneered by Howard, had notable successes at Bournville in Birmingham and New Earswick in York, both suburbs developed on garden city lines by the chocolate manufacturers, Cadburys and Rowntree, in the early part of the twentieth century. Yet much suburban development of the interwar period owed more to speculative interest on the part of private enterprise than to Howard's and Morris's principles of collective ownership. As economic recession deepened and government subsidies dwindled, builders were more concerned with cutting costs than with adhering to garden city principles.

6.7

Study figure 6.5 carefully. It is one of a series of advertisements by London Transport promoting the pleasures of suburban life. What meanings and values are encoded in this advertisement? Does it address a particular social group? Whose vision of suburbia does it seem closer to: that of Masterman or that of Morris and Howard or neither? Is it possible to read against the dominant meaning? If necessary, remind yourself how to answer this by referring back to activity 3.4 and the ensuing discussion of encoding and decoding. We have given you some headings under which to organize your responses.

- Subject matter: what does the picture depict?
- Connotations: list all the ideas that you associate with the images in the advertisement.
- Narrative: can you make up a story around this picture? What happened before and what might happen next?
- Written text: how does this link to the visual images?
- Style: can you say anything about the way it is drawn? Look, for example, at the shapes, lines, light and shade, perspective etc.

The images are rural and idealized: trees, a winding road, rosebushes and sunflowers, and a cottage-style house with lattice windows, half-timbering and dormer windows. Copy from a poem by the eighteenth-century poet William Cowper is inserted to anchor the meanings of the images. Entitled 'Sanctuary', the poem extols the tranquillity of rural life. It is significant that the words of an eighteenth-century poet have been chosen: Cowper (1731–1800) lived and wrote much of his poetry before the full consequences of nineteenth-century industrialization had been realized. Cowper represents, in this advertisement, a rural, pre-industrial England that, although lost, can be, at least in part, recovered by living in a suburb such as Golders Green. Thus suburban Golders Green is represented as a peaceful, domestic haven in a timeless, semi-rural setting; one that is welcoming to young families and close enough to the workplaces of the city. Above all, of course, this idyll has been made possible by London Transport, with its quick and accessible train service to London.

Figure 6.5   Golders Green London Transport poster, early 1900s

However, it does seem as if there are certain contradictions that could allow for alternative readings. Foremost is the fact that in order to savour the delights of Golders Green it is necessary to use the very technology (the railway) that, at least in part, destroyed the particular aspects of rural life being celebrated here – peace, tranquillity and sanctuary. At the same time, while the advertisement appears to endorse a nostalgic return to a lost Arcadia,[1], its style is predominantly modern, relying as it does on sharp, clean lines, geometric shapes and bright, clear colours. The caption 'A Place of Delightful Prospects' is also ambiguous. On the one hand, the word 'prospects' can refer to the view, but it can, of course, also refer to possibilities for career promotion, as in the phrase 'career prospects'. Is the advertisement suggesting that a move to the suburbs can improve your job prospects as well as providing a haven of domestic tranquillity? Finally, if you look up William Cowper in a reference work such as *The Oxford Companion to English Literature*, you will discover that he suffered from periodic bouts of suicidal depression, requiring treatment in various asylums, throughout his life. Once this is known, the phrase 'A Place of Delightful Prospects' appears highly ironic, especially as we know that for some people, particularly women, suburban life could lead to depression and anxiety. It is also a reminder that using reference books to find out more about people, captions, phrases, historical events etc. can sometimes provoke interesting lines of thought. This exercise should have given you some insights into how advertisers were able to use the rural utopianism of the Garden City Movement to promote the use of suburban transport and the purchase of suburban homes. At the same time, the advertisement appears to be suggesting that the purchase of a home at Golders Green promises the detached and aspirational lifestyle satirized by Masterman, rather than the communitarian spirit envisioned by Howard and Morris.

London Transport were not the only people to use rural nostalgia to sell suburbia. House builders extolled the advantages of 'healthy drudge-less living', in which the benefits of modern technology combined with rural beauty to offer 'a site of unspoilt beauty, modern convenience, dependable services', where it was possible to 'open your window to the tonic air of Kent's healthiest estates' (advertisements for suburban housing estates cited in Oliver *et al.*, 1981, pp. 85, 95). Names such as Belmore Farm, Selsdon Garden Village, Perivale Wood and Palmers Green reinforced the link with a bygone rurality and tapped into what were believed to be the desires of second-or third-generation city dwellers for their rural roots. Look back at the 1936 map of Northfield and note the names of the new residential streets. If you are able, note the names used for new housing estates in the area you live. Do they continue to draw on the idea of a rural past? Housewives, and no doubt their husbands, were more pragmatic. Suburbia, for them, represented an attractive, healthy environment in which it was possible to enjoy the benefits of labour-saving homes and to raise children safe from the pollution and crime of the city. Many working-class women who had watched their mothers struggle against the dirt and overcrowding of inner-city housing aspired to the better living conditions offered in suburbia, even if it meant financial sacrifices (Giles, 1995).

---

[1] Arcadia was the idealized location of the pastoral for writers from the Renaissance onwards.

As suburban development expanded throughout the twenties and thirties, a number of social commentators continued Masterman's satiric attack on the 'Suburbans'. It is worth spending some time identifying what it was about the suburbs that repelled so many writers of the period.

6.6

The first extract is by an architect, Clough Williams-Ellis, written in 1928.

Everyone knows that England has changed violently and enormously within the last few decades. Since the War, indeed, it has been changing with an acceleration that is catastrophic, thoroughly frightening the thoughtful amongst us, and making them sadly wonder whether anything recognizable of our lovely England will be left for our children's children . . . For – need it be said? – it is chiefly the spate of mean building all over the country that is shrivelling up the old England – mean and perky little houses that surely none but mean and perky little souls should inhabit with satisfaction. (Clough Williams-Ellis, quoted in Burnett, 1986, p. 273)

The second reading is by the journalist, novelist and critic J. B. Priestley, from his book *English Journey*, which charts his travels around England in the 1930s. Priestley is describing his experience of taking a tram journey along one of the arterial roads out of Birmingham City Centre.

Then followed one of the most depressing little journeys I ever remember making . . . In two minutes its [Birmingham's] civic dignity, its metropolitan airs, had vanished; and all it offered me, mile after mile, was a parade of mean dinginess . . . I only know that during the half-hour or so I sat staring through the top windows of that tram, I saw nothing, not one single tiny thing, that could possibly raise a man's spirits. Possibly what I was seeing was not Birmingham but our urban and industrial civilization. The fact remains that it was beastly. It was so many miles of ugliness, squalor, and the wrong kind of vulgarity, the decayed anaemic kind . . . For there was nothing, I repeat, to light up a man's mind for one single instant. I loathed the whole long array of shops, with their nasty bits of meat, their cough mixtures, the *Racing Specials*, their sticky cheap furniture, their shoddy clothes, their fly-blown pastry, their coupons and sales and lies and dreariness and ugliness. I asked myself if this really represented the level reached by all those people down there on the pavements. I am too near them myself, not being one of the sensitive plants of contemporary authorship, to believe that it does represent their level. They have passed it. They have gone on and it is not catching up. Why were the newest and largest buildings all along this route either picture theatres or pubs? (Priestley, 1934, pp. 85–6)

The third extract is from an article in *The Lancet* by Dr Stephen Taylor. In this article Dr Taylor identifies what he calls 'the suburban neurosis', a neurosis suffered, he claims, by many women who live in the suburbs. He lists some of the presenting symptoms. These include a lump in the throat, trembling, continuous headache, a swollen stomach, back pain, shortness of breath, insomnia and weight loss. The article offers reasons for these psychosomatic symptoms.

Let me translate this miserable little story into medical jargon. The deep seated aetio-logical factors of the suburban neurosis are, no doubt, extremely complex. The stom-ach which swells represents perhaps an unconscious urge to further motherhood, the sleepless nights a longing for a full sex life. Existence in the suburbs is such that the self-preserving, race-preserving and herd instincts can be neither adequately satisfied nor sublimated . . .

The superficial causes are as follows: –

1. *Boredom* occasioned by –

(a) *Lack of friends* – Few who have not worked or lived in the suburbs can realise the intense loneliness of their unhappy inhabitants. There is no common meeting ground like the pub and the street of the slum dwellers, and the golf and tennis club of the middle classes. There is no community of interest such as is found in the village. Lack of individual enterprise, shyness and bashfulness prevent calling, and the striking up of friendships. It is respectable to keep oneself to oneself. The Englishman's home is still his castle, but for the Englishwoman too often her gaol . . .

We have, I fear, let matters go too far in the jerry-building, ribbon-development line to institute an entirely satisfactory prophylaxis. We have allowed the slum which stunted the body to be replaced by a slum which stunts the mind. Perhaps, like a pack of cards, these rotten little houses will in due course collapse. Perhaps, when the children grow up, they will break down the barriers which separate family from fam-ily. But even this hope may prove false. Instead, the child may see through the values of its family and come to despise it. Or its over-proud parents may push it into a job for which is it intellectually unqualified – and one more neurotic will be launched on its way . . .

The prevention of the suburban neurosis, then, is in the hands of the social workers and politicians. And if they require a purely self stimulus, one would remind them that, in the latent feelings and strivings of the new mental slum-dwellers, there is waiting a most hopeful field for the teachers of new, and possibly dangerous, political ideologies.
(Taylor, 1938, reprinted in Giles and Middleton, 1995, pp. 230–9)

The final extract is from the novel *Coming up for Air* (1939) by George Orwell, in which the narrator, George Bowling, an insurance salesman, living in suburbia, tries to make sense of his life as the Second World War looms.

Do you know the road I live in – Ellesmere Road, West Bletchley? Even if you don't, you know fifty others exactly like it.

You know how these streets fester all over the inner-outer suburbs. Always the same. Long, long rows of little semi-detached houses – the numbers in Ellesmere Road run to 212 and ours is 191 – as much alike as council houses and generally uglier. The stucco front, the creosoted gate, the privet hedge, the green front door. The Laurels, the Myrtles, the Hawthorns, Mon Abri, Mon Repos, Belle Vue. At perhaps one house in fifty some anti-social type who'll probably end in the workhouse has painted his front door blue instead of green . . . We're all respectable householders – that's to say Tories, yes-men, and bumsuckers. Daren't kill the goose that lays the gilded eggs! And the fact that actually we aren't householders, that we're all in the middle of paying for our houses and eaten up with the ghastly fear that something might happen before we've made the last payment, merely increases the effect. Every one of those poor downtrodden bastards, sweating his guts out to pay twice the proper price for a brick doll's house that's called Belle Vue because there's no view and the bell doesn't ring – every one of those poor suckers would die on the field of battle to save his country from Bolshevism. (Orwell, 1939, pp. 13–14)

6.8

- Can you identify the aspects of suburbia that are of concern to these writers? Pay particular attention to the language and images used. What do they tell us about the writers' attitudes?
- What is your response to these writers' views on suburbia? Do you agree with them? Do you feel they are unreasonable? Do you think they are partly true but . . .?
- What do you understand by the term 'suburban' today? Can you think of recent or contemporary TV programmes, films or books that use suburbia as a location? If you can, how is suburbia represented in these?
- Taylor suggests that women are more likely to display 'neurotic' symptoms as a result of living in suburbia than men. How do you respond to this?

All these writers stress the uniformity of suburbia – its sameness and its monotony. All of them, although they express it in different ways, are concerned that the uniformity and monotony, the 'meanness', of suburbia is linked to a spiritual and moral bankruptcy, which Taylor suggests may express itself as mental illness. As Orwell's George Bowling remarks at the end of *Coming up for Air*, 'Nothing's real in Ellesmere Road except gas bills, school fees, boiled cabbage and the office on Monday' (Orwell, 1939, p. 231). For these writers, and the many who sympathized with them, suburbia represented the values of acquistiveness, detachment, respectability and conformity – a moral desert in which individuality allied to spiritual and aesthetic sensibility was dead. For all the writers this moral void is also linked to national and political identity: 'the shrivelling up' of 'our lovely England', the 'beastly . . . ugliness' of 'our urban and industrial civilization' or, in Orwell's vision, the reduction of heroic patriots to 'poor suckers' who would 'die on the field of battle to save his country from Bolshevism'. Unlike Orwell, Taylor suggests that the suburbs, rather than producing political acquiescence to the status quo, may in fact provide the breeding ground for 'dangerous' ideologies. In 1938 he would have had in mind fascism and communism. Taylor also suggests that there are gender differences in responses to suburbia. In the early 1960s, Betty Friedan, an American feminist, drew her analysis of women's oppression from her observations of women living in the suburbs of the USA. She identified their dissatisfaction with their lives as 'the problem that has no name' (Friedan, 1965).

Two other writers, the cartoonist and illustrator, Osbert Lancaster and the poet, John Betjeman, envisaged, in tongue-in-cheek mode, a drastic solution to the 'problem' of suburbia,

It is sad to reflect that so much ingenuity should have been wasted on streets and estates which will eventually become the slums of the future. That is, if a fearful and more sudden fate does not obliterate them prematurely, an eventuality that does much to reconcile one to the prospect of aerial bombardment. (Lancaster, quoted in Oliver *et al.*, 1981, p. 46).

Come, friendly bombs, and fall on Slough;
It isn't fit for humans now,
There isn't grass to graze a cow
Swarm over, Death!
(Betjeman, 1937, p. 24)

The ways in which the writers and advertisers that we have just discussed represented suburbia have to be understood in relation to other discourses of the period: for example, of home and family and of modern 'mass' society. We can only attend briefly to these in the space provided, but if you wish to take this further you will find plenty of ideas in the suggestions for further reading. Let us take home and family first.

The First World War had revealed that a great many of the young recruits conscripted for armed service were medically unfit. As a result, successive governments throughout the twenties and thirties, as well as social reformers and the medical profession, were concerned to improve the general health of the nation's citizens. There was general agreement that the best place to achieve this was through concentrating on childcare, preventative hygiene in the home and improved housing. Mothers were targeted as the people who could most readily achieve these improvements through attention to cleanliness, nutrionally balanced meals and careful monitoring of their children's progress. Where they were 'uneducated' in mothercraft, as it came to be called, health visitors and infant welfare clinics would provide guidance and advice. Motherhood was extolled as a social responsibility and a service to one's country. As one childcare manual proclaimed, 'take care of the babies and the nation will take care of itself' (*The Motherhood Book*, 1934, p. 752). Although this period was not unique in linking home and nation, it did so in ways which focused on physical care and the physical environment. Home was increasingly seen as the foundation of good health and stable citizenship. The attraction of suburbia for so many families has to be understood in relation to this discourse of domesticity. Moreover, in the immediate aftermath of the First World War, decent homes were represented as a reward for returning servicemen. The slogan 'homes fit for heroes' fed into the very real needs of men returning from the horrors of active service – home offered safety, solace and respite, as well as a much-earned reward. The dominant discourse of home in the period was one that emphasized safety, security, health and a better future for the nation's citizens, newly enfranchised by the 1918 Representation of the People Act. This way of thinking about home was commonly held, even by those political groupings – for example, feminism – who might have been expected to oppose it (Beddoe, 1989; Light, 1991; Bourke, 1994; Giles, 1995).

As we saw in chapter 1, the Cambridge academics F. R. and Q. D. Leavis expressed concern in this period about the growth of 'mass' culture. This anxiety, which was common among the intelligentsia of the day, extended itself to the new institutions of 'mass' society. In particular, this anxiety focused on a more comprehensive education system and the newly established centres of cultural power, such as the enormously influential newspaper owners, Hollywood and radio broadcasting, over which the traditional intellegentsia, formed in Oxbridge and the public schools and linked by kinship ties from birth, had little control. There were two predominant discourses of cultural change in the period and it very much depended on where and how one positioned oneself as to whether the products of democratization and culture were represented as, pessimistically, 'mass' or, more optimistically, 'modern'. Within the discourse of 'mass' culture the suburban semi could symbolize the worst manifestations of 'mass' aesthetics, marking a new boundary between the 'middlebrow' tastes of the general population and the 'highbrow' concerns of the professionally educated (Baxendale and Pawling, 1996, pp. 20–1, 48–50). Within the 'modern' discourse of culture suburbia represented progress, a break with Victorianism and its attendant squalor and poverty.

We hope that we have shown you something of the variety of meanings that **mediated** the geographical location known as suburbia and the discourses within which these were understood. We have summarized some of these meanings for you below and suggest that you spend some time linking these to the two discourses outlined above.

- Suburbia was a geographical location under the general control of the city but developed on what was previously the countryside.
- Suburbia combined the convenience of urban living with the advantages of the countryside – *rus in urbe* or the the country in the city.
- A well planned suburban environment based on collective ownership of land would produce garden cities, which would enhance, rather than destroy, the landscape.
- Suburbia could provide a healthy environment in which to live and rear children.
- Suburbia offered a tranquil sanctuary away from the noise, disorder and pollution of the city.
- Suburban homes offered improved design and the amenities of modern technology.
- Suburbia produced homogeneity and conformity.
- Suburban streets were aesthetically unpleasing, 'ugly' and monotonous. The houses were badly designed and cheaply built.
- The monotony and conformity of suburbia killed individuality.
- Suburbia was fertile ground for the growth of political ideologies such as fascism or communism.
- Suburbia was a moral desert in which spiritual sensibility had been replaced by the values of acquisitiveness and a spurious gentility, particularly in women.
- Life in a suburban environment might lead to mental illness.
- Suburbia was particularly stifling for women.
- Private enterprise 'duped the masses' into purchasing homes on mortgages, thereby ensuring their continued acquiesence to the social structures of capitalism.

6.9

Do you think any one meaning is more dominant than the others: (a) then; (b) now? How do these meanings relate to or conflict with the discourses discussed above. We have started you off with examples.

- Taylor's concern with the mental health of women in suburbia could contradict the discourse of motherhood as a fulfilling service to the nation.
- The idea of suburbia as a moral desert seems to link with the pessimistic discourse of 'mass' society.
-
-
-
-

The semi-detached, identity and individuality

Places, as you will recall from chapters 2 and 5, are spaces where identities are formed, whether they be national or social: in Thrift's words (above) 'places have meanings for us'. In this section we can begin to explore how far the identities represented by the writers above (lonely misfit, neurotic, smug materialist, for example) were lived out in the suburbs and to what extent these representations can be challenged. Let us begin by identifying who precisely inhabited suburbia.

In 1949, Roy Lewis and Angus Maude published 'a critical survey of the history, present conditions and prospects of the middle classes, from whom come most of the nation's brains, leadership and organizing ability'. In *The English Middle Class* they state that 'a fairly high proportion of the houses built by private enterprise between the wars went to the middle classes' (Lewis and Maude, 1949, p. 169). According to Lewis and Maude the middle classes comprised civil servants, business managers, those in the professions, farmers, shopkeepers and traders. Between the wars the middle class, thus defined, increased by 10 per cent as a changing economy demanded more public officials, more managers and more professionals. At the same time, however, there was a huge expansion in the numbers of clerical workers, foremen and supervisors. John Burnett comments on the emergence of this particular group as follows.

Here was a great army of new recruits to the class, keenly anxious to demonstrate their arrival by the adoption of a life-style which separated them from the respectable poverty from which many had risen. To live in a new suburb rather than an old, overcrowded town, in a detached or semi-detached villa rather than a terraced or back-to-back house, above all, to be able to buy a house instead of merely renting it, and to luxuriate in the sense of security and achievement which property-owning brought, were their predominant ambitions. The new arrivals shared with the older members of the class the belief that family and home were the central life interests, and that the house, which enshrined these institutions, had an importance far beyond other material objects. (Burnett, 1986, p. 251)

147

The next reading is taken from Seebohm Rowntree's social survey of York, undertaken in the late 1930s. Rowntree was concerned to identify the causes of poverty and establish what improvements in the circumstances of working-class life, if any, had occurred since his earlier (1901) survey of poverty in York. In this extract Rowntree is commenting on the quality of housing in the city of York. The suburban semi-detached house comes under Category 1, which, for Rowntree, is the highest category: 'post-war semi-detached houses with their new standard of comfort and amenity'.

6.7

Approximately 4,330 of these have been built between 1920 and 1939. Most of them, however, are occupied by families not covered by our survey, but it covered 670 of them . . .

Of the 670 families in this category, 118 have bought their houses, 388 are buying them on the instalment system, and 164 are renting them. The average amount paid in weekly instalments plus rates is 17s. 6d. [87½p] and the median is 16s. 11d. [about 85p]. Corresponding figures for houses rented are 15s. 9d. [about 79p] and 15s. 11d. [about 80p].

In comparing these figures it must be remembered that the owner of a house is responsible for 'landlord's repairs', depreciation and property tax, which together may be estimated at about 3s. [15p] per week. Thus the average all-in cost to the buyer is about 20s. [£1], or 4s. [20p] more than the average rent.

It must not be assumed that all those occupying houses in this category are well-off, though this true of the great majority. Many of those who have bought, and more of those who are buying their houses were forced to adopt this course owing to the shortage of houses to let, and the latter have a great struggle to keep up their payments.

It will be interesting to see what are the occupations of those living in Category 1 houses. The following list, which refers to 200 householders taken at random, may be regarded as representing the class as a whole.

37 clerks
20 joiners
17 engine drivers
15 coach builders
12 fitters and engineers
11 printers, lithographers, etc.
 8 factory workers
 7 travellers
 7 coach painters
 7 railway guards
 5 in business on own account
 4 insurance agents
 4 electricians
 4 retired people with children earning
 3 each – blacksmiths, salesmen, signalmen, teachers

2 each – carriage inspectors, foremen, factory supervisors, policemen, cabinet makers, draughtsmen, carriage trimmers

1 each – station porter, ticket inspector, painter, cashier, army officer, organ builder, plumber, dentist's assistant, goods checker, musician, male nurse. (Rowntree, 1941, pp. 229–30)

6.10

- What information does this reading give you: (a) about the cost of living in the suburbs; (b) the people who lived in the suburbs in York.
- Does this support the view that the suburbs comprised a homogeneous group of people?

It does seem, doesn't it, that, at least in York, there was a wide range of people even within the social group defined by Rowntree as working class? Of 200 people, only 37, fewer than 25 per cent, were clerks and the rest came from a diversity of occupations. Were you surprised to see 'clerks' defined as working class? Masterman identifies clerical work as one of the occupations that comprises what is sometimes called the lower middle class. Lewis and Maude identify clerks as belonging to a social group concerned to distance themselves from the urban working class. Rowntree, on the other hand, locates clerks in the working class, defined by him according to earnings. Those on less than £250 a year are categorized as working-class 'for the purposes of simplicity' (Rowntree, 1941, p. 11). This suggests that the classifications and categorizations around which identities are formed are rarely rigid, often disputed and constantly open to redefinition. In his earlier survey of York, Rowntree defines the working class as those unable to keep a servant: employing a servant relieved wives of the burden of housework, thus transforming them from 'women' into 'ladies', with all the implications of leisured gentility thus suggested. By 1941, he is using income as a classifying system which may, of course, relate to 'servant keeping', but is not bound by it.

Second, you may also have noticed that at least 55 of the 200 (25 per cent) worked in occupations associated with the railway. Rowntree does not use this as a means of categorizing people, but he might have done. The main sources of work for the people of York were at Rowntrees' chocolate factory or with the railways. York was a crucial railway junction as well as a site for the building of rail stock. As well as working for the railways, employees might turn to social clubs, like the Railway Institute, in their leisure time. This seems to raise the possibility that some people in York might have aligned themselves to local networks – for example, as railway workers – through which local identities might be formed. Such local identities might cut across the so-called homogeneity of the suburbs and might extend beyond classifications based on residence or income to include other railway workers who did not live in the suburbs.

You may also have noted Rowntree's point that many of those opting for home ownership, instead of renting, did so because of a shortage of houses to rent, rather than because they aspired to the status of home owners. This is worth noting, because it suggests that, while there were many people who did aspire to the independence conferred by home ownership, there may have been equally as many for whom the decision was more pragmatic. The price of buying a house of one's own was high and often required considerable financial sacrifice:

> Well, nobody bought their own house in those days. Everybody put their names down on the housing list and then got a corporation house. If you planned and got your own house, which quite a few women and girls did, that was another thing. 'It's putting a noose around your neck.' But it didn't matter. The done thing was to buy your own house, be independent, so it was nice. And you was looked up to if you was buying your own house. You know. 'She's buying her own house.' We had a house like a palace. And people used to come and visit us and say, 'Oh isn't their house posh.' And everything was spot on, it was so lovely. (Wife of a painter and decorator, quoted in Roberts, 1995, p. 28)

Finally, as Rowntree points out, the majority of semi-detached houses in York were not occupied by those he defines as working class. It seems safe to assume that the remaining 3560 houses were occupied by as diverse a population as the 670 on which he focuses, and encompassed an equally wide range of occupations and affiliations.

Turn back now to the maps of Northfield. Although the predominant feature of these maps is the growth of residential housing, there are houses, large and small, that predate this expansion. If you have the opportunity wander around any suburban area established before the Second World War. In many places you will see a mixture of housing types: Victorian and Edwardian villas, pockets of local authority council housing and large, older houses like the ones in Northfield (Beechcroft, Bella Vista, Bosmere). Although there were suburbs almost completely made up of streets of semi-detached houses, there were also many that contained a variety of houses and therefore, presumably, a diversity of social groups and lifestyles. We hope it is becoming clear that it might be difficult to locate as 'typical' the suburban identities offered by writers such as Masterman, Orwell or Taylor, and that the range of social groups, types of housing, financial motivations and associated lifestyles found in suburbia suggests a more complex set of relations than such writers presuppose.

Remind yourself of the criticisms levelled against suburbia by the writers in the previous section. You will recall that they deplored the uniformity of the semi-detached house, which they saw as stifling individuality and creativity. Now read the following extract, which is from Osbert Lancaster's *Pillar to Post, the Pocket Lamp of Architecture*, in which the author satirizes the demand of house purchasers for individual design manifcsted in a hotch-potch of suburban house styles that he dubs 'By-pass variegated'. Lancaster was a cartoonist and illustrator who worked for the *Architectural Review*

6.8

As one passes by, one can amuse one's self by classifying the various contributions which past styles have made to this infernal amalgam; here are some quaint gables culled from Art Nouveau surmounting a façade that is plainly Modernistic in inspiration; there the twisted beams and leaded parts of Stockbroker's Tudor are happily contrasted with bright green tiles of obviously Pseudish origin; next door some terra-cotta plaques, Pont Street Dutch in character, enliven a white wood Wimbledon Transitional porch, making it a splendid foil to a red-brick garage that is vaguely Romanesque in feeling. But while he is heavily indebted to history for the majority of his decorative and structural details (in almost every case the worst features of the style from which they were filched), in the planning and disposition of his erections the speculative builder displays a genius that is all his own. Notice the skill with which the houses are disposed, that insures that the largest possible area of countryside is ruined with the minimum of expense; see how carefully each householder is provided with a clear view into the most private offices of his next-door neighbour and with what studied disregard of the sun's aspect the principal rooms are planned.
(Lancaster, quoted in Graves and Hodge, 1940, p. 174)

6.11

- What does Lancaster's satiric attack on suburban housing criticize?
- Does his account suggest uniformity and monotony?
- What is his objection to the variety of styles he describes?
- Find out about modernism in art and architecture in the early twentieth century, and see if this helps you to understand Lancaster's position. Suggestions for reading: B. Hillier, *The Style of the Century 1900–1980*; C. Bloom (ed.), *Literature and Culture in Modern Britain: 1900–1929*, M. Bradbury and J. McFarlane (eds), *Modernism; 1890–1930*; S. Tillyard, *The Impact of Modernism: the Visual Arts in England*.
- Is it possible to see the diversity and mix of styles in a positive light?

The last question above is one we want to explore further. We are going to ask how far the inhabitants of suburbia were able to exercise choice and expressions of individuality, even in areas dominated by rows of identical semi-detached houses. Were the condemnations of critics accurate? Did the occupiers of semi-detached houses adhere to what Taylor called 'the herd mentality' or a set of stifling conformities that denied individual creativity while celebrating individual detachment – 'keeping yourself to yourself'. Or were there opportunities for individual identities to express themselves? Now look at table 6.1.

Table 6.1 The Dunroamin house: planes of choice

Plane of choice	Examples	Characteristics	Range of choice	Price 1920s and 1930s	Freedom of choice
First, the house as habitable shell	3-bedroom semi. 4-bedroom semi. Also bungalow; chalet in some districts	Permanent, structural. Privately owned or sometimes rented	Variations of plan; with/without garage, outbuilding. Plot sizes	From £450 to £900 normal. Higher in 'select' areas	Limited by district and numbers of builders
Second, repertoire of alternative major features	Windows, bays, gables, porches	Semi-permanent, distinctive, large-scale. Seldom changed	As offered by builder. Often 5–10 types	As offered by builder; might add £100 to £150 to price of house	Restricted to variants offered by builder
Third, repertoire of alternative details and fixtures	Stained-glass windows, tiled fireplaces, bath-room suite	Distinctive, non-structural. Changed very rarely	10–50 variants of each might have been offered by builder	£1 (stained-glass) to £20 (fireplace)	Controlled by availability from builders' merchant
Fourth, items of primary function	Cooker, carpets, bedroom suite, dining-room suite	Large, heavy. Could have been moved. Occasionally might be replaced	5–20 variants obtainable in large stores	£20 or above, according to quality and style of materials	Consider-able conditioned by store stock and transport
Fifth, articles of secondary function	Radiogram, toaster, standard lamp, electric fire	Practical, portable. Might have been changed, parts might have been replaced	10 (radios) to 50 (light fittings) available in local shops	£2 to £5	Extensive, local shops and stores. Delivered or carried
Sixth, accessories of symbolic function	Ornaments, pictures, bird table, garden figurines	Portable, decorative. Often not durable. Frequently supplemented	100s. available in shops or as souvenirs	2s. [10p] to £2 or above	Unrestricted choice. Travel (e.g. holidays) might have extended it

Source: Bentley (1981b, p. 139).

6.12

- Using table 6.1, can you suggest areas where individual home owners might exercise creativity?
- Were there constraints on what could be achieved? What were they?
- How do you think critics of the suburban semi would respond to the choices represented by table 6.1?

It would appear that there was a certain amount of choice available for people to embellish, furnish and decorate their homes in ways that express individuality. However, Orwell's George Bowling, you will remember, comments that the householder who paints the front door a different colour is likely to be labelled 'antisocial'. This is an exaggeration, but it was probably true that anyone exceeding the limits of acceptable taste would risk criticism. There are two general points worth making on this.

First, individual taste would be shaped to some extent by what was actually offered by builders and in the shops; to seek out something very different would require time and money. Individual taste could also, of course, be influenced by fashion trends, particularly those adopted by members of the same social group – stained glass panels which made a feature of the front door were particularly popular. But, equally, the 'modern', flat-roofed, functional semis designed by architects influenced by European modernism were generally not popular. Whether they shared a common identity or not, the purchasers of suburban semi-detached houses made it clear that they preferred traditional embellishments (gables, lattice windows, stained glass) to modern streamlining. In doing so, they were not simply manipulated by advertising and market forces but were able to influence the design and construction of their homes in their role as consumers.

Second, while the home offered a site for a certain amount of creativity and expression, this involved material consumption rather than reading philosophy or listening to Mozart. As such, the very areas in which individuals might express themselves were frowned upon by critics as lacking 'culture' and refinement, thus reinforcing the idea among the intelligentsia, writers like Osbert Lancaster, that 'the suburban mentality' was acquisitive, materialistic and fetishistic, and, of course, different from their own. Chapter 9 offers a more extended discussion of consumption as an aspect of contemporary culture.

In this section we have begun to suggest that attacks on suburbia relied on certain myths and stereotypes about its inhabitants: that they constituted a homogenous group, were motivated by aspirations to gentility, were acquisitive, conformist and lacking in 'higher' sensibilities. These myths (see chapter 4) hide the complex, fluid and multi-layered nature of suburban experience and identity.

6.13

- If those who condemned the suburban semi-detached drew on and produced myths of suburbia, does this invalidate their views? Should we simply dismiss their view as elitist and snobbish?
- Are there any elements of the myth which you feel are 'true'?
- Whose need for identity and belonging does the myth serve, and how?
- Can you identify other myths of suburbia touched upon in this chapter? Look back to the summary of meanings if it helps.
- Whose need for identity and belonging might these other myths serve?

We will leave you to make your own responses to these questions. However, it is worth making the point that to represent the suburbs as places to avoid at all costs or to escape from as quickly as possible is to construct a distance from those who live there and to assert an identity based on being different from 'them'. Equally, for those who wished to escape the dirt and squalor of inner-city housing, the myth of suburbia as a semi-rural paradise of order and tranquillity might be particularly potent. To return to what we said at the start of this section: places have meanings for us, and these meanings not only produce shared understandings but in doing so shape the identities open to us. We end by quoting the words of someone for whom suburbia has been a significant aspect of her identity in ways that are profoundly complex. Read the following extract from an essay by Valerie Walkerdine, currently Professor of the Psychology of Communication at Goldsmiths' College, University of London. Walkerdine is writing about her childhood in Derby in the 1950s.

6.9

It was the summer of 1983. In a suburb of Derby I sat in the car and looked at the inter-war semi that had been my home since I was born. A little girl on a tricycle cycled along the drive and out on to the pavement. It was as though I were seeing myself in a time warp.

This was the first time that I had been able to go back and look at this place, the house that was the basis of my childhood memories and dreams, the last remaining testament to that secret past of a proletarian provincial childhood. I had wanted to keep its nooks and crannies, its supreme ordinariness, safe as a place I could remember, where the past would not be lost.

And yet, everything about it, its sense of safety, had felt for so long like a trap, the site and origin of an ordinariness both hated and desired. It was the place in which, if I were not careful and being so vigilant, I might turn into my mother.

It was in that moment, in the fifties, when I felt set up, set up to want, to want to be different, special, when I was chosen to be one of the children of the post-war boom, who would leave the safe innocence of the suburbs for the stripped-pine promises of the new middle class, for the glamour of the metropolis and the desperate lure of the academy. (Walkerdine, 1985, p. 63).

The point we are trying to make is that the meanings which attach themselves to the suburban semi-detached house, even by those who live, or have lived, in them, are not fixed. History does not necessarily repeat itself; nor is 'human nature' the same throughout history. The experiences and meanings that shape consciousness in one decade can be very different in another. Identity and consciousness are, as we saw in chapter 2, created, in part, by the social, geographical and historical circumstances in which we find ourselves. The ways in which people make sense of these circumstances and the identities to which they subscribe are drawn from the different meanings of a shared historically specific culture, as the final reading in this section demonstrates.

6.10

[T]he Internet is freeing people from their work-related prison of suburbia. If the daily need for commuting to work were removed, most of suburbia's exiles would no doubt choose to move either to villages or, indeed, back to the cities.

Suburbia has managed to deliver the worst of all worlds – too much traffic, not enough greenery, too far from work, not far enough from neighbours. Planners have failed to create communities that have more in common than their distance from Kings Cross or Victoria station. Not surprising, then, that given half a chance – and a decent Internet connection – many of us would not hesitate to flee from the soul-destroying streets of identical semi-detached houses . . .

Over the past four years many of my contemporaries have moved from places such as Clapham and Richmond to Central London, in the search of a community of like-minded people and a flat within walking distance to Dillons or Café Bohème.

A lot of these people work for companies that are based in the Thames Valley, Reading triangle – the English version of Silicon Valley. Since daily face-to-face contact with their co-workers is not a requirement of their jobs, why not move to Soho, where life is significantly more fun than it is in suburbia? The Internet has given people the opportunity to make that choice, and many are taking it. (Eva Pascoe, *The Independent*, 28 October 1997).

The semi-detached as national heritage

The example of heritage that we shall examine in this section is not one of the interwar semis we have been discussing, but was built earlier. Nevertheless, thinking about the questions raised by it will extend our discussion of heritage and history in chapter 4 and connects well with the questions raised in this chapter. Mr Straw's house in Worksop, Nottinghamshire, was left, by him, to the National Trust on his death in 1990. It is one of a pair of semi-detacheds, built around 1905–7, in 'a pleasant street just being developed on the outskirts of town among the residences of professional people' (National Trust, 1993, p. 5). Visitors are able to see round the house for a small charge, there is a short video presentation and postcards and 'an illustrated souvenir' can be purchased. Now read the introduction to the souvenir booklet.

6.11

No. 7 Blyth Grove, Worksop, the home of the Straw family from 1923, is, from the outside at least, a typical example of a well-to-do tradesman's house in a provincial town at the beginning of this century. But because the family which lived here were so averse to change, it has remained almost entirely unaltered since the early 1930s. Down to the 1932 calendar on the wall of the Dining Room, there is hardly a trace of the last 60 years.

It was in 1932 that William Straw, a grocer and seeds merchant and father of two sons, William and Walter, died suddenly whilst gardening. The blow was so devastating to the family that they allowed nothing to be changed in the house from that day forward. Father's pipes and tobacco pouch still hang beside the fireplace, his hats and coats on the pegs in the Hall.

Seven years later Florence Straw, the boys' mother, also died and the embalming was complete. The curtains were always kept drawn in her Sitting Room with its piano, small low chairs in their faded case covers, and china and glass ornaments. From this time on, her two sons lived on the surface of the house, existing, it seems, entirely in the past. While Walter, the younger son, continued to run the family business, William gave up his teaching job in London and returned to look after the house. The brothers had no telephone, radio, television or central heating, and entering the house today, one steps back three-quarters of a century.

When William, the last of the Straw family, died in 1990 at the age of 92, he left the contents of 7 Blyth Grove, other property in Worksop, and the bulk of his estate to the National Trust, although he had never been a member. (He said he had considered joining but, faced with the choice between the Trust and the Thoroton Society in Nottingham, had picked the latter as having the lower subscription!) The National Trust was able to buy the freehold of both Nos 5 and 7 Blyth Grove, which had been left elsewhere, and has made every effort to preserve the house exactly as it was found. (The National Trust, 1993, p. 3).

6.15

- What does the National Trust see as the particular significance of this house?
- What is the Trust's aim with regard to the house?

The National Trust sees the house as 'a typical example of a well-to-do trades-man's house'. The commentary accompanying the video presentation, which can be watched on visiting the house, speaks of a whole way of life 'locked in time' and 'captured' for posterity. You may think there is a tension between the stress on typicality and the 'locked-in-timeness' of 7 Blyth Grove. This particular house is unusual because it has remained unaltered since the 1930s: a more 'typical' house might show signs of change and alteration as well as traces of its past. Moreover, as the National Trust makes clear, it intends to 'preserve the house exactly as it was found'. In order to achieve this aim it is necessary to charge visitors an en-trance fee and sell associated commodities. Yet, in order to protect the stair car-pet, for example, from wear occasioned by visitors' feet, it has been necessary to take it up and replace it with something similar. In order to preserve Mr Straw's house 'as it was found' it is necessary to remove and alter things (the stair carpet). And the act of preserving it, of course, makes it no longer, if it ever was, typical. The history of the house and its inhabitants is unique and unusual – hence its fascination, as we shall see.

Look now at figure 6.6. This photograph is on the back cover of the souvenir booklet and depicts the Lumber Room at the top of the house, a room that would once have been used to house a maidservant, but was used by the Straws, who

Figure 6.6 'Junk room', Mr Straw's house, Nottinghamshire

dispensed with domestic help after the deaths of their parents, as a junk room. What strikes you as interesting in this picture and why?

When we first scrutinised the picture we noticed the ARP warden's helmet, the 'Baby Daisy' vacuum cleaner, the brown paper bag from the family firm, the bottled fruit, the hat box and the jug and ewer, all of which suggest both a private and a public history (family activities and work, alongside the intrusion of the Second World War). This junk room was, we can assume, a place where objects were continually added and stored, and very possibly some were removed. The 'Baby Daisy' vacuum cleaner may have been put there earlier than the ARP warden's helmet or the bottled fruit. Yet the impression given by the photograph is static and fixed: the past, represented by the various objects, has been frozen and 'captured'. It is presented to posterity as a spectacle upon which we may gaze and perhaps exclaim at its oddities.

6.16

Can you suggest what meanings the National Trust is conveying about history in its statements about 7 Blyth Grove and in the picture from the souvenir booklet?

It would be possible to argue, wouldn't it, that the National Trust represents history as a static, frozen body of knowledge, separated from the present and only available to us as spectacle? This version of history does not encourage us to engage in critical dialogue: instead it invites us to look and marvel.

However, when I (Judy Giles) visited Mr Straw's house I was as fascinated by the story of the Straw family as by the house and its objects. I was not the only one: the stewards who showed us round told different anecdotes about the Straws and the other visitors asked numerous questions about William and Walter. For example, after the death of their mother, William and Walter lived as bachelors and dismissed the maidservant, and no women were allowed in the house thereafter. Was this misogyny, was it connected to the period's ideas of respectability and morality, what did it mean then and how do we understand it now? William took over the domestic management of the house after his mother's death: cooking, cleaning and shopping. How was this viewed by others: was it seen as 'odd', were the brothers respected in the town despite their eccentricities, or even because of them, or were they avoided? These questions involved all of us there engaging with the past in terms of our understandings of gender, morality and sexuality in the present. This enabled us to be involved in making sense of and reconstructing the past, rather than simply consuming it as a finished product. In doing so we, the consumers of heritage, were not the passive 'dupes' suggested by some critics of heritage (see chapter 4). Not only were we able to engage critically with what seemed to us pertinent issues, we were also involved in negotiating and adapting the version of history offered by the National Trust.

6.17

Think about other properties owned by the National Trust. In what ways is Mr Straw's house different? Does the acquisition of Mr Straw's house by the National Trust therefore have implications for what is understood as 'national heritage'?

We will leave you to answer this question.

Conclusions

We hope that this chapter has shown you how the ideas introduced in part I of this book can be applied to the study of a particular cultural formation – in this case the suburban semi-detached. There is a lot more we could have said on the subject with more space, and we hope you may be stimulated to carry out your own projects on this topic or related areas. You should find plenty of interesting material in the suggestions for further reading.

PART II

CHAPTER 7

High Culture/Popular Culture

As we have seen, culture can be viewed as a contested field of interaction within which people make and encounter meanings. This chapter will examine what is often seen as a tension between popular and so-called 'high' culture via work on everyday life, and also through discussion of two perspectives on the place of literature studies in the education system. We conclude the chapter with a re-reading of Kenneth Grahame's *The Wind in the Willows*, in which we draw upon a number of recent approaches to the culturally grounded study of literary texts. Our approach cannot neglect questions of popular culture but, by focusing on 'high' culture, we want to address – in this chapter at least – the apparent over-emphasis on popular culture in many introductory works (for another perspective on the focus on popular culture in contemporary British cultural studies, see Storey, 1993, pp. 181–202; also see McGuigan, 1992). Before you begin to work on the material in this chapter you might find it useful to read or re-read chapter 1 in this volume.

Discriminations

For Raymond Williams, 'culture has two aspects: the known meanings and directions, which its members are trained to; the new observations and meanings, which are offered and tested' (Williams, 1958a, p. 6). There is a tension here which arises from the idea that cultures can *train* or shape individuals, but that these same individuals retain the ability to test and otherwise discriminate between forms of culture and meaning. Williams devoted a major study, *Culture and Society; 1780–1950* (1958b), to the examination of this issue, and his work remains essential reading for anyone interested in the development of the link between the older sense of culture as 'the tending of natural growth', and the late eighteenth and early nineteenth-centuries' idea, in which:

> It came to mean, first, 'the general state or habit of a mind, having close relations with the idea of human perfection'. Second, it came to mean 'the general state of intellectual development, in a society as a whole'. Third, it came to mean 'the general body of the arts'. Fourth, later in the century, it came to mean 'a whole way of life, material, intellectual and spiritual'. It came also, as we know, to be a word which often provoked, either hostility or embarrassment. (Williams, 1958b, p. 16)

What is useful in this assertion is the idea of historically competing definitions of and meanings for the concept of culture. One version of cultural studies in the late twentieth century takes as its object of study everyday life and its related material culture. In consequence, the role of 'high' culture, its artefacts and practices, and the political effects of these are, perhaps, less readily addressed in many introductory works on the subject. It should, of course, be noted that there are a number of different versions of cultural studies currently operating and, often, competing for dominance: cultural studies in the USA has a very different, and some would argue a less politicized, agenda to cultural studies in South Asia, for example (Lal, 1996).

In this chapter we want to concentrate upon aspects of 'high' culture, not because we think this is a more important area than any of the other aspects of culture which we have been addressing in this book, but rather because to forget so-called 'high' culture in any analysis of a given epoch or society means offering a distorted picture of its cultural sphere. We have found that while many introductory works deal with popular fiction and equip students to tackle such texts (Storey, 1996, pp. 29–53; Fiske, 1991, pp. 103–27), less space is given to exploring the ways in which so-called 'high' culture is part of the process whereby meanings are produced and circulated within a society.

In many ways, studying culture is inevitably going to be about making plain the discriminations and hierarchies of value through which a given culture operates. For example, you may recall that in his definition of culture Williams suggests a view which appears to leave out many areas of activity and formations. According to Williams, culture refers to:

i.   the general process of intellectual, spiritual and aesthetic development
ii. a particular way of life, whether of a people, a period or a group.
iii. the works and practices of intellectual and especially artistic activity. Williams, 1976, pp. 87–93)

In his short commentary on Williams's definition, John Storey (1993, p. 2) argues that:

- Williams's category i is unrelated to popular culture.
- Williams's category ii covers what Storey calls 'lived cultures' or cultural practices (i.e. ways in which everyday activities and events can be seen as specific to a particular group, and as such partake of the beliefs and values of that group): here Storey includes activities like Christmas or seaside holidays.
- Williams's category iii includes 'signifying practices' (i.e. ways of encoding and/or communicating a set of meanings/ideas/values): for Storey these include soap operas, pop music, comics, novels, ballets, fine art etc.

Storey's stress on culture as a set of processes and practices offers a contemporary (1990s) interpretation of Williams's work. This view of culture as continually in process is evident elsewhere in Williams's own work, in which he refines his original position and argues that cultural formations can be grouped under three broad headings: *dominant, residual* and *emergent* (Williams, 1981 p. 204).

7.1

READING

Cultural reproduction, in its simplest sense, occurs essentially at the (changing) level of the dominant . . . The residual, by contrast, though its immediate processes are reproductive, is often a form of cultural alternative to the dominant in its most recent . . . forms . . . At the opposite end of the range, the emergent is related to but not identical with the innovatory. Some kinds of innovation . . . are movements and adjustments within the dominant, and become its new forms. But there is usually tension and struggle in this area. Some innovations – kinds of art and thought which emerge and persist as disturbing – would tend to destroy the dominant in any of its forms, just as some new social forces would tend to destroy the social order rather than reproduce or modify it.

No analysis is more difficult than that which, faced by new forms, has to try to determine whether these are new forms of the dominant or are genuinely emergent. In historical analysis the issue gets settled: the emergent becomes the emerged . . . and then often the dominant. But in contemporary analysis, just because of the complex relations between innovation and reproduction, the problem is at a different level. (Williams, 1981, pp. 204–5)

As Williams suggests, art is a good area in which to observe this phenomenon in action. In the nineteenth century, as today, some forms of conceptual and abstract art, by not fitting the period's dominant notion of what constituted art, were mocked as 'daubings that a child could do', or simply dismissed as 'that's not art!' Yet the impressionist and post-impressionist art of the later nineteenth and early twentieth centuries, once condemned by some sections of the art establishment, is now one of the dominant forms of art. Indeed, reproductions of impressionist paintings are now endlessly recycled in shopping bags, greetings cards and posters on sale in the high street (you can explore some of these debates via Flint, 1984; Bullen, 1988; Harrison and Wood, 1992). Using Williams's three concepts (residual, dominant, emergent) we could argue that nineteenth-century impressionism began as an emergent form, became a dominant form and may now, at least within the art establishment if not in popular imagination, be seen as a highly influential but residual form.

7.1

ACTIVITIES

Think about the following in terms of whether they seem to be residual, dominant or emergent forms of culture. We have started you off with an example.

- Indie music. Began as independent, alternative to mainstream popular music: has now become mainstream? Therefore an emergent form which is becoming dominant?
- Karaoke.
- The art of Damien Hurst.
- *The Wind in the Willows*.
- The Beatles.

When we examine the ways in which we understand the cultural practices and associated signifying systems of contemporary societies, there are, clearly, no right or wrong answers: what we are looking at is the way in which we read cultural practices and the judgements we might make about people who express themselves through/in relation to different cultural formations. However, it is interesting to note how far you feel able to state your own view point (your 'individual' meanings) and how far you feel constrained by your awareness of what you are expected to think about a topic (the 'common-sense' meanings).

7.2

- Group about five of the following aspects of British culture, according to whether you believe them to be facets of 'high', mass or popular culture. You might also like to think about the perspective you are working from would your parents, your grandparents share your views? Would someone from a different ethnic group from yourself share your views? Would someone from a different part of the world from you share your views?

Shopping at Marks and Spencer
Shopping at The Gap
Shopping at Harvey Nichols in Leeds
Shopping at Harvey Nichols in Knightsbridge
Shopping at Superdrug
Shopping at Boots
Shopping at Kwik Save
Shopping at Sainsbury's
Shopping at The Co-Op
Eating at McDonald's
Watching *EastEnders*
Watching *Neighbours*
Watching BBC News
Watching ITV News
Listening to Radio 1
Listening to Radio 3
Listening to Radio 4
Listening to Classic FM
Poster of Monet's water lilies purchased from Athena
Poster of Monet's water lilies purchased from Tate Gallery shop
Looking at Monet's painting in an art gallery
Reading *The Times*
Reading the *Guardian*
Reading the *Sun*
Reading *Take a Break*
Reading *Vogue*
Reading *NME*
Listening to The Prodigy

Listening to Mozart
Listening to U2

- How did you know which category to put each practice into?
- Try to decide if the cultural practice is dominant, residual or emergent.

Given Williams's insistence that dominant cultural forms are always integral to the social structures of a society – in the sense that they interact with economic factors, family structures and the education system to produce, reinforce and sustain its social relations and stratifications – you might want to consider the extent to which popular culture could ever be said to be in a dominant position in contemporary British society. How far does the perspective which you, and perhaps your circle of friends, have on aspects of contemporary culture suggest that beliefs about the value of cultural forms and practices are shared by people of, say, the same age, class, region, gender or ethnic group? To what extent does cultural value get decided by you and how far might it be imposed by the mass media, by family practices, by peer pressures etc.? You might like to follow up this activity by reading the work of the French sociologist, Pierre Bourdieu, on this area (Bourdieu, 1984; see also Storey, 1993, pp. 187–90; Frow, 1995, pp. 27–47).

The divisive nature of culture may well have been foregrounded by activity 7.2, in which you attempted to classify various aspects of culture and society in 1990s Britain. Culture is shaped by patterns of social power, and its divisiveness is part and parcel of the social milieu in which we find ourselves: one in which difference carries with it social meanings that can shape our interaction with our world. Now read the following extract by John Fiske.

7.2

Bourdieu's work is valuable because in his account of proletarian culture he reveals cultural practices that are typical of subordinate allegiances. So women, regardless of their class, can and do participate in soap operas in a way that parallels what Bourdieu has identified as a mark of proletarian culture, but that can be generalised out to refer to the culture of the subordinate, or popular culture. Similarly, . . . [a study] in Germany has shown how women's tastes in news are functional (another characteristic of proletarian taste identified by Bourdieu): women prefer the local news to the national because they can use its accounts of burglary and assaults in the local streets, or road accidents, and of missing children as part of their maternal function of preparing their children to face their immediate social world. Women's tastes and proletarian tastes are similar not because women are proletarian or because the proletariat are feminine, but because both are disempowered classes and thus can easily align themselves with the practices of popular culture, for the people are formed by social allegiances among the subordinate.

Everyday life is constituted by the practices of popular culture, and is characterised by the creativity of the weak in using the resources provided by the disempowering system while refusing finally to submit to that power. (Fiske, 1991, p. 47)

7.3

- What was your reaction to the passage by Fiske? How would you describe the image of women and of the working class which emerges from this extract?
- Would you want to counter Fiske's assertions? What arguments would you use?
- Can you think of any examples of the ways in which people creatively use the resources of a disempowering system? You could consider, for example, the ways in which gay culture has recycled a mainstream film like *The Wizard of Oz* or the ways in which different forms of popular music are consumed by different audiences.

Fiske's summary of some of Bourdieu's ideas suggests that popular culture is the arena in which the disempowered and subordinate operate. In *Understanding Popular Culture* he attempts to celebrate the potential of forms of culture (like soap operas) which do not have the sanction of state or semi-state organisations such as the education system. Fiske goes on to explore how people can relate creatively to mass forms of entertainment in ways that allow them to resist categorization and classification by those who are better positioned to produce dominant forms of knowledge (you might at this point remind yourself of the discussion on discourse and power in chapter 3). Fiske's outline of popular culture as a contested and dynamic terrain draws upon the work of Michael de Certeau:

7.3

The everyday life of the people is where the contradictory interests of capitalist societies are continually negotiated and contested. De Certeau (1984) is one of the most sophisticated theorists of the culture and practices of everyday life, and running through his work is a series of metaphors of conflict – particularly ones of strategy and tactics, of guerrilla warfare, of poaching, of guileful ruses and tricks. Underlying all of them is the assumption that the powerful are cumbersome, unimaginative, and over organized, whereas the weak are creative, nimble and flexible. So the weak use guerrilla tactics against the strategies of the powerful, making poaching raids upon their texts or structures, and play constant tricks upon the system.

The powerful construct places where they can exercise their power – cities, shopping malls, schools, workplaces and houses, to name only some of the material ones. The weak make their own spaces within those places; they make the places temporarily theirs as they move through them, occupying them for as long as they need or have to. A place is where strategy operates; the guerrillas, who move into it, turn it into their space; space is practiced place. (Fiske, 1991, pp. 32–3)

You might at this point want to remind yourself of the discussion on places and spaces in chapter 5. If, as Fiske suggests, popular culture is the product of a sequence of skirmishes with a dominant and official 'high' culture, it would seem important to know what it is that the popular is defining itself against. The postmodernist idea that hierarchies have been abolished in the contemporary cultural sphere seems to have little impact on, for example, debates about the National Curriculum, which requires students of GCSE English to study a complete Shakespeare play as part of their studies, but does not, for example, stipulate that students must study any work by recent black British writers. For the state, the work of a writer who died well over three hundred years ago is seen as an essential element of a school curriculum for pupils preparing for citizenship in a multi-ethnic, predominately urban, culture. Popular culture's raids on 'Shakespeare' include the production of such artefacts as fridge magnets of swear words, cigars, T-shirts etc., and while, for some, these guerrilla tactics function to make 'Shakespeare' part of a more contemporary and familiar world, such tactics fail to engage productively with what it is that makes his works an essential component of the National Curriculum: wearing a 'Big on the Bard' sweatshirt to your English class is hardly an act of guerrilla expropriation.

A helpful way of describing the processes of cultural interaction and negotiation, which can, perhaps, avoid some of the pitfalls of the popular = good, 'high' = bad or, indeed, the popular = bad, 'high' = good approach, can be found in the work of the influential Russian thinker Mikhail Bakhtin.

For Bakhtin, the individual consciousness is the product of a multiplicity of interactions within a social context in which meanings are contested. We have seen already the ways in which we can be aware of a difference between those values held by society in general and those we might use individually when it comes to such things as shopping or listening to music. We may personally not own any recording of work by Mozart, but we are very likely to be aware that his work has a status within our culture which is very different to that afforded to The Prodigy or Oasis. The diversity of positions – the fact that in the 1990s there are people who are passionate about Mozart and would not consider The Prodigy music, as well as people who are passionate about The Prodigy and would not consider Mozart music, as well as those who consider both music – at a given moment in history is conceptualized by Bakhtin as **heteroglossia**: a 'diversity of languages' (Todoroy, 1984, p. 56). The multiple interactions an individual has with the discourses which operate within her or his social milieu are described as a process of **dialogism**. Dialogism, which is engendered by the interaction of a range of perspectives on the same subject, makes it possible continually to subvert any claims, on the part of a particular ideology, for the existence of its single, or **monological**, value system. For example, if you have just left home to attend university, your parents may urge you to spend your evenings doing your course work; your friends may urge you to join them in the student union; your tutor may urge you to read more feminist theory; your landlord may urge you to clean up your kitchen; and your bank manager may urge you to get a part-time job. All these competing claims could be part of your experience of being at university and, as such, will tend to challenge the idea that being at university is only about study or sorting out your own finances or drinking in the union bar.

However, some of the discourses that seek to shape your activities as a student have more power than others. For Bakhtin, the dominance of certain discourses within a specific cultural or social space can be seen as an actualization, at the micro-level, of the socio-economic divisions within the society that produces them. Thus you may find that your parents or school teachers warned you away from studying a subject like cultural studies or media studies at university, perhaps urging you to do a 'proper' degree in an area like history or a 'useful' degree in areas like business management or leisure sciences. You may find that your landlord has similar views to your parents about what a degree ought to be and, on reflection, you can probably see that these perspectives stem from ideas that assume a link between higher education and employment prospects. These ideas may clash with the values expressed, implicitly and explicitly, by your tutors, for whom the idea of a university focuses on its role as a place in which knowledge can be pursued for its own sake. Your friends, in opposition to these ideas of what it means to be at university, may assert that university is about mixing with your peer group in the pub, student union or a club. Dominant discursive positions (represented here by the beliefs and values espoused by your landlord, parents and tutors) seek to suppress opposition because more is at stake than a communication system: a group's identity and status (as parents, as tutors) is maintained by the wide acceptance of the validity of its set of values. The positions represented by parents and tutors in this example are **hegemonic** in so far as they are able to secure a measure of consent from you, and this is true of the education system as a whole. Hence, it is constantly reasserted that working hard and preparing for employment are 'in your best interests'. Opposition to these ideas constitutes a way of subverting and resisting these dominant or hegemonic meanings. And, of course, in practice it is likely that your perspective as well as that of your parents and tutors will include, to greater or lesser extents, possibly warring elements of all the foregoing ideas. Thus, as Bakhtin argued, individual consciousness is itself produced from the interaction of multiple voices within a particular social context.

Let us now link this to thinking about the dialogics of cultural value and how competing claims for status can be linked to a particular group's way of seeing the world. A useful illustration of this is the ongoing persistence of Arnoldian views regarding the place of literary culture in the education system.

Versions of literary culture: 1921 and 1994

One of the early definitions of culture which we looked at in chapter 1 of this book was that of Matthew Arnold, who defined culture as the best that has been thought and read. We want now to look at two texts which seek to define what constitutes 'the best'.

7.4

From *The Newbolt Report on the Teaching of English in England* (1921), introduction.

We believe that . . . an education based upon the English language and literature would have important social, as well as personal, results; it would have a unifying tendency. Two causes, both accidental and conventional rather than national, at present distinguish and divide one class from another in England. The first of these is a marked difference in their modes of speech. If the teaching of the language were properly and universally provided for, the difference between educated and uneducated speech, . . . which at present causes so much prejudice and difficulty of intercourse on both sides, would gradually disappear. Good speech and great literature would not be regarded as too fine for use by the majority, nor, on the other hand, would natural gifts for self-expression be rendered ineffective by embarrassing faults of diction or composition. The second cause of division amongst us is the undue narrowness of the ground on which we meet for the true purposes of social life. The associations of sport and games are widely shared by all classes in England, but with mental pleasures and mental exercises the case is very different. The old education was not similar for all, but diverse. It went far to make of us not one nation, but two, neither of which shared the associations or tastes of the other. An education fundamentally English would, we believe, at any rate bridge, if not close, this chasm of separation. The English people might learn as a whole to regard their own language, first with respect, and then with a genuine feeling of pride and affection. More than any mere symbol it is actually a part of England: to maltreat it or deliberately to debase it would be seen to be an outrage; to become sensible of its significance and splendour would be to step upon a higher level. In France, we are told, this pride in the national language is strong and universal; the French artisan will often use his right to object that an expression is not French. Such a feeling for our own native language would be a bond of union between classes, and would beget the right kind of national pride. Even more certainly would pride and joy in the national literature serve as such a bond. This feeling, if fostered in all our schools without exception, would disclose itself far more often and furnish common meeting ground for great numbers of men and women who might otherwise never come into touch with one another. We know from the evidence of those who are familiar with schools of every type that the love of fine style and the appreciation of what is great in human thought and feeling is already no monopoly of a single class in England, that it is a natural and not an exceptional gift, and that though easily discouraged by unfavourable circumstances it can also, by sympathetic treatment, be easily drawn out and developed. Within the school itself all scholars, though specialising perhaps on different lines, will be able to find a common interest in the literature class and the debating or dramatic society. And this common interest will be likely to persist when other less vital things have been abandoned. The purely technical or aesthetic appeal of any art will, perhaps, always be limited to a smaller number but, as experience of life, literature will influence all who are capable of finding recreation in something beyond mere sensation. These it will unite by a common interest in life at its best, and by the perpetual reminder that through all social differences human nature and its strongest affections are fundamentally the same.

7.4

- What, for the authors of this report, is the function of the study of English literature and language?
- Draw up a list of the positive terms which the report uses in connection with the kind of education it seeks to promote: to what extent can you begin to make judgements about the political beliefs and values of the report from this listing?

ACTIVITIES

7.5

From *The Newbolt Report*, chapter VIII, Literature and Adult Education: Literature and the Nation.

We were told that the working classes, especially those belonging to organised labour movements, were antagonistic to, and contemptuous of, literature, that they regarded it merely as an ornament, a polite accomplishment, a subject to be despised by really virile men. Literature, in fact, seems to be classed by a large number of thinking working men with, antimacassars, fish knives and other unintelligible and futile trivialities of middle class culture, and, as a subject of instruction, is suspect as an attempt to side-track the working class movement. We regard the prevalence of such opinions as a serious matter, not merely because it means, the alienation of an important section of the population from the *confort and mirthe* of literature, but chiefly because it points to a morbid condition of the body politic which if not taken in hand may be followed by lamentable consequences. For if literature be, as we believe, an embodiment of the best thoughts of the best minds, the most direct and lasting communication of experience by man to men, a fellowship which binds together by passion and knowledge the vast empire of human society, as it is spread over the whole earth, and over all time, then the nation of which a considerable portion rejects this means of grace, and despises this great spiritual influence, must assuredly be heading to disaster . . .

At the same time we are unable to subscribe to the dictum that literature, as generally interpreted, is a part of middle-class culture. We sincerely wish it were. We find, on the contrary, an indifference among middle-class persons to the claims of literature, even more disheartening than the open hostility which we are told exists among certain circles of working-class opinion. Here, quite as much as there, is to be found a striking contrast with mediaeval conditions . . . Does poetry play anything like the same part in the domestic economy of the average well-to-do household to-day? The question answers itself. Children at the Secondary or Public School learn to pay a certain lip-service to literature, but it is safe to say that more than 90 per cent. of middle-class people have ceased to read poetry in adult life. Why is this? We can find no more satisfactory answer than that already given in dealing with the attitude of the working man, namely, that poetry is not recognised as having any vital connection with a workaday world.

237. It is natural for man to delight in poetry; the history of mediaeval society, to say nothing of all primitive societies, proves this. Further, we claim that no personality can be complete, see life steadily and see it whole, without that unifying influence, that purifying of the emotions, which art and literature can alone bestow. It follows from what we have said above that the bulk of our people, of whatever class, are unconsciously living starved existences, that one of the richest fields of our spiritual being is left uncultivated – not indeed barren, for the weeds of literature have never been so prolific as in our day. It is easy to blame Education for this, but Education cannot proceed far in advance of the general outlook of its age. The true cause lies deeper, is rooted among the very foundations of our civilisation. Yet we believe that it belongs to a transitory phase of human development and will, therefore, in course of time cease to operate . . .

238. The interim, we feel, belongs chiefly to the professors of English literature. The rise of modern Universities has accredited an ambassador of poetry to every

important capital of industrialism in the country, and upon his shoulders rests a responsibility greater we think than is as yet generally recognised. The Professor of Literature in a University should be – and sometimes is, as we gladly recognise – a missionary in a more real and active sense than any of his colleagues. He has obligations not merely to the students who come to him to read for a degree, but still more towards the teeming population outside the University walls, most of whom have not so much as heard whether there be any Holy Ghost. The fulfilmnt [sic] of these obligations means propaganda work, organisation and the building up of a staff of assistant missionaries. But first, and above all, it means a right attitude of mind, a conviction that literature and life are in fact inseparable, that literature is not just a subject for academic study, but one of the chief temples of the human spirit, in which all should worship. We say all, for there is a tendency to suppose that literature is the preserve of the cultured, a tendency from which Matthew Arnold, the apostle of culture, was himself not entirely free. The great men of culture, he wrote, are those who have had a passion for diffusing, for making prevail, for carrying from one end of society to the other, the best knowledge, the best ideas of their time; who have laboured to divest knowledge of all that was harsh, uncouth, difficult, abstract, professional, exclusive; to humanise it, to make it efficient outside the clique of the cultivated and learned, yet still remaining the *best* knowledge and thought of the time, and a true source, therefore, of sweetness and light. A noble ideal, yet one that is incomplete without Henry Sidgwick's comment upon it: If any culture really has what Mr. Arnold in his finest mood calls its noblest element, the passion for propagating itself, for making itself prevail, then let it learn to call nothing common or unclean. It can only propagate itself by shedding the light of its sympathy liberally; by learning to love common people and common things, to feel common interests. Make people feel that their own poor life is ever so little beautiful and poet-ical; then they will begin to turn and seek after the treasures of beauty and poetry outside and above it. Culture, like all spiritual gifts, can only be propagated by enthusiasm; and by enthusiasm that has got rid of asperity, that has become sympathetic; that has got rid of Pharisaism, and become humble. The ambassadors of poetry must be humble, they must learn to call nothing common or unclean, not even the local dialect, the clatter of the factory, or the smoky pall of our industrial centres.

7.5

- Comment on the extract's views of the working and middle classes and the attitude towards literature attributed to these groups.
- Why does the report value poetry so highly?
- What problems can you envisage facing a professor attempting to take up the challenge to missionary action set out in the report. Would the situation in the 1920s be any different from that which exists today? What, if any, are the relations between your higher education institution and its nearby towns or surrounding city?

ACTIVITIES

Now read the extract from the School Curriculum and Assessment Authority's review of the National Curriculum's provision for English (HMSO, 1994). As part of the review, this document contains specific recommendations for the kinds of literature which school age pupils should encounter; the report's authors note that the 'provisions ensure that all pupils read texts by some authors of central importance to the literary heritage . . . the lists represent a widely shared consensus of authors who deserve to be read' (HMSO, 1994, p. iv).

7.6

5.1 Pupils should be introduced to literature of 'high' quality, including works written in previous centuries, those from earlier in the twentieth century and contemporary writing. Pupils should be encouraged to appreciate the distinctive qualities of such works through activities which emphasise the interest and pleasure of reading them rather than necessitating a detailed, line-by-line study. Pupils working at Levels 1, 2 and 3 should be introduced to these significant authors and works in the English literary heritage by means appropriate to the pupils maturity and reading abilities.

5.2 During each of Key Stages 3 and 4, pupils should read:
- a range of drama, including a play by Shakespeare;
- a range of fiction, including
    i. One work published before 1900 by an author listed in 5.3;
    ii. one work published since 1900 by an author listed in 5.4;
- a range of poetry, including
    i. poems by two significant poets whose works were published before 1900, listed in 5.5;
    ii. poems by three significant poets whose works were published since 1900, listed in 5.6;
- a range of non-literary and non-fiction texts

5.3 Authors whose fiction works were published before 1900:
Jane Austen, Charlotte Bronte, Emily Bronte, John Bunyan, Wilkie Collins, Arthur Conan Doyle, Stephen Crane, Daniel Defoe, Charles Dickens, George Eliot, Henry Fielding, Elizabeth Gaskell, Thomas Hardy, Nathaniel Hawthorne, Henry James, Edgar Allan Poe, R. L. Stevenson, Jonathan Swift, Anthony Trollope, Mark Twain, H. G. Wells.

5.4 Authors whose fiction works were published since 1900:
Stan Barstow, H. E. Bates, Nina Bawden, Arnold Bennett, Ray Bradbury, Joseph Conrad, Majorie Darke, Berlie Doherty, Gerald Durrell, Ford Maddox [sic] Ford, E. M. Forster, Leon Garfield, Alan Garner, William Golding, Grahame Greene, Rosa Guy, L. P. Hartley, Ernest Hemingway, Susan Hill, Ann Holm, Janni Howker, Richard Hughes, Aldous Huxley, Ruth Prawer Jhabvla [sic], James Joyce, D. H. Lawrence, Harper Lee, Laurie Lee, Rosamond Lehmann, Ursula Le Guin, Doris Lessing, Joan Lingard, Penelope Liveley, Michelle Magorian, Olivia Manning, Katherine Mansfield, Jan Mark, Somerset Maugham, Iris Murdoch, Beverley Naidoo, V. S. Naipaul, Edna O' Brien, George Orwell, Phillipa Pearce, Jean Rhys, Rukshana Smith, Muriel Spark, John Steinbeck, Mildred Taylor, Gwyn Thomas, J. R. R. Tolkein, Evelyn Waugh, H. G. Wells, Virginia Woolf, John Wyndham.

5.5 Poets whose works were published before 1900:
Matthew Arnold, Elizabeth Barrett Browning, William Blake, Robert Bridges, Robert Browning, Robert Burns, Lord Byron, Geoffrey Chaucer, John Clare, S. T. Coleridge, Emily Dickinson, John Donne, John Dryden, Thomas Gray, George Herbert, Robert Herrick, G. M. Hopkins, John Keats, Christopher Marlowe, Andrew Marvell, John Milton, Alexander Pope, Christina Rossetti, Shakespeare (sonnets), Percy Bysshe Shelley, Edmund Spenser, Alfred Lord Tennyson, William Wordsworth, Sir Thomas Wyatt.

5.6 Poets whose works were published since 1900:
Dannie Abse, Fleur Adcock, W. H. Auden, James Berry, John Betjeman, Charles Causley, Gillian Clarke, Wendy Cope, Douglas Dunn, T. S. Eliot, U. A. Fanthorpe, Robert Frost, Robert Graves, Thom Gunn, Thomas Hardy, Seamus Heaney, Ted Hughes, Elizabeth Jennings, Jenny Joseph, Philip Larkin, D. H. Lawrence, Liz Lochhead, Norman MacCaig, Louis MacNeice, Edwin Muir, Grace Nichols, Leslie Norris, Wilfred Owen, Brian Patten, Sylvia Plath, Siegfried Sassoon, Vernon Scannell, Stephen Spender, Anne Stevenson, Dylan Thomas, Edward Thomas, R. S. Thomas, Derek Walcott, W. B. Yeats.

5.7 The range of non-literary and non-fiction texts should include
- autobiographies, e.g. Winston Churchill, Gerald Durrell, Edmund Gosse, J. S. Mill, R. K. Narayan, journals and diaries, e.g. Daniel Defoe, Anne Frank, Samuel Pepys, Dorothy Wordsworth, pamphlets, letters and travel writing, e.g. Bruce Chatwin, James Cook, Freya Stark, Paul Theroux;
- reference books, leaflets, magazines, databases, brochures, radio and television.
(HMSO, 1994, pp. 17–18)

7.6

- Using a reference work like *The Oxford Companion to English Literature*, examine the authors listed in any one section. Consider the ratio of men to women; the number of non-white authors; the lack of any dramatists other than Shakespeare.
- Look at a bestseller list (usually to be found in a broadsheet Sunday newspaper): do any of the authors listed in the curriculum appear? What reasons can you suggest for their presence or absence?
- Draw up a list of the books you have read in the past six months; try to categorize them (by genre, e.g. literary fiction, horror, thriller, romance). Can you also distinguish between books read for pleasure and those read as part of course requirements. Do any of the authors whose works you have read for pleasure appear on the lists above?
- How important do you think it is that school pupils study the range of literary works outlined? What role do you think the study of literature has in today's society? Now look back at your comments on the material from the Newbolt Report. Can you identify points of difference and points of similarity between the two?

We have spent some time thinking about these two statements regarding the place of literature in the education system, as they point up the ways in which the official ideas of the state have retained a remarkable degree of coherence over a long period of time. Both reports foreground the ways in which the state legitimates and promotes a particular set of texts. Indeed, so powerful is this process that when people begin to study culture it is very often assumed that 'high' culture will be the focus of their studies. *The Newbolt Report* and *English in the National Curriculum* promote a set of values which suggest that there is only one version of literary history, and that there is no real argument about what constitutes literary studies or, indeed, the purpose of a literary education. In fact, within university literature departments, fierce debates have raged over the past twenty years about the nature and relevance of literature, and anyone who has followed the sometimes acrimonious deliberations of the Booker Prize judges knows that literary worth is not always easily agreed upon. Moreover, teachers who are charged with implementing the curriculum may not always agree fully either as individuals or as an organized body with the version of literary study represented in the National Curriculum.

In both documents there is an assumption that the inculcation of a literary culture is part of the state's duty; a duty which, for the Newbolt Committee and, it would appear, for today's curriculum advisors, still seems to rest on Arnoldian notions of the benefits of encountering cultivated minds. We are not suggesting that schoolchildren should not study and benefit from the writings of Shakespeare or Dickens, but we are drawing your attention to the ways in which the debate is framed and the assumptions that underpin it. Further, as we have pointed out, the official version is not the only version but it may certainly be the most powerful, partly because it can draw on history and tradition, and partly because it is legitimated through the power of government.

Within the education system, then, there appears to be an idea that despite a disparate and heterogeneous social sphere, there remain shared values which can be disseminated through education. While literary culture may no longer be the exclusive preserve of a particular socio-economic class, it clearly remains part of the cultural baggage which goes with the notion of being educated. Think about the phrases that people use to describe what they are reading: 'something to read on the train'; 'holiday reading'; 'it's only a thriller'. You might feel awkward talking about a certain kind of reading you enjoy, not because anything is wrong with that sort of text but because, in the specific context you have been asked to think about it, that kind of writing is regarded as of 'lesser' status. This is also true for films, theatre, opera, popular music and television. As Simon Frith observes,

> the crucial 'high'/low conflict is not that between social classes but that produced by the commercial process itself at *all* levels of cultural expression, in pop as well as classical music, in sports as well as the cinema. 'High'/low thus describes the emergence of consumer elites or cults on the one hand (the bohemian *versus* the conformist), and the tension between artists and their audiences . . . on the other (the modernist and the avant garde against the orthodox and main stream). (Frith, 1991, p. 109).

7.7

- Look in local newspapers, broadsheet newspapers and the tabloids at the pages which advertise entertainments and cultural events, or read a selection of reviews of music, art, films and theatre. Can you identify those that might have cult status or appeal to certain consumer elites? How far do you think the media creates a cult or an elite?
- Choose a film, TV programme, musical or art event that you think of as cult or elite. Try and list the characteristics that produce this status. For example, if it is a film, it might be shown only in an art house or independent cinema.

You could take this further by undertaking a project on a well documented recent cult TV series, like *Twin Peaks* or *The X-Files*. To explore the reasons for its success and discover more about who watched it, try looking up references to the series in CD-ROM editions of national newspapers or accessing Web sites devoted to the programme. Try to think about not only the content of the programme but also who watched it, when it was screened and how it was treated by the media.

Re-reading literature: 1990s approaches

As we have seen, Raymond Williams's work on cultural history foregrounded 'high' culture, especially literary culture, as a means of opening up the workings of hegemony (Williams, 1958b). The contemporary version of Williams's approach might be found in **new historicist** and **cultural materialist** re-readings of literary works, which examine texts as embedded in and produced by specific cultural contexts. In between and alongside these positions there exists a range of other approaches that treat texts which are just as likely to be sold in a supermarket as they are in a bookshop: work on romance, on comics, on thrillers, for example. A characteristic of these approaches is that the text comes to be seen as a commodity or material object, produced at a particular time, in a particular place, under particular social and economic conditions, as opposed to being studied solely for its aesthetic value.

Among the most influential of the new approaches to texts which have been adopted by those engaged in looking at literary works are new historicism and its variant cultural materialism (for accessible overviews of these approaches, see Barry, 1995, pp. 172–90; Knowles, 1996, pp. 586–92). Alongside these approaches there has been a great deal of interest in postcolonial theory and queer theory (for an accessible overview of these approaches, see Barry, 1995: on lesbian and gay criticism, pp. 139–55; on postcolonial criticism, pp. 191–201). This chapter concludes its discussion of 'high' culture with discussion of the ways in which contemporary approaches to literary texts can lead to a re-reading of a classic text of the kind promoted by the National Curriculum in ways that re-engage it with the particular culture in which it was produced. We have chosen to work with the Edwardian children's classic. *The Wind in the Willows* (1908), which tells the story of Mole, Rat and Toad and their adventures along the riverbank. Locating this text in relation to the heteroglossia of its era can suggest alternative ways in which it may be read that can contribute to a greater understanding of the interrelation between text and context. Such an approach can go some way to blurring the high – popular divide because it insists upon the interpenetration of text and wider society.

Re-reading texts: *The Wind in the Willows* (1908) and English masculinity

This section draws upon a **new historicist** approach to develop a contextualized reading of Grahame's novel. It also makes use of ideas from **queer theory** to illuminate the bonds of male friendship at the centre of the novel. In what follows we provide signposts for a re-reading of Grahame's novel which draws upon these new approaches to texts and suggests something of their power to challenge. To get the most out of this section we recommend that you read the whole of *The Wind in the Willows* before you work through the remainder of this chapter. We begin with a short introductory overview of the topic, which is designed to help you work with the material in the various activity sections.

A crisis of English masculinity?

The novel's central characters are all male, and their relationships can be read in the light of the ongoing debates in the 1900s about the nature of English masculinity. At this time there was considerable anxiety about the stability of gender roles, and several books and articles were written on the subject, including Edward Carpenter's *The Intermediate Sex: a Study of Some Transitional Types of Men and Women*, one of the first English studies of homosexuality, which appeared in the same year as Grahame's novel. The anxiety about the changing nature of gendered identity was particular acute in Britain in the later nineteenth century, as it was given impetus by events like the passing of the Labouchere Amendment of 1885 (which made homosexual acts criminal) and the trial and imprisonment of Oscar Wilde in 1895. In the later 1890s there was something of a backlash against certain kinds of 'decadent' behaviour – a decadence which was closely related to the beliefs and attitudes expressed in work featured in the magazine the *Yellow Book*, a literary and artistic periodical for which Graham was writing in the 1890s (for further information on the cultural background to this see Ledger, 1997, pp. 94–121).

In Britain, this backlash against decadence and degeneration was given added impetus by anxieties about Empire: Britain's imperial holdings were increasingly seen as threatened by expansionist activities by other powers, notably Germany. The idea of national degeneracy as a threat to Britain's imperial mission informs the period's fears about the fate of the Englishman, especially after the drawn out events of the second Boer War (1899–1902), when officers regularly wrote home and to the press to lament the poor physical condition of their troops. Related to this was a growing perception that modern urban living was morally and physically damaging. This middle-class anxiety fed a sense of a growing gulf between the classes which is evident throughout the later nineteenth century and the early Edwardian period (Marriott, 1996; Schwarz, 1996); something of this fear is manifested in Grahame's novel in the portrayal of the Wild Wooders.

Fears of national decline in the face of what were seen as growing internal and external threats led to increased emphasis on normalcy; on being a proper English man or woman. Signs of deviance from these social codes were mocked – the free thinking New Women of the 1880s and 1890s were consistently satirized because they were seen as a threat to traditions of femininity. These, largely middle-class, women, by acting autonomously and resisting traditional patterns of feminine respectability, were often seen as setting a bad example to the 'lower orders': of failing in their duty as 'mothers of the nation'. With the rise of so-called new women there came to be perceived a range of new men: henpecked, down trodden at best or actively camp and effeminate (the urban middle-class dandy) at worst, these masculine roles were seen as just as much of a threat to the future of the nation (Ledger, 1997, pp. 94–121).

It is in this context that, during the later nineteenth century, the concept of 'the gentleman' becomes more inclusive. It was extended to cover public school educated middle-class men (as opposed to members, however minor, of the hereditary aristocracy) and, from 1880 onwards, the public school gentleman became the dominant stereotype of English masculinity. Educated to a limited level, instilled with a version of muscular Christianity, the late nineteenth-century English gentleman became perceived as the backbone of the administrative class at home and abroad, and an environment was created in which male solidarity was valorized:

> masculine privilege was sustained by male friendships within institutions like the public schools, the older universities, the [gentleman's] clubs and the professions. Because, however, the continuing dominance of bourgeois males also required that they marry and produce offspring, the intensity and sufficiency of male bonding needed to be strictly controlled by homophobic mechanisms. (Dellamorra, 1996, p. 83)

The Wind in the Willows focuses upon a small clique of privileged males, living a leisured existence in a rural Arcadia. This world is threatened by the irrational pursuit of pleasure by the spendthrift Toad, which encourages the encroachment of the underprivileged masses, represented here by the Wild Wooders. The novel ends with order restored through the 'heroic' activity of the central males, acting together to re-establish the status quo. What this tale of the fruits of male bonding appears to overlook is any sense that the male middle-class values of comradeship and solidarity were, in some quarters, being recast as part of the wider problem of gender identity.

The Edwardian homosexual

Edward Carpenter's ground-breaking study of lesbians and gay men, *The Intermediate Sex: a Study of Some Transitional Types of Men and Women* (1908), can provide us with contextualizing material from the period which addresses itself to the nature of gender identity. Just as Grahame's novel evokes a rural Arcadia confidently able to resist the threats of the wider world and Wild Wood, so Carpenter's work evokes a lost era of sexual freedom when queerness was not marginalized: both men implicitly critique modern social conditions, albeit from different perspectives and for different ends (Mason, 1994, p. 12). Carpenter's work was taken up in left-wing circles, but was to be especially influential with members of the Bloomsbury 'group' a little later (Weeks, 1981, p. 174). In the extract that follows, Carpenter offers his views on the gender crisis of the early twentieth century.

7.7

If the modern woman is a little more masculine in some ways than her predecessor, the modern man (it is to be hoped), while by no means effeminate, is a little more sensitive in temperament and artistic in feeling than the original John Bull. It is beginning to be recognised that the sexes do not or should not normally form two groups hopelessly isolated in habit and feeling from each other, but that they rather represent the two poles of one group – which is the human race; so that while certainly the extreme specimens at either pole are vastly divergent, there are great numbers in the middle region who (though differing corporeally as men and women) are by emotion and temperament very near to each other . . .

More than thirty years ago, however, an Austrian writer, K. H. Ulrichs, drew attention in a series of pamphlets . . . to the existence of a class of people who strongly illustrate the above remarks, and with whom specially this paper is concerned. He pointed out that there were people born in such a position – as it were on the dividing line between the sexes – that while belonging distinctly to one sex as far as their bodies are concerned they may be said to belong mentally and emotionally to the other; that there were men, for instance, who might be described as of feminine soul enclosed in a male body . . . or in other cases, women whose definition would be just the reverse. And he maintained that this doubleness of nature was to a great extent proved by the special direction of their love-sentiment. For in such cases, as indeed might be expected, the (apparently) masculine person instead of forming a love-union with a female tended to contract romantic friendships with one of his own sex; while the apparently feminine would, instead of marrying in the usual way, devote herself to the love of another feminine.

People of this kind (i.e., having this special variation of the love-sentiment) he called Urnings;[1] and though we are not obliged to accept his theory about the crosswise connexion between 'soul' and 'body,' since at best these words are somewhat vague and indefinite; yet his work was important because it was one of the first attempts, in modern times, to recognise the existence of what might be called an Intermediate sex, and to give at any rate some explanation of it.

Since that time the subject has been widely studied and written about by scientific men and others, especially on the Continent (though in England it is still comparatively unknown), and by means of an extended observation of present-day cases, as well as

---

[1] Note: From Uranos, heaven; his idea being that the Uranian love was of a higher order than the ordinary attachment . . . [original note].

the indirect testimony of the history and literature of past times, quite a body of general conclusions has been arrived at – of which I propose in the following pages to give some slight account . . .

It is partly for these reasons, and to throw a little light where it may be needed, that I have thought it might be advisable in this paper simply to give a few general characteristics of the Intermediate types.

As indicated then already, in bodily structure there is, as a rule, nothing to distinguish the subjects of our discussion from ordinary men and women; but if we take the general mental characteristics it appears from almost universal testimony that the male tends to be of a rather gentle, emotional disposition – with defects, if such exist, in the direction of subtlety, evasiveness, timidity, vanity, etc.; while the female is just the opposite, fiery, active, bold and truthful, with defects running to brusqueness and coarseness. Moreover, the mind of the former is generally intuitive and instinctive in its perceptions, with more or less of artistic feeling; while the mind of the latter is more logical, scientific, and precise than usual with the normal woman. So marked indeed are these general characteristics that sometimes by means of them (though not an infallible guide) the nature of the boy or girl can be detected in childhood, before full development has taken place; and needless to say it may often be very important to be able to do this . . .

We have so far limited ourselves to some very general characteristics of the Intermediate race. It may help to clear and fix our ideas if we now describe in more detail, first, what may be called the extreme and exaggerated types of the race, and then the more normal and perfect types. By doing so we shall get a more definite and concrete view of our subject.

In the first place, then, the extreme specimens – as in most cases of extremes – are not particularly attractive, sometimes quite the reverse. In the male of this kind we have a distinctly effeminate type, sentimental, lackadaisical, mincing in gait and manners, something of a chatterbox, skilful at the needle and in woman's work, sometimes taking pleasure in dressing in woman's clothes; his figure not unfrequently betraying a tendency towards the feminine, large at the hips, supple, not muscular, the face wanting in hair, the voice inclining to be 'high'-pitched, etc.; while his dwelling-room is orderly in the extreme, even natty, and choice of decoration and perfume. His affection, too, is often feminine in character, clinging, dependent and jealous, as of one desiring to be loved almost more than to love . . .

These are types which, on account of their salience, everyone will recognise more or less. Naturally, when they occur they excite a good deal of attention, and it is not an uncommon impression that most persons of the homogenic nature belong to either one or other of these classes. But in reality, of course, these extreme developments are rare, and for the most part the temperament in question is embodied in men and women of quite normal and unsensational exterior. Speaking of this subject and the connection between effeminateness and the homogenic nature in men, Dr. Moll says: 'It is, however, as well to point out at the outset that effeminacy does not by any means show itself in all Urnings. Though one may find this or that indication in a great number of cases, yet it cannot be denied that a very large percentage, perhaps by far the majority of them, do not exhibit pronounced Effeminacy.' And it may be supposed that we may draw the same conclusion with regard to women of this class – namely, that the majority of them do not exhibit pronounced masculine habits. In fact, while these extreme cases are of the greatest value from a scientific point of view as marking tendencies and limits of development in certain directions, it would be a serious mistake to look upon them as representative cases of the whole phases of human evolution concerned.

If now we come to what may be called the more normal type of the Uranian man, we find a man who, while possessing thoroughly masculine powers of mind and body, combines with them the tenderer and more emotional soul-nature of the woman – and sometimes to a remarkable degree. Such men, as said, are often muscular and well-built, and not distinguishable in exterior structure and the carriage of body from others of their own sex; but emotionally they are extremely complex, tender, sensitive, pitiful and loving, 'full of storm and stress, of ferment and fluctuation' of the heart; the logical faculty may or may not, in their case, be well-developed, but intuition is always strong; like women they read characters at a glance, and know, without knowing how, what is passing in the minds of others; for nursing and waiting on the needs of others they have often a peculiar gift; at the bottom lies the artist-nature, with the artist's sensibility and perception. Such a one is often a dreamer, of brooding, reserved habits, often a musician, or a man of culture, courted in society, which nevertheless does not understand him – though sometimes a child of the people, without any culture, but almost always with a peculiar inborn refinement . . .

That men of this kind despise women, though a not uncommon belief, is one which hardly appears to be justified. Indeed, though naturally not inclined to 'fall in love' in this direction, such men are by their nature drawn rather near to women, and it would seem that they often feel a singular appreciation and understanding of the emotional needs and destinies of the other sex, leading in many cases to a genuine though what is called 'Platonic' friendship. There is little doubt that they are often instinctively sought after by women, who, without suspecting the real cause, are conscious of a sympathetic chord in the homogenic which they miss in the normal man . . .

I have now sketched – very briefly and inadequately it is true – both the extreme types and the more healthy types of the 'Intermediate' man . . . types which can be verified from history and literature, though more certainly and satisfactorily perhaps from actual life around us. And unfamiliar though the subject is, it begins to appear that it is one which modern thought and science will have to face. Of the latter and more normal types it may be said that they exist, and have always existed, in considerable abundance, and from that circumstance alone there is a strong probability that they have their place and purpose. (Carpenter, 1908, pp. 17–37)

7.8

Create a checklist of the characteristics of the male Urning; you may find it helpful to do this in two categories (e.g. 'extreme' and 'normal').

You will refer to your notes on Carpenter in further work on Grahame's novel.

The English gentleman

Carpenter's work seeks to identify the characteristics of what, for the period, might be imagined as the antithesis of the English gentleman. He is careful to stress the 'normality' of the average Urning, and while this might be intended to reassure, in the climate of anxiety which existed in Edwardian Britain this capacity to appear normal while being different might well have occasioned concern. In order to take further our work on the male roles of *The Wind in the Willows*, we will now spend a little time considering the extent to which the values and behaviour of the novel's central characters can be related to some definition of the English gentleman. While reading the following extracts, note what each writer suggests are the main characteristics of this type.

7.8

The idea of the gentleman is not a class idea . . . it is an idea which has had its mutations. In the eighteenth century a gentleman knew his tenants, his fields, and his foxes: he helped to govern his country, and might sit in parliament at Westminster; he might even be interested in architecture and painting, and indulge himself in music. He was an amateur furnished with ability – the apotheosis of the amateur. But the essence was a code of conduct – good form: the not doing of the things which are not done: reserve: a habit of understatement. The code became disengaged, and explicit, with the spread of boarding or 'public' schools during the nineteenth century. It was in many ways a curious code. It was hardly based on religion, though it might be instilled in sermons: it was a mixture of stoicism with mediaeval lay chivalry, and of both with unconscious national ideals half Puritan and half secular. Yet if it contained such national ideals, it was not a national code, in the sense that it embraced the nation: it was the code of an elite (from whatever classes the elite was drawn) rather than a code of the nation at large. On the other hand elites will always count; and 'social idealism', or snobbery at its best, made the code of the gentleman pervasive. It is impossible to think of the character of England without thinking also of the character of the gentleman. But it is also impossible to think of the character of the gentleman clearly. It has an English haze. The gentleman is shy, yet also self confident. He is the refinement of manliness; but the manliness is sometimes more obvious than the refinement . . . (Barker, 1947, reprinted in Giles and Middleton, 1995, 59)

The Englishman feels very deeply and reasons very little. It might be argued, superficially, that because he has done little to remedy the state of things on the Congo, that he is lacking in feeling. But, as a matter of fact, it is really because he is aware – subconsciously if you will – of the depth of his capacity to feel, that the Englishman takes refuge in his particular official optimism. He hides from himself the fact that there are in the world greed, poverty, hunger, lust or evil passions, simply because he knows that if he comes to think of them at all they will move him beyond bearing. He prefers, therefore, to say – and to hypnotise himself into believing – that the world is a very good – an all-good-place. He would prefer to believe that such people as the officials of the Congo Free State do not really exist in the modern world. People, he will say, do not do such things . . . the especial province of the English nation is the evolution of a standard of manners. For that is what it comes to when one says that the province of the English is to solve the problem of how men may live together . . . It is true that in repressing its emotions this people, so adventurous and so restless, has discovered the secret of living

. . . this people which has so 'high' a mission in the world has invented a saving phrase which, upon all occasions, unuttered and perhaps unthought, dominates the situation. For, if in England we seldom think it and still more seldom say it, we nevertheless feel very intimately as a set rule of conduct, whenever we meet a man, whenever we talk with a woman: 'You will play the game.' (Ford Madox Ford, 1907, reprinted in Giles and Middleton, 1995, pp. 46–52)

ACTIVITIES

7.9

These passages can serve us as a checklist of English masculinity in the early twentieth century and so give a context for understanding the representation of masculinity in *The Wind in the Willows*. The Englishman is shy but self confident, manly rather than refined, and while capable of feeling deeply, is unreflective about his emotions; indeed, rather than face contradictions he will take refuge in what Ford calls official optimism.

- How far do these traits relate to the characteristics of the main characters in Grahame's novel? Make a list of the characteristics of each character: we have started you off.

Rat	Mole	Badger	Toad
Poet and warlike	Domestic	Free spirit	Shows off

- How far did the characters fit Barker's and Ford's definitions of the English gentleman?
- What features do the characters have that are not part of the listing provided by your notes on the extracts? How do you explain apparent contradictions like the fact that rat is both a dreamy poet and, when the occasion calls for it, apt to be very warlike?
- Look back at your notes on Carpenter: how far are the characteristics he identifies visible in the novel? Can you, for example, make a case for Rat as a type of Urning? Which scenes and sequences would you refer to to make out your case? What material might you use to refute such a reading?

Homosociality in The Wind in the Willows

When we are juxtaposing material on 'the gentleman' with Carpenter's work on queerness it is important to recall Dellamora's point about protecting and controlling homosexuality via homophobia. What your notes may reveal is that the masculinity of a character like Rat is far less fixed and stable than might at first appear. At this stage it is helpful to step back from the text and reflect briefly upon some of the approaches associated with queer theory, before turning once more to Grahame's novel. Eve Sedgwick, an influential critic working in this field, has argued that patriarchal society requires homophobia – a fear of homosexuality – and that this is inevitable in a male-dominated culture. Sedgwick uses the term 'homosocial' when talking about male-dominated cultural milieus:

> Homosocial is a word which is today gaining a wider currency; it is used in history and the social sciences to describe social bonds between persons of the same sex: it is a neologism, obviously formed by analogy with homosexual, and just as obviously meant to be distinguished from homosexual. In fact, it is applied to such activities as male bonding, which may . . . be characterised by intense homophobia, fear and hatred of homosexuality. (Sedgwick, 1985, p. 1)

Given that society is often organized by men promoting the interests of other men, homosociality has been constructed as especially antagonistic towards the idea of men loving men (homosexuality) (Sedgwick, 1985, pp. 4–5). By focusing upon the ways in which heterosexual male dominance requires the marginalization of the queerness which threatens its social dominance, critics like Sedgwick and other queer theorists have facilitated a re-reading of masculinity which is alert to the role's contradictions and complicity in the status quo. As Koestenbaum has argued, queer theory 'questions heterosexuality's privileges and forces masculine writing to take seriously the threat of queerness . . . within male texts of all varieties lurks a homosexual desire [often disguised as homosociality] which, far from reinforcing patriarchy, undermines it, and offers a way out' (Koestenbaum, 1989, p. 5). Bearing in mind Koestenbaum's argument about the ways in which homosexuality can 'lurk' within homosociality, read the following argument and then consider the questions which follow it.

7.9

Mole comes out of the closet

If we trace the movement of Mole in this novel we see him travel from a position where he is associated with private domesticity to one in which he has become a respected member of the riverbank world. The story first places Mole with Rat as his companion but it is through his liaison with the more uncomplicatedly masculine Badger that he achieves his mature status.

Mole is an interesting figure in the contexts afforded by the debates about masculinity in the period. His terror in the Wild Wood, his irrationality whilst Rat deduces the location of Badger's home and his readiness to adopt helper-type roles all mark him off as somewhat short of the period's masculine ideal. Mole's house is a further register of this slippage. Perhaps the most striking feature of this house is its statuary:

> In the middle was a small round pond containing goldfish and surrounded by a cockle shell border. Out of the centre of the pond rose a fanciful erection clothed in more cockle shells and topped by a large silvered glass ball that reflected everything all wrong and had a very pleasing effect. (Grahame, 1983, p. 52)

Mole's tastes are indicative of his sensuality and a privileging of the aesthetic over the practical. His cockle shell erection is in a style that today might be called kitsch and, given the wider social context (partially reflected in the novel) in which hierarchies are to be maintained, his delight in an artefact which 'reflected everything all wrong' and in consequence had a 'very pleasing effect' is suggestive.

Our first meeting with Mole sees him running from this domestic locale, casting aside his 'feminine' duties to embrace the bachelor life of the river; a locale which is associated with a loss of maturity and of the related need for adult responsibility:

> By the side of the river he trotted as one trots, *when very small, by the side of a man, who holds one spellbound by exciting stories.* (Grahame, 1983, p. 2; emphasis added)

Mole meets Rat, who offers to show him more of the river and to take him on a picnic. The river world of Rat is one of freedom and leisure, recalling (perhaps) the world of middle class coteries which were often circles in which gay men met in the later nineteenth century (on this see Weeks, 1989, p. 260). In one sense the book clearly diverges from the idealised homosexual world of the fin de siècle in that the working class body is not the focus of middle class interest as it certainly was in Wilde's circle (Weeks, 1989, p. 262). In E. M. Forster's novel of homosexual awakening, *Maurice*, written a few years after Grahame's novel, it is the rural working class male who is the physical lover that Maurice has sought – a lover whose closeness to nature allows Maurice to express his animal lusts (as they are seen in the text) in the specifically rural, idealised setting of the Greenwood. In Grahame's text, however, Mole and Rat set up their bachelor existence in a seemingly sexless Arcadia.

Yet what are noticeable in these early chapters are the ways in which Mole takes up the domestic and 'feminine' role: he is the one who is strongly emotional – little ecstasies over unpacking the picnic hamper, tears of remorse; his ineptness at rowing – and his repeated flights of emotion are signs of a failure of manly self-restraint. Rat, on the other hand, is both the man of action and the poet – the very type of masculinity promoted by the public school and made flesh for many a few years after this novel was written in the person of the warrior-poet Rupert Brooke. We see Rat taking charge of situations and frequently laden with phallic weaponry (guns, pistols etc.) whilst the Mole is left to deal with the dishes.

In Chapter 2 they go caravanning with Toad and amongst everything else that happens during this trip we have an illustration of the way in which homosociality (i.e. male bonding) might be read as homosexual. Fed up with Toad's demands and the effort of life on the road, the two chums hold hands in the dark and plan to escape to their dear old hole by the river (Grahame, 1983, p. 18). This scene evokes both a public school experience of isolation and male friendship and also hints at the kind of escapist turn evident in Forster's turn to the Greenwood; both texts establish the rural as the locale in which the middle class male can do as he pleases.

In Mole and Rat we have, then, what Sedgwick might term a homosocial couple and their relationship cannot stand apart from the wide-spread gender panic of the early twentieth century. This is not to say that Grahame was gay nor that this text is about homosexuality: it is to suggest that placing the novel in the wider context afforded by the culture of the period and Grahame's biography we can start to read its account of homosociality in ways that he may not have intended but which are certainly relevant to an account of the shifting perceptions of English masculinity in the period. The richness and ambiguity of text like *The Wind in the Willows* allows for a diversity of decodings, some of which, like the reading above, may run counter to its intended meaning, but nevertheless offer insights into the discourses that produced certain understandings of masculinity at a particular historical moment ... (Taken from an unpublished lecture by Tim Middleton)

7.10

- What was your reaction to this extract? If you thought it was misguided (or even stupid), can you think about why you reacted in this way?
- How far does it support the findings of your own work on the version of Grahame's novel which emerges after its central character's traits have been set alongside those described by Barker, Carpenter and Ford?

The persistence of high culture

Did your response to the lecture extract have anything to do with your sense of the status of the novel? The 1983 edition published by the Oxford University Press World's Classics series (a title which in itself seems to guarantee the text's prestige and global importance) offers the reader the following back cover blurb as part of its sales pitch:

> *The Wind in the Willows* (1908) is a book for those 'who keep the spirit of youth alive in them; of life, sunshine, running water, woodlands, dusty roads, winter firesides'.
> So wrote Kenneth Grahame of his timeless tale of Toad, Mole, Badger, and Rat in their beautiful and benevolently ordered world. But it is also a world under siege, threatened by dark and unnamed forces – 'the Terror of the Wild Wood' with its 'wicked little faces' and 'glances of malice and hatred' – and defended by the mysterious Piper at the Gates of Dawn. *The Wind in the Willows* has achieved an enduring place in our literature: it succeeds at once in arousing our anxieties and in calming them by giving perfect shape to our desire for peace and escape.

This firmly suggests that *The Wind in the Willows* is a 'classic' children's book, and this status may well shape the ways in which we respond to readings of it. Notice how the blurb sets up oppositions as a means of describing the text's content: we have started you off but you can add in oppositions you identified in your own reading to create a more detailed account.

Favoured – River Bank	Not favoured – non-River Bank
beautiful	dark
benevolent	wicked

The novel organizes itself around what were, and what by and large remain, oppositions fostered by the dominant culture. As a text written for a middle-class child (and, in fact, a particularly difficult and unhappy child), the preaching of peace and happiness through adherence to River Bank values is clearly part of an overtly ideological message. Any reading of the novel has to take on board the fact that the River Bank world is threatened, but what the kind of reading we have been investigating here can do is to shift attention away from the obvious source of trouble (Toad's selfishness, the threat of the 'working-class' Wild Wooders) to a more deep-seated threat (as the dominant discourse of the period might have perceived it) to the middle-class males who dominate the River Bank milieu – a threat which, ironically, is actually inherent in the very nature of the all-male milieu they fight to preserve. The fact that the kind of reading sketched here may (at first) appear to be 'unthinkable' can be seen as a register of the lengths to which the dominant culture of patriarchy goes in order to bury any hint of homo-sexuality in its celebration of homosociality.

Conclusions

In this discussion of the homosocial in *The Wind in the Willows* we have, of course, only begun to explore the ways in which a text changes when situated in its ori-ginal cultural context. To take the reading we have been considering further, you will need to find out more about the period and the debates about gendered iden-tity which were current at the time. It will also help if you learn more about Grahame's own life: the suggested reading and other resources listed below can help you to make a start on this.

This chapter has examined some of the ways in which cultural studies has ap-proached a divided and disparate cultural sphere. In this chapter we have tended to concentrate upon literary culture, but other areas of 'high' culture, like classical music, opera, painting or dance, can all provide rich sites for your own investiga-tions. An approach to literary as well as popular texts that involves seeing both as inextricably linked aspects of the production and circulation of meanings at a specific historical moment can identify not only the ways in which dominant dis-courses manifest themselves, but also latent trends, nuances and tendencies that run counter to the dominant.

Suggested further reading

This list covers suggestions for further reading on new historicism, queer theory and approaches to gender and literature in the period. For works cited in the chapter as a whole please see the references at the end of this book

Peter Barry (1995) *Beginning Theory: an Introduction to Literary and Cultural Theory*. Man-chester: Manchester University Press. Has a good discussion of new historicism and its UK variant, cultural materialism, and a chapter on what he terms Lesbian and Gay criticism: a good starting point.
Peter Green (1959) *Kenneth Grahame: a Study of His Life, Work and Times*. London: John Murray. The standard biography.

Steve Humphries and Pamela Gordon (1996) *A Man's World: from Boyhood to Manhood, 1900–1960*. London: BBC Books. Based on oral history work for a TV series, this book offers a wide range of recollections about aspects of masculinity in the period, including discussion of homosexuality.

Lyn Pykett (1995) *Engendering Fictions: the English Novel in the Early Twentieth Century*. London: Arnold. A very readable account of the debates about gender as they manifested themselves in the fiction of the era: contains an appendix of quotations from a range of period sources on the topic which can be productively juxtaposed with material from Grahame and the extracts from Barker, Carpenter and Ford provided here.

Eve Kosofsky Sedgwick (1994) *Epistemology of the Closet*. London: Penguin. Not an easy read but worth perserving with: this book is a landmark in queer theory.

Martin Taylor (1989) *Lads: Love Poetry of the Trenches*. London: Constable. This book offers an example of another approach to the kind of re-reading we sketch here. Thomas's work examines homosocial poetry from the First World War and teases out its homosexual aspects.

Web sites

Queer Resources Directory has links to a range of queer theory/culture sites at: http://www.qrd.org/qrd/culture/

People with a History: an Online Guide to Lesbian, Gay, Bisexual and Transsexual History is a wonderfully rich site, with masses of material and links to hundreds of other sites: http://www.fordham.edu/halsall/pwh/index.html

CHAPTER 8

Subjects, Bodies, Selves

Introduction

You will recall that in chapter 2 we separated identity and subjectivity, promising to return to subjectivity later. We hope that the ideas introduced in this chapter will not simply be added on to your understanding of identity but will also cause you to reflect back on and rethink your ideas about identity in the light of this discussion. Although the terms identity and subjectivity are sometimes used interchangeably, they are not quite synonymous but neither are they entirely separated concepts. Indeed, thinking about the different ways in which the terms are used and the nuances of meaning, which may defy definition, will focus your mind on what is at stake when cultural and social theorists write about these issues. This chapter refers to some of the most influential theorists of the self in the twentieth century: Sigmund Freud, Jacques Lacan, Michel Foucault, Louis Althusser. However, it is not our intention to offer comprehensive accounts of complex theories or areas of knowledge. These are readily available elsewhere and should be the subject of in-depth study as your interests dictate. Our aim, in this chapter, is to flag up important areas for your further consideration, to introduce you to the possibilities in such areas and to stimulate your thinking based on your own experience.

In chapter 2 we introduced you to humanist ideas of the self, which hold that individual consciousness is the centre from which meaning, identity and language originate. We went on to problematize this idea by suggesting that identities are not simply a matter of individual choice; nor are we born with a core self. Instead, we argued, identity is socially and historically formed. In doing so we adopted an **anti-humanist** position that challenges common-sense beliefs about the nature of selfhood and identity. Subjectivity, in this context, signifies differently from orthodox understandings of the term, such as that given by the *Oxford English Dictionary*: 'proceeding from personal idiosyncrasy or individuality; not impartial or literal'. Instead, 'against this humanist notion, the concept of subjectivity decentres the individual by problematizing the simplistic relationship between language and the individual which common sense presumes' (Easthope and McGowan, 1992, p. 67). Now read the following definition.

8.1

'Subjectivity' can be defined as that combination of conscious and unconscious thoughts and emotions that make up our sense of ourselves, our relation to the world and our ability to act in that world. Unlike the individualist notion of people as rational, self-motivated individuals in pursuit of their own clear and stable self-interest, the concept of subjectivity can capture both the notion of people as intentional subjects – actors in the world – and at the same time as subject to forces beyond their conscious control. For that reason, it has proved very useful to feminist theory, which has recognized that as women we behave in ways which we do not intend and are not always in our own interests. Such 'irrational' behaviour has been experienced by women as their own failure to make personal and emotional changes that politically and intellectually seem desirable. A need to understand why this happens, or how what is called a contradictory subjectivity is produced, led feminists to examine, among other accounts, psychoanalytic theories of the unconscious . . .

Even though our subjectivity is, by definition, what we experience as most personal and most individual, our desires and expectations are acquired in a social context. (Crowley and Himmelweit, 1992, p. 7).

There are two points we can make here, which will be discussed further in later sections. First, you may have noted that Crowley and Himmelweit point to a significant meaning of the term 'subject', that is the sense of being 'subject to'. As they suggest, people are 'subject to forces beyond their conscious control'. When we act 'irrationally' or apparently against our best interests, either as women or as men, we are not the coherent, centred selves presupposed by humanism, but may experience a lack of control, a fragmentation of who we think we are and a sense of confusion – 'a contradictory subjectivity'. We will look at the psychoanalytic theories of Jacques Lacan, which have been used to examine how this sense of a fractured self is produced.

Second, the extract refers to the idea we met in chapter 2 that, while consciousness is experienced at a personal and individual level, our desires, needs and hopes are produced within the parameters of the social and historical context in which we are situated. Thus, apparently 'irrational' behaviours can be examined from a social as well as a psychoanalytic perspective. This is important. If 'irrational' motivations are a product of unconscious impulses that can only be interpreted by the analyst in the process of psychoanalysis, we may find ourselves locked into unchangeable behaviours that could be as determining as those ascribed to biological imperatives. Thinking about the relation between social and unconscious processes in the production of subjectivities allows for the possibility of change. In order to examine how subjectivity is constituted by the structures of society, we shall consider Foucault's theories of the **discursive** construction of subjectivity. You will remember that we introduced you to Foucault's theory of discourse in chapter 3. It would be useful to remind yourself of this. You might also find it helpful to reread the brief discussion of Althusser's theory of the subject in chapter 2.

Before we continue, here is a summary of the main ideas of anti-humanist conceptions of **decentred** subjectivity. We shall be extending our discussion of these in the sections that follow.

- The subject 'I' is not a unified, coherent identity but a sometimes contradictory set of multiple or fragmented selves.
- Individual subjectivities do not precede language but are themselves constituted in language.
- Subjects are both able to act in the world and subject to forces outside their control.
- The constitution of a particular subjectivity involves a relationship between unconscious motivations and social structures.
- Subjectivity is also constituted in relation to our physical bodies.

One other important point we want to raise here is that, while we have adopted an anti-humanist position with regard to subjectivity, we are aware of the possible difficulties of such a position for political movements concerned with combating oppression and the subordination that accompanies this. Feminism, for example, has argued that women have always experienced a sense of fragmentation and find it difficult, in a male-dominated culture, to express an authentic sense of self. One aspect of feminist endeavour has been to create spaces in which women could construct representations of women that were more valid than the images frequently reproduced in literature and the media. Women, like other oppressed groups, may need to validate themselves as coherent beings with a voice of their own in order to counter the misrepresentations of dominant culture. There has been considerable debate within feminism about the advantages and disadvantages of adopting an anti-humanist stance towards subjectivity, but whatever the difficulties many feminists now recognize the impossibility of speaking or writing in a single voice – that of 'woman'. Instead there is an awareness that 'I' may encompass a diversity of intersecting subjectivities: for example, among others, those of generation, 'race', ethnicity, sexual orientation, class (Fuss, 1989; Butler, 1990; hooks 1991).

ACTIVITIES

8.1

You may have noted in this paragraph that we have moved from writing about 'fragmentation' to writing about 'diversity'. Does 'diversity' suggest a more positive way of seeing subjectivities? If so, how?

Fragmented or multiple selves?

Because individual subjectivity is formed from the unconscious and the social, any apparently coherent conscious selfhood remains precarious and fragile, relying, as it does, on the repression of the unconscious. Most of us have behaved at some time or another in ways that took us by surprise or threatened our sense of the kind of the person we believed ourselves to be. Have you ever found yourself thinking or saying, 'Why did I do that – it's not like me at all'?

8.2

Can you think of examples in your own life when your sense of self might be **destablized** in this way? We have suggested some possibilities. Try to add to these.

- At an interview for a job that you really want you 'find' yourself saying something that you know will lessen your chances of getting the job.
- Catching sight of your reflection in a shop window or mirror you think for a moment that it is someone else.
- Knowing that you are very short of money this month you 'find' yourself buying an expensive item of clothing.
-
-
-
-

In any of the situations above we 'find' ourselves behaving as if we were a different person – someone we don't 'know', a stranger – and we appear to have no control over this. We just 'find' ourselves acting or looking in ways that appear to contradict what we know about ourselves at the level of conscious thinking. The point to grasp is that this is not a matter of moving between different aspects of a fixed, pre-given personality or adopting certain roles in specific situations. Instead, subjectivity is constantly in flux, constantly in process and only ever briefly stabilized. Equally, following Althusser's concept of interpellation, situations offer us or 'recruit' us to socially appropriate modes of subjectivity. For example, a woman who has just had a baby is invited to take up the socially appropriate subject position that constitutes being a mother in late twentieth-century Western societies, and she may 'recognize' herself in this invitation (see the section on language and subjectivity below). However, she may experience, simultaneously, intense feelings of hostility towards her newborn baby that threaten this subject position. She may feel unaccountably guilty: 'Why, when I've got a beautiful baby, do I feel so unhappy and depressed? What's wrong with me? I must be a bad mother.' The subject position 'mother' into which she has been interpellated and where she has located herself cannot contain or incorporate these contradictory feelings and impulses, and the result for the woman may be a sense of splitting or fragmentation, what is sometimes described as a sense of 'falling apart'. She does not experience herself as the coherent individual of humanist thought but in multiple ways: as subject to uncontrollable forces; as the subject of society's narratives about mothers and motherhood; and as the subject of her own actions and feelings (she physically cares for the baby, she loves the baby).

The point to grasp is that the concept of subjectivity always implies an unconscious dimension. It is not synonymous with personality or selfhood but offers a way of connecting conscious and unconscious dimensions of the self with the social world in which these are formed and acted out. Certain forms of mental illness are characterized by extreme manifestations of 'split personality' in which the sufferer may be partially or totally unaware of extreme shifts in persona. Close relatives can be devastated by the loss of the person they once knew and find it difficult to accept that 'he's not the man I married' or 'she's not my mother any longer'. We also say similar things about changes in people we know, changes brought about as a result of illness, social mobility, political commitment and even excess alcohol. To summarize:

- subjectivities may be assumed temporarily;
- a particular subjectivity may be more dominant in specific contexts but may remain as traces in other situations;
- the positions in which we locate ourself at any one moment may be fragile, open to disruption from other subject positions and from those desires, impulses and needs that form the unconscious;
- we may be invited to assume certain subject positions and this will involve issues of power and dominance (we shall discuss this later in the chapter).

Now read the following poem, *Recognition*, by Carol Ann Duffy.

8.2

Recognition

Things get away from one.
I've let myself go, I know.
Children? I've had three
and don't even know them.

I strain to remember a time
when my body felt lighter.
Years. My face is swollen
with regrets. I put powder on,

but it flakes off. I love him,
through habit, but the proof
has evaporated. He gets upset.
I tried to do all the essentials

on one trip. Foolish, yes,
but I was weepy all morning.
Quiche. A blond boy swung me up
in his arms and promised the earth.

You see, this came back to me
as I stood on the scales.
I wept. Shallots. In the window,
creamy ladies held a pose

which left me clogged and old.
The waste. I'd forgotten my purse,
fumbled; the shopgirl gaped at me,
compassionless. Claret. I blushed.

Cheese. Kleenex. *It did happen*.
I lay in my slip on wet grass,
laughing. Years. I had to rush out,
blind in a hot flush, and bumped

into an anxious, dowdy matron
who touched the cold mirror
and stared at me. Stared
and said I'm sorry sorry sorry.
(Duffy, 1994, pp. 40–1)

8.3

What contradictory selves are experienced by the speaker of the poem? Is she able to reconcile these in the poem? What are the speaker's feelings about these conflicting selves? What contradictions are there between her sense of herself and the ways in which she is seen by others? What subject positions are offered to her in the social world she inhabits?

The speaker of the poem tries to hold on to memories of herself as a young girl in love with, presumably, her husband. She remembers herself as slim and attractive – a sexually desirable woman. In the present, however, she knows herself to be 'an anxious, dowdy matron', menopausal and overweight, for whom sex has become 'habit'. She experiences these two senses of herself as in conflict. Note how the structure of the poem constantly juxtaposes past and present realities by using the items of her shopping list to trigger off memories and make connections, 'Claret. I blushed. Cheese. Kleenex. it did happen.' She experiences herself as both joined to her younger self and cut off from it; a sense of fragmentation which causes her sadness and guilt. Looking in the mirror, her older self apologizes to her younger self, thus reinforcing the sense of irreconcilable split with which the poem ends. The shopgirl sees her simply as a silly middle-aged lady who has forgotten her purse, or that is how the speaker believes she is perceived. Her husband 'gets upset' – by her indifference to sex, by the fact she is no longer the youthful girl he courted? And her children have grown up and gone away. Other people's perceptions of who she is shape her own view of herself but do not constitute it totally. The subject positions available to her are wife, mother and middle-aged woman, but she cannot fit herself neatly into these, nor can she any longer see herself or be seen as a young, sexually desirable woman.

You might note that the speaker/poet does not suggest anywhere that one of these selves is the 'real' self. Instead the poem expresses a powerful sense of dislocation and fragmentation. And, something we shall return to, she experiences this sense of dislocation through her body: she weeps, she blushes, she wears make-up to hide her feelings, she is saddened by her thickening body, she experiences a hot flush and remembers her body being swung in his arms. The memories and traces of her different selves are marked bodily as well as known cognitively. How did you respond to this? Did you feel saddened by the speaker's confusion and loss of selfhood? Is it possible to see conflicting selves in a more positive way? Now read the following extract by Gloria Anzaldúa, a Chicano and lesbian-feminist poet and writer who works in the United States. Anzaldúa mixes a range of dialects and languages in her work, including North Mexican, Castilian Spanish and English, in order to draw attention to the relationship between subjectivity and language. Anzaldúa suggests a new subject, neither woman, nor lesbian, nor American, nor Chicano, that 'has to shift out of habitual formations' of rational thinking and move towards a mode of 'divergent thinking . . . one that includes rather than excludes'. She calls this new consciousness *la mestiza*.

8.3

The new *mestiza* copes by developing a tolerance for contradictions, a tolerance for ambiguity. She learns to be an Indian in Mexican culture, to be Mexican from an Anglo point of view. She learns to juggle cultures. She has a plural personality, she operates in a pluralistic model – nothing is thrust out, the good, the bad and the ugly, nothing rejected, nothing abandoned. Not only does she sustain contradictions, she turns the ambivalence into something else.

She can be jarred out of ambivalence by an intense, and often painful, emotional event which inverts or resolves the ambivalence. I'm not sure exactly how. The work takes place underground – subconsciously. It is work the soul performs. The focal point of fulcrum, that juncture where the mestiza stands, is where phenomena tend to collide. It is where the possibility of uniting all that is separate occurs. This assembly is not one where severed or separated pieces merely come together. Nor is it a balancing of opposing powers. In attempting to work out a synthesis, the self has added a third element which is greater than the sum of its severed parts. The third element is a new consciousness – a mestiza consciousness – and though it is a source of intense pain, its energy comes from continual creative motion that keeps breaking down the unitary aspect of each new paradigm. (Anzaldúa, 1987, pp. 79–80).

8.4

- This reading offers a more positive and radical way of seeing the conflicts and tensions of subjectivity. Can you identify words and phrases which suggest this?
- How do you respond to this?
- Does this passage have anything in common with Carol Ann Duffy's poem?

ACTIVITIES

You may have noted the emphasis on movement and creativity: 'performs', 'creative motion'. There is an energy in this piece which contrasts with the static, trapped sense of Duffy's poem. Yet both speakers desire or seek some kind of unity or synthesis. For Anzaldúa it is this quest for synthesis that offers creative and dynamic opportunities; for Duffy's speaker the experience leads to despair. You might also note that in both there is an awareness of a split between an outer, 'public' self and an inner, 'private' self. Remind yourself of what we said e lier about the relationship between social and unconscious processes in the construction of subjectivity. Recognition that individual subjectivity is split and fractured need not be cause for despair, as Anzaldúa demonstrates. Instead it can offer opportunities for new ways of thinking – we can, according to Anzaldúa, 'learn to juggle cultures' and, albeit painfully, create new forms of consciousness that embrace ambivalence and contradiction rather than seeking to resolve these.

In your reading you will encounter examples of subjectivity represented as fragmentation and atomization, and subjectivity represented as fluid, flexible and plural. Although the distinction between optimism and pessimism may not always be as stark as we have made it here, it is worth pausing to think carefully about where on the continuum (optimistic–pessimistic) the writer/speaker positions herself or himself.

8.5

Can you think of images or motifs that are used in writing, films and the media in attempts to capture this sense of the self as something constructed but fluid and potentially fragile. We have started you off. Try to find examples of the motifs we have listed in novels, advertisements, autobiographies, TV drama, poems, films, photographs and paintings and think about whether they suggest pleasure in multiplicity or whether they suggest a negative fragmentation, or something between. Make notes of your responses and ideas. You could add to this list as you come across other images and motifs.

- Mirrors (see Duffy's poem above)
- Clothes
- Body parts
- Borders (see Anzaldúa above)
- Masks

ACTIVITIES

- Twins/doubles
- Child in an adult body/adult in a child's body
- Metamorphoses – animal to human, human to animal, for example
- Robots, machines, technology
-
-
-

Language and subjectivity

We said earlier in this chapter that 'individual subjectivities do not precede language but are themselves constituted in language'. At this point it would be useful to remind yourself of the discussion about language and representation in chapter 3. The theories of the French psychoanalyst Jacques Lacan (1901–83) give language a far more prominent place in the construction of the psyche than did Freud. Freud suggested that the newborn baby has no sense of itself as a separate entity, that it lives in a symbiotic relationship with the mother (or mother surrogate) in which there are no boundaries between the self and another. Not only does the baby experience itself in this amorphous way, it also has no sense of being male or female. For Lacan, the acquisition of a gender identity occurs, significantly, at the same time as the baby is acquiring language.

At what point and how does the baby recognize itself as a bodily form, separate from the mother? According to Lacan this occurs around the age of six months when the child sees its reflection in a mirror and identifies with an imaginary image of itself as a 'self' with boundaries. Lacan uses the mirror as a metaphor to suggest how this moment of awareness is both recognition and misrecognition. The baby, who has up until now experienced itself as fluid and unbounded, sees, in the mirror, an image of a bounded entity. This image is experienced as seductive and pleasurable, but also as false – the baby still *feels* undefined and unbounded. The mirror image is both the baby and not the baby, both subject (myself) and object (image of myself). Think of the sentence 'I see myself'. The 'I' who is doing the looking cannot at the same time be the object (myself) that is being looked at. The mirror reflection gives the baby a coherent image of itself with which it can identify; yet, at the same time that this mirror image offers a sense of a separated, bounded self, it also occasions a split between the desired image/illusion (object) and the experiencing subject (the 'I' who looks). We 'misrecognize' the mirror reflection as an authentic identity when, in fact, it gives us only *an imaginary sense* of self. Throughout our lives, according to Lacan, we seek authenticity and identity in illusions of selfhood that depend upon the ways in which other people (mirrors) offer us reflections of ourselves or are seen as images of who we think we are. The primary reflector is, of course, the mother (or surrogate mother). As Rosalind Minsky explains. 'this taking of an identity from outside will form the basis of all [the baby's] other identifications. The baby narcissistically arrives at some kind of sense of "I" only by finding an "I" reflected back by something outside itself and external – its (m)other' (Minsky, 1992, p. 189).

The use of the mirror as a metaphor for the way in which the small child comes to perceive itself as 'I', separate from its mother and others, is one of Lacan's most accessible ideas. However, it is in Lacan's highly original re-working of Freud's Oedipal moment (which occurs later than the mirror phase) that the significance of language is introduced and we want to turn to this now.

8.4

To go back to the mirror phase in the imaginary pre-Oedipal period for a moment, the child contemplating itself in the mirror can be seen as something that bestows meaning – a kind of 'signifier' – and the image in the mirror as a kind of 'signified' . . . The image of the child in the mirror is for the child apparently the meaning of itself – when it *felt* it had only a very chaotic, unbounded meaning before this moment. We can also see what Lacan calls 'the mirror phase' as a kind of metaphor: one item, the child, discovers a likeness of itself in something else, an 'other' (the reflection). This is really for Lacan how he sees everything that happens in the imaginary: objects repeatedly reflect themselves in a kind of sealed unit where there are no apparent differences or divisions, where everything is fluid. The mirror images in the 'Imaginary' are ones of fullness, wholeness, totality, complete identity. There is no separation or gap between the experience of the child and the world it inhabits. For Lacan this is the imaginary world of 'demand' where, through identification with the other, the self is actually annihilated while imagining itself complete and full because it is *completely* dependent on the mother. It is also the world where satisfaction is never entirely complete: the baby never feels that the mother's response to its demand is ever quite enough; there is always an element of dissatisfaction.

With the entry of the father onto the scene [at the Oedipal moment], the child is precipitated into a crisis. It has to recognize that identities can only come into being, as Saussure argued, as a result of the perception of *difference*. One term or subject only has meaning because it is different from other terms and other subjects, and excludes them. At the time when the small child is first discovering sexual difference it is also, highly significantly, acquiring language. And in the discovery of language the child unconsciously learns that a sign (in this case a word) only has meaning because it is different from other signs (words) and that signs always stand for, or represent, the absence of what they signify. The words in language stand in for objects, and in this sense operate like metaphors . . . And here we get to perhaps the central point in Lacan's theory. As the child learns about language standing in for objects in the world, it is also unconsciously learning about them in the psychic world of sexuality – in the discovery of sexual difference. The father, symbolized by the phallus, legislates to the child that it must take its place within a family which is defined by sexual difference, by exclusion (it cannot be its parents' lover) and by absence (it must give up its relationship with its mother). Its identity as a human subject capable of operating viably within the family and in society depends on its recognition that it is different from some people and the same as others. In its recognition of this pre-determined social fact, the child is enabled to move from a world of fantasy, into the world of language and the symbolic. The intrusion of the third term into the child's world turns out to be not only the father – the possessor of the phallus – but also, in Lacan's theory, the law of how we *perceive* the world, that is language and culture. In this way Lacan links the sexual psychic world with the social world – the dimension of language. The child recognizes the meaning of the phallus as a signifier (as something which bestows meaning although empty in itself) – as crucially the signifier of *difference* and at the same time the signifier of the *power* to break into the child's world with the mother and shatter it. Only this allows the child to enter into the rest of the chain of empty signifiers which bestow meaning – language.

The small child becomes a human subject capable of identifying with, seeing itself reflected in, the 'I' of language by means of this joint entry into language and at the same time sexual ordering and identity ('he', 'him', 'she', 'her' are positions which pre-exist and lie in wait to receive the child when it 'steps into' language). The child finds the idea of its gendered self awaiting it in language and can then identify with the sense of coherence and self it bestows, just as it did with the image in the mirror. (Minsky, 1992, pp. 191–3).

ACTIVITIES

8.6

This extract has a lot of complex ideas in it so take time to reread and think about it. Go through it once and make notes of what you see as the three or four main points. Then reread it, but this time try to fill in some detail for each of your main points. Finally, reread the extract again and note down your response to it. Does it make sense to you? Do Lacan's theories help to explain the acquisition of identity? What specifically do you find difficult to accept, if anything? Why? Does it help to remind yourself that Lacan is using the mirror and the phallus metaphorically – he is not referring to an actual, visible penis.

Lacan's theories have been taken up by feminist theorists who see, in the focus on language, potential for disrupting the negative representation of femininity posited in Freud's accounts of sexual difference. Julia Kristeva, for example, has focused attention on the way in which the language of the pre-Oedipal Imaginary – a language of babble and fluidity, which she has termed 'semiotic' – can disrupt and transgress the laws of the symbolic order. Kristeva links the 'semiotic' with the feminine and the symbolic with the masculine, but not in ways which fix these positions to biological sex. Men as well as women can seek to rediscover the language of the Imaginary that is lost at the moment when the child 'steps into' language and the symbolic order. If this interests you, we suggest you look at Toril Moi's *A French Feminist Reader*, which will introduce you to the ideas of Kristeva and other influential French feminists, Luce Irigaray and Hélène Cixous.

READING

8.5

What I call 'the semiotic' takes us back to the pre-linguistic states of childhood where the child babbles the sounds s/he hears, or where s/he articulates rhythms, alliterations, or stresses, trying to imitate her/his surroundings. In this state the child doesn't yet possess the necessary linguistic signs and thus there is no meaning in the strict sense of the term. It is only after the mirror phase or the experience of castration in the Oedipus complex that the individual becomes subject-ively capable of taking on the signs of language, of articulation as it has been pre-scribed – and I call that 'the symbolic' . . .

What I call 'the semiotic' is a state of disintegration in which patterns appear but which do not have any stable identity: they are blurred and fluctuating. The processes which are at work here are those which Freud calls 'primary': processes of transfer. We have an example of this if we refer once again to the melodies and babblings of infants which are a sound image of their bodily instability. Babies and children's bodies are made up erotogenic zones which are extremely excitable, or, on the contrary, indiffer-ent, in a state of constant change, of excitation, or extinction, without there being any fixed identity.

A 'fixed identity': it's perhaps a fiction, an illusion – who amongst us has a 'fixed' identity? It's a phantasm; we do nevertheless arrive at a certain type of stability. There are several steps which lead to this stability and one step which has been accentuated by the French psychoanalyst Jacques Lacan is the specular identification which he calls 'the mirror phase'. In this phase one recognizes one's image in a mirror as one's self-image. It is a first identification of the chaotic, fragmented body, and is both violent and jubilatory. The identification comes about under the domination of the maternal image, which is the one nearest to the child and which allows the child both to remain close and to distance itself.

I see a face. A first differentiation takes place, and thus a first self-identity. This iden-tity is still unstable because sometimes I take myself to be me, sometimes I confuse myself with my mother. This narcissistic instability, this doubt persists and makes me ask 'who am I?', 'is it me or is it the other?' The confusion with the maternal images as first other remains.

In order for us to be able to get out of this confusion, the classical pattern of devel-opment leads us to a confrontation inside the Oedipal triangle between our desire for the mother and the process of loss which is the result of paternal authority. In the ideal case, this finishes by stabilising the subject, rendering her/him capable both of pro-nouncing sentences which conform to the rules, to the law, and of telling her/his own story – of giving her/his account. (Kristeva, 1986, in Eagleton, 1996, pp. 352–3).

8.7

- Go back to the list of motifs you began to compile in the previous section. Can these motifs be explained with reference to the ideas discussed above?
- Select a film, advertisement, novel etc. Try to 'read' it using ideas and concepts from Lacan and/or Kristeva.

Discourse and the subject

So far we have looked at theories of the constitution of subjectivity that focus on the individual psyche and on language. We suggested earlier in this chapter that 'we may be invited to assume certain subject positions and this will involve issues of power and dominance.' Althusser drew on Lacan's theory of the mirror stage in order to explain how and why people invest in those specific social relationships that enable the perpetuation of the capitalist mode of production, and that may not be in their best interests. According to Althusser, we 'recognize' ourselves in the subject positions we are invited to occupy and may experience a sense of (illusory) security and belonging in the process of intepellation into a specific subject position (Althusser, 1971). Equally, however, we may experience our 'self' as oscillating between contradictory subject positions as we are 'hailed' or inter-pellated by competing subject positions, or we may attempt to resist a particular address because it invites us to take up a position of powerlessness.

Foucault's theories of discourse hold that the individual subject is produced in and through the specific discourses that circulate in any society at any given mo-ment. Thus, for example, according to Foucault, subject categories, such as 'lun-atic' or 'criminal', do not pre-exist their construction in language and discourse. People differentiated as 'lunatics' only begin to know themselves as such and are known as such in and through the discourses of science and medicine that con-struct bodies of knowledge about a subject named as 'the lunatic' or 'the criminal' (Foucault, 1967, 1975).

Let us illustrate this with an example. Before the late nineteenth century there were, of course, people who engaged in same-sex sexual practices, but there was not a specific identity 'homosexual' that described and circumscribed certain in-dividuals on the basis of their sexual behaviour. The late nineteenth and early twentieth centuries, however, witnessed the emergence of a category of person, named homosexual, in the vocabularies of medical and psychological knowledge and in legal practices. It was this homosexual person or 'subject', rather than the sexual practices, that became the focus of concern for medicine, psychology and the law. Thus, a new subject, 'the homosexual', emerged and, having been named, could be observed and regulated by the medical profession and the law. The fu-rore surrounding the trials of Oscar Wilde in 1895 produced a public image of the newly emerging identity, 'homosexual', an image that was to be used as a scape-goat during outbursts of moral panic. Yet, at the same time, the production of 'the homosexual' in the medical, psychological and legal discourses of sexuality opened up possibilities for homosexuals themselves, who adopted the term 'ho-mosexual' in order to assert their own sense of identity and right to name them-selves. The subject position 'homosexual' classified, and thereby had the power to survey and circumscribe, individual behaviours, while at the same time offering a subject position from which to assert the dignity of a homosexual subjectivity. By the end of the nineteenth century the outline of a ' "modern" male homosexual identity was beginning to emerge', offering possibilities for self-expression as well as producing an intensely oppressive definition that legitimated punitive moral regulation (Weeks, 1989, pp. 96–122).

Foucault was concerned with what he called disciplinary power and the means by which this is exercised. His focus is on the emergence in the nineteenth and twentieth centuries of new large-scale institutions that regulate, govern, discipline and 'police' modern populations: schools, prisons, clinics, hospitals, factories. This disciplinary power is asserted through administrative systems, professional expertise and the knowledge provided by 'disciplines' such as psychology. Unlike

Althusser's concept of interpellation, which 'recruits' subjects through and in ideology, constructed in language, Foucault's discourse has a materiality in that it is about language *and* practice. Discourse is not, as you will remember from chapter 3, simply at the level of address and representation: it involves social practices and institutions. Discourse, according to Foucault, not only addresses us as subjects in language, as 'woman', 'man', 'homosexual', 'lunatic', 'criminal', 'witch', 'immigrant' and so forth, but functions to position us materially as embodied subjects. Its aim is to produce human beings who can be treated as 'docile bodies' to be labelled, measured, trained, cured, punished, imprisoned, exiled, tortured (Foucault, 1967, 1973, 1975). It is not necessary to accept all the details of Foucault's theories of power and discourse to accept the usefulness of these for understanding some of the paradoxes and complexities of power relations in modern societies. Now read the next extract, in which Stuart Hall draws upon his own experience in order to think about the ways in which 'a particular complex of discourses' generates certain sets of power relations around the concepts of 'race' and colour.

8.6

At different times in my 30 years in England, I have been 'hailed' or interpellated as 'coloured', 'West Indian', 'Negro', 'black', 'immigrant'. Sometimes in the street; sometimes at street corners; sometimes abusively; sometimes in a friendly manner; sometimes ambiguously. (A black friend of mine was disciplined by his political organization for 'racism' because, in order to scandalize the white neighbourhood in which we both lived as students, he would ride up to my window late at night and, from the middle of the street, shout 'Negro!' very loudly to attract my attention!) All of them inscribe me 'in place' in a signifying chain which constructs identity through the categories of colour, ethnicity, race.

In Jamaica where I spent my youth and adolescence, I was constantly hailed as 'coloured'. The way that term was articulated with other terms in the syntaxes of race and ethnicity was such as to produce the meaning, in effect, 'not black'. The 'blacks' were the rest – the vast majority of the people, the ordinary folk. To be 'coloured' was to belong to the 'mixed' ranks of the brown middle class, a cut above the rest – in aspiration if not in reality. My family attached great weight to these finely-graded classificatory distinctions and because of what it signified in terms of distinctions of class, status, race, colour insisted on the inscription. Indeed, they clung to it through thick and thin, like the ultimate ideological lifeline it was. You can imagine how mortified they were to discover that, when I came to England, I was hailed as 'coloured' by the natives there precisely because, as far as they could see, I *was* 'black', for all practical purposes . . . It is the position within the different signifying chains which 'means' not the literal, fixed correspondence between an isolated term and some denotated position in the colour spectrum . . .

As a concrete lived individual, am I indeed any one of these interpellations? Does any one of them exhaust me? In fact, I 'am' not one or another of these ways of representing me, though I have been positioned as all of them at different times and still am some of them to some degree. But, there is no essential, unitary 'I' – only the fragmentary, contradictory subject I become. Long after, I encountered 'coloured' again, now as it were from the other side, beyond it. I tried to teach my son he was 'black' at the same as he was the learning the colours of the spectrum and he kept saying to me that he was 'brown'. Of course, he was *both*.

Certainly I am from the West Indies – though I've lived my adult life in England. Actually, the relationship between 'West Indian' and 'immigrant' is very complex for me. In the 1950s, the two terms were equivalents. Now, the term 'West Indian' is very romantic. It connotes reggae, rum and coke, shades, mangoes, and all that canned tropical fruit salad falling out of the coconut trees. This is an idealized 'I'. (I wish I felt more like that more of the time.) 'Immigrant' I also know well. There is nothing remotely romantic about that. It places one so equivocally as *really belonging somewhere else*. 'And when are you going back home?' Part of Mrs. Thatcher's 'alien wedge'. Actually I only understood the way this term positioned me relatively late in life – and the 'hailing' on that occasion came from an unexpected direction. It was when my mother said to me, on a brief visit home: 'I hope they don't mistake you over there for one of those immigrants!' The shock of recognition. I was also on many occasions 'spoken' by that other, absent, unspoken term, the one that is never there, the 'American' one, undignified even by a capital 'N'. The 'silence' around this term was probably the most eloquent of them all. (Hall, 1996, pp. 27–9)

8.8

- What do you think Hall means when he says of the term 'black' that it 'is the position within the different signifying chains which 'means' not the literal, fixed correspondence between an isolated term and some denotated position in the colour spectrum'?
- What do you make of Hall's point that the silence around the term 'Nigger' was 'the most eloquent of them all'? Can you suggest how and in what ways a silence can be 'eloquent'?
- Can you suggest ways in which 'the fragmentary, contradictory subject [Hall] become[s]' is positioned materially as well as linguistically?

Embodied selves

Let us look now at another, very different, example of how narratives of the self may have social effects. The following extract, from a paper by Emily Martin, is concerned with the social implications of scientific and popular images of biological reproduction in humans. As well as scientific textbooks and journal articles, Martin has studied a range of biology teaching materials and films that have been produced in order to educate the public about reproductive physiology. She argues that this material consistently uses stereotypes in which egg and sperm are represented in terms of the human characteristics conventionally attributed to femininity and masculinity. Thus, the egg is represented as passive, a Sleeping Beauty who 'once released from the supportive environment of the ovary . . . will die within hours unless rescued by a sperm' (cited in Martin, 1992, p. 413). Martin also shows how this imagery is used in a popular film, *Look Who's Talking*.

8.7

Other popular materials also do their part: the recent film *Look Who's Talking* begins with a simulation of a hugely magnified egg floating, drifting, gently bouncing along the fallopian tube of a woman who is in the midst of making love with a man. The soundtrack is 'I Love You So' by the Chantals. Then we see, also hugely magnified, the man's sperm barreling down the tunnel of her vagina to the tune of 'I Get Around' by the Beach Boys. The sperm are shouting and calling to each other like a gang of boys: 'Come on, follow me, I know where I am, keep up, come on you kids, I've got the map'. Then as the egg hoves into view, they shout, 'This is it, yeah, this is definitely it, this is the place, Jackpot, right here, come on, dig in you kids'. And when one sperm finally pushes hard enough to open a slit in the egg (a slit that looks remarkably like a vulva), that sperm (as his whole self is swallowed up) cries out, 'Oh, oh, oh, I'm in!'

When I got to this point in my research, I was already wondering what social effects such vivid imagery might be having. I thought perhaps this imagery might encourage us to imagine that what results from the interaction of egg and sperm – a fertilized egg – is the result of intentional 'human' action *at the cellular level*. In other words, whatever the intentions of the human couple in this microscopic 'culture', a cellular 'bride' (or *femme fatale*) and a cellular 'groom' (or her victim) make a cellular baby . . . Endowing egg and sperm with intentional action, a key aspect of personhood in our culture, lays the foundation for the point of viability [of life in abortion debates] being pushed back to the moment of fertilization.

Why would this matter? Because endowing cells with personhood may play a part in the breaking down of boundaries between self and the world, and a pushing back of the boundary of what constitutes the inviolable self. In other words, whereas at an earlier time, the skin might have been regarded as the border of the individual self, now these microscopic cells are seen as tiny individual selves. This means that the 'environment' of the egg and sperm, namely the human body, is fair game for invasion by medical scrutiny and intervention. It is not, of course, that the interior of our bodies was not the object of study and treatment until now. But we may be experiencing an intensification of those activities (made more potent by state support) which are understood as protecting the 'rights', viability, or integrity of cellular entities. It would not be that endowing cells with personhood by means of imagery in biology automatically *causes* intensification of initiatives in the legislature and elsewhere that enable protection of these new 'persons'. Rather, I am suggesting that this imagery may have a part in creating a general predisposition to think of the world in a certain way that can play an important role whenever legal and other initiatives do take place.

It is possible that in the 1990s what was the patient (or person) has itself begun to become *an environment* for a new core self, which exists at the cellular level. This change may be adding to our willingness to focus ever more attention on the internal structures of this tiny cellular self, namely its genes. In turn, such a shift in attention may encourage us to permit dramatic changes in the 'environment' of the genes in the name of maintaining their welfare. (Martin, 1992, pp. 414–15)

Martin's analysis demonstrates how a particular way of talking about the world becomes naturalized. We are so used to the language used to describe the functions and actions of cells in our bodies that we barely notice its metaphoric function. In making visible the images and metaphors used to describe human reproduction, Martin stops us taking these for granted and requires us to think about the social implications of seeing our bodies as the home of cellular 'persons'. In doing so she also raises questions about what characterizes personhood and individuality. But she does so from a very different perspective than that of Lacan: her concern is with the human body rather than the human psyche.

The previous sections have considered how subjectivity is produced through the unconscious and through the ways we are positioned in relation to social formations. In this section we want to extend our discussion by looking at the relationship between the bodies we inhabit and the social context in which these are experienced. In chapter 2 we introduced you to the idea of biological essentialism and suggested, via the reading from Linda Birke (reading 2.6), the possibilities involved in challenging orthodox conceptions of the dualistic relationship of mind to body. Recent sociological thinking has begun to theorize how our bodies not only sustain physical life, but also shape identity and a sense of self. Such theorizing attempts to explore how the body as a material object is shaped by social processes as well as biology, and how social processes and practices are, in turn, shaped by the materiality of actual physical bodies. In recent years the human body has been more and more intensely scrutinized, reconstructed and investigated by scientists, educationalists, the state, consumer culture and individuals. In Foucault's terms, we could say the human body has become the subject of disciplinary power – it is regulated, surveilled, 'policed' by medical expertise, scientific knowledge and bureaucratic systems.

ACTIVITIES

8.9

Spend a few minutes compiling examples of the ways in which science and technology can have an impact on physical bodies and biological functions. We have started you off with two examples.

- Organ transplants
- Fitness regimes via aerobic classes, gyms, sport etc.
-
-
-
-

Recent technological and medical advances have begun to threaten the previously stable boundaries between human and machine, between nature and technology. The day may not be far off when computer chip brain implants will be available, while medical science has already made it possible for us to change our bodies over our lifetimes by exchanging diseased organs for donated organs or by replacing worn out limbs with new, artificial ones. Genetic engineering, recently thrown into prominence by the cloning of a sheep, threatens traditional ideas of individual uniqueness, and *in vitro* fertilization has already removed the need for heterosexual intercourse in human reproduction. Many of these advances have the potential to benefit humanity, and many remain in the future and may never happen. Nevertheless, the rapid development of these technologies has thrown into uncertainty our knowledge of the body as a natural entity. Science and technology have replaced religious belief as the means by which we know the world, but rather than providing new certainties they have destabilized our understanding of what constitutes a bodily self (Shilling, 1997, pp. 67–9). As a result, as Shilling points out, 'we potentially have the means to exert an *unprecedented degree of control* over bodies, [but] we are also living in an age which has *thrown into radical doubt* our knowledge of the consequencess of this control, and of *how we should control* our bodily selves' (p. 67, original emphasis).

Scientific interventions into bodies raise complex moral issues which will require extensive debate legally and politically. Questions about responsibility for the actions of a body which is not biologically 'owned' but made up of artificial parts or parts from the bodies of others will produce moral and legal dilemmas about issues of individual responsibility and ownership (Turner, 1992). Recent developments not only create new moral and legal dilemmas around the concept of the individual, but can also permit radical changes to what have traditionally been seen as 'natural' functions. Martin cites an example of a recently patented method by which a man's sperm can be 'washed' to remove those sperm that carry a gene complex which may predispose the individuals thus reproduced to ccrtain diseases. She comments that this method 'profoundly affects and fragments the act of sexual intercourse for both men and women, replacing it with masturbation followed by chemical operations on the sperm and then artificial insemination' (Martin, 1992, p. 419). Equally, scientific advances can have far-reaching implications for social practices. Genetic testing for predisposition to certain diseases could be extended to the workplace, with employers including genetic assessment as part of the selection process for new appointments.

The ability to change one's body is neither new nor limited to science and medicine. Individuals have, from choice or coercion, frequently altered their bodies in a variety of ways. For example, the binding of women's feet in China to reshape the foot, the wearing of corsets to alter a woman's bodily shape in nineteenth-century Western societies, body piercing and tattooing, weight training to develop muscles, male and female circumcision and cosmetic surgery are all ways in which the body is altered for social rather than medical reasons. Such practices have consequences for self-identity. A nineteenth-century middle-class Western woman bound tightly into a corset (fashionable waist sizes in the 1880s were thirteen to sixteen inches) experiences her body as confined, a bodily experience that is reinforced by social conventions that require her to undertake little physical activity. The physical discomfort and even illness caused by overtight lacing is understood as emanating from her general fragility and predisposition to sickness rather than from the effects of excessive corsetry. If she has to sit down and rest frequently this is understood in terms of her 'natural' femininity rather than as a consequence of the artificial manipulation of her body. Thus, being a Western woman in the nineteenth century may come to mean feeling confined and often unwell.

The following letter to the agony column of a broadsheet newspaper suggests how closely body image is associated with self-identity.

You'll think this a trivial problem, but last week I had beautiful long hair and I went to the hairdresser asking for a trim and he persuaded me to have it all cut off in a new, short style. Since then I have been beside myself with unhappiness. I cry every time I look in the mirror. People will say it will grow again, but it could take months or even years. I can't bear the idea of wearing a wig. I just don't look like me any more. But I can't understand why I am so depressed. I have even felt suicidal though I would never go ahead with it. (The *Independent*, 6 November 1997)

8.10

- Do you think the writer of the letter above is male or female? Give reasons for your answer.
- How would you respond to the writer's problem? Write a reply. If you are able, compare your response to that of other people. What assumptions about body image do these responses reveal?
- Try to imagine the effect on self-identity if you had never seen yourself in a mirror (or photograph). How might you experience your body? Would it be different?

In affluent contemporary Western societies the body has become a site for asserting or transforming identity. Like our homes, the body can be reconstructed in order to convey messages about who we are and how we want to be seen. Consumer culture encourages us to see our bodies as projects to be worked on through fitness regimes, diet, nutrition, clothing, make-up, body building and general self-care of our bodies (Rosen, 1983; Shilling, 1993). These projects are not only about protecting our bodies from disease but also intimately connected with self-confidence and self-image. While there are undoubted advantages in the increased focus on our bodies, we should not forget that there is a lot of money to be made from selling body projects; nor, as yet, can we halt the inevitability of ageing. The modern concern with bodily perfection has implications for how we see ourselves as we get older and for how old age, physical disability and ageing are perceived and represented.

8.11

- Are fitness clinics, gyms and beauty clinics more accessible to certain groups of people than others?
- What consequences might there be for the way in which we see older people as a result of modern concerns with fitness, 'the body beautiful' and health?
- Are there implications for how older people might be treated (legally, medically, politically, socially) as a result of the ways in which ageing is constructed and represented?

Finally, we want to consider how the body functions as what Mary Douglas calls 'a symbol of society' (Douglas, 1966, p. 115).

Figure 8.1   An illustration from *Fit Body*, number 16

8.8

In advanced consumer capitalism, as Robert Crawford has elegantly argued, an unstable agonistic construction of personality is produced by the contradictory structure of economic life [Crawford, 1985]. On the one hand, as producers of goods and services we must sublimate, delay, repress desires for immediate gratification; we must cultivate the work ethic. On the other hand, as consumers we must display a boundless capacity to capitulate to desire and indulge in impulse; we must hunger for constant and immediate satisfaction. The regulation of desire thus becomes an ongoing problem, as we find ourselves continually besieged by temptation, while socially condemned for overindulgence. (Of course, those who cannot afford to indulge their desires as consumers, teased and frustrated by the culture, face a much harsher dilemma.)

Food and diet are central arenas for the expression of these contradictions. On television and in popular magazines, with a flip of the page or barely a pause between commercials, images of luscious foods and the rhetoric of craving and desire are replaced by advertisements for grapefruit diets, low-calorie recipes, and exercise equipment. Even more disquieting than these manifest oppositions, however, are the constant attempts by advertisers to mystify them, suggesting that the contradiction doesn't really exist, that one can 'have it all'. Diets and exercise programs are accordingly presented with the imagery of instant gratification ('From Fat to Fabulous in 21 Days', 'Size 22 to Size 10 in No Time Flat', 'Six Minutes to an Olympic-Class Stomach') and effortlessness ('3,000 Sit-Ups Without Moving an Inch . . . 10 Miles of Jogging Lying Flat on Your Back' . . . '85 Pounds Without Dieting', and even, shamelessly, 'Exercise Without Exercise'). In reality, however, the opposition is not so easily reconciled. Rather, it presents a classic double bind, in which the self is torn in two mutually incompatible directions. The contradiction is not an abstract one but stems from the specific historical construction of a 'consuming passion' from which all inclinations toward balance, moderation, rationality, and foresight have been excluded.

Conditioned to lose control at the mere sight of desirable products, we can master our desires only by creating rigid defenses against them. The slender body codes the tantalizing ideal of well-managed self in which all is kept in order despite the contradictions of consumer-culture. Thus, whether or not the struggle is played out in terms of food and diet, many of us may find our lives vacillating between a daytime rigidly ruled by the 'performance principle' and nights and weekends that capitulate to unconscious 'letting go' (food, shopping, liquor, television, and other addictive drugs). In this way, the central contradiction of the system inscribes itself on our bodies, and bulimia emerges as a characteristic modern personality construction. For bulimia precisely and explicitly expresses the extreme development of the hunger for unrestrained consumption (exhibited in the bulimic's uncontrollable food binges) existing in unstable tension alongside the requirement that we sober up, 'clean up our act', get back in firm control on Monday morning (the necessity for purge – exhibited in the bulimic's vomiting, compulsive exercising, and laxative purges). (Bordo, 1990, 96–7)

8.12

- Collect examples of exhortations to (a) 'let go', (b) restrain ourselves, (c) 'have it all' in advertisements, on TV, in magazines and newspapers. Do you find these messages contradictory?
- Can you find examples in your own experience of patterns of 'binge and purge'?
- Can you suggest ways in which the ideal of the 'slender body' regulates or 'disciplines' human populations? Consider figure 8.1.

Bordo suggests that 'the self is torn in two mutually incompatible directions'. This connects with the discussions of fragmented selves with which we began this chapter. However, can you see how Bordo's fragmented self is experienced through the physical body as well as known cognitively and patterned unconsciously? Subjectivity here is manifested in bodily practices – eating, drinking, exercise, purging – which are also social practices – enjoying leisure and going to work. Our bodies, what we do to them and how we use them are subject to social as well as biological processes. Thus, it becomes possible to speak of human beings as **embodied subjects**. Not only are we invited to locate ourselves linguistically, psychologically and cognitively in certain subject positions, but the body is 'directly involved in a political field; power relations have an immediate hold upon it; they invest it, mark it, train it, torture it, force it to carry out tasks, to perform ceremonies, to emit signs' (Foucault, 1975, p. 25).

Bordo cites Crawford's claim that the structures of economic capitalism produce an unstable personality formation, oscillating between 'immediate gratification' and self-discipline. Does this focus on a specific economic structure as the determining factor in the formation of a collective personality negate Lacan's theory of the mirror stage, the Imaginary and the self constituted in language? Is it possible to construct links between Lacan's theories and the points made here about embodied subjects? Can thinking about a particular form of economic life at a certain moment in history counteract the universalizing, ahistorical tendency of Lacan's theories of identity acquisition? These are not easy questions and, although we will leave you to think about them, we hope you will return to them by extending your reading in what is a complex but rewarding area. Refer to the suggestions for further reading for this chapter.

Conclusions

In conclusion we offer you a summary of the main points we have covered here.

- Subjectivity means our sense of ourself as separate from others, with the ability to act in the world we inhabit. It also, at the same time, involves a sense of being subject to, under the control of, something external to ourself, and at the mercy of desires, fantasies, impulses that are lodged deep in the unconscious and inaccessible to the conscious thinking mind of the subject (the unconscious is accessible only through the interpretations of the analyst in the process of psychoanalysis). In this way the subject does not create the social world he or she inhabits but is produced by it, through language and culture.
- Post-structuralist theories focus on the precariousness and unfinished nature of subjectivity. The idea of multiple and fragile subjectivities can be understood as cause for despair or the source of new forms of subjectivity which could challenge existing oppressions.
- Lacan's theories of how subjectivity is acquired rework Freudian ideas of the unconscious by focusing on the way language acts to constitute the subject. He also stresses the illusory and utopian nature of our desire for coherence and wholeness, represented by the mirror image.
- Subjectivity is not only acquired at the level of the unconscious. According to Althusser, ideology invites us, through language, to take up and 'recognize' ourselves in subject positions that are socially appropriate for specific situations. Foucault's concept of disciplinary power asserts that we also 'know' ourselves through our relations with others as constituted in the discourses

that produce the material practices of 'race', sexuality, gender, nationality, class etc. It should be noted here that Foucault does not himself deal directly with 'race', gender or nationality, but other theorists have drawn upon his ideas in order to offer analyses and challenges in these areas.

- We do not only experience ourselves through our minds and feelings but equally through our bodies. The body is not separated from thought and feeling but is a material entity on which struggles over identity and selfhood may be inscribed. For example, those who have undergone sex change operations often testify that they could not 'really' claim male or female identity, despite feeling themselves to be a woman or man, until their bodies were marked as female or male.

- The body can act as a 'symbol of society', representing society's anxieties and preoccupations. In this sense the body is not simply a biological entity but a social body structured by the formations of a particular social and economic system.

CHAPTER 9

Consumption

Introduction

In chapter 8 we ended our discussion with the argument that 'the contradictory structure of economic life' produces a 'preoccupation with the "internal" management of the body' (Bordo, 1990, p. 96). As Bordo explains, 'On the one hand, as "producer-selves", we must be capable of sublimating, delaying, repressing desires for immediate gratification; we must cultivate the work ethic. On the other hand, as "consumer-selves" we serve the system through a boundless capacity to capitulate to desire and indulge in impulse.'

This chapter focuses on 'consumer-selves': that is, our role as purchasers of commodities and services, audiences for films and TV, and readers of visual and written texts such as advertisements. Bordo's point about the tension between 'producer-selves', bound by the work ethic, and 'consumer-selves', able to 'indulge in impulse', raises two important points which we are going to ask you to think about in this chapter. First, the two processes, production and consumption, are intimately and inextricably connected. Second, our willingness and capacity to consume is linked to deeply felt desires and impulses. Although much of our discussion is focused on the consumption of commodities, we are also consumers of a diversity of cultural forms, such as TV programmes, films, books, leisure activities and, as we discussed in chapter 4, history in the form of museums, artefacts and other 'heritage' products. Throughout this chapter we shall be asking you to consider how far, in our roles as consumers, we are able to appropriate such products as symbols of a desired identity, and how far choices about use and meaning are shaped by the concerns of producers.

If you keep these questions in mind as you work through the material it may help you to make sense of the arguments we are presenting. A final point: the recent focus on practices of consumption in sociology and cultural studies has led to the use of qualitative, ethnographic methods of research in which people are invited to talk about their own practices or are observed in everyday situations that involve consumption, such as shopping or watching television. Such approaches have proved valuable in complementing research methods that employ quantitative data or focus on textual analysis. The following studies are stimulating analyses that use qualitative, ethnographic research methods: Radway (1987), Gillespie (1989), Gullestad (1992) and Morley (1986, 1992).

What is a consumer?

The *Oxford English Dictionary* offers the following definitions of consumption:

1 The action or fact of consuming by use, waste, etc.
2 Decay, wasting away or wearing out; waste.
3 Wasting of the body by disease; now applied specifically to pulmonary consumption.
4 The destructive employment of industrial products, the amount of them consumed.

As you can see, there is a rather negative set of ideas being associated with the process of consumption. Raymond Williams's outline of the shifting meanings of the word 'consumer' can help us to think about the processes involved in a little more detail.

9.1

In modern English *consumer* and *consumption* are the predominant descriptive nouns of all kinds of use of goods and services. The predominance is significant in that it relates to a particular version of economic activity, derived from the character of a particular economic system, as the history of the world shows.

Consume has been in English since C14 . . . In almost all its early uses, *consume* had an unfavourable sense, it meant to destroy, to use up, to waste, to exhaust. This sense is still present in 'consumed by fire' and in the popular description of pulmonary phthisis as *consumption*. Early users of *consumer*, from C16, had the same general sense of destruction or waste.

It was from [the mid] . . . C18 that *consumer* began to emerge in a neutral sense in the description of bourgeois political economy. In the new pre-dominance of an organised market, the acts of making and of using goods and services were newly defined in the increasingly abstract pairings of *producer* and *consumer*, *production* and *consumption*. (Williams, 1976, pp. 78–9)

In a capitalist economy consumption is the necessary obverse of production. Goods are produced by using the (exploited, in Marxist terms) labour of people. These goods are bought and used (consumed), thereby creating profit for the producers. Following Marx, production – the economic base – was seen as determining the ways in which commodities and cultural forms were received and used. As we saw in chapter 1, the emergence of mass media and mass production gave rise to concerns that people were being manipulated into forms of consumption that were not necessarily in their best interests, but simply served to maintain and reproduce capitalist and materialistic societies at the expense of any real morality and/or individual autonomy. A good example of this approach is Vance Packard's *The Hidden Persuaders*, published in 1957, in which the advertising industry is represented as a dangerous force that conditions and manipulates the responses of a passive populace. More recently studies have focused on the role of the consumer and debates about the degree of autonomy and choice, as well as the potential available in practices of consumption to resist and negotiate the power relation between producer and consumer. We shall look at some of these arguments later in the chapter but for now the point to think about is how production and consumption, rather than being in a relationship of direct cause and effect (production determines consumption) are constantly engaged in a process of negotiation. For example, in the 1980s when Coca-Cola tried to introduce a 'new' taste Coke, in response to competition from Pepsi, this was commercially unsuccessful and they were forced by consumer resistance to return to the taste of 'classic Coke' (Miller, 1998, p. 171).

Buying a newspaper

To help us think through an act of consumer choice and its place in the wider processes of cultural life, let us look at the act of buying a newspaper.

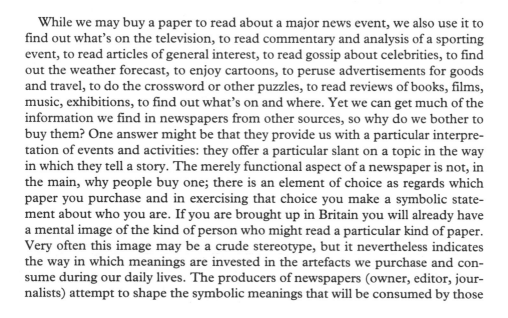

9.1

- If you regularly buy or read a newspaper, can you identify the different kinds of information you expect to be offered?
- Are there other places where you could, as easily, gain this information?
- What do you turn to first when you read a newspaper? Are there things you never read?
- Which newspapers do you read, and why?

ACTIVITIES

While we may buy a paper to read about a major news event, we also use it to find out what's on the television, to read commentary and analysis of a sporting event, to read articles of general interest, to read gossip about celebrities, to find out the weather forecast, to enjoy cartoons, to peruse advertisements for goods and travel, to do the crossword or other puzzles, to read reviews of books, films, music, exhibitions, to find out what's on and where. Yet we can get much of the information we find in newspapers from other sources, so why do we bother to buy them? One answer might be that they provide us with a particular interpretation of events and activities: they offer a particular slant on a topic in the way in which they tell a story. The merely functional aspect of a newspaper is not, in the main, why people buy one; there is an element of choice as regards which paper you purchase and in exercising that choice you make a symbolic statement about who you are. If you are brought up in Britain you will already have a mental image of the kind of person who might read a particular kind of paper. Very often this image may be a crude stereotype, but it nevertheless indicates the way in which meanings are invested in the artefacts we purchase and consume during our daily lives. The producers of newspapers (owner, editor, journalists) attempt to shape the symbolic meanings that will be consumed by those

215

who buy the papers by using language and codes which evoke the beliefs and values of its audience (Hartley, 1982, p. 96). In the next activity you can examine some of the ways in which this is apparent via a comparative study of two daily papers.

ACTIVITIES

9.2

Buy a popular tabloid paper like the *Sun* or the *Mirror* and a broadsheet paper like the *Guardian*, the *Independent* or the *Daily Telegraph*. If you wish, you could use a local or regional daily paper instead of one of the nationals.

- Compare the front pages: what is the ratio of stories to pictures? Which stories are foregrounded?
- What kind of products are advertised? Is there a difference in the kinds of product advertised in the two papers you are comparing?
- Can you find any apparent contradictions in terms of opinion, belief, values etc., both within an individual paper and between the two. For example, does the tabloid celebrate the sporting achievements of a black-British player while containing an argument hostile to other sectors of the black-British community? Does the broadsheet comment include images of women on its fashion pages which contradict arguments on its editorial pages?
- Can you summarize the differences and similarities between the two papers' approach to news? What percentage of their stories are about political events; how many deal with elements of popular culture (the lives of soap, film or other celebrities; the stories of 'ordinary' people)?

By working through your chosen newspapers you should begin to build up a sense of the ways in which a given paper presented 'the news' on a particular day. While buying the paper on that day does not automatically mean that you subscribe wholeheartedly with the full spectrum of its views (you may, for example, have purchased a paper for this activity which you wouldn't normally read), the newspaper corporations themselves, and the advertisers who buy space in newspapers, clearly do believe that certain groups of people read certain kinds of papers. When we buy a newspaper we are involved in an act of consumer choice that is also about expressing a sense of or desire for a particular self-identity. For example, advertisers who buy space in newspapers increasingly use **psychographic** variables, such as the ones listed below, in order to classify and target specific consumers.

Trendies	Those who crave the admiration of their peers
Egoists	Those who seek pleasure
Puritans	Those who wish to feel virtuous
Innovators	Those who wish to make their mark
Rebels	Those who wish to remake the world in their image
Groupies	Those who just want to be accepted

Drifters	Those who are not sure what they want
Drop outs	Those who shun commitments of any kind
Traditionalists	Those who want things to stay as they are
Utopians	Those who want the world to be a better place
Cynics	Those who have to have something to complain about
Cowboys	Those who want easy money

(Selby and Cowdery, 1995, p. 25)

9.3

Can you identify ways in which your chosen newspapers from activity 9.2 target any of these groups?

You may have noted that buying and reading a newspaper is a good example of consumption as 'using up' and often 'waste'. Think about what happens to your daily newspaper when you have finished with it. Newspapers are a particular example of a disposable commodity: they are not meant to be durable or lasting. This applies literally – the material object can be thrown away or used to wrap rubbish or fish and chips in – and metaphorically – the items of news, gossip and information are ephemeral and quickly replaced by new stories and information. Environmentalists have advocated the re-cycling of used paper, including newspapers, and many people, concerned with the ethics of a 'throw-away' society, now actively choose this option rather than simply disposing of newspapers as rubbish. Choices about buying and reading a specific newspaper are not the only ones available to us: we are also invited to assert certain ethical values in the ways in which we choose to dispose of the paper.

My high street and your high street

Figure 9.1 is a schematic diagram of a suburban shopping area. This map is of a suburban area just outside the centre of York; it is only half a mile from the centre of the city which has a much greater range of shops, and is only just over a mile from a large supermarket by car or bus. The area around the shops includes Victorian and Edwardian terraced housing, 1930s and 1940s semi-detached homes with gardens and more modern developments, ranging from an estate of semi-detached properties, immediately behind the shopping area illustrated, to low rise flats and sheltered accommodation. At the time of writing, smaller terraced properties are on the market for between £50,000 and £60,000, while some of the larger Victorian houses are on sale for over £100,000.

In the past week, I (Tim Middleton) have gone into properties 2, 5, 18 and 23. Over the past year, I have been into all properties bar numbers 3, 6, 7, 8, 11, 19, 20, 22, 27, 28, 30 and 32. I have lived in this area for over five years and in

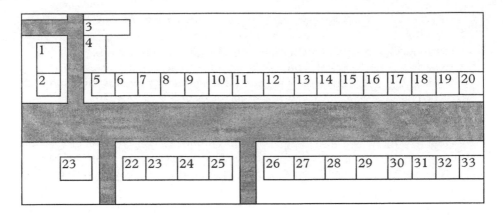

Key

1 Delicatessen.
2 Small supermarket.
3 Carpet and bed shop.
4 Hairdresser.
5 Newsagent and Post Office.
6 Optician.
7 Card shop.
8 Solicitor.
9 Video rental shop.
10 Chinese restaurant.
11 Charity shop.
12 Freezer shop.
13 Indian restaurant.
14 Greengrocer.
15 Pizza takeaway.
16 Ironmonger.
17 Cafe.

18 Bicycle shop.
19 Estate agent
20 Bookmaker.
21 Antique shop.
22 Italian takeaway.
23 Newsagent.
24 Pharmacy.
25 Fish and chip shop.
26 Small supermarket.
27 Pet shop.
28 Butcher.
29 Greengrocer.
30 Beer and wine making supplies.
31 Chinese takeaway.
32 Laundrette.
33 Antique shop.

Figure 9.1 A suburban shopping area

that time I have visited all the properties bar 6, 7, 20, 22, 30 and 32. In this shopping area I have purchased items ranging from stamps through to a house, but in the main I use the shops for convenience: buying items I have run out of; buying takeaway food when I can't be bothered to cook. The bulk of my shopping is done on a weekly basis in a large supermarket on the edge of town, and many other purchases, including products for sale near to my home, are also made elsewhere.

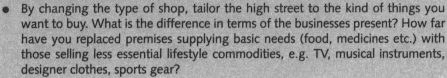

9.4

- Using the map in figure 9.1 track the journeys you would make if you were reliant upon this range of shops alone for your purchasing over a month. What things can't you buy? What would you normally buy elsewhere?
- All the businesses featured (apart from the Post Office) are local to York. What would be the difference if the businesses were national chains?
- By changing the type of shop, tailor the high street to the kind of things you want to buy. What is the difference in terms of the businesses present? How far have you replaced premises supplying basic needs (food, medicines etc.) with those selling less essential lifestyle commodities, e.g. TV, musical instruments, designer clothes, sports gear?

The link between consumption and consumer choice raises a number of issues. When we shape a complex of shops in our own image we are very likely to deny the needs of others: at a basic level you can examine this by exploring the difference between your responses to the exercise above and those of a friend or colleague. In the example above, replacing the small supermarkets with a branch of Harvey Nichols, turning the charity shop into a branch of Jaeger and the Chinese into a Michelin three-star restaurant might suit us if we are used to a comfortable life in South Kensington but is unlikely to be of much use if our income is restricted to meeting basic needs as cheaply as possible.

What makes Harvey Nichols a different place to shop for clothes from a charity shop, in the end, comes down to economic factors, but these cannot be easily separated from issues of ideology and identity. And, while consumers can create identities for themselves and for social groups from the range of material objects and cultural products available, such as theatres, football and cinema, the consumer is not always, nor inevitably, in complete control of either the meanings of products or their availability. When, in 1996, Harvey Nichols opened a store in Leeds there were many jokey columns in the press about whippet loving flat-capped Northerners being bewildered by Southern glamour, but the company clearly did not spend huge amounts of money on its Leeds shop without feeling confident that the Yorkshire consumer wanted more from a clothes shop than something to keep out the weather. To this end it had no doubt undertaken considerable market research in the area. However, Harvey Nichols was also undoubtedly influenced by the fact that Leeds was growing fast as 'the financial and commercial centre of the North', and could expect a continuing influx of upwardly mobile migrants from all areas of Britain, in particular the South East, especially if it was able to offer a rival culture to the metropolis. The example of a semi-suburban shopping zone in York points up the varied needs of a consuming public by suggesting that acts of consumption can be occasions when we do make meanings out of the world around us. However, these take place through a process of negotiation between the requirement to service our needs and desires and the demands of producers to ensure profitability.

9.5

If you have access to newspapers on either CD-ROM or microfiche you could search for articles on the setting up of Harvey Nichols in Leeds in mid-to late 1996, and think about the various interests being catered for. This could be the start of a longer research project on department stores. (See, for example, Du Gay, 1997, for an analysis of the fashion store Benneton.)

Having introduced you to the idea of consumer choice and its connection to production and identity, let us begin to explore some of the critical perspectives that explain the relationship between consumption and production.

Theories of consumption

Broadly speaking, thinking about consumption can focus upon:

- the economic and global impact of consumer activity, positioning consumers as the passive victims of capitalism;
- the ways in which acts of consumption are a creative and active way in which individuals articulate their own identity;
- the ways in which economic and global structures of production are inextricably linked with individual acts of consumer choice.

It is unlikely in contemporary cultural or sociological studies that you will encounter the first position extremely stated. Between these three positions there are a wide range of intermediate positions, and in this chapter we are interested in how far consumption can be an active practice through which people are able to influence what is produced, as well as using 'taste', artefacts and products to construct and express certain identities.

As Williams observed (reading 9.1), the emergence of the consumer as a distinct social role has been a major factor in the shift to a capitalist mode of production, and one approach to the study of consumption has been derived from Marxist thinking about the relationship between individuals and society under capitalism. This approach to the study of consumption, which derives from Marx's ideas about political economy, is one which stresses individuals as trapped within a system of exchange over which ultimately they have little control. John Storey offers the following summary of Marxist ideas regarding consumption.

9.2

The cultural analysis of consumption begins in the political concerns of Marxism. In order to understand the classical Marxist account of consumption, we must know something about how it conceives the difference between capitalist and pre-capitalist social formations. Pre-capitalist societies (feudalism in Britain, for example) were not consumer societies in that goods were made mostly for immediate consumption or use or to be exchanged for other goods. It is only after the collapse of feudalism and the emergence of capitalism, a system based on the market, on money and on profit, that consumption becomes detached from simple needs and emerges as a significant aspect of human activity.

For Karl Marx and Frederick Engels, the transition from feudalism to capitalism was a transition from production driven by need to production driven by profit. Moreover, in capitalist societies, workers make goods in return for wages. They do not own the goods; the goods are sold on the market at a profit. Therefore to get goods, workers have to buy them with money. Thus: workers become 'consumers', and we have the emergence of 'consumer society'. To ensure the making of profits, people must consume. Therefore consumption is artificially stimulated by advertising. One consequence of this is 'alienation'. According to Marx . . . alienation results from 'the fact that labour is external to the worker . . . the worker feels himself only when he is not working . . . His labour is therefore . . . not the satisfaction of a need but a mere means to satisfy needs outside itself' . . .

In other words, men and women are denied identity in (uncreative) production, and are therefore forced to seek identity in (creative) consumption. But this is always little more than a hollow substitute (a fetish). Moreover, the process is encouraged by the so-called ideology of consumerism – the suggestion that the meaning of our lives is to be found in what we consume, rather than in what we produce. Thus the ideology legitimates and encourages the profit-making concerns of capitalism (a system demanding an ever increasing consumption of goods). (Storey, 1996, pp. 113–14)

Marx's ideas may seem a little abstract and, certainly, seem to suggest that as a consumer we are merely powerless functionaries of a grand capitalist master plan. There seems to be little space for what many people might see (perhaps hedonistically) as the enjoyable dimension to consumption. People actually do enjoy consuming and do believe that consumption has significant meaning in terms of their identity. Slavenka Drakulic quotes a frequent complaint from women in Eastern Europe: 'Look at us – we don't even look like women. There are no deodorants, perfumes, sometimes even no soap or toothpaste. There is no fine underwear, no pantyhose, no nice lingerie. Worst of all, there are no sanitary napkins. What can one say except that it is humiliating' (Drakulic, 1992: 31).

9.6

Drakulic writes about conditions prior to the collapse of communism in Eastern Europe. Do you think that the desire of Eastern European women for consumer goods is 'a hollow substitute' for a 'real' identity that has been lost with the advent of capitalism? How do you respond to their feeling that the lack of consumer products is humiliating?

The first serious attempt to study the role of consumers was by Thorstein Veblen, who studied the consumption patterns of the newly affluent North American bourgeois in the late nineteenth century (Veblen, 1899). Veblen's studies demonstrated that, rather than being at the mercy of capitalist production, people were able to assert their social status, not only through the wealth they accumulated, but also via a display of the products and services they purchased – what he termed 'conspicuous consumption'. Commodities and services acted as symbolic markers of affluence and status in addition to or regardless of their functional necessity. An example will serve to illustrate this. In Britain in the late nineteenth and early twentieth centuries, owning a piano was a sign of status and respectability, as well as having use-value as a form of leisure. Even families with little spare money aspired to owning a piano, which was often displayed in the 'parlour' or best room. Possessing a piano was a form of 'conspicuous consumption' and some people were prepared to spend beyond their means in order to be able to demonstrate their identity as respectable, piano-owning members of society. You might remind yourself of the case study in chapter 6, where we discussed the ways in which purchasing a home and selecting design features and furnishings operated as a means of asserting distance from some social groups and allegiance with others. It could be argued that people did not 'need' pianos or stained glass windows in their front doors any more than people in contemporary societies 'need' stereo systems or Laura Ashley wallpaper. The cultural theorist Herbert Marcuse claimed that these are 'false needs' orchestrated by advertisers and the manufacturers of pianos, wallpapers or stereo systems in order to lure us into a cycle of consumer desire and gratification (Marcuse, 1964). For example, the argument runs, we buy convenience foods because the demands of paid work leave little time to cook, but the money we earn is spent on expensive foods that could be made more cheaply at home if we were not 'forced' to spend so much time at work earning the money to pay for these expensive foods, as well as other consumer items we have been manipulated by producers and advertisers into believing we 'need'. In this way consumption is seen as determined by the overriding logic of capitalist production: put crudely, we only consume because manufacturers require us to. Now read the following extract from an essay by Theodor Adorno and Max Horkheimer which argues that the cultures we consume, in the same ways as material commodities, are equally determined by the mechanisms of consumer capitalism.

READINGS

9.3

The sociological theory that the loss of the support of objectively established religion, the dissolution of the last remnants of precapitalism, together with technological and social differentiation or specialization, have led to cultural chaos is disproved every day; for culture now impresses the same stamp on everything. Films, radio and magazines make up a system which is uniform as a whole and in every part. Even the aesthetic activities of political opposites are one in their enthusiastic obedience to the rhythm of the iron system . . . Under monopoly all mass culture is identical, and the lines of its artificial framework begin to show through. The people at the top are no longer so interested in concealing monopoly: as its violence becomes more open, so its power grows. Movies and radio need no longer pretend to be art. The truth that they are just business is made into an ideology in order to justify the rubbish they deliberately produce. They call themselves industries; and when their directors' incomes are published, any doubt about the social utility of the finished products is removed . . .

[T]he basis on which technology acquires power over society is the power of those whose economic hold over society is greatest. A technological rationale is the rationale of domination itself . . . It has made the technology of the culture industry no more than the achievement of standardization and mass production, sacrificing whatever involved a distance between the logic of the work and that of the social system. This is the result not of a law of movement in technology as such but of its function in today's economy. The need which might resist central control has already been suppressed by the control of the individual consciousness. The step from the telephone to the radio has clearly distinguished the roles. The former still allowed the subscriber to play the role of subject, and was liberal. The latter is democratic: it turns all participants into listeners and authoritatively subjects them to broadcast programmes which are all exactly the same. (Adorno and Horkheimer, 1947, extracted in During, 1993, pp. 30–1)

9.7

- Consider the significance of the phrase 'culture industry'. Remind yourself of our discussions in chapter 1 about Arnold and about mass culture. Why do you think Adorno and Horkheimer, writing in the mid-1940s, chose this phrase? Is it purely descriptive?
- Adorno and Horkheimer were living in the United States when they wrote this essay. They were refugees from Hitler's Germany and had experienced state control of cultural production. Can you think of any ways (or examples) in which US cultural production in the 1940s might have led them to their conclusions about the determining force of capitalist production? In order to answer this you may need to consult further reading. The following are suggestions: Gomery (1976), Schatz (1981), Bordwell et al. (1985), Turner (1993, pp. 14–18).

ACTIVITIES

There are a number of points to note in what has been called 'the production of consumption' perspective (du Gay et al., 1997, p. 86). First, as we have seen, this perspective treats consumption as *an effect* of production, thus denying the possibility of human agency. As consumers, it is argued, we have 'needs' that are created and then satisfied by the producers of goods, services and media, and as such are 'false' or inauthentic. Second, consumption has been perceived as less serious than the work of producing goods, services and culture. As well as being seen as a passive activity, consumption is linked to hedonism, pleasure, frivolity – it is less important than the serious work of industry, or finance, or commercial administration. Furthermore, consumption is seen as something that takes place in the private sphere of home and family, whether it be buying a house, watching a TV programme, reading a book, purchasing a piano or replacing a car. As such, it is less authentic as a way of creating a sense of identity than the world of paid work, where a 'real' sense of self can be established. You may have begun to notice an implied gender dimension: consumption appears to be allied to conventional feminine attributes, such as passivity and domesticity, and production to mascu-line attributes, such as paid labour and activity. The 'production of consumption' perspective relies on a set of oppositional terms in which one term of the opposi-tion is always more dominant or highly valued: production/consumption; true needs/false needs; work/pleasure; active/passive; public/private; art/mass culture; male/female.

Extending the work of Veblen, two recent theorists have contested the 'produc-tion of consumption' approach, offering ways in which consumption can be seen, more positively, as linked to culture and identity, rather than as simply the effect of economic phenomena. Jean Baudrillard contested Marcuse's typology of 'false' and 'natural' needs, arguing that while producers do attempt to create markets and therefore a 'need' for a certain product, particularly through advertising, con-sumers are able to resist the precise blandishments and injunctions of advertising and instead 'play with "needs" on a keyboard of objects' (Baudrillard, 1988, 45). As Baudrillard argues, 'We know that advertising is not omnipotent and at times produces opposite reactions: and we know that in relation to a single 'need', ob-jects can be substituted for one another.' Consumption, rather than being simply an economic practice, is also a system of signs that produce meaning in ways similar to language (see chapter 3). Indeed, Baudrillard suggests that 'marketing, purchasing, sales, the acquisition of differentiated commodities and object/signs – all of these presently constitute our language, a code with which our entire society communicates and speaks of and to itself' (Ibid.).

As you read the next extract, from a piece by the journalist Suzanne Moore, try to formulate responses to the following questions:

- Is her discussion of these adverts about the ostensible product being mar-keted? Is it about something else? If so, why does she focus on advertisements for Lee jeans, Nissan cars and Wallis clothes shop?
- Can you connect Baudrillard's point that commodities and objects, advertis-ing and purchasing constitute a language in which we speak of and to our-selves with the point Moore is making about three recent adverts?

READING

9.4

What Girl Power Means

I am as concerned as the next woman about adverts which show women being violent towards men. I don't think there are anything like enough of them.

The three ads that have been singled out by the Advertising Standards Authority – for Lee Jeans, showing a woman's stiletto-heeled boot resting on the buttock of a naked man, with the slogan 'Put the Boot in', the Nissan ad with a man clutching his crotch and the line 'Ask Before You Borrow It' and the Dress to Kill campaign for Wallis which shows men in danger of being killed because they are distracted by beautiful women – have attracted almost 100 complaints. The complaints were not upheld, but the ASA has warned advertising agencies that they should think twice about using such 'Girl Power' imagery . . .

It is fitting that Girl Power should be a concept picked up by the ad industry. For Girl Power is, in essence, a kind of re-branding [of feminism] . . .

The fragility of contemporary masculinity is wondrous to behold. Is it such a delicate thing, that it must be protected at all times by bodies such as the Advertising Standards Authority? Women, I suppose, are simply hardened by being bombarded by imagery about what women should be, so they take it all rather lightly – unless of course they acquire an eating disorder and kill themselves. (Moore, 1997)

Moore uses advertisements as a way of discussing gender relations more widely. In doing so she is assuming a shared understanding on the part of her readership about how advertisements work. Part of this shared understanding is the recognition that advertisements play on our preoccupations, our fantasies and our desires – we all 'know' that advertising is trying to manipulate us. At the same time, we 'know' that advertisements use puns, storylines and imagery that offer visual and other pleasures. We also 'know' how to resist advertisers' exhortations to take up the positions offered in advertisements. Watching the Nissan advertisement, in which it is suggested that a man has been subjected to violence for borrowing his girlfriend's car, is unlikely to result in widescale attacks on males by young women. Yet, as Moore points out, it speaks to unconscious desires around domination and submission and is expressing something about the relations between the sexes in the late 1990s. If you doubt this think about whether this advertisement would have been possible or comprehensible ten or twenty years earlier. We are able to 'read' the advertisements Moore refers to because we understand the visual and graphic languages in which the ideas are inscribed. The advertisements constitute a language or a code with which we communicate just as much as the language or codes of political institutions or medical science. Moore engages with this language in order to explore how British society in the 1990s 'speaks of and to itself' on the subject of gender relations. At the same time, the advertisements themselves invite us to buy not only the product but also the desires that they encode. When we buy cars, jeans or fashion clothes we are not able to do so from outside this communicative exchange. It would be very difficult to be entirely neutral or ignorant of the marketing and advertising of the products we purchase. This does not mean we are unable to resist these strategies: we can and do, buying products for other purposes than advertised, appropriating them for our own use and needs, but whenever we do so we cannot but remain aware of what it is we are resisting or adapting. For example, I (Judy Giles) might buy a pair of Lee jeans because they are comfortable and hardwearing, not because advertising tells me they are the fashionable attire of a young, modern *femme fatale*. Nevertheless, at some level I am aware of these coded meanings in order to resist them and insist to myself that middle-aged women can also buy Lee jeans, that they are not only for the young nor is their function purely a sexual one. In doing so, I am saying something about the world I live in and who I am, and I am doing so using the language of material objects, in this case a pair of jeans.

We want to turn now to the ideas of the French sociologist Pierre Bourdieu. So far we have talked about the consumption of objects such as cars or jeans without considering how people are situated differently with regard to their consumption of such products. Obviously, the richer people are, the more choice they have about what, where and when they purchase material objects. This is also true of cultural products: the price of a ticket for the opera may prohibit many people from enjoying this form of culture. Bourdieu developed Veblen's theory of 'conspicuous consumption' by linking consumption more tightly to social class in a study of patterns of consumption in France in the 1960s and 1970s. In order to introduce you to Bourdieu's ideas, we have chosen an extract from his study of the consumption of what he calls 'sports products' in France. However, before you read this we offer a brief introduction to some of his key ideas in order to help you to get the most out of the reading.

Bourdieu argues that any individual's capacity to consume is determined by variations in economic capital (the amount of money for disposal) and cultural capital (what we learn from the family and education). We develop 'tastes' for certain objects as a result of what he calls **habitus**. Habitus refers to a web of knowledge that we gain from the family, our understanding of classification systems such as class and the 'common-sense', taken for granted assumptions we operate with, which together predispose us to see objects in terms of whether or not they are appropriate for us as particular kinds of persons. For example, it could be argued that the habitus of some people predisposes them to develop a 'taste' for books, which are then consumed in terms of how much money is available but also in terms of the symbolic value of possessing books and the knowledge therein – what Bourdieu calls 'cultural capital'. Bourdieu shows how French working-class people preferred food that expressed abundance and solidity – red meat, bread and cheese and 'rough' red wine – while middle-class food tastes were for a healthy diet, aesthetic presentation and 'correct' preparation. The point to grasp is that Bourdieu is not suggesting that consumption is a direct reflection of class, but that class differences are constructed through people's ideas about the 'appropriate' products for consumption. A final note: when Bourdieu writes of 'fractions of the dominant class' he has in mind a distinction between those whose social position results from economic capital – wealth and affluence – and those whose social position is derived from cultural capital – education and learning.

9.5

I think that, without doing too much violence to reality, it is possible to consider the whole range of sporting activities and entertainments offered to social agents . . . as a *supply* intended to meet a *social demand*. If such a model is adopted, two sets of questions arise. First, is there an area of production, endowed with its own logic and its own history, in which 'sports products' are generated . . . Secondly, what are the social conditions of possibility of the appropriation of the various 'sports products' that are thus produced . . . In other words, how is the demand for 'sports products' produced, how do people acquire the 'taste' for sport, and for one sport rather than another, whether as an activity or as a spectacle? . . .

Thus, most of the team sports – basketball, handball, rugby, football – which are most common among office workers, technicians and shopkeepers, and also no doubt the most typically working-class individual sports, such as boxing or wrestling, combine all the reasons to repel the upper classes. These include the social composition of their public which reinforces the vulgarity implied by their popularization, the values and virtues demanded (strength, endurance, the propensity to violence, the spirit of 'sacrifice', docility and submission to collective discipline, the absolute antithesis of the 'rôle distance' implied in bourgeois rôles, etc.), the exaltation of competition and the contest, etc. To understand how the most distinctive sports, such as golf, riding, skiing or tennis, or even some less recherché ones, like gymnastics or mountaineering, are distributed among the social classes and especially among the fractions of the dominant class, it is even more difficult to appeal solely to variations in economic and cultural capital or in spare time. This is firstly because it would be to forget that, no less than the economic obstacles, it is the hidden entry requirements, such as family tradition and early training, and also the obligatory clothing, bearing and techniques of sociability which keep these sports closed to the working classes and to individuals rising from the lower-middle and even upper-middle classes; and secondly because economic constraints define the field of possibilities and impossibilities without determining within it an agent's positive orientation towards this or that particular form of practice. In reality, even apart from any search for distinction, it is the relation to one's own body, a fundamental aspect of the habitus, which distinguishes the working classes from the privileged classes, just as, within the latter, it distinguishes fractions that are separated by the whole universe of a life-style. On one side, there is the *instrumental* relation to the body which the working classes express in all the practices centred on the body, whether in dieting or beauty care, relation to illness or medication, and which is also manifested in the choice of sports requiring a considerable investment of effort, sometimes of pain and suffering (e.g. boxing) and sometimes a *gambling with the body itself* (as in motor-cycling, parachute-jumping, all forms of acrobatics, and, to some extent, all sports involving fighting, among which we may include rugby). On the other side, there is the tendency of the privileged classes to treat the body as an *end in itself*, with variants according to whether the emphasis is placed on the intrinsic functioning of the body as an organism, which leads to the macrobiotic cult of health, or on the appearance of the body as a perceptible configuration, the 'physique', i.e. the body-for-others. Everything seems to suggest that the concern to cultivate the body appears, in its most elementary form, i.e. as the cult of health, often implying an ascetic exaltation of sobriety and dietetic rigour, among the lower-middle classes, i.e. among junior executives, clerical workers in the medical services and especially primary-school teachers, who indulge particularly intensively in gymnastics, the ascetic sport *par excellence* since it amounts to a sort of training (*askesis*) for training's sake . . .

It is doubtless among the professions and the well-established business bourgeoisie that the health-giving and aesthetic functions are combined with social functions; there, sports take their place, along with parlour games and social exchanges (receptions, dinners, etc.), among the 'gratuitous' and 'disinterested' activities which enable the accumulation of social capital. This is seen in the fact that, in the extreme form it assumes in golf, shooting, and polo in smart clubs, sporting activity is a mere pretext for select encounters or, to put it another way, a technique of sociability, like bridge or dancing. (Bourdieu 1978, reprinted in During, 1993, pp. 340, 353–5)

9.8

- Look for examples in magazines, on TV and in the newspapers of the distinctions between 'sports products' that Bourdieu identifies.
- Think about the sports that you, and those you know, engage in either as a spectator or as a participant. Are Bourdieu's assertions about the relationship between class and different sports borne out in your experience?
- Can you suggest ways in which gender, disability, ethnicity or age cut across the class distinctions that are, according to Bourdieu, constructed through the consumption of sports?
- Remind yourself of the discussion of identity and the body in chapter 8. Can you make connections between what was said there and what Bourdieu is saying?

We would suggest that while Bourdieu draws attention to the ways in which practices of consumption are simultaneously economic *and* symbolic acts, thus avoiding the pessimism of theorists like Adorno and Horkheimer, he none the less remains constrained by his focus on the structural forces of class. He is therefore unable to explain the variety of ways in which people actively use the products they consume, be it a particular sport, a TV programme, a pair of jeans or a car, in creating meaningful identities for *themselves*. For example, the recent engagement in football, as spectators, by upwardly mobile young men, as part of the construction of a 'laddish' identity, involves the appropriation of a sport traditionally associated with the working classes. And this new identity can be seen as a response to changing gender relations rather than a need for young men to ally themselves with the working classes or to reproduce distinctions between classes.

Bourdieu's approach, which used questionnaires, is not dissimilar to that used by market research companies and the media in order to profile social stereotypes for the purposes of monitoring consumer behaviour and identifying lifestyles. Look carefully at figure 9.2, which represents a typology of 1990s male lifestyles. Notice how much of the profiling is linked to what each stereotype supposedly consumes.

9.9

List the different forms of consumption that are identified in this typology. We have started you off.

- Drinks
- Holidays
-
-
-
-
-
-

Is there any evidence in these profiles of the 'taste' for different sports identified by Bourdieu?

9/NEW MEN

Happy? No, they're just drinking to forget the angst and confusion brought on by the existential ills facing the modern male …

Nineties Man is angst-ridden, confused and selfish. According to marketing experts, "New Man" is a figment of female imagination, while "New Lad" is a cop-out. Kathy Marks charts a dismal diagnosis of the existential ills of the modern male.

It was so simple a few decades ago. Men were men, and the world was constructed in such a way that they never doubted it. The institutions of state, family and work combined to create and nurture their masculine identity.

Massive social and economic changes since the 1960s have played havoc with the old certainties, shattering men's confidence and leaving them floundering for a sense of self.

This is the dire picture painted by Chad Wollen, an analyst at the Henley Centre for Forecasting. Men are doomed, Mr Wollen told a conference organised by Channel 4, unless they emulate women and learn to cope with an insecure and volatile world. In earlier times, men have exactly why they are: to impregnate their wives, bring home the money and protect their families. But all three functions have been profoundly ...

Pity the Nineties Man who derives self-esteem from being the breadwinner. Nearly 70 per cent of women aged 20 to 59 now work. In their procreational capacity, too, men are far from indispensable, given the latest advances in reproductive science (not to mention falling sperm counts). As for the strong figure protecting his family from danger – research

by the Henley Centre shows that men are increasingly fearful about their own safety.

The institutions which reinforced the classic male image have disintegrated, Mr Wollen argued. The job for life, the traditional family and the paternalistic state no longer exist. In their place are far more fluid and unpredictable structures.

How then, does modern man handle his identity crisis? Does he rise to the challenge, seek fresh role models in a shifting society? No, he buries his head, ostrich-like, and pretends that it will all go away.

Day to day, he relies on Nineties Woman to pick up the pieces. "Women are now looking after families, jobs, and – most importantly for men – men," said Mr Wollen.

Alternatively, the contemporary male buys his way out of responsibilities. If his wife is not around to cook, he orders in a pizza. If there is housework or childcare to be dealt with, he engages domestic help and nannies.

More and more, he seeks relief from stress through drink and drugs. "Nineties Man is trying to pretend that the world hasn't changed," Mr Wollen said. "When all else fails, he goes out for a beer."

He dismissed New Man – the caring, sharing, nappy-changing 1980s male – as a product of wishful female thinking, and poured scorn on New Lad – the football, sex and booze-obsessed 1990s man – as a puerile backlash.

"Men are regressing to a time when the old stereotypes still held true. The Lad is an incredibly powerful image, but it's not an adult response. Men have to learn about flexibility and uncertainty. They have to understand that they can't be masters of the universe."

Keeping up appearances: For all his bravado, experts believe that Nineties Man may be suffering a unprecedented identity crisis stemming from the demise of traditional certainties

WHICH TYPE OF NINETIES MAN ARE YOU?

Sean Kelleher, business development manager at Channel 4, has identified five "social stereotypes"

Nathan:
Aged 15-34, mainly from ABC1 class. Appearance is important to Nathan; he enjoys spending money on clothes and skin-care products. He goes out to clubs and wine bars, and is athletic and sporty. Nathan's body and temple. He regards cooking as a virtue, likes eating out in ethnic restaurants and drinks strong beers and lagers such as Lowenbrau. He loves hi-tech gadgets and computers, watches ER and Brookside, and is bad at managing money.

Dave:
Mainly 15-34, with a C2DE bias. Dave is more settled, likes his home comforts and spends a lot of time on the sofa, particular when there is football or wrestling on the television. He wears designer labels, shops at Sainsbury and enjoys a night out in the pub, drinks lagers such as Labatts and believes that real men should down numerous pints at one sitting. He goes to dog races and plans to buy a satellite dish next year.

Mark:
Mainly 35-54, with an ABC1 bias. Mark is self-assured and confident, a top earner and a National Lottery enthusiast. He knows what he wants out of life and works hard to achieve it. He has said tastes in fashion, plays squash or tennis once a week and drives a family saloon car. Mark enjoys food, sometimes to the point of over-indulgence, and drinks French imported beers. He watches The Girlie Show and probably has a pension.

Brian:
Mainly aged 35-54, C2DE class. Brian has "downmarket" cultural tastes. He watches a lot of television, particularly Sky football, and reads newspapers to keep up with showbusiness gossip rather than world affairs. He likes expensive aftershaves, takeaway meals and cigars. Brian goes on package holidays and when abroad, wants only to eat, drink and lie in the sun. He despises vegetarians and believes low-alcohol lager is not a man's drink.

Philip:
Aged 55 plus, mainly ABC1. Philip wants to be a Nineties Man, but has deeply-rooted traditional male values. He loves fine wines and gardening, and reads the financial pages to keep tabs on his investments. He takes holidays in Europe, buys organic produce and may buy a vegetarian. He exercises by taking long walks, is not obsessed with his appearance and is financially sophisticated. He is a homebird who drinks beers such as Theakstons.

Figure 9.2 'New Men'

Selling identities

Let us pursue the relationship between acts of consumption and individual identity further via a reading from travel writer Jonathan Raban's account of the modern city as an 'emporium of styles'.

9.6

In the city, we are barraged with images of the people we might become. Identity is presented as plastic, a matter of possessions and appearances; and a very large proportion of the urban landscape is taken up by slogans, advertisements, flatly photographed images of folk heroes – the man who turned in to a sophisticated dandy overnight by drinking a particular brand of vodka, the girl who transformed herself in to a latter day Mata Hari with a squirt of cheap scent. The tone of the wording of these advertisements is usually pert and facetious, comically drowning in its own hyperbole. But the photographs . . . are brutally exact: they reproduce every detail of a style of life, down to the brand of cigarette lighter, the stone in the ring, and the economic row of books on the shelf . . .

For the new arrival, this disordered abundance is the city's most evident and alarming quality. He feels as if he has parachuted into a funfair of contradictory imperatives. There are so many people he might become, and a suit of clothes, a make of car, a brand of cigarettes, will go some way towards turning him in to a *personage* even before he has discovered who that personage is. Personal identity has always been deeply rooted in property, but hitherto the relationship has been a simple one – a question of buying what you could afford, and leaving your wealth to announce your status. In the modern city, there are so many things to buy, such a quantity of different kinds of status, that the choice and its attendant anxieties have created a new pornography of taste. The leisure pages of the Sunday newspapers, fashion magazines, TV plays, popular novels, cook books, window displays all nag at the nerve of our uncertainty and snobbery . . . The piece of furniture, the pair of shoes, the book, the film, are important not so much in themselves but for what they communicate about their owners; and ownership is stretched to include what one likes or believes in as well as what one can buy. (Raban, 1974, pp. 64, 66)

Raban may have been writing over twenty years ago, but his account of the relationship between consumption and identity still seems to ring true today. The Weekend section of the *Guardian*, for example, has a style section which includes three regular columns on what is currently fashionable. These are entitled, in best late 1990s tongue in cheek, 'Style Slave', 'Style Dictator' and 'Style Insider': one of them is written by someone using the pseudonym 'Dee Siner'. All three work to inform readers about what, from the perspective of the presumably youngish, London-based journalists writing the columns, is currently trendy. The 'Style Slave' column for 4 October 1997, for example, tells us that 'the big china mug no longer has a place in the multi-cultural interior', before going on to extol the virtues of the tea bowl and tell us that we can get them at Selfridges. While it would be naïve to assume that Selfridges was inundated with desperate *Guardian* readers in search of tea-bowls on 4 October it is obvious that this kind of column works by linking a certain kind of identity (one that favours multicultural interiors) with reading the *Guardian*. As a *Guardian* reading, futon sleeping, kilim owning, wok cooking individual, I (Tim Middleton) probably fall into the 'typical reader' position assumed by the article in question, and so may admit to an 'oh, that's an interesting idea' response, but I have yet to chuck out my china mugs. What this suggests is that the stereotypes and profiles used by the media are not simply figments of a journalist's or advertiser's imagination. They frequently do have some basis in the world outside marketing; otherwise, how would we recognize aspects of ourselves or people we know in them? Stereotypes work by selecting certain characteristics from the multitude of ways in which people are constituted, and asserting these as all there is to be known about a person. In doing so they reduce complicated and fluid identities to one or two 'typical' features, which then come to represent the whole person. Thus, while stereotypes are not direct reflections of real people, they are connected to the external world in complex ways.

9.10

- Look back at the profiles of 'nineties man' in figure 9.2. Do you recognize parts of yourself or anyone you know in these descriptions?
- Try to produce your own profiles of 'nineties man' or 'nineties woman'. This would work best if done with other people. Identify the problems you encounter in doing this and try to analyse why you encountered the particular problems you did.
- Look through magazines, advertisements and newspapers. Do you find yourself identifying, at least in part, with any of the stereotypes you encounter.
- Look at the Saturday edition of a range of daily papers. What columns and sections appear only at the weekend? What does this suggest about the projected readership in terms of leisure pursuits etc.
- Look at the review sections of daily papers or monthly magazines. Compare, for example, the *Sunday Times* book section with the books section of *Marie Claire* magazine. Are any of the same texts reviewed? What are the differences between the reviews? How does the range of works covered construct the idea of a typical reader? You can do the same kind of activity comparing style or cookery pages.
- Use a CD-ROM edition of the *Guardian* and search through the various style columns: what items emerge as 'must have' products for the 'style slave'? Can you find any of these in the homes of yourself or people you know?

ACTIVITIES

Look now at the advertisement for Tilda's Madhur Jaffrey range of Indian sauces (figure 9.3). Even if you do not know who Madhur Jaffrey is, the photograph shows an Asian woman placing a herb on the side of a dish of curry: this works to suggest the idea of 'home cooking'. While most readers, if they stop to think, will realize that it is unlikely that Madhur Jaffrey has anything to do with the actual manufacture of the product, this advert seeks to reassure us of the authenticity of

Figure 9.3 Advertisement for Tilda sauces

the sauce. The advert allows for at least two answers to its opening question, 'Who makes yours?': 'I do' or 'The takeaway down the road does.'

This advert wants to sell us authenticity and the idea of quality. It also has behind it the idea of convenience, but cannot readily address this because of the potentially negative association of that idea as well as the contradictions between convenience and quality. 'Quality' and 'authenticity' are attributes to be worked for – they suggest in this context 'home cooking' and 'real ingredients' – while 'convenience' suggests the possibility of compromising on 'quality'. The text of the advert stresses the status of the cook – 'the World's leading authority on Indian cuisine' – and the product – 'greeted enthusiastically by lovers of authentic Indian food' – and then works to stress quality and taste – 'exquisite', 'outstanding', 'sheer mouth-watering opulence [*sic*]'. The image plays an important role as well: the sauces are grouped with a number of fresh ingredients in order to imply some kind of link between them; the cutting board contains a number of items which have been cut up along with a knife; all of which reinforces the idea of Madhur Jaffrey making the curry. The freshness of the products, along with the cleanliness of the environment featured, is emphasized by the glass and gleaming steel shelving behind her, the water beads on the tomatoes and peppers, the gloss of the seemingly just cut lime. Having Madhur Jaffrey in the picture also works for the authenticity of the product, partly because it shows her making it, but also because we have a picture of an Asian woman dressed in a sari (think how the meaning would change if she were pictured in chef's whites or in the coverall clothing used in the factory which actually produces the sauce). Tilda is selling an idea about a product. Buying the product doesn't necessarily mean you subscribe to that idea, but a cursory examination of a range of store magazines does seem to suggest that ideas about quality and authenticity are very much to the fore in 1990s food retailing. Can you think of other areas of contemporary life in which 'quality' and 'authenticity' are promulgated as important values? For example, the business corporation Mars lists 'quality' as one of the five guiding principles that underpin every aspect of its business operations: 'quality, responsibility, mutuality, efficiency and freedom' (Mars promotion booklet for Graduate Management Training Programme, 1997).

9.11

- Examine a range of magazines, including store magazines and popular women's magazines like *Bella* and *Take a Break*. Examine the ways in which food is being advertised – noting in particular the stress placed on authenticity and quality and any contradictions arising from this.
- Take another type of product and compare and contrast the ways in which it is advertised. It might be best to work on a range, to include both practical items like toilet paper or sanitary towels and luxury products like exotic cars or designer clothes. Are certain values given particular significance?
- Remind yourself of the discussion on Bourdieu's idea of habitus and 'taste'. Can you identify ways in which any of the advertisements construct differentiated (according to social groups) 'tastes'?

Agency, appropriation and ethics

As we have seen, the contemporary consumer has a bewildering array of products with which to interact. We want now to return to the work of Jean Baudrillard, from whom we quoted earlier. In the following extract the cultural historian Roy Porter provides an introductory overview of some key points in Baudrillard's ideas about consumption.

9.7

The modern consumer society . . . [is] a system in which analysis of the laws of production has become obsolete. Consumption is all important, and consumption has to be understood in a novel manner. Thanks to the twentieth century revolutionization of consciousness – through mass communications, hi-tech media, the advertising and publicity industries, the empire of images throughout the global village – modern human beings now inhabit an artificial, hermetically sealed pleasure dome . . . nothing any longer possesses intrinsic value, in and for itself. Meaning is produced by endless, symbolic exchanges within a dominant code, whose rhetoric is entirely self-referential; a sexy woman is used to sell a car; a car sells cigarettes, cigarettes sell machismo; machismo is used to sell jeans; and so the symbolic magic circle is sealed. (Porter, 1993, pp. 1–2)

9.12

How far do you think that the world of advertising is purely self-referential? Are there ways in which adverts actually relate to 'the real world'? How would advert-like posters for campaigns like the promotion of slower speeds in built up areas, the promotion of safe-sex practices or anti-drink-driving campaigns be purely self-referential?

Baudrillard's ideas seem to work more readily when we look at consumer products as opposed to campaigns. Many car advertisements feature a picture of the car in isolation, whereas the reality of driving in the late twentieth century is crowded roads and traffic queues. Designer clothing is often advertised in ways which are reminiscent of the photo-shoot images used by glossy magazines in their reporting on a fashion line. Both these examples can be said to be self-referential in that the world of car sales does not want to remind its audience of the problems of car ownership in the 'real' world, and the fashion industry has a very symbiotic relationship with the fashion press (Braham, 1997).

Baudrillard wrote, as we have seen, that consumption functions like a language, with its own self-referential codes and signs. Bourdieu argued that as consumers we play an important part in creating the meaning of products, be they football or jeans, and are thus active agents in determining who buys what and for what purpose, even if we do so within his rather static version of social class. Both theorists were concerned to assert that the producers of, for example, football or jeans do not have complete control over the ways in which their products are thought about, spoken about and used. Daniel Miller offers an interesting example of how a localized community can appropriate (consume) an object – the steel drum of Trinidadian steel bands – and in doing so invest it with meanings that assert a specific identity in resistance to the meanings conventionally associated with the steel drum, which is used to transport oil. Trinidad depends economically on the exportation of oil and, as a result, has been at the mercy of the fluctuating price of oil in the world economy. The steel oil drum can be seen as a symbol of Trinidad's economic dependency, but by using these drums as musical instruments to create a musical form known internationally, Trinidadians have appropriated the symbol of their dependence as a symbol of local identity. Trinidadians have reused an object associated with their everyday work and their economic poverty to produce a particular style of music that has allowed them to acquire a dignity and status in the global as well as local community. As Miller points out, Trinidadians guard jealously their status as the originators of the steel band (Miller, 1997, p. 32). The manufacturers of the steel oil drums appropriated by Trinidadian steel bands could hardly have envisaged their products being used in this way. Indeed, as we know, business corporations spend enormous sums of money on marketing and advertising in attempts to 'persuade' consumers to see their products in specific ways. If consumers were simply passive dupes manipulated by the forces of economic capitalism, producers would not have to spend such vast sums of money on marketing their products.

One strand of thinking that has developed from the work of Bourdieu and Baudrillard has been to see consumption as a source of pleasure, as a way in which, particularly, young people are enabled to assemble identities creatively from a diversity of styles, products and appropriation of cultural forms – fashion, popular music, sport and material objects. This appropriation and reworking of self-selected cultural forms and commodities is referred to as **bricolage** and is offered as a strategy by which people are able to resist, subvert and negotiate consumer capitalism. An influential proponent of this view is John Fiske, who argues that

> consumer choice between similar commodities is often not between competing use-values, despite the efforts of consumer advice groups, but between cultural values: and the selection of one particular commodity over others becomes the selection of meanings, pleasure and social identity for the consumer . . . Meanings and pleasures circulate . . . without any real distinction between producers and consumers. (Fiske, 1987, pp. 311, 312)

Fiske is discussing TV rather than shopping for commodities. However, if we focus for a moment on shopping, it is fairly obvious that this is not a simple matter of pleasure, with producers and consumers equally aligned. As we saw in the section on the high street, most of our shopping is routinely done to meet food and household needs rather than selecting a lifestyle. Shopping frequently involves frustration, exhaustion and anxiety. A single mother may experience considerable anxiety, both on behalf of her children and in terms of her identity as a parent, if she is unable to afford the latest toy fashion or the particular brand of trainers perceived as *de rigueur* among her children's peer group. Parents frequently experience difficult tensions around the desire to 'treat' their children and the equally strong need to teach non-materialistic values. Anxieties about debt and overspending, about the consumer excess that currently constitutes Christmas, at least in Britain and the USA, and about affording a holiday are common experiences. Equally, parents may worry, if they cannot afford the school skiing trip or the theatre visit, that they are depriving their children of valuable 'cultural capital' (to use Bourdieu's term).

The dominance of the motor car in industrialized countries as a symbol of identity and independence, despite the reality of owning and maintaining a car, has repercussions not only for those for whom cars are an inaccessible luxury, but also for the health, safety and environmental resources of the world.

Finally, we need to think about consumption in terms of the global economy. Most people are not consumer hedonists engaged in a constant cycle of purchasing; nor are most people completely free to consume whatever, whenever and wherever they wish. When people shop they are frequently motivated by thrift and the need to get value for money. Increasingly, it could be argued, there is a concern among 'First World' consumers to be responsible 'global' citizens and not to waste the world's resources or pollute the environment. Daniel Miller has suggested that 'what we see is a desire on the part of consumers to reconstruct small moral worlds that tame [the] vast forces [of modern capitalism]' (Miller, 1997, p. 47). Nevertheless, this focus on 'small moral worlds' – that is, local dilemmas and identities – may impact, in ways which remain unknown to most of us, on other localized groupings in the less industrialized areas of the world. The concern of multinational corporations to provide consumer choice in the form of low prices for a range of different commodities in the 'First World' relies on supporting the cheapest producer. Producing cheap goods is most easily achieved by paying low wages, and the most likely places where this can happen are in developing countries. Mars, for example, is currently developing manufacturing businesses in the former Eastern Bloc countries Russia, Poland and Hungary. Hence, the thriftiness of the 'First World' consumer may impact upon those who work in less affluent countries.

9.13

- Next time you go shopping, notice, if you can, where the goods you buy have come from. From which countries do high street shops like Marks and Spencer, the Body Shop, Tesco and Sainsbury buy the commodities they sell?
- Do you think we should be willing to pay more for the commodities we consume in order to generate higher wages for those in developing countries? If we did agree to this, how would we know where the extra money we paid went? How could you find out the profit margins of those who sell many of the commodities we buy? How easy would it be to shop ethically? Should there be monitoring and regulation of exploitation by governments or by a global body? How could this be achieved?
- Can you think of other forms of 'ethical consumerism': for example, recycling newspapers.
- Can you think of examples of business corporations that promote themselves as 'ethical producers': for example, the Body Shop?

Conclusions

Rather than summarizing the material we have covered, we want to leave you with a number of questions to think about and research further.

- Corporations like Coca-Cola, McDonalds and Sony are global enterprises. Do they tailor their products to specific, local consumers in different countries or do they simply offer a homogeneous product worldwide? You could usefully look at *Doing Cultural Studies: the Story of the Sony Walkman* (du Gay et al., 1997), which discusses many of the issues raised in this chapter with reference to a particular product, the Sony Walkman.
- Do you think that most of us tend to think about and respond to the issues of a 'small, moral world' – that is family, neighbourhood, friendship group, workplace, nation – rather than global concerns? If your answer is 'yes', why do you think this is? If you answered 'no', can you give reasons for your answer?
- People who work in marketing, media and advertising, producing TV programmes, magazines, advertisements and branded consumer products are also consumers of the products they produce. For example, according to Mars publicity material, Damian Guha, who graduated in Philosophy, Politics and Economics from Oxford, now works as a brand manager for Pedigree Petfoods, a subsidiary of Mars. He describes the business culture he is part of as one that 'offers a world of opportunities for high energy people who thrive on interaction and challenge and like to set and achieve demanding personal goals'. He is part of a team producing and marketing branded petfood but he is also, presumably, a consumer who buys a range of branded products, many of which may have been targeted at young people like himself: young people who are highly skilled at reading and manipulating the language of consumerism. Is it, therefore, more accurate to see the relationship between production and consumption as circular rather than one of cause and effect? An interesting article which discusses this in relation to magazines for young women is '*More!* New sexualities in girls' and women's magazines' (McRobbie, 1996).

The subject of consumption is a complex one and we have been able only to offer you a taste here of the debates and issues it raises. If the subject interests you, and we hope it will, look at the suggestions for further reading. However, as well as reading further in the area, you could do worse than reflect upon your own experience as a consumer of both material objects and cultural forms. The questions posed above may help you to begin this process.

CHAPTER 10

Case Study 2. From TV to PC: Culture and Technology in the Late Twentieth Century

Introduction

[T]echnology means the will to virtuality, and virtuality is about the recline of western civilization, an historical non-time marked by recurrent bouts of spasmodic violence and random crashes of all big referents, which are horizoned by the ascendant politics of liberal and retro-fascism. Unlike the 1890s with its romantic invocation of catastrophe scenarios, the 1990s emerge as an era of general cultural recline: a time of cynical romanticism and cold love, where the body disappears into a virtual imaging system, and where even catastrophes are reversed by the media-net into specular publicity for a crash that will never happen. (Kroker and Weinstein, 1994, p. 2)

In this book we have been working with a definition of culture which stresses the practices and processes of daily life. As Kroker and Weinstein suggest, in the late twentieth century the electronic culture of the Internet is so pervasive that our technology comes to be a register of social and cultural trends, as well as a means by which such trends develop. Even if we do not personally surf the net, our daily lives are caught up in electronic technology; whether in the form of credit card transactions, loyalty card data, library swipe-cards or the apparently simpler form of watching TV, heating a meal in a microwave or listening to a CD.

In the late twentieth century many aspects of life in industrialized countries are reliant upon technology to an extent that even twenty years ago might have seemed surprising. In this final chapter we will be looking at the TV and computer as key pieces of technology in contemporary cultures and providing discussion material, activities and suggested further reading to help you develop your own case study of either technological form. If TV culture has been a mainstay of cultural studies in Britain, Australia and the USA, the electronic culture of the Internet and World Wide Web has only recently become the subject of analysis and debate (see, for example, Mackay, 1997).

We want to begin our discussion with some assertions – in tabular form – from Derrick de Kerckhove, director of the McLuhan Program in Culture & Technology at the University of Toronto; a man hailed by some as today's version of Sixties media commentator Marshall McLuhan.

10.1

Social Trends

1960s–70s	1980s
Producerism	Consumerism
Self-centredness (me decade)	Environmentalism
Relationships	Fitness
Hippies	Yuppies
Feminism	DINKS (double income, no kids)
Social (and not so social) drugs	Non smokers
Ideological drive	Bottom line

Television and computers conquered the industrial world, carrying and shaping corporate psychology according to their own highly distinctive criteria which, in turn, formed and informed distinctive policies within the culture that helped to develop others . . .

Psychological Trends

	Television	Computer
	(saturation during 70s)	(penetration during 80s)
Dominant Concepts	Mass culture	Speed culture
	Mass production	Instant communication
	Being everywhere at once	Being here and now where it counts
Main Patterns of Communication	Broadcasting (one way) (*Give people what they want*)	Networking (two way) (*Find out what people want*)
Dominant Marketing Attitudes	Seduction	Precision
Dominant Business Strategy	Promoting	Accounting
Main source of metaphors	Body – senses – touch (Touch me, feel me)	Brain/central nervous system (The Soul of the *New Machine*)
Favourite Buzzwords	Myths, icons, images	Logic, AI, expert systems
Popular Mythological Representation	Superman (X Ray vision, flying)	2001's HAL (command and control)

If you replace the category headings in the first . . . [table] by Television on the left and Computer on the right, you will be surprised that the new headings actually yield more information. They make even more sense than the classification by periods. TV turned us into inveterate consumers, by bringing the outside world inside our homes, inside the self. We developed a kind of voracious appetite for images and goods. But computers, by projecting outwards from our central nervous systems, giving us access and power over any point in the environment, at any time, for any purpose, made producers of us. The younger generation of men and women got high on small business and new ventures instead of drugs. The computerization of the economy is also key to all the other changes, being the nerve centre of the present body politic. (de Kerckhove, 1995, p. 131–2).

---

de Kerckhove is an optimist about technology and might be criticized for having a rather loose sense of the actual history of the periods he identifies. Wasn't there a recession in the late 1980s? Didn't yuppies symbolize excess, including excessive drug taking? How can a computer from a 1970s film be the dominant mythological figure for the 1990s? (How many people reading this book have seen Kubrick's film?) We agree with him that these two technological media are central to any understanding of the cultures of the decades he identifies, but would hesitate over some of his claims.

What do you think? Can you begin to extend de Kerckhove's ideas by drawing up your own tables for the dominant social trends of the 1990s (some of the earlier sections in this book may help you with this)? Who would be the 1990s zeitgeist social group: Eco warriors, New Lads, Riot Grrls? Is Ecstasy the nineties drug? What (if anything) has replaced consumerism? By thinking about your own view of the social trends of the 1990s and, more particularly, of the role of TV and computers in them, you will have begun to work towards your own view of the interface between the technological and the social in contemporary culture. It is this interface which the activities and discussion offered in this chapter let you begin to explore. If you don't feel ready to tackle the broad questions raised by de Kerckhove's claims at this stage, then we hope that by the end of the chapter you will be more able to debate and discuss the claims made by him and commentators in this area.

Technology and contemporary culture: the television

It is something of a cliché that we live in an era in which the visual dominates over other forms of representation. While TV viewing figures show a slight decline in the 1990s, the audience for cinema is rising and thousands of people interact with screen-based media, including Tamogochi electronic pets, Sony Playstations, CD-ROM simulations, on-line gaming and other World Wide Web based activity. These examples are linked by a new conception of the viewer as an active participant in the screened events; TV and cinema still tend to work by positioning the viewer as spectator, but even here things are changing.

Table 10.1 Commonly owned technological products

	Age (years)						
	Teenager (own/years)	20–29 (own/years)	30–39 (own/years)	40–49 (own/years)	50–59 (own/years)	60–69 (own/years)	70+ (own/years)
Colour TV							
Microwave							
Answerphone							
Cordless phone							
Mobile phone							
Personal computer							
Portable CD player							
Scanner							
Digital camera							

In the 1950s and 1960s going to the cinema meant collective viewing in an environment which was not dissimilar to many theatres; cinema spaces included stalls, balcony and cheap seats high up. Cinemas seated hundreds of people and viewing was often a shared, community experience (an example of this would be the reaction to the film *Rock Around the Clock*, which was released in 1955). Today, cinemas are much smaller spaces, often seating only 100 people; several showings of the same film each day have replaced the previous pattern of a single showing with a 'matinee' at weekends. With TV there have been equally far reaching changes: the expansion of terrestrial networks and the opening up of satellite and cable channels has created a plethora of choice. The TV remote control device and mass production techniques have meant that in many households there are several televisions; viewing has become a solitary and often fragmentary experience. TV remote control devices allow channel surfing, and some types of TV show have adapted to a newly active viewer by working through short sequences: for example, the many 'youth' TV shows such as those distributed by MTV.

You can explore the ways in which daily life has become more technologized by surveying the experience of your peers and that of your parent and grandparents. Table 10.1 lists some commonly owned items.

ACTIVITIES

10.1

- Which of the items listed in table 10.1 do your own?
- How many years have you used an item of this type?

This crude survey will reveal broad patterns of ownership, perhaps suggesting the extent to which the sample polled is part of a technologized culture, but will also point up differences in the experience of technology according to age. As anyone who has ever bought a computer will know, technology moves very rapidly and the latest piece of equipment quickly becomes out-paced by newer technology. One of the problems of this pace of technological change is that we have machines which allow us to do things that we could not do before, and this is often cited as an argument for the pointlessness of technology. This proliferation is also evident in that facet of technologized culture which touches most people's lives on a daily basis: the television.

In the 1970s, cultural studies tended to see TV as something which sought to impose ideological positions upon a largely passive audience. Studies such as Brunsdon and Morley's (1978) analysis of the early evening TV news show *Nationwide* stressed the ways in which the medium sought to shape and construct itself in line with the beliefs and values of its ideal audience: the show created an idealized spectator and, the study suggests, worked by trying to position viewers in this role. More positive accounts of TV from this period still tended to see the medium as controlling its audience. Here is Graeme Turner's summary of Fiske and Hartley's work in their influential *Reading Television* (1978):

10.2

Fiske and Hartley approach television as an oral, rather than a literate, medium . . .

> Every medium has its own unique set of characteristics, but the codes which struc-
> ture 'the language' of television are much more like those of speech than of writing.
> Any attempt to decode a television 'text' as if it were a literary text is thus not only
> doomed to failure but is also likely to result in a negative evaluation of the medium
> based on its inability to do a job to which it is in fact fundamentally unsuited. [Fiske
> and Hartley, 1978, p. 15]

Their description of the function of television draws on Hall's encoding/decoding model
[see Hall, 1990, and chapter 3]:

> The internal psychological state of the individual is not the prime determinant in the com-
> munication of television messages. These are decoded according to individually learnt but
> culturally generated codes and conventions, which of course impose similar constraints of
> perception on the encoders of the messages. It seems, then, that television functions as a
> social ritual, overriding individual distinctions, in which our culture engages in order to
> communicate with its collective self. (85)

Television, they suggest, performs a 'bardic function' for the culture. Just as the bard
translated the central concerns of his day into verse, television renders 'our own everyday perceptions' into its specialised language system. It serves the needs of the culture
in particular ways: it addresses collective audiences rather than the individual; it is
oral rather than literate; it operates as a centring discourse, appearing as the voice of
the culture with which individuals can identify; and it takes its place in the cycle of
production and reproduction of the culture's dominant myths and ideologies. Fiske and
Hartley divide television's bardic function into categories that include the articulation of
a consensus about reality; the implication of individuals into membership of the culture;
the celebration, explanation, interpretation, and justification of the doings of individuals within the society; the demonstration of the practical adequacy of the culture's
ideologies and mythologies, and, conversely, the exposure of any practical inadequacy
resulting from changed social conditions; and the guarantee of audience members'
status and identity. There is some overlap in these categories, but the general notion of
the bardic function continues to be useful. (Turner, 1992, pp. 101–2)

10.2

- What do you think the differences are between systems of communication
  based upon speech and those based upon writing? How far can TV today
  be seen as a speech-based form of communication? What is the 'grammar' of TV (its rules of organization)? What about forms (bragging,
  gossip, proclamations etc.)? Is there a 'vocabulary' of TV which differs
  between programmes? Try comparing a TV adaptation of a 'classic' novel with
  an episode of a soap opera, for example (for a useful guide on how to analyse
  TV, see Selby and Cowdery, 1995).

- Fiske and Hartley were writing before the advent of the remote control: given this technology, how far would you want to argue that the 'internal psychological state of the individual' has now become a major factor in a TV communication?
- How far do you think the idea of a bardic function remains viable today? Think about state, legal and sporting events broadcast on TV (e.g. the funeral of Diana, Princess of Wales, the O. J. Simpson trial in America, the Louise Woodward trial in Autumn 1997, coverage of the Gulf War, election broadcasts, international sporting events) and the ways in which these might fit into Fiske and Hartley's categories. Take another type of TV programme, like a quiz show, the Ophrah Winfrey show or even a soap opera, and think about the extent to which it can be discussed as possessing a 'bardic function'.

The institution of TV

Television is the applied technology of a late form of capitalist society that is increasingly complex and increasingly mobile. It is the chosen communication of a particular kind of household. It is the dominant form of communication in a society where information and communication are centralized in their origin. (O'Connor, 1989, p. 94).

Now read Stuart Price's discussion of TV as an institution.

10.3

What is the meaning of the term 'institution'? It is all too easy to attempt to explain the term by giving an *example* of a familiar media institution, like the BBC, rather than a *definition*. In *A Dictionary of Communication and Media Studies* (p. 87), Watson & Hill define institution quite differently, as '[a] term generally applied to patterns of behaviour which are established, approved an usually of some permanence'.

Here we have an idea which might help us to break the habit of imagining institutions simply as large buildings in Central London. 'Patterns of behaviour' suggests that there is a human dimension to all institutions. In *Mass Communication Theory*, McQuail writes that various media have become institutionalised, which means that (p. 37) 'they have acquired a stable form, structure and set of functions and related public expectations.'

The key to both definitions is to be found in words like 'patterns' and 'structure', 'established' and 'stable'. In other words, institutions are bodies which have a settled structure and a set way of functioning. Alvarado, Gutch and Wollen (*Learning the Media*, p. 48) use the definition employed by Raymond Williams:

Institution is one of several examples of a noun of action or process which became, at a certain stage, a general and abstract noun describing something apparently objective and systematic; in fact, in the modern sense, an *institution*.

Table 10.2 Output on two days by BBC1 and Channel 4 television

Programme type	BBC 1 Saturday (24 hours 16 minutes of programmes)		BBC 1 Wednesday (24 h 25 min)		Channel 4 Saturday (21 h 40 min)		Channel 4 Wednesday (21 h 15 min)	
	Hours	%	Hours	%	Hours	%	Hours	%
Children's	5 h 8 min	21	1 h 55 min	8	2 h	9	1 h 40 min	8
News*	5 h 55 min	24	8 h 40 min	35	1 h	5	55 min	4
Weather	8 min	1	10 min	1	0		0	
Sport	6 h 15 min	26	0		4 h	18	3 h 10 min	15
Light entertainment	2 h 50 min	12	6 h 10 min	25	2 h 25 min	11	9 h 5 min	43
Popular drama (including soaps	49 min	3	3 h 30 min	14	3 h 45 min	17	3 h 50 min	18
Film	2 h 50 min	12	3 h 25 min	14	7 h 50 min	36	1 h 40 min	8
Quiz/game shows	21 min	1	15 min	1	0		30 min	2
Education	0		0		0		30 min	2
Current affairs	0		30 min	2	1 h	5	0	

*BBC news figure includes the output of BBC News 24.

These authors create no surprises when they insist (p. 49) that:

> . . . no text without production and without audience is possible, and to teach about institutions is to teach about the relations . . . between those three.

Here, the idea of institution as a *relationship* is stressed – a relationship between production, text and audience. (Price, 1993, pp. 297–8).

One way of thinking about TV's relationship with its audience is in terms of its supposed 'bardic' function. If this function exists, the range of programmes ought to reflect what culture regards as significant and relevant: that is, it ought to reflect 'a consensus about reality' (Turner, 1992, p. 102). Table 10.2 details the hours of programming by type of programme and also the percentage of the output devoted to a particular type.

The advent of the BBC's News 24 as a filler in the overnight slot (5 hours and 15 minutes of the total news output for Saturday and 3 hours and 45 minutes of the output on Wednesday on the sample days) does rather distort the picture. If you asked someone which channel had more news coverage many people might have said Channel 4. The figures also point up a gap between popular preconception and actuality: Channel 4 schedules far more popular drama and popular light entertainment than the BBC. The data do not include any timings for advertisements – how far do you think that this is a serious omission?

This is the TV output but it is unlikely to equate with individual viewing habits. For example, on the days in question I (Tim Middleton) watched nothing on either channel on Saturday and on Wednesday watched EastEnders on the BBC and taped a Channel 4 cookery programme which I watched on another day. There is a difference between the output of a TV channel and the cultural consumption of a given individual which makes it hard to accept Fiske and Hartley's claims for TV as 'bardic' or the notion of TV as somehow shaping and dictating how we use it. Without video recorders to allow us to shape and structure our viewing we probably could not access the diversity of programming now available. The following lists some of the choice available at 8 p.m. one Wednesday evening:

BBC 1: *EastEnders* (soap).
BBC 2: *Rick Stein's Fruits of the Sea* (cookery).
ITV: *Des O'Connor Tonight* (light entertainment).
Channel 4: *TV Dinners* (cookery).
Channel 5: *Survivor* (documentary).

In the early 1980s viewers would have had only three choices; Channel 4 was launched in the early 1980s and Channel 5 in 1997. Following the launch of the Astra satellite in the late 1980s, it became possible to view satellite broadcasts via a 'dish' receiver and decoder. If we add in some of the major satellite channels to our listing the choice offered grows to:

BBC 1: *EastEnders* (soap).
BBC 2: *Rick Stein's Fruits of the Sea* (cookery).
ITV: *Des O'Connor Tonight* (light entertainment).
Channel 4: *TV Dinners* (cookery).
Channel 5: *Survivor* (documentary).
Sky Screen 1: *Muppet Treasure Island* (last hour of film).
Sky Screen 2: *Family of Cops* (film).
Carlton Select: *Desmond's* (sitcom).
Discovery: *Solar Empire* (documentary).
Eurosport: *Live boxing* (continued sports coverage).
Granada Plus: *The Adventures of Sherlock Holmes* (popular drama).
Sky 1: *Rescue Paramedics* (documentary).
UK Gold: *2point4 Children* (continued sitcom).

Deregulation of broadcasting in 1993 led to the spread of cable channels; at present these are confined to larger conurbations. There is also the possibility of pay-per-view services being developed using Internet-like computer technology, which would further extend choice. At present, however, the Internet offers few TV-like live forums, tending instead to offer text-based services. On the Wednesday night selected there were some Internet sites which contained a variety of material, including a chat show, a music programme and a football discussion programme. Charting the ways in which you access and interact with TV can be a useful starting point for a reflection upon the role of broadcast media in contemporary culture.

10.3

Price's account of TV as institution is one which stresses interaction between viewer and channel. You could explore this by drawing up a table of channel output over a week and then filling in details of what you watched as a percentage of the output of that programme type. You could also collect data from friends and colleagues; in order to provide a broader picture you should try to ensure that your survey covers different age, gender and ethnic groups. You might like to compare the results of your viewing habits survey with national viewing figures (these can often be found in the Monday edition of the *Guardian*, among others).

You may find that there are patterns in your results which can indicate assumptions about the role and function of TV made by a particular age or socio-economic group. For more detailed work you could try observing a single subject watching a taped programme and noting all the things which she or he does in addition to watching the TV. You could think about the ways in which people use technology to construct new identities or to reassert 'traditional' identities. The following extract, from Marie Gillespie's study of the ways in which South Asian families in west London viewed and used home videos, offers insights into the complex use to which new technologies can be put with relation to 'Indian' identities.

10.4

In Southall [west London] the rapid expansion of the home video market needs to be considered not only as providing an extension to an already important and dynamic film culture [consisting of popular Hindi films, known as 'Bombay' films shown in local cinemas] but also very much a response on the part of a black community to life in Britain. Southall, like many other black communities, has come into existence in the first instance as a result of racist immigration and housing policies. Such communities have developed as 'sanctuaries' against the racism they experience. The exclusion and marginalization of many people in Southall from mainstream British society, coupled with the failure to provide adequate leisure/culture facilities, has . . . contributed to the development of an important home video culture . . .

For the older members of the community, nostalgia is a key element in the pleasure experienced through film. In one particularly moving account by a man in his seventies, tears welled in his eyes as he recounted: 'When we see black-and-white films it reminds us of our childhood, our school days, our school mates, of what we were thinking, of what we did do, of our heroes . . . and I tell you this gives us great pleasure.' The films would appear to act as a form of collective popular memory and some parents are able to convey a sense of their past in India to their children . . .

Various degrees of scepticism are registered among the boys [interviewed by Gillespie] about parents' attempts to 'artificially maintain a culture' through film: 'Parents want their children to maintain certain religious values, beliefs and customs but that doesn't mean that Indian films are necessarily going to educate them in that way. They may well do the opposite . . . I think the moral standards in most recent films is pretty appalling.' But clear distinctions are made between religion and a sense of cultural identity and whilst firmly upholding the Sikh faith one boy claims: 'Parents use the films to represent their culture to their children but that will not work because those are not my roots, that place [India] has nothing to do with me anymore.'

Many parents lament what they see as a process of progressive 'cultural loss' in each generation of children. Looking to the past they attempt to re-create 'traditional culture'. Meanwhile young people, with eyes to the future, are busy re-creating something 'new'. The striving after cultural continuity and the negoiation of cultural identity are thus inescapably dialectical processes and they must, moreover, be seen in the widest possible context. The notion of viewing as a social activity which takes place in families needs to be extended to include more detailed explorations of the wider social, cultural, and ideological contexts and uses of the VCR. (Gillespie, 1989)

Technology as contemporary culture

Douglas Rushkoff has coined the term 'screenager' to describe the visually literate generation 'born into a culture mediated by the television and computer (Rushkoff, 1997, p. 3), and his work on contemporary culture suggests that mediating the multiplicity (or, in computer terms, 'multitasking') of programmes on offer is an essential skill for survival in today's culture. Just as the audiences for early talking cinema had to become accustomed to the conventions of a new medium, so we are gradually accustoming ourselves to channel surfing on the TV interactive sites on the Internet. If contemporary TV offers a bewildering array of options to the viewer, then the World Wide Web can, at times, seem to offer an overwhelming choice of sites.

One of the reasons why computers remain a rather closed off area for many people (aside, that is, from their cost) is their association with science. Unlike the TV set, which has been part of the furniture of most households since the 1950s or 1960s, the computer has yet to become quite so familiar. It is marketed as an educational device, as a home office or as an entertainment centre. Consumers are frequently bewildered by the jargon of RAM and ROM and processors and cache memory. No one goes into a TV shop and expects to be given information about the tube or speaker output, but most PCs are sold as items of high technology. With operating systems like that of the Apple Macintosh in the 1980s and Windows 95 and 98 in the 1990s, most systems are relatively simple to operate and do not need any more skill to interact with than a TV set. What is more, unlike with TV, the user can actually create material which contributes to the medium (World Wide Web pages, inputs to newsgroups etc.): networked computing is a very interactive form of technological culture.

Below is the hypertext markup language (html) version of a portion of a World Wide Web page:

```
<HTML>
<!--This file created 18/1/99 10:00 am by Claris Home Page version 3.0-->
<HEAD>
    <TITLE>Literature Studies</TITLE>
    <META NAME=GENERATOR CONTENT="Claris Home Page 3.0">
    <X-CLARIS-WINDOW TOP=66 BOTTOM=600 LEFT=8 RIGHT=693>
    <X-CLARIS-TAGVIEW MODE=minimal>
</HEAD>
<BODY BGCOLOUR=" #FFFFFF" BACKGROUND="images/backgr1.jpg">
<H2><CENTER><FONT SIZE="+4" COLOR=" #FF0000">Literature
Studies@UCRYSJ<A NAME=top></FONT></CENTER></H2>
<P> </P>
<P> </P>
<P><TABLE BORDER=1 BGCOLOR=" #FFFFFF" WIDTH="92%"
HEIGHT=179 BACKGROUND="images/backgr1.jpg">
    <TR>
    <TD>
        <H4><CENTER><A HREF="Discipline%20Web/people.htm"><FONT
SIZE="+3" COLOR=" #FF0000">People</FONT></A></CENTER></H4>
    </TD>
    <TD BACKGROUND="Conrad%20%26%20new%20front/
Parchment%20(light)">
        <H4><CENTER><A HREF="Discipline%20Web/people.htm"><FONT
```

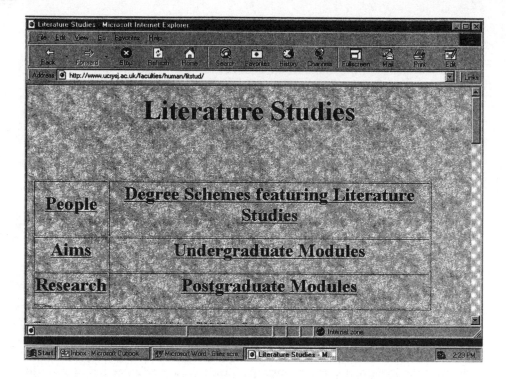

Figure 10.1   College of Ripon & York St John, Literature Studies web site

SIZE="+3" COLOR=" #FF0000">Degree
Schemes featuring Literature Studies</FONT></A></CENTER></H4>
   </TD>
  </TR>
  <TR>
   <TD>

Figure 10.1 shows the same site viewed through the *Internet Explorer* browser. To create the latter I did not have to get involved in all the program codes of the first example; text is simply entered and then given attributes (a particular type of heading, colour, size) and status (a link to another World Wide Web page, for example) via a program (*Claris Homepage* 3.0) that is easy to interact with. If you can use a word-processing package then you can write a web page. The ability to create a document and file it on to a server means that individuals can interact with on-line media to an extent not currently possible with other screen-based broadcasts. Instead of watching, as we do with TV, we interact with the computer, using the browser programme to 'enter' into cyberspace:

> Cyberspace. A consensual hallucination experienced daily by billions of legitimate operators, in every nation . . . A graphic representation of data abstracted from the banks of every computer in the human system. Unthinkable complexity. Lines of light ranged in the nonspace of the mind, clusters and constellations of data. Like city lights, receding . . . (Gibson, 1984, p. 67)

Gibson's creation of the term 'cyberspace' in the mid 1980s and its widespread adoption shortly after to describe the (slightly less mind-bogglingly visual) Internet alerts us to the speed with which his science fiction fast became science fact. Writing in 1997, the journalist Douglas Rushkoff offers the following view of the development of cyberspace.

10.5

The realm of computer networks is a created world, built upon an intentionally organic, anarchy-inspiring skeleton . . . When the practical application gave way to pure pleasure, participants created bulletin boards and conferences dedicated to extremely personal, intensely spiritual, and highly philosophical subjects. It was as if going on-line somehow opened up a person to a more chaotic sensibility. Fifty year old businessmen got into conversations about Carl Jung with teenagers whose dreadlocks and piercings would repulse them in the street. New kinds of forums arose to give people a chance to interact in more dreamlike ways. Multi-User Dimensions (MUDs) allowed users to engage in text based fantasy games with strangers from around the world. Physically, it was as safe as sending e-mail; psychologically, well, it was as depraved as the participants wanted it to get.

At the moment we realize that the computer medium is not just for reading and consuming but for posting and participating, and an entirely new set of responsibilities confronts us: what do we want to say and do, and what effect will our words have on the consensual hallucination?

With increasing rapidity, the hierarchically structured databases, newsgroups, and file sharing systems (FTP, Usenet, gopher servers) are giving way to more freeform style Internet browsers, that encourage users to chart their own, almost random paths through the world of computer networks. The World Wide Web lets people participate on-line in a manner much more consistent with the underlying network. Any person or institution can create a 'home page' – a bunch of data, images, text, and 'links' to other Web pages throughout the network. Because these pages are linked to one another, users roam from one place to another, exploring the Web in the manner they would explore a natural environment: go to a tree, inspect its bark, see a bug, follow it to its nest. On the Web, one might start by accessing a computer in New York with a page someone created about Marshall McLuhan. He can click on a picture of the book *Understanding Media* and get connected to another Web page containing the text of the book. On that page, he may find links to other media theorists, television museums, or the University of Toronto. A click of the mouse takes you to the new site.

Exploring the Web requires a surfer's attitude toward data and ideas. Maybe this is why it took a kid to develop the software most people now use to navigate it. Back in 1993 at the age of twenty-two, Marc Andreessen, an avid PC game player, co-wrote the first version of Mosaic, the first widely used and user friendly graphical interface for

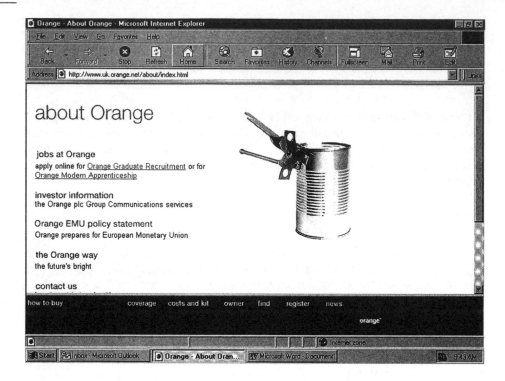

Figure 10.2   Orange web site

the World Wide Web. His stated aim has always been to create software that allows people to get the most out of existing technologies. Currently called Netscape, the later version of Andreessen's programme allows users to access sound, graphics, and video over their phone lines. (Rushkoff, 1997, 183–5)

It is interesting to note that Netscape, one of the computer industry's more successful new companies in the early 1990s, is now locked in a struggle for supremacy with the mega-corporation Microsoft; a struggle which centres on the provision of a graphical based software which allows user to access the Web. Netscape posted loses of US$113 million in 1997 (*Guardian* 6 January 1998, p. 16), the year in which Microsoft aggressively marketed its rival Internet browser, *Internet Explorer*.

All of this points up the extent to which the net is very much a commercial space and seems to challenge Rushkoff's vision of it as a site of personal freedom. Look through issues of national newspapers or magazines and spot the number of web site addresses. How many of them are for companies? Are any for individuals?

You might like to trace the history of Netscape from its first appearance in 1994 through to its recent battles with Microsoft: the history of this company can reveal

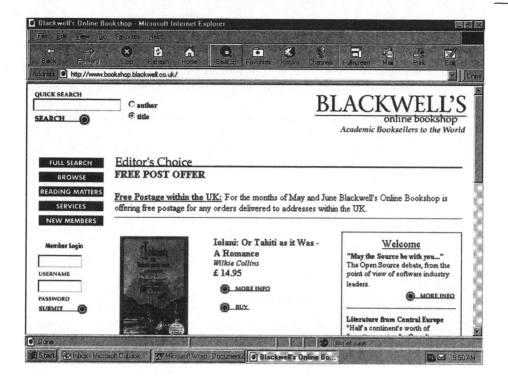

Figure 10.3 Blackwell's Online Bookshop

much about the expansion of the World Wide Web and the sudden rush to exploit its commercial potential which occurred in the 1990s. Use CD-ROMs of newspapers to gather information or try visiting some World Wide Web sites. For data and commentary on the Internet as a commercial medium see, among others, the following World Wide Web sites:

GVU's WEB User Survey: http://www.cc.gatech.edu/gvu/user_surveys/
Values and Life Styles: http://future.sri.com
MIDS: http://www.mids.org

Figures 10.2 and 10.3 give some examples of World Wide Web pages produced by commercial organizations.

Organizations are still working towards an appropriate format for Internet sites: some, as in the examples from Orange here, seem to treat the web page as a kind of brochure; offering images from the company's advertising which users may have seen in print media or on TV. There is a definite attempt to give the user a sense of the corporate identity – can you describe some of the ways in which this operates in the examples featured? You might like to look at other sites produced by technological companies like Sony or Apple, for example, which are more dynamic and interactive than the example from Orange given here, with links to short samples of games, films and music as well as product data. Indeed, the fact that the web site itself features animation and eye catching colours, which make it impossible to reproduce in a book, suggests some of the ways in which the publication of advertising on the Web can enhance connotations of dynamic, techno-savvy activity.

The Blackwell's book service site is more typical of many commercial World Wide Web sites and those of educational establishments in that it is largely text-based and built around hyper-links to other pages in the Blackwell site or to other locations on the World Wide Web. Such sites require users to interact via a mouse or keyboard and allow them to seek out information only after they sift through a number of often irrelevant pages. The text-based nature of the World Wide Web means that Rushkoff's suggestion that we interact with the Web as we might explore a natural environment is, at present, an overstatement. Even with portable phones and laptop or palmtop computers we cannot easily interact with the Web other than through a screen; even VR headsets and body suits require screens and most of the data are text-based.

The high-tech web sites of commercial organizations, like the prime time shows on terrestrial TV, are not the best places to look for alternatives to the dominant culture. If the Net started out as a military communications system and has become an overloaded electronic market place, there are none the less spaces in which individuals and groups can operate. As Rushkoff's article suggests, it is in the interactive sites which rely upon postings (like MUDs and newsgroups) that net culture of this sort is at its most diverse and visible. These centres of activity are closer to local cable TV shows, fanzines and the like; they make use of a sophisticated technological infrastructure for often subversive ends. In addition, these spaces can often be threatening and, in some ways, dangerous. Perhaps, at the level of metaphor, Rushkoff's claims do have some merit.

10.6

READING

Virtual reality can mean different things to different people. Commercial, military and academic technological developments, which include head-mounted displays, data gloves and certain interactive video games, have been regarded in the popular press since about 1989 as the present and future of virtual reality. Although this type of technology has been well funded, academically theorized and vociferously hyped in pop-culture lifestyle publications . . . projected as a dangerous, scary fantasy in mainstream movies such as *Lawnmower Man*, or else as a sci-fi wet dream involving sex in wired body suits, very little of it is developed beyond preliminary stages, affordable or available to the general public.

Another type of virtual reality involves much less high tech hardware and is made up by its many users as they go along. This type of VR includes the user created environments found on telephone and online chatlines, bulletin board systems, newsgroups, and any of the number of commercial online service providers that have proliferated in the past several years. Of this type, the richest, most complex and most comprehensively elaborate environments are MUDs: multi-user dimensions (or dungeons).

MUDs are text based, interactive databases located on the Internet that allow many users to communicate with each other at the same time by typing text into their computers. Everybody in the same 'room' sees whatever you type, and you can see what everybody else is typing as well. You can look at other people and the room you're in, walk or teleport into another place, pick up objects, even dance and get drunk in a virtual club. The only technology required is a computer and a modem or a means of direct access to the Internet. The only skills required are patience enough to learn a few simple commands, some programming ability or willingness to learn, and good writing skills to craft highly complex, vivid environments in which you begin to feel as if you are actually there. Unlike better known chat-line systems, in which the users can openly converse as if on a telephone, players on MUDs are also objects; they have bodies they can describe as simply, attractively or fantastically as the skill and imagination of the individual writer allow . . .

When you newly arrive on a MUD, your first act is to decide on a name for yourself. On some MUDs, people go by their real names, but on most, people invent new identities. You can be a character from your favourite book, movie or TV show, or invent a persona of your own. You describe yourself and choose a gender. You can 'morph' (change from one description and/or gender to another) with a single command, and change your mind and rewrite yourself at any time. Communication with other players is just as easy. If you want to say something, you type *say* followed by whatever it is you want to say.

If you (. . . [in your role as] character Amalea) wanted to make a face or a gesture, you might type:

emote looks baffled and her lip quivers slightly.

Everyone in the room would then see:

Amalea looks baffled and her lip quivers slightly.

Emoting allows for a richness and variety of communicative nuances not easily conveyable in other electronically mediated environments. Players become conscious of having 'bodies' and, just as they do in 'real life', express themselves with physical gestures as often as they speak. Sometimes the sense of presence is so vivid that you feel as if you are really touching, smelling, tasting, seeing whatever is around you, in a complex interchange of experience between a physical and an imaginary body. (McRae, 1996, pp. 245–7)

10.7

Upload your electronic body via Internet into a MUD, and you are suddenly exited into a strange, spectral, disembodied space. In this floating fiction-packet you choose your own 'handle' and take verbal hits emerging from unexpected points in the virtual geometry from other nomadic travellers on the electronic frontier (voices come at you from up, down, behind, sideways, and even from inside your skin as the schizoid electronic self clammers [*sic*] to get out and play in the MUD). The discussion in the MUD playground is banal, high school existentialism:

'What's the meaning of cyberspace?' 'Is this all there is?' 'What are we going to do now we are here?' But the verbal screen is just that: a *trompe l'oeil* that disguises the shocking intensity of the feeling of dislocation from the flesh as your electronic mind floats around in cyber space. The sensation is like treading aerial water in a dark nowhere space where digital bodies converge momentarily like iridescent bubbles, and then just as suddenly burst and disappear . . .

Playing in the MUD is the pataphysics of New Age culture. It is how the western (technocratic) mind likes to think of itself in the dying days of the twentieth century: evanescent foam in the evolutionary story of virtualized life. (Kroker and Weinstein, 1994, 128–30)

ACTIVITIES ✓

10.4

- Look back at chapters 2 and 8 and think carefully about:
  (a) The relationship between notions of the subject and the (apparent) freedom of the MUD environment. What is your response to the idea of having an 'electronic mind'?
  (b) The extent to which MUD personae could alter the ways in which individuals think of themselves particularly in relation to their physical body.
- If you have access to the Internet try visiting and interacting in some MUDs: LambdaMOO is a good starting point. Alternatively, you can use the search term 'MUD' on your Internet browser's search facility and follow up links that interest you.
- One thinker who has explored the implications of virtual space for identity is Donna Haraway. To take your investigation further you might like to read her 1992 essay 'The promises of monsters: a regenerative politics for inappropriate/d others' (see especially pages 324–9). This essay is a more recent stage in a vein of thought which began in Haraway's (1985) 'A manifesto for cyborgs'; the essay, and interesting supporting discussion, is available in Weed (1989, pp. 173–217).g

While the one-line world of MUDs and MOOs (MUDs, object-oriented) can enable people to interact in new and challenging ways, there is much evidence that the culture of the Internet replicates many of the tensions and divisions of the non-electronic world. For some commentators, the Internet and World Wide Web are male dominated precisely because of their technological base; a base which has traditionally been regarded as a male preserve. While the diversity of the World Wide Web means that there is space for everyone, the apparent lack of hierarchies does not mean that it is wholly utopian. People joining a MUD and asking questions which have been dealt with by other participants in the past may well find that they are deluged with masses of hostile comments from other participants (a process known as flaming).

In the collection of essays *Wired Women: Gender and New Realities in Cyberspace* (Cherny and Weisse, 1996), many contributors reflect upon the white male heterosexual hegemony which exists on the Internet and in computer-related culture in general. For Karen Coyle, the computer joystick is a penis substitute: something the male gamer grips to pleasure himself as he interacts with the images on the computer screen (pp. 47–8). Susan Clerc's survey of fan-based Internet sites for such shows as *Star Trek*, *Babylon 5* and *The X-Files* reveals a predominantly male user profile. Even when women access such sites and related newsgroups they are less active than the male fans, largely because of the sexist and macho culture created by the dominant male users (pp. 81–8).

10.8

One young woman I spoke with, a college senior majoring in English, decided to put 'MRS!' next to her name on all her electronic correspondence because of the constant requests for dates. Her comments on sexism on line included:

> I think (the Internet) is the last bastion of real ugly sexism because it's unmoderated and faceless. I've received more 'wanna fucks' . . . and 'shut up bitch' mail than I care to count. I've posted to *alt.feminism* and had men posting me back screamingly hateful e-mail calling me everything from a lesbian to a whore. One man told me that as a woman 'you have so little to complain about in real life that you stay on the net all day whining about how bad things are' . . .

While it can be said that 'wanna fuck' e-mail is 'only words' and 'not real', I can't help but wonder how many women are discouraged from speaking up online for fear of being targeted for some sort of sexual advance or another . . .

Harassment isn't just a women's issue. In this kind of free-for-all climate, the only people who will have free speech are those who have the gall to stand up to threats or frequent requests for sex, and those who have been lucky enough not to step on the wrong person's toes yet . . . Sandy [another victim of on-line harassment] compares the current atmosphere online to . . . [that of a] dark science fiction movie . . .

> It's like another world, it's like another planet. It's like a totally unregulated dirty nasty little underworld. It's got some really nice, great shining pockets of humanity and education and conversation, and then its got this horrible seamy gutter-ridden filth . . . they're spreading like a cancer. As far as how to eradicate that without cutting out the good, I don't know what's going to happen to it. I really sincerely do not think censorship and government regulation is the way to go, I just wish people were a little nicer to each other. (Brail, 1996, pp. 151–5)

Conclusions

Technology can be both empowering and overpowering. This chapter has offered you a number of ways into the debates around culture and technology, but to take your studies further you will need to spend some time gathering information about TV culture or the Internet. In this chapter we have tried to think about technology via discussion of two dominant forms – the TV and the computer – and our suggestions for further reading reflect this focus. In addition to printed sources we have complied a list of World Wide Web sites and related material. When you have had a chance to look at some of these you might like to turn back to the start of the chapter and reread the material from Derrick de Kerckhove, mapping out your own account of the social trends of the 1990s and commenting upon the role of the TV and computer technology.

Conclusion

We hope that you have found things in this book that have enriched and enhanced your study of culture and set you thinking about the areas you would like to explore in more detail.

If you have worked through some or all of the chapters in this book, you will know by now that we are much more interested in the processes by which culture can be studied than we are in arguing for a particular approach or theoretical position. You will also be aware that we have particular areas of interest and that these have shaped our account of how you might set about studying culture.

This book has sought to equip you with a range of approaches to some of the main aspects of contemporary culture in Britain today. We have tried to look at material from across the cultural terrain, focusing our discussions on people, places and practices that seem to us to be significant in any approach to the study of our culture. As teachers of cultural studies we have, inevitably, engaged in debates within the subject area, and this book's emphasis on the need to reflect upon the relationship between a still dominant high culture and that of everyday life, and its concern to establish a dialogue with the traces of the cultures of different epochs which still inform our society today, are just two of the ways in which we have tried to make a case for areas that are often marginalized or neglected in introductions to British cultural studies.

Where next?

If you have been reading this book as part of a programme of study in a college or university then the answer to this question may well seem to be mapped out for you. Whether or not this is the case, we would like to make a few suggestions about the ways in which you might want to follow up the arguments and ideas introduced in this work. It may be that the areas we highlight below are not the ones that caught your interest or attention, and if this is the case we refer you to the further reading suggestions for the chapter dealing with the topics that particularly interested you.

The following suggestions provide some ways of further refining and developing your approach to the study of culture:

- Follow the debates about the nature, focus and use of cultural studies in the *Times Higher Education Supplement* and also in specialist journals like *Cultural Studies, Feminist Review, Journal of Popular Culture, Postmodern Culture, Theory, Culture and Society* and *Women's Studies International Forum*. You will also find articles and reports on items of relevance to cultural studies in the mainstream press, although these are often sensationalized and rely on 'sound-bite' reporting.

- Questions of cultural value have been touched upon a number of times in this book and provide an area of intense debate within cultural studies. Works which have important things to say about this issue include Steven Connor, *Theory and Cultural Value* (Oxford: Blackwell, 1992), John Frow, *Cultural Studies and Cultural Value* (Oxford: Oxford University Press, 1995) and Jim McGuigan, *Cultural Populism* (London: Routledge, 1992). For an approach that focuses upon the ways in which the issue of cultural values arises in relation to responses to film and TV adaptations of 'classic' literary works see the essays in Deborah Cartmell et al. (eds), *Pulping Fictions: Consuming Culture across the Literature/Media Divide* (London: Pluto Press, 1996).

- Cultural studies has, by and large, embraced postmodern theory in its account of contemporary culture, and many introductory works rely upon postmodernist assumptions which are not always debated. The following works will help you come to your own conclusions: Lawrence Cahoone, *From Modernism to Postmodernism: an Anthology* (Oxford: Blackwell, 1996), Steven Connor, *Postmodernist Culture: an Introduction to Theories of the Contemporary* (Oxford: Blackwell, 1989), Terry Eagleton, *The Illusions of Postmodernism* (Oxford: Blackwell, 1996), Scott Lash and Jonathan Friedman (eds), *Modernity and Identity* (Oxford: Blackwell, 1992), Mica Nava and Alan O'Shea (eds), *Modern Times: Reflections on a Century of English Modernity* (London: Routledge, 1996) and Alan Sinfield, *Literature, Politics and Culture in Postwar Britain* (London: Athlone Press, 1997).

- The cultural legacy of imperialism and colonialism and the cultures of post-colonialism are further key areas of debate. You can explore some of the issues in this complex field via the essays in Bill Ashcroft, Gareth Griffiths and Helen Tiffin (eds), (1995) *The Post-colonial Studies Reader* (London: Routledge, 1995) or Patrick Williams and Laura Chrisman, *Colonial Discourse and Post-colonial Theory: a Reader* (Hemel Hempstead, Harvester Wheatsheaf, 1993). Two important books in this field worth reading in their own right are Homi Bhabha, *The Location of Culture* (London: Routledge, 1994) and Edward Said, *Culture and Imperialism* (London: Chatto and Windus, 1993). For a focus on the culture of British imperialism see, among others, the essays in John M. MacKenzie, *Imperialism and Popular Culture* (Manchester: Manchester University Press, 1986), and the primary-source texts in Elleke Boehmer, *Empire Writing* (Oxford: Oxford University Press, 1998).

- One area we have not focused on in great detail is the question of how cultural artefacts are produced and distributed. The part played by multinational and global corporations, such as Sony or Rupert Murdoch's News Corporation, in producing what we can see, listen to, participate in and so on is an important topic. You could explore the ways in which the global media is organized and how it is shaped by international, national and local politics. Useful texts to get you started include P. Du Gay (ed.), *Production of Cultures/Cultures of Production* (London: Sage/Open University, 1997), M. Real, *Exploring Media Culture: a Guide* (London: Sage, 1996), J. Street, *Politics and Popular Culture* (Cambridge: Polity Press, 1998) and K. Thompson, *Cultural Regulation and Media* (London: Sage/Open University, 1997).

References and Further Reading

Chapter 1

Arnold, M. (1869) *Culture and Anarchy*. London: Cambridge University Press.

Bourdieu, P. (1984) *Distinction: a Social Critique of the Judgement of Taste*, trans. R. Nice. Cambridge, MA: Harvard University Press.

du Gay, P. et al. (eds) (1997) *Doing Cultural Studies: the Story of the Sony Walkman*. London: Sage/Open University.

Ford, B. (ed.) (1992) *The Cambridge Cultural History of Britain. Volume 9: Victorian Britain*. Cambridge: Cambridge University Press.

Hoggart, R. (1957) *The Uses of Literacy*. Harmondsworth: Penguin.

Houghton, W. (1957) *The Victorian Frame of Mind 1830–1870*. New Haven, CT, and London: Yale University Press.

Jordan, G. and Weedon, C. (1995) *Cultural Politics: Class, Gender, Race and the Postmodern World*. Oxford: Blackwell.

Kuper, A. and Kuper, J. (eds) (1985) *The Social Science Encylopedia*. London: Routledge.

Leavis, F. R. (1930) *Mass Civilization and Minority Culture*. Cambridge: Minority Press.

Leavis, Q. D. (1932) *Fiction and the Reading Public*. London: Chatto and Windus.

Macdonald, D. (1957) A theory of mass culture. In B. Rosenberg and D. Manning White (eds), *Mass Culture: the Popular Arts in America*. New York: Macmillan.

Ortner, S. (1974) Is female to male as nature is to culture? In M. Z. Rosaldo and L. Lamphere (eds), *Women, Culture and Society*. Stanford, CA: Stanford University Press.

Said, E. (1993) *Culture and Imperialism*. London: Vintage.

Storey, J. (1993) *An Introductory Guide to Cultural Theory and Popular Culture*. London: Harvester Wheatsheaf.

Strinati, D. (1995) *An Introduction to Theories of Popular Culture*. London: Routledge.

Williams, R. (1958a) Culture is ordinary. Reprinted in A. Gray and J. McGuigan (eds, 1993), *Studying Culture: an Introductory Reader*. London: Edward Arnold.

Williams, R. (1958b) *Culture and Society: Coleridge to Orwell*. London: Chatto and Windus.

Williams, R. (1961) *The Long Revolution*. London: Chatto and Windus.

Williams, R. (1976) *Keywords: a Vocabulary of Culture and Society*. London: Fontana.

Chapter 2

African Rights (1994) *Rwanda: Death, Despair and Defiance*. London: African Rights.

Althusser, L. (1971) Ideology and ideological state apparatuses. In *Lenin and Philosophy and Other Essays*, trans. B. Brewster. London: New Left Books.

Birke, L. (1992) Transforming biology. In H. Crowley and S. Himmelweit (eds), *Knowing Women: Feminism and Knowledge*. Cambridge: Polity Press.

Bordo, S. (1993) *Unbearable Weight: Feminism, Western Culture and the Body*. Berkeley: University of California Press.

Carby, H. (1982) White woman listen! Black feminism and the boundaries of sisterhood. In Centre for Contemporary Cultural Studies, *The Empire Strikes Back: Race and Racism in 70s Britain*. London: Hutchinson.

Cashmore, E. and Troyna, B. (1990) *Introduction to Race Relations*. London: Falmer Press.

Coward, R. (1984) *Female Desire: Women's Sexuality Today*. London: Paladin.

Crowley, H. and Himmelweit, S. (eds) (1992) *Knowing Women: Feminism and Knowledge*. Cambridge: Polity Press.

Daly, M. (1979) *Gyn/Ecology: the Metaethics of Radical Feminism*. London: The Women's Press.

Fanon, F. (1986) *Black Skins, White Masks* (trans. C. L. Markman). London: Pluto.

Featherstone, M., Hepworth, M. and Turner, B. S. (eds) (1991) *The Body: Social Process and Cultural Theory*. London: Sage.

Freud, S. (1933) New introductory lectures on psychoanalysis. In J. Strachey (ed.), *The Standard Edition of the Complete Works of Sigmund Freud, volume 22*. London: Hogarth Press.

Gates, H. L. Jr (1986) *'Race', Writing and Difference*. Chicago: Chicago University Press.

Giddens, A. (1990) *The Consequences of Modernity*. Cambridge: Polity Press.

Gilroy, P. (1987) *'There Ain't No Black in the Union Jack': the Cultural Politics of Race and Nation*. London: Hutchinson.

Glissant, E. (1992) Caribbean discourse: reversion and diversion. In A. J. Arnold and K. Drame (eds), *Caribbean Discourse: Selected Essays*. Charlottesville: University Press of Virginia.

Haythorne, E. (1990) *On Earth to Make the Numbers Up*. Yorkshire Arts Circus.

Heron, L. (ed.) 1985) *Truth, Dare, Promise: Girls Growing up in the Fifties*. London: Virago.

Jordan, G. and Weedon, C. (1995) *Cultural Politics: Class, Gender, Race and the Postmodern World*. Oxford: Blackwell.

Kureishi, H. (1990) *The Buddha of Suburbia*. London: Faber and Faber.

Marx, K. (1859) *A Contribution to the Critique of Political Economy*. Reprinted in *Marx/ Engels: Selected Works in One Volume*. London: Lawrence and Wishart (1968).

Mercer, K. (1990) Welcome to the jungle: identity and diversity in postmodern politics. In *Identity, Community, Culture, Difference*. London: Lawrence and Wishart.

Minh-ha, Trinh T. (1989) *Woman, Native, Other: Writing, Postcoloniality, and Feminism*. Bloomington: Indiana University Press.

Robins, K. (1997) What in the world's going on? In P. du Gay (ed.), *Production of Culture/ Cultures of Production*. London: Sage/Open University.

Rutherford, J. (ed.) (1990) *Identity: Community, Culture, Difference*. London: Lawrence and Wishart.

Shilling, C. (1993) *The Body and Social Theory*. London: Sage.

Shilling, C. (1997) The body and difference. In K. Woodward (ed.), *Identity and Difference*. London: Sage.

Simons, M. and Bleiman, B. (1987) *More Lives*. London: ILEA English Centre.

Stanley, L. (1992) *The Auto/biographical I: the Theory and Practice of Feminist Auto/biography*. Manchester: Manchester University Press.

Stevens, R. (1994) Evolutionary origins of identity. In J. Anderson and M. Ricci (eds), *Society and Social Science: a Reader*. Milton Keynes: The Open University.

Weeks, J. (1990) The value of difference. In J. Rutherford (ed.), *Identity: Community, Culture, Difference*. London: Lawrence and Wishart.

Woodward, K. (ed.) (1997) *Identity and Difference*. London: Sage/Open University.

Chapter 3

Allen, R. C. (ed.) (1987) *Channels of Discourse*. Chapel Hill and London: University of North Carolina Press.

Barthes, R. (1967) *Elements of Semiology*. London: Jonathan Cape.

Barthes, R. (1973) *Mythologies*. London: Granada.

Belsey, C. (1980) *Critical Practice*. London: Methuen.

Beneveniste, E. (1971) *Problems in General Linguistics*. Miami: University of Miami Press.

Berger, J. (1972) *Ways of Seeing*. London: BBC/Penguin.

Betterton, R. (ed.) (1987) *Looking on: Images of Femininity in the Visual Arts and Media*. London: Pandora.

Bobo, J. (1988) *The Color Purple*: black women as cultural readers. Reprinted in Dines and Humez (1995).

Bonner, F., Goodman, L., Allen, R., Janes, L. and King, C. (eds) (1992) *Imagining Women: Cultural Representations and Gender*. Cambridge: Polity Press.

Branston, G. and Stafford, R. (1996) *The Media Student's Book*. London: Routledge.

Coward, R. (1984) *Female Desire: Women's Sexuality Today*. London: Paladin.

Dines, G. and Humez, J. M. (eds) (1995) *Gender, Race and Class in Media: a Text-reader*. London: Sage.

Duncker, P. (1992) *Sisters and Strangers: an Introduction to Contemporary Feminist Fiction*. Oxford: Blackwell.

Dyer, R. (1983) Seen to be believed: some problems in the representation of gay people as typical. *Studies in Visual Communication*, 9(2). Reprinted in Dyer (1993).

Dyer, R. (1993) *The Matter of Images: Essays in Representation*. London: Routledge.

Fiske, J. (1987) *Television Culture*. London: Routledge.

Foucault, M. (1972) *The Archaeology of Knowledge*. London: Tavistock.

Foucault, M. (1973) *The Birth of the Clinic*. London: Tavistock.

Foucault, M. (1975) *Discipline and Punish: the Birth of the Prison*. London: Allen Lane.

Foucault, M. (1978) *The History of Sexuality*. Harmondsworth: Penguin.

Frederickson, G. (1987) *The Black Image in the White Mind*. Hanover, NH: Wesleyan University Press.

Gates, H. L. (1988) *The Signifying Monkey*. Oxford: Oxford University Press.

Gledhill, C. (1984) Klute I: a contemporary film noir and feminist criticism. In E. A. Kaplan (ed.) *Women in Film Noir*. London: British Film Institute.

Golby, J. (1986) *Culture and Society in Britain 1850–1890*. Oxford: Oxford University Press/ The Open University.

Gray, A. and McGuigan, J. (eds) (1993) *Studying Culture: an Introductory Reader*. London: Edward Arnold.

Grossberg, L. (1984) Strategies of Marxist cultural interpretation. *Critical Studies in Mass Communication*, 1.

Hall, S. (1997) *Representation: Cultural Representations and Signifying Practices*. London: Sage/Open University.

Hall, S. (1992) The West and the rest. In S. Hall and B. Gieben (eds), *Formations of Modernity*. Cambridge: Polity Press/The Open University.

Hall, S. (1990) Encoding/decoding in television discourse. In S. Hall, D. Hobson, A. Lowe and P. Willis (eds), *Culture: Media: Language*. London: Hutchinson. Reprinted in S. During (ed., 1993), *The Cultural Studies Reader*. London: Routledge.

hooks, b. (1992) *Black Looks: Race and Representation*. Boston: South End Press.

Isaacs, S. (1948) *Childhood and After*. London: Routledge and Kegan Paul.

Levack, B. (1995) *The Witch-hunt in Early Modern Europe*, 2nd edn. New York: Longman.

McClintock, A. (1995) *Imperial Leather*. London: Routledge.

McCracken, E. (1993) *Decoding Women's Magazines: from 'Mademoiselle' to 'Ms'*. London: Macmillan.

McDonald, M. (1995) *Representing Women: Myths of Femininity in the Popular Media*. London: Edward Arnold.

Mackenzie, J. (ed.) (1986) *Imperialism and Popular Culture*. Manchester: Manchester University Press.

Morley, D. (1989) Changing paradigms in audience studies. In E. Seiter (ed.), *Rethinking Television Audiences*. Chapel Hill: University of North Carolina Press.

O'Sullivan, T., Hartley, J., Saunders, D. and Fiske, J. (1983) *Key Concepts in Communication*. London: Methuen.

Said, E. (1978) *Orientalism*. Harmondsworth: Penguin.

Seiter, E. (1990) Different children, different dreams: racial representation in advertising. Reprinted in Dines and Humez (1995).

Showalter, E. (1997) *Hystories: Hysterical Epidemics and Modern Culture*. New York: Columbia University Press.

Spence, J. (1980) What do people do all day? Class and gender in images of women. *Screen Education*, 29. Reprinted in Spence (1995).

Spence, J. (1995) *Cultural Sniping: the Art of Transgression*. London: Routledge.

Saussure, F. de (1974) *Course in General Linguistics*, trans. W. Baskin. London: Fontana.

Williamson, J. (1978) *Decoding Advertisements: Ideology and Meaning in Advertising*. London: Marion Boyars.

Chapter 4

Ascherson, N. (1987) 'Heritage' as vulgar English nationalism. *Observer*, 29 November; and Why 'heritage' is right-wing. *Observer*, 8 November.

Barthes, R. (1973) *Mythologies*. London: Granada.

Baxendale, J. and Pawling, C. (1996) *Narrating the Thirties: a Decade in the Making, 1930 to the Present*. Basingstoke: Macmillan.

Benjamin, W. (1973) *Illuminations*. London: Collins.

Calder, A. (1992) *The Myth of the Blitz*. London: Pimlico.

Clarke, J., Crichter, C. and Johnson, R. (eds) (1979) *Working Class Culture: Studies in History and Theory*. London: Hutchinson.

Giles, J. and Middleton, T. (1995) *Writing Englishness 1900–50: an Introductory Sourcebook on National Identity*. London: Routledge.

Hewison, R. (1987) *The Heritage Industry: Britain in a Climate of Decline*. London: London University Press.

Jenkins, K. (1991) *Re-thinking History*. London: Routledge.

Johnson, R. (1982) *Making Histories: Studies in History-writing and Politics*. London: Hutchinson.

Marwick, A. (1970) *The Nature of History*. London and Basingstoke: Macmillan.

Marwick, A. (1986) Introduction to history. *Unit 1–3 A102, Arts Foundation Course*. Milton Keynes: Open University.

Paxman, J. (1998) *The English: a Portrait of a People.* London: Michael Joseph.

Rowbotham, S. (1973) *Hidden from History.* London: Pluto Press.

Samuel, R. (1994) *Theatres of Memory.* London: Verso.

Spence, J. (1980) What do people do all day? Class and gender in images of women. *Screen Education,* 29. Reprinted in J. Spence (1995) *Cultural Sniping: the Art of Transgression.* London: Routledge.

Steedman, C. (1992) *Past Tenses: Essays on Writing Autobiography and History.* London: Rivers Oram.

Thompson, E. P. (1963) *The Making of the English Working Class.* Harmondsworth: Penguin.

Tosh, J. (1984) *The Pursuit of History: Aims, Methods and New Directions in the Study of Modern History.* London and New York: Longman (rev. edn 1991).

White, II. (1973) *Metahistory: the Historical Imagination in Nineteenth Century Europe.* Baltimore: Johns Hopkins University Press.

Williams, R. (1976) *Keywords: a Vocabulary of Culture and Society.* London: Fontana.

Wright, P. (1985) *On Living in an Old Country: the National Past in Contemporary Britain.* London: Verso.

Chapter 5

Achebe, C. (1977) An image of Africa: racism in Conrad's *Heart of Darkness.* Reprinted in R. Kimborough (ed., 1988), *Heart of Darkness.* New York and London: Norton.

Agnew, J. (1993) Representing space: space, scale and culture in social science. In J. Duncan and D. Ley (eds), *Place/Culture/Representation.* London: Routledge.

Barnes, T. J. and Duncan, J. (1992) *Writing Worlds: Discourse, Text and Metaphor in the Representation of Landscape.* London: Routledge.

Best, S. and Kellner, D. (1991) *Postmodern Theory: Critical Interrogations.* London: Macmillan.

Bhabha, H. (1994) *The Location of Culture.* London: Routledge.

Boehmer, E. (1995) *Colonial and Postcolonial Literature: Migrant Metaphors.* Oxford: Oxford University Press.

Conrad, J. (1902) *Heart of Darkness,* ed. R. Kimborough (1988). New York and London: Norton.

de Certeau, M. (1984) *The Practice of Everyday Life.* Berkeley: University of California Press.

Duncan, J. and Ley, D. (eds) (1993) *Place/Culture/Representation.* London: Routledge. (See, especially, Introduction: representing the place of culture, pp. 1–24.)

During, S. (ed.) (1993) *The Cultural Studies Reader.* London: Routledge.

Eagleton, T. (1974) Introduction to Thomas Hardy, *Jude the Obscure.* London: Macmillan.

Fiske, J. (1992) Cultural studies and the culture of everyday life. In L. Grossberg, C. Nelson and P. Treichler (eds), *Cultural Studies.* London: Routledge.

Foucault, M. (1984) Space, power, knowledge. In S. During (ed., 1993), *The Cultural Studies Reader.* London: Routledge.

Foucault, M. (1986) Of other spaces. *Diacritics,* 16, 22–7.

Hardy, F. E. (1928) *The Life of Thomas Hardy: 1840–1928.* London: Macmillan.

Hardy, T. (1896) *Jude the Obscure.* London: Macmillan.

Harley, J. B. (1992) Deconstructing the map. In T. J. Barnes and J. Duncan (eds), *Writing Worlds: Discourse, Text and Metaphor in the Representation of Landscape.* London: Routledge.

Jackson, P. (1989) *Maps of Meaning: an Introduction to Cultural Geography*. London: Routledge.

Jameson, F. (1984) Postmodernism, or the cultural logic of late capitalism. *New Left Review*, 146, 53–93.

Joyce, J. (1916) *A Portrait of the Artist as a Young Man*. London: Paladin.

Keith, M. and Pile, S. (eds) (1993) *Place and the Politics of Identity*. London: Routledge. (See, especially, Introduction, part 1: the politics of place, pp. 1–21, and Introduction, part 2: the place of politics, pp. 22–40.)

Kowinski, W. S. (1985) *The Malling of America: an Inside Look at the Great Consumer Paradise*. New York: Pantheon.

Laclau, E. (1990) *New Reflections on the Revolutions of Our Time*. London: Verso.

Lave, J. (1988) *Cognition in Practice*. Cambridge: Cambridge University Press.

Lefebvre, H. (1991) *The Production of Space* (trans. D. Nicholson Smith). Oxford: Blackwell. (First published in French as *Production de l'espace*. Paris: Editions Anthropos, 1974.)

Little, J., Peake, L. and Richardson, J. (eds) (1988) *Women in Cities: Gender in the Urban Environment*. London: Hutchinson.

Massey, D. (1991) A global sense of place. *Marxism Today*, June. Reprinted in A. Gray and J. McGuigan (eds, 1993), *Studying Culture: an Introductory Reader*. London: Edward Arnold.

Morris, M. (1988) Things to do with shopping centres. In S. Sheridan (ed.), *Grafts: Feminist Cultural Criticism*. London: Verso.

Pickles, J. (1992) Texts, hermeneutics and propaganda maps. In T. J. Barnes and J. Duncan (eds), *Writing Worlds: Discourse, Text and Metaphor in the Representation of Landscape*. London: Routledge.

Pred, A. (1983) Structuration and place; on the becoming sense of place and structure of feeling. *Journal for the Theory of Social Behaviour*, 13, 45–68.

Pred, A. (1984) Place as historically contingent process: structuration and the geography of becoming places. *Annals of the Association of American Geographers*, 279–97.

Ryan, S. (1994) Inscribing emptiness. In C. Tiffin and A. Lawson (eds), *De-Scribing Empire*. London: Routledge.

Said, E. (1978) *Orientalism*. Harmondsworth: Penguin.

Shunner-Smith, P. and Hannam, K. (1994) *Worlds of Desire, Realms of Power: a Cultural Geography*. London: Edward Arnold.

Smith, N. and Katz, C. (1993) Grounding metaphor: towards a spatialized politics. In M. Keith and S. Pile (eds), *Place and the Politics of Identity*. London: Routledge.

Soja, E. (1989) *Postmodern Geographies: the Reassertion of Space in Critical Social Theory*. London: Verso.

Soja, E. and Hooper, B. (1993) The spaces that difference makes: some notes on the geographical margins of the new cultural politics. In M. Keith and S. Pile (eds), *Place and the Politics of Identity*. London: Routledge.

Thrift, N. (1997) 'Us' and 'them': re-imagining places, re-imagining identities. In H. Mackay (ed.), *Consumption and Everyday Life*. London: Sage/Open University

Vujakovic, P. (1995) The Sleeping Beauty complex: maps as text in the construction of national identity. In T. Hills and W. Hughes (eds), *Contemporary Writing and National Identity*. Bath: Sulis Press.

Willis, S. (1991) *A Primer for Daily Life*. London: Routledge.

Chapter 6

Anon. (1934) *The Motherhood Book*. London: Amalgamated Press.

Baxendale, J. and Pawling, C. (1996) *Narrating the Thirties. A Decade in the Making: 1930 to the Present*. Basingstoke: Macmillan.

Beddoe, D. (1989) *Back to Home and Duty: Women between the Wars, 1918–39*. London: Pandora.

Bentley, I. (1981a) Arcadia becomes Dunroamin: suburban growth and the roots of opposition. In P. Oliver et al. (eds), *Dunroamin*. London: Barrie and Jenkins.

Bentley, I. (1981b) The owner makes his mark, choice and adaptation. In P. Oliver et al. (eds), *Dunroamin*. London: Barrie and Jenkins.

Betjeman, J. (1937) Slough. Reprinted in J. Guest (ed., 1978), *The Best of Betjeman*. Harmondsworth: Penguin.

Bloom, C. (ed.) (1993) *Literature and Culture in Modern Britain: 1900–1929*. London: Longman.

Bourke, J. (1994) *Working-class Cultures in Britain 1890–1960*. London: Routledge.

Bradbury, M. and McFarlane, J. (eds) (1976) *Modernism: 1890–1930*. Harmondsworth: Penguin.

Burnett, J. (1986) *A Social History of Housing 1815–1985*, 2nd edn. London: Methuen.

Friedan, B. (1965) *The Feminine Mystique*. Harmondsworth: Penguin.

Giddens, A. (1989) *Sociology*. Cambridge: Polity Press.

Giles, J. (1989) Something that bit better: women, domesticity and respectability 1919–39. Unpublished DPhil, University of York.

Giles, J. (1995) *Women, Identity and Private Life in Britain 1900–50*. Basingstoke: Macmillan.

Giles, J. and Middleton, T. (1995) *Writing Englishness 1900–50: an Introductory Sourcebook on National Identity*. London: Routledge.

Graves, R. and Hodge, A. (1940) *The Long Weekend: a Social History of Great Britain 1918–1939*. London: Cardinal.

Hillier, B. (1983) *The Style of the Century 1900–1980*. London: The Herbert Press.

Howard, E. (1902) *Garden Cities of Tomorrow*. London: Faber.

Jackson, A. (1973) *Semi-detached London: Suburban Development, Life and Transport, 1900–39*. London: Allen and Unwin.

Lewis, R. and Maude, A. (1949) *The English Middle Classes*. Harmondsworth: Penguin.

Light, A. (1991) *Forever England: Femininity, Literature and Conservatism between the Wars*. London: Routledge.

Mackay, H. (ed.) (1997) *Consumption and Everyday Life*. London: Sage/Open University.

Masterman, C. F. G. (1909) *The Condition of England*. London: Methuen.

Morris, W. (1890) *News from Nowhere*. London: Routledge and Kegan Paul.

National Trust (1993) *Mr Straw's House: an Illustrated Souvenir*. National Trust Enterprises.

Oliver, P., Davis, I. and Bentley, I. (1981) *Dunroamin: the Suburban Semi and Its Enemies*. London: Barrie and Jenkins.

Orwell, G. (1939) *Coming up for Air*. Harmondsworth: Penguin.

Priestley, J. B. (1934) *English Journey*. Harmondsworth: Penguin.

Roberts, E. (1995) *Women and Families: an Oral History 1940–70*. Oxford: Blackwell.

Rowntree, B. S. (1901) *Poverty: a Study of Town Life*. London: Longman.

Rowntree, B. S. (1941) *Poverty and Progress*. London: Longman.

Thorns, D. (1972) *Suburbia*. London: McGibbon and Kee.

Thrift, N. (1997) 'Us' and 'them': re-imagining places, re-imagining identities. In H. Mackay (ed.), *Consumption and Everyday Life*. London: Sage/Open University

Tillyard, S. (1988) *The Impact of Modernism: the Visual Arts in England*. London: Routledge.

Walkerdine, V. (1985) Dreams from an ordinary childhood. In L. Heron (ed.), *Truth, Dare, Promise*. London: Virago.

Chapter 7

Barker, E. (1947) An attempt at perspective. In E. Barker (ed.), *The Character of England*. Oxford: Clarendon Press.

Barry, P. (1995) *Beginning Theory: an Introduction to Literary and Cultural Theory*. Manchester: Manchester University Press.

Bourdieu, P. (1986) *Distinction: a Social Critique of the Judgement of Taste*, trans. R. Nice. Cambridge, MA: Harvard University Press.

Brooker, P. and Widdowson, P. (1986) A literature for England. In R. Colls and P. Dodds (eds), *Englishness: Politics and Culture 1880–1920*. London: Croom Helm.

Bullen, J. B. (1988) *Post-impressionists in England*. London: Routledge.

Carpenter, E. (1908) *The Intermediate Sex: a Study of Some Transitional Types of Men and Women*.

Clark, K, and Holquist, M. (1984) *Mikhail Bakhtin*. Cambridge, MA: Harvard University Press.

Colls, R. and Dodds, P. (eds) (1986) *Englishness: Politics and Culture 1880–1920*. London: Croom Helm.

Crowther, M. A. (1992) The tramp. In R. Porter (ed.), *Myths of the English*. Cambridge: Polity Press.

Dawson, G. (1994) *Soldier Heroes*. London: Routledge.

de Certeau, M. (1984) *The Practice of Everyday Life*. Berkeley: University of California Press.

Dellamora, R. (1996) Homosexual scandal and compulsory heterosexuality in the 1890s. In L. Pykett (ed.), *Reading Fin de Siècle Fictions*. London: Longman.

Eagleton, T. (1987) The end of English. *Textual Practice*, 1(1).

Fiske, J. (1989) *Reading the Popular*. London: Unwin Hyman.

Fiske, J. (1991) *Understanding Popular Culture*. London: Unwin Hyman.

Flint, K. (1984) *Impressionists in England*. London: Routledge.

Ford, F. M. (1907) Extract from *The Spirit of the People*. In J. Giles and T. Middleton (eds, 1995), *Writing Englishness 1900–1950*. London: Routledge.

Forster, E. M. (1971) *Maurice*. Harmondsworth: Penguin.

Frith, S. (1991) The good, the bad, and the indifferent: defending culture from the populists. *Diacritics*, 21(4).

Frow, J. (1995) *Cultural Studies and Cultural Value*. Oxford: Oxford University Press.

Giles, J. and Middleton, T. (1995) *Writing Englishness 1900–50: an Introductory Sourcebook on National Identity*. London: Routledge.

Grahame, K. (1908) *The Wind in the Willows*. Oxford: World's Classics.

Harrison, C. and Wood, J. (eds) (1992) *Art in Theory*. Oxford: Blackwell.

Hirschkop, K. and Shepherd, D. (eds) (1989) *Bakhtin and Cultural Theory*. Manchester: Manchester University Press.

HMSO (1994) *English in the National Curriculum: Draft Proposals, May 1994*. London: HMSO.

Holquist, M. (1990) *Dialogism: Bakhtin and His World*. London: Routledge.

Hughes, R. (1993) *The Culture of Complaint: the Fraying of America*. Oxford: Oxford University Press.

Knowles, J. (1996) Marxism, new historicism, cultural materialism. In R. Bradford (ed.), *Introducing Literary Studies*. London: Harvester.

Koestenbaum, W. (1989) *Double Talk*. London: Routledge.

Lal, V. (1996) *South Asian Cultural Studies*. Delhi: Manohar.

Ledger, S. (1997) *The New Woman: Fiction and Feminism at the Fin de Siècle*. Manchester: Manchester University Press.

McGuigan, J. (1992) *Cultural Populism*. London: Routledge.

Marriott, J. (1996) Sensation of the abyss: the urban poor and modernity. In M. Nava and A. O'Shea (eds), *Modern Times: Reflection on a Century of English Modernity*. London: Routledge.

Mason, M. (1994) *The Making of Victorian Sexuality*. Oxford: Oxford University Press.

Montgomery, M. et al. (1992) *Ways of Reading: Advanced Reading Skills for Students of English Literature*. London: Routledge.

Newbolt Committee (1921) *The Teaching of English in England*. London: HMSO.

Schwarz, B. (1996) Night battles: hooligan and citizen. In M. Nava and A. O'Shea (eds), *Modern Times: Reflection on a Century of English Modernity*. London: Routledge.

Sedgwick, E. (1985) *Between Men: English Literature and Male Homosocial Desire*. New York: Columbia University Press.

Showalter, E. (1991) *Sexual Anarchy*. London: Bloomsbury.

Storey, J. (1993) *An Introductory Guide to Cultural Theory and Popular Culture*. London: Harvester Wheatsheaf.

Storey, J. (1996) *Cultural Studies and the Study of Popular Culture*. Edinburgh: Edinburgh University Press.

Todorov, T. (1984) *Mikhail Bakhtin: The Dialogical Principle*, trans. W. Godzich. Manchester: Manchester University Press.

Twitchell, J. B. (1992) *Carnival Culture: the Trashing of Taste in America*. New York: Columbia University Press.

Weeks, J. (1981) *Sex, Politics and Society*. London: Longman.

Weeks, J. (1989) The idea of sexual minorities. In R. Samuel (ed.), *Patriotism: the Making and Unmaking of British National Identity. Volume 2: Minorities and Outsiders*. London: Routledge.

Williams, R. (1958a) Culture is ordinary. Reprinted in A. Gray and J. McGuigan (eds), *Studying Culture: an Introductory Reader*. London: Edward Arnold.

Williams, R. (1958b) *Culture and Society: Coleridge to Orwell*. London: Chatto and Windus.

Williams, R. (1976) *Keywords: a Vocabulary of Culture and Society*. London: Fontana.

Williams, R. (1981) *Culture*. London: Fontana.

Chapter 8

Althusser, L. (1971) Ideology and ideological state apparatuses. In *Lenin and Philosophy and Other Essays*, trans. B. Brewster. London: New Left Books.

Anzaldúa, G. (1987) La conciencia de la mestiza/towards a new consciousness. In *Borderlands/La Frontera: the New Mestiza*. San Francisco: Spinsters/Aunt Lute.

Bordo, S. (1990) Reading the slender body. In M. Jacobus, E. Fox Keller and S. Shuttleworth (eds), *Body/Politics: Women and the Discourse of Science*. New York and London: Routledge, pp. 83–112.

Butler, J. (1990) *Gender Trouble: Feminism and the Subversion of Identity*. London: Routledge.

Crawford, R. (1985) A cultural account of 'health' – self-control, release, and the social body. In J. McKinlay (ed.), *Issues in the Political Economy of Health Care*. New York: Methuen.

Crowley, H. and Himmelweit, S. (eds) (1992) *Knowing Women: Feminism and Knowledge*. Cambridge: Polity Press.

Douglas, M. (1966) *Purity and Danger: an Analysis of Concepts of Pollution and Taboo*. London: Routledge.

Duffy, C. A. (1994) *Selected Poems*: Harmondsworth: Penguin.

Eagleton, M. (ed.) (1996) *Feminist Literary Theory: a Reader*, 2nd edn. Oxford: Blackwell.

Easthope, A. and McGowan, K. (eds) (1992) *A Critical and Cultural Theory Reader*. Buckingham: Open University Press.

Featherstone, M., Hepworth, M. and Turner, B. S. (eds) (1991) *The Body: Social Process and Cultural Theory*. London: Sage.

Foucault, M. (1967) *Madness and Civilization*. London: Tavistock.

Foucault, M. (1973) *The Birth of the Clinic*. London: Tavistock.

Foucault, M. (1975) *Discipline and Punish: the Birth of the Prison*. London: Allen Lane.

Fuss, D. (1989) *Essentially Speaking: Feminism, Nature and Difference*. London: Routledge.

Hall, S. (1996) Signification, representation, ideology: Althusser and the post-structuralist debates. In J. Curran, D. Morley and V. Walkerdine (eds), *Cultural Studies and Communications*. London: Edward Arnold.

hooks, b. (1991) *Yearning: Race, Gender and Cultural Politics*. London: Turnaround (also extracted in Eagleton, 1996).

Kristeva, J. (1986) A question of subjectivity (interview with Susan Sellers). *Women's Review*, 12 (also extracted in Eagleton, 1996).

Lacan, J. (1949) *Écrits: a Selection*, trans. Alan Sheridan. London: Tavistock and Norton.

Martin, E. (1991) The egg and the sperm: how science has constructed a romance based on stereotypical male-female roles. *Signs: Journal of Women in Culture and Society*, 16, 1–18.

Martin, E. (1992) Body narratives, body boundaries. In L. Grossberg, C. Nelson and P. Treichler (eds), *Cultural Studies*. New York: Routledge.

Minsky, R. (1992) Lacan. In H. Crowley and S. Himmelweit (eds), *Knowing Women: Feminism and Knowledge*. Cambridge: Polity Press.

Moi, T. (ed.) (1986) *The Kristeva Reader*. Oxford: Blackwell.

Moi, T. (ed.) (1987) *French Feminist Thought: a Reader*. Oxford: Blackwell.

Nicholson, L. (ed.) *Feminism/Postmodernism*. New York: Routledge.

Rosen, T. (1983) *Strong and Sexy: the New Body Beautiful*. London: Columbus Books.

Shilling, C. (1993) *The Body and Social Theory*. London: Sage.

Shilling, C. (1997) The body and difference. In K. Woodward (ed.), *Identity and Difference*. London: Sage.

Turner, B. S. (1992) *Regulating Bodies: Essays in Medical Sociology*. London: Routledge.

Weeks, J. (1989) *Sex, Politics and Society: the Regulation of Sexuality since 1800*. London: Longman.

Chapter 9

Adorno, T. and Horkheimer, M. (1947) The culture industry: enlightenment as mass deception. In *Dialectic of Enlightenment*. London: Verso.

Adorno, T. (1991) *The Culture Industry: Selected Essays on Mass Culture*, ed. J. M. Bernstein. London: Verso.

Baudrillard, J. (1988) *Selected Writings*. Cambridge: Polity Press.

Bordo, S. (1990) Reading the slender body. In M. Jacobus, E. Fox Keller and S. Shuttleworth (eds), *Body/Politics: Women and the Discourse of Science*. New York and London: Routledge, pp. 83–112.

Bordwell, D., Steiger, J. and Thompson, K. (1985) *The Classical Hollywood Cinema: Film Style and Mode of Production to 1960*. New York: Columbia University Press.

Bourdieu, P. (1978) How can one be a sports fan? *Social Science Information*, 17(6).

Braham, P. (1997) Fashion: unpacking a cultural production. In P. du Gay (ed.), *Production of Culture/Cultures of Production*. London: Sage/Open University.

Drakulic, S. (1992) *How We Survived Communism and Even Laughed*. London: Vintage.

du Gay, P. (ed.) (1997) *Production of Culture/Cultures of Production*. London: Sage/Open University.

du Gay, P. et al. (eds) (1997) *Doing Cultural Studies: the Story of the Sony Walkman*. London: Sage/Open University.

During, S. (ed.) (1993) *The Cultural Studies Reader*. London: Routledge.

Dyer, R. (1979) The role of stereotypes. In J. Cook and M. Lewington (eds), *Images of Alcoholism*. London: British Film Institute.

Fiske, J. (1987) *Television Culture*. London: Routledge.

Giddens, A. (1990) *The Consequences of Modernity*. Cambridge: Polity Press.

Gillespie, M. (1989) Technology and tradition – audio-visual culture among South Asian families in West London. *Cultural Studies*, 3(2). Reprinted in A. Gray and J. McGuigan (eds, 1993), *Studying Culture: an Introductory Reader*. London: Edward Arnold.

Gomery, D. (1976) Writing the history of the American film industry: Warner Bros and Sound. *Screen*, 1.

Grossberg, L. (1984) Strategics of Marxist cultural interpretation. *Critical Studies in Mass Communication*, 1.

Gullestad, M. (1992) *The Art of Social Relations: Essays on Culture, Social Action and Everyday Life in Modern Norway*. Oslo: Scandinavian University Press.

Gullestad, M. (1996) *Everyday Life Philosophers: Modernity, Morality and Autobiography in Norway*. Oslo: Scandinavian University Press.

Hartley, J. (1982) *Understanding News*. London: Methuen.

Hebdige, D. (1979) *Subculture: the Meaning of Style*. London: Methuen.

King, A. (ed.) (1991) *Culture, Globalization and the World System*. Basingstoke: Macmillan.

Lury, C. (1996) *Consumer Culture*. Cambridge: Polity Press.

McRobbic, A. (1996) *More!* New sexualities in girls' and women's magazines. In J. Curran, D. Morley and V. Walkerdine (eds), *Cultural Studies and Communications*. London: Edward Arnold.

Marcuse, H. (1964) *One Dimensional Man*. London: Routledge.

Miller, D. (1997) Consumption and its consequences. In H. Mackay (ed.), *Consumption and Everyday Life*. London: Sage/Open University.

Miller, D. (1998) Coca-Cola: a black sweet drink from Trinidad. In D. Miller (ed.), *Material Cultures*. London: University College London Press.

Morley, D. (1986) *Family Television: Cultural Power and Domestic Leisure*. London: Comedia.

Morley, D. (1992) *Television, Audiences and Cultural Studies*. London: Routledge.

Moore, S. (1997) What girl power means. *The Independent*, 14 November.

Nava, M., Blake, A., MacRury, I. and Richards, B. (eds) (1997) *Buy This Book: Studies in Advertising and Consumption*. London: Routledge.

Packard, V. (1957) *The Hidden Persuaders*. London: Longmans, Green and Co.

Perkins, T. E. (1979) Rethinking stereotypes. In M. Barrett, P. Corrigan, A. Kuhn and J. Wolff (eds), *Ideology and Cultural Production*. London: Croom Helm.

Porter, R. (1993) Baudrillard: history, hysteria and consumption. In C. Rojek and B. S. Turner (eds), *Forget Baudrillard?* London and New York: Routledge, pp. 1–21.

Raban, J. (1974) *Soft City*. London: Fontana.

Radway, J. (1987) *Reading the Romance: Women, Patriarchy and Popular Literature*. London: Verso.

Schatz, T. (1981) *Hollywood Genres: Formulas, Filmmaking, and the Studio System*. New York: Random House.

Selby, K. and Cowdery, R. (1995) *How to Study Television*. Basingstoke: Macmillan.

Storey, J. (1996) *Cultural Studies and the Study of Popular Culture: Theories and Methods*. Edinburgh: Edinburgh University Press.

Thompson, K. (ed.) (1997) *Media and Cultural Regulation*. London: Sage/Open University.

Turner, G. (1993) *Film as Social Practice*. London: Routledge.

Veblen, T. (1899) *The Theory of the Leisure Class: an Economic Study of Institutions*. New York: Macmillan.

Williams, R. (1976) *Keywords: a Vocabulary of Culture and Society*. London: Fontana.

Chapter 10

TV and media culture

Alvarado, M., Gutch, R. and Wollen, T. (1987) *Learning the Media*. London: Macmillan.

Brunsdon, C. and Morley, D. (1978) *Everyday Television: Nationwide*. London: BFI.

Fiske, J. and Hartley, J. (1978) *Reading Television*. London: Methuen.

Gillespie, M. (1993) Technology and tradition – audio-visual culture among south Asian families in west London. In A. Gray and J. McGuigan (eds), *Studying Culture: an Introductory Reader*. London: Edward Arnold, pp. 147–60. (First published in *Cultural Studies*, 3(2), 1989.)

Hall, S. (1990) Encoding/decoding in television discourse. In S. Hall, D. Hobson, A. Lowe and P. Willis (eds), *Culture: Media: Language*. London: Hutchinson.

Hartley, J. (1982) *Understanding News*. London: Methuen.

Mackay, H. (1997) Consuming communication technologies at home. In H. Mackay (ed.), *Consumption and Everyday Life*. London: Sage/Open University.

McLuhan, M. (1964) *Understanding Media*. New York: McGraw.

McQuail, D. (1987) *Mass Communication Theory*. London: Sage.

Morley, D. (1992) *Television, Audiences and Cultural Studies*. London: Routledge.

O'Connor, A. (1989) *Raymond Williams: Writing, Culture, Politics*. Oxford: Blackwell.

Price, S. (1993) *Media Studies*. London: Pitman.

Real, M. R. (1996) *Exploring Media Culture: a Guide*. London: Sage.

Selby, K. and Cowdery, R. (1995) *How to Study Television*. London: Macmillan.

Turner, G. (1992) *British Cultural Studies: an Introduction*. London: Routledge.

Watson, J. and Hill, A. (1989) *A Dictionary of Communication and Media Studies*. London: Arnold.

Internet/cyber culture

Brail, S. (1996) The price of admission: harassment and free speech in the Wild, Wild West. In L. Cherny and E. R. Weisse (eds), *Wired Women: Gender and New Realities in Cyberspace*. Seattle: Seal Press.

Cherny, L. and Weisse, E. R. (eds) (1996) *Wired Women: Gender and New Realities in Cyberspace*. Seattle: Seal Press.

de Kerckhove, D. (1995) *The Skin of Culture: Investigating the New Electronic Reality*. London: Kogan Page.

Gibson, W. (1984) *Neuromancer*. London: Victor Gollancz.

Greenfield, P. M. (1984) *Mind and Media: the Effects of Television, Video Games, and Computers*. Cambridge, MA: Harvard University Press.

Haraway, D. (1992) The promises of monsters: a regenerative politics for inappropriate/d others. In L. Grossberg et al. (eds), *Cultural Studies*. London: Routledge.

Haraway, D. (1985) A manifesto for cyborgs: science, technology, and socialist feminism in the 1980s. *Socialist Review*, 15(18). Reprinted in Weed (1989) and in L. J. Nicholson (ed., 1990), *Feminism/Postmodernism*. London: Routledge.

Herring, S. (1993) Gender and democracy in computer-mediated communication. *Electronic Journal of Communication*, 3(2).

Jones, S. G. (1995) *Cybersociety: Computer-mediated Communication and Community*. London: Sage.

Kantrowitz, B. (1994) Men, women and computers. *Newsweek*, 16 May.

Kennedy, A. J. (1998) *The Internet and World Wide Web: the Rough Guide*, 4th edn. Harmondsworth: Penguin.

Kroker, A. and Weinstein, D. (1994) *Data Trash: the Theory of the Virtual Class*. Montreal: New World Perspectives.

Leary, T. (1979) *Chaos and Cyber Culture*. Berkeley, CA: Ronin Publishing.

McRae, S. (1996) Coming apart at the seams: sex, text and the virtual body. In L. Cherny and E. R. Weisse (eds), *Wired Women: Gender and New Realities in Cyberspace*. Seattle: Seal Press.

Rushkoff, D. (1997) *Children of Chaos: Surviving the End of the World as We Know It*. London: Flamingo.

Sheff, D. (1993) *Game Over: How Nintendo Sapped an American Industry, Captured Your Dollars, and Enslaved Your Children*. New York: Random House.

Shields, R. (ed.) (1996) *Cultures of the Internet: Virtual Spaces, Real Histories, Living Bodies*. London: Sage.

Skerrow, G. (1986) Hellivision: an analysis of two video games. In C. McCabe (ed.), *High Theory/Low Culture*. Manchester: Manchester University Press.

Turkle, S. (1988) Computational reticence: why women fear the inanimate machine. In C. Kramarae (ed.), *Technology and Women's Voices*. London: Routledge.

Weed, E. (ed.) (1989) *Coming to Terms: Feminism, Theory, Politics*. London: Routledge.

World Wide Web sites

This is an eclectic listing of sites which may be useful for work on Internet culture or in cultural studies more generally: follow links from these sites to explore the culture of the Internet.

All Movie guide (on-line film guide): http://www.Allmovie.com

Alt.culture (an A to Z of 1990s culture): http://www.altculture.com

Iain Banks (unofficial web site devoted to the works of the popular Scottish author): http://www.phlebas.com

Ctheory (an online journal devoted to cyber and postmodern culture): http://www.ctheory.com

The Eighties Server (an A to Z of 1980s culture): http://www.80s.com

GeekGirl (Australian cyber-feminist 'zine): http://www.geekgirl.com.au/
Hotwired (*Wired* magazine's on-line site): http://www.hotwired.com
Kovacs' Directory of Scholarly and Professional E-Conferences: http://www.n2h2.com/
  KOVACS
Post Modern Culture (on-line journal): http://jefferson.village.virginia.edu/pmc/
Salon Magazine (American arts and culture magazine): http://www.salonmag.com
The trAce project (cyber writing site): http://trace.ntu.ac.uk
Web Virtual Library E-journal Catalogue: http://www.edoc.com/
Yahoo Women's Studies server: http://www.yahoo.com/social_science/women_s-studies

Usenet discussion groups

Discussion groups on every subject you can imagine (as well as on topics you have never heard of) abound – just don't expect too much from the discussion and read the FAQs (frequently asked questions) before you post a question. There is a useful guide, with links, at:

http://alabanza.com/kabacoff/Inter-links/listserv.html

Bibliography

Readers

Anon. (1994) *The Polity Reader in Cultural Theory*. Cambridge: Polity Press.

Baehr, H. and Gray, A. (eds), *Turning It on: a Reader in Women and Media*. London: Edward Arnold.

Curran, J., Morley, D. and Walkerdine, V. (eds) (1996) *Cultural Studies and Communications*. London: Edward Arnold.

Dines, G. and Humez, J. M. (eds) (1995) *Gender, Race and Class in Media: a Text-reader*. London: Sage.

During S. (ed.) (1993) *The Cultural Studies Reader*. London: Routledge.

Easthope, A. and McGowan, K. (eds) (1992) *A Critical and Cultural Theory Reader*. Buckingham: Open University Press.

Eagleton, M. (ed.) (1996) *Feminist Literary Theory: a Reader*, 2nd edn. Oxford: Blackwell.

Franklin, S., Lury, C. and Stacey, J. (eds) (1991) *Off-centre: Feminism and Cultural Studies*. London: HarperCollins.

Gray, A. and McGuigan, J. (eds) (1993) *Studying Culture: an Introductory Reader*. London: Edward Arnold.

Grossberg, L., Nelson, C. and Treichler, P. (eds) (1992) *Cultural Studies*. New York: Routledge.

Skeggs, B. (1995) *Feminist Cultural Theory: Process and Production*. Manchester: Manchester University Press.

Storey, J. (ed.) (1994) *Cultural Theory and Popular Culture: a Reader*. London: Harvester.

Introductory texts

Bonner, F., Goodman, L., Allen, R., Janes, L. and King, C. (eds) (1992) *Imagining Women: Cultural Representations and Gender*. Cambridge: Polity Press.

Branston, G. and Stafford, R. (1996) *The Media Student's Book*. London: Routledge.

Crowley, H. and Himmelweit, S. (eds) (1992) *Knowing Women: Feminism and Knowledge*. Cambridge: Polity Press.

Selby, K, and Cowdery, R. (1995) *How to Study Television*. Basingstoke: Macmillan.

Storey, J. (1993) *An Introductory Guide to Cultural Theory and Popular Culture*. London: Harvester Wheatsheaf.

Sardar, Z, and Loon, B. V. (1997) *Cultural Studies for Beginners*. Cambridge: Icon Books.

Strinati, D. (1995) *An Introduction to Theories of Popular Culture*. London: Routledge.

Turner, G. (1990) *British Cultural Studies: an Introduction*. London: Routledge.

Reference books

These are some examples, but browsing in the reference section of a library will suggest many others.

The Concise Oxford Dictionary.

Cook, C. and Stevenson, J. (1988) *The Longman Handbook of Modern European History 1763–1985.* London: Longman.

Cook, C. and Stevenson, J. (1988) *The Longman Handbook of British History 1714–1987.* London: Longman.

Drabble, M. (ed.) *The Oxford Companion to English Literature.* Oxford: Oxford University Press.

Walker, J. (ed.) (annual) *Halliwell's Film Guide.* London: HarperCollins.

Kuper, A. and Kuper, J. (eds) (1985) *The Social Science Encylopedia.* London: Routledge.

Riff, M. A. (ed.) (1987) *Dictionary of Modern Political Ideologies.* Manchester: Manchester University Press.

Rose, P. (ed.) (1995) *The Penguin Book of Women's Lives.* Harmondsworth: Penguin.

Williams, R. (1976) *Keywords: a Vocabulary of Culture and Society.* London: Fontana.

Index